W9-BNH-344

Your Personal Net Series available from Dell

NETGUIDE
NETSTUDY
NETSPORTS
NETSCI-FI
NETMONEY
NETDOCTOR

net study

Your Complete Guide to Academic Success Using the Internet and Online Service

A Michael Wolff Book

A Dell Book

Published by
Dell Publishing
a division of
Bantam Doubleday Dell Publishing Group, Inc.
1540 Broadway
New York, New York 10036

The authors and publisher have used their best efforts in preparing this book. However, the authors and publisher make no warranties of any kind, express or implied, with regard to the documentation contained in this book, and specifically disclaim, without limitation, any implied warranties of merchantability and fitness for a particular purpose with respect to listings in the book, or the techniques described in the book. In no event shall the authors or publisher be responsible or liable for any loss of profit or any other commercial damages, including but not limited to special, incidental, consequential, or any other damages in connection with or arising out of furnishing, performance, or use of this book.

Trademarks A number of entered words in which we have reason to believe trademark, service mark, or other proprietary rights may exist have been designated as such by use of initial capitalization. However, no attempt has been made to designate as trademarks or service marks all personal-computer words or terms in which proprietary rights might exist. The inclusion, exclusion, or definition of a word or term is not intended to affect, or to express any judgment on, the validity or legal status of any proprietary right which may be claimed in that word or term.

NetSci-Fi, NetSpy, NetCollege, NetStudy, NetDoctor, NetMarketing, NetVote, NetJobs, NetGames2, NetTravel, NetTaxes, NetMusic, NetGames, NetChat, NetMoney, NetTech, NetSports, Your Personal Net, the Your Personal Net Logo, NetBooks, NetHead, NetSpeak, NetBest, and CyberPower are trademarks of Wolff New Media LLC. The Net Logo, What's On In Cyberspace, and YPN are registered trademarks of Wolff New Media LLC. The trademark NetGuide, created by Michael Wolff & Company, Inc., is now owned by CMP Media, Inc., and is used under a license from CMP. The book *NetGuide* is an independent publication not affiliated with CMP or any CMP publication.

The trademark Dell® is registered in the U.S. Patent and Trademark Office.

ISBN: 0-440-22429-2

Printed in the United States of America

Published simultaneously in Canada

October 1997

10 9 8 7 6 5 4 3 2 1

OPM

WOLFF NEW MEDIA

Michael Wolff
Publisher and Editor in Chief

Kelly Maloni
Executive Editor

Ben Greenman
Creative Director

Stevan Keane
Editor

Research Editor: Kristin Miller
Senior Editor: Dina Gan
Production Editor: Donna Spivey

Associate Art Director: Eric Hoffsten
Assistant Art Director: Jay Jaffe

Associate Editors: Molly Confer, Hylton Jolliffe, Bennett Voyles
Assistant Editors: Deborah Cohn, Rachel Greene
Staff Writers: Wendy Nelson, Stephanie Overby, Wendy Phillips
Editorial Assistants: Vicki Tsolomytis, Eric Zelko
Production Assistants: Alex Fogarty, Amy Gawronski

Contributing Writers: Cristine Cooper, Juan Gan, Laurie Kalmanson,
Elizabeth Kemler, Jeff O'Brien, Susan Pottinger, Hillary Rosner
Copy Editor: Sonya Donaldson

Vice President, Marketing: Jay Sears
Advertising Director: Michael Domican
Marketing Assistants: Nicholas Bogaty, Amy Winger

WOLFF NEW MEDIA LLC

Michael Wolff
President

Alison Anthoine
Vice President

Joseph Cohen
Chief Financial Officer

Special thanks:

And, as always, Aggy Aed

TABLE OF CONTENTS

Part 11: School Library

Appendices

FAQ

Frequently asked Questions about the Net and NetStudy

1. What is the Net, anyway?

The Net is the electronic medium composed of the millions of computers networked together throughout the world. Also known as cyberspace, the information highway, the IWay, or the Infobahn, the Net comprises four types of networks—the Internet, a global, noncommercial system with more than 30 million computers communicating through it; commercial online services, such as America Online and CompuServe; the set of discussion groups known as Usenet; and the thousands of regional and local bulletin board services (BBSs). Although the most common use of the Net is the exchange of email, the past year has seen the development of increasingly sophisticated methods for displaying and sharing information. More and more, the Internet refers to the World Wide Web, and more and more the Web unites all the diverse locations and formats that make up the Net.

2. How can the Net help me get better grades?

Students can conduct research, take sample tests, and meet with an online tutor for just about every subject they'll encounter in school. They can read novels, access dictionaries and encyclopedias, and search library catalogs. They can post their creative writing efforts online and correspond with other students from around the world by email. With multimedia and interactive lessons, getting an education has never been more effective or enjoyable. The Net makes education easier for educators, too. Teachers can get lesson plans, curriculum guides, and instruction on using the Internet in the classroom. They can also access other schools on the Net and find out how to become part of the global community of cybereducators. Part 1 of this book has a section called Teachers' Lounge, which has general education online resources for teachers. Most sections in this book also have a Teachers' Lounge subheading with subject-specific resources. Using the Internet, networking with other teachers has never been easier.

3. I'm learning something already. What do I need to get started?

A computer and a modem, and a few tricks to find your way around.

4. Can you help me decide what computer and modem I'll need?

If you've bought a computer fairly recently, it's likely that it came with everything you need. But let's assume you have only a bare-bones PC. In that case you'll also need to get a modem, which will allow your computer to communicate over the phone. So-called 14.4 modems, which transfer data at speeds up to 14,400 bits per second (bps), are standard. You should be able to get one for less than $100. But 28,800 bps modems are fast replacing them, and the prices are dropping rapidly. Next, you'll need a communications program to control the modem. This software will probably come free with your modem, your PC, or—if you're going to sign up somewhere—your online service. Otherwise, you can buy it off the shelf for under $25 or get a friend to download it from the Net. Finally, you'll want a telephone line (although if you plan to use the Net with any regularity, you'll probably want to consider installing a second phone line, because the cost of logging on repeatedly can mount quickly). If that's still not good enough, you can contact your local telephone utility to arrange for installation of an ISDN line, which allows data to be transmitted at even higher speeds. ISDN isn't as expensive as you think.

5. What kind of account should I get?

You'll definitely want to be able to get email; certainly want wide access to the Internet; and possibly want membership to at least one online service.

On the following pages you'll find some of your access choices.

Email Gateway

This is the most basic access you can get. It lets you send and receive messages to and from anyone, anywhere, anytime on the Net. Email is quickly becoming a standard way to communicate with friends and colleagues. (Yesterday: "What's your phone number?" Today: "What's your email address?") Email gateways are often available via work, school, or the online services listed here.

Online Services

Priciest but often easiest, these services have a wealth of options for the cyberstudent. Online services are cyber city-states. The large ones have more "residents" (members) than most U.S. cities—enough users, in other words, to support lively discussions and games among their membership, and enough resources to make a visit worthwhile. They generally require their own special start-up software, which you can buy at any local computer store or by calling the numbers listed in this book. (Hint: Look for the frequent starter-kit giveaways.) AOL and CompuServe, the largest online services, both provide access to many of Usenet's more than 10,000 newsgroups, email gateways through which you can subscribe to any Internet mailing lists, and access to the World Wide Web (WWW). America Online is even incorporating links to Web sites in its own forums.

Internet Providers

There are a growing number of full-service Internet providers (which means they offer email, Usenet, FTP, IRC, telnet, gopher, and WWW access). In practical terms, the Internet lets you lose yourself in the expanse of the Smithsonian museums or the authoritative Bartlett's Quotations; subscribe to a mailing list that helps you understand calculus or follow the latest research on particle physics; or find a newsgroup where the participants share their experiences with the dreaded SAT. Dial-up SLIP (serial line Internet protocol) and PPP (point-to-point protocol) accounts are currently the most popular types of Internet connections. They have all but replaced text-only, standard dial-up accounts and offer significantly faster access as well as graphically-enchanced point-and-click programs for Windows, Macintosh, and other platforms.

BBSs

BBSs range from mom-and-pop, hobbyist computer bulletin boards to large professional services. What the small ones lack in size they often make up for in affordability and homeyness. In fact, many users prefer these scenic roads to the increasingly commercial information highway. BBSs are easy to get started with, and if you find one with Internet access or an email gateway, you'll get the best of local color and global reach at once. You can locate local BBSs through the Usenet discussion groups alt.bbs.lists and comp.bbs.misc, or the BBS forums of the commercial online services. Many, if not most, local BBSs now offer Internet email, as well as live chat, and file libraries.

Direct Network Connection

Look, Ma Bell: no phone lines! The direct network connection is the fast track of college students, computer scientists, and a growing number of employees of high-tech businesses. It puts the user right on the Net, bypassing phone connections. In other words, it's a heck of a lot faster. If you're downloading hundreds of articles on Shakespeare or trying to follow a Net simulcast of a symposium, you'll need this kind of connection speed.

6. By the way, exactly how do I send email?

With email, you can write to anyone on a commercial service, Internet site, or Internet-linked BBS, as well as to those people connected to the Net via email gateways, SLIPs, and direct-network connections.

Email addresses have a universal syntax called an Internet address. An Internet address is broken down into four parts: the user's name (e.g., gan), the @ symbol, the computer and/or company name, and what kind of Internet address it is: **net** for network, **com** for a commercial enterprise—as with Your Personal Network (ypn.com) and America Online (aol.com)—**edu** for educational institutions, **gov** for government sites, **mil** for military facilities, and **org** for nonprofit and other private organizations. For instance, the address for the senior editor of this book, who has since earned the nickname Miss Jean Brodie, would be gan@ypn.com.

7. What about the Web?

The World Wide Web is a hypertext-based information structure that now dominates Internet navigation. The Web is like a house where every room has doors to a number of other rooms, or an electronic magazine where elements on the page are connected to elements on other pages. Words, icons, and pictures on a page link to other pages, not only on the same machine, but anywhere in the world. You have only to click on the appropriate word or phrase or image, and the Web does the rest. With invisible navigation, you can jump from a comprehensive list of libraries to a chat session focused on French to a commercial page touting the latest in math software. All the while you've FTPed, telnetted, gophered, and linked without a thought to case-sensitive Unix commands or addresses.

Your dial-up Internet provider undoubtedly offers programs that allow you to access the Web. Lynx and WWW are pretty much the standard offerings for text-only Web browsing. Usually you choose them by typing lynx and www and then <return>. What you'll get is a "page" with some of the text highlighted. These are the links. Choose a link, hit the return key, and you're off.

If you know exactly where you want to go on the Net and don't want to wade through Net directories and indexes, you can type a Web page's address, known as a URL (uniform resource locator). The URL for the education hubsite Global SchoolNet, for example, is http://www.gsn.org. On some Web browsers, such as the current version of Netscape, "http://" is not required. In our example, you could simply type www.gsn.org.

8. What about graphical Web browsers? What are these things?

With the emergence of new and sophisticated software like Netscape Navigator (http://www.netscape.com), the Web looks and sounds the way its architects imagined—pictures, icons, appetizing layouts, downloadable sound clips, and even animation. Some commercial services have developed customized Web browsers for their subscribers, but all will soon allow their users to choose from the most popular versions. If you subscribe to one of these services, head to the service's Internet forum for instructions on how to get on the Web. Web browsers are more than just presentation tools. Most of them allow Netsurfers to see all kinds of sites through a single interface. Want to read newsgroups? Need to send email? Interested in participating in real-time chat? You can do it all with your browser. And many Internet providers, including America Online, allow subscribers to build their own Web pages, which then reside semi-permanently in cyberspace.

9. And these newsgroups?

There are many places in cyberspace where netsurfers can post their opinions, questions, and comments, but the most widely read bulletin boards are a group of some 10,000-plus "newsgroups" collectively known as Usenet. Usenet newsgroups traverse the Internet, collecting thousands of messages a day from whomever wants to "post" to them. More than anything, the newsgroups are the collective, if sometimes babel-like voice of the Net—everything is discussed here. And we mean everything. On the soc.history newsgroup, people chat about everything from the post-Columbian pandemic to the necessity of using the A-bomb in World War II; on alt.sewing, seams, darts, and knife pleats are afforded center stage. While delivered over the Internet, Usenet newsgroups are not technically part of the Internet. Smaller BBSs that have news feeds sometimes store only a couple dozen newsgroups, while most Internet providers and online services offer thousands. (If there's a group missing that you really want, ask your Internet provider to add the newsgroup back to the subscription list.)

The messages in a newsgroup, called "posts," are listed and numbered chronologically—in other words, in the order in which they were posted. You can scan a list of messages before deciding to read a particular message. If someone posts a message that prompts responses, the original and all follow-up messages are called a thread. The subject line of subsequent posts in the thread refers to the subject of the original message. For example, if you were to post a message with the subject "Fake Volcanoes as a Science Project: Good idea or bad?" to sci.geo.geology, all responses would read "Re: Fake Volcanoes as a Science Project: Good idea or bad?" In practice, however, topics wander in many directions.

Popular newsgroups generate hundreds of messages daily. To cut back on repetitive questions, newsgroup members often compile extensive lists of answers to frequently asked questions (FAQs). Many FAQs have grown so large and so comprehensive that they are valuable resources in their own right, informal encyclopedias (complete with hypertext links) dedicated to the newsgroup's topic. For example, the alt.usage.english FAQ not only addresses the basics of words usage and grammar, but also focuses on specific topics like usage disputes and the origins of clichés.

10. Mailing lists?

Mailing lists are like newsgroups, except that they are distributed by Internet email. The fact that messages show up in your mailbox tends to make the discussion group more intimate, as does the proactive act of subscribing. Mailing lists are often more focused, and they're less vulnerable to irreverent and irrelevant contributions. For instance, students and teachers interested in Andean Folk Music can exchange information on discographies and Latin culture on the Andino mailing list.

To subscribe to a mailing list, send an email to the mailing list's subscription address. Often you will need to include very specific information, which you will find in this book. To unsubscribe, send another message to that same address. If the mailing list is of the listserv, listproc, or majordomo variety, you can usually unsubscribe by sending the command **unsubscribe <listname>** or **signoff <listname>** in the message body. If the mailing list instructs you to "Write a request" to subscribe ("Dear list owner, please subscribe me to…"), you will probably need to write a request to unsubscribe.

Once you have subscribed, messages are almost always sent to a different address than the subscription address. Most lists will send you the address when you subscribe. If not, send another message to the subscription address and ask the owner.

11. And telnet, FTP, gopher? Can you explain?

Telnet:

When you telnet, you're logging on to another computer somewhere else on the Internet. You then have access to the programs running on the remote computer. If the site is running a library catalog, for example, you can search the catalog. If it's running a live chat room, you can communicate with others logged on. Telnet addresses are listed as URLs, in the form **telnet://domain.name:port number**. A port number is not always required, but when listed it must be used.

FTP:

FTP (file transfer protocol) is a method of copying a file from another Internet-connected computer to your own. Hundreds of computers on the Internet allow "anonymous FTP." In other words, you don't need a unique password to access them. Just type "anonymous" at the user prompt and type your email address at the password prompt. The range of material available is extraordinary—from archives of journal articles to collections of anatomical images. Since the advent of Web browsers, net-surfers can transfer files without using a separate FTP program. In this book, FTP addresses are listed as URLs, in the form **ftp://domain.name/directory/filename.txt**. And here's an extra bonus—logins and passwords aren't required with Web browsers.

Gopher:

A gopher is a program that turns Internet addresses into menu options. Gophers can perform many Internet functions, including telnetting and downloading files. Gopher addresses throughout this book are listed as URLs, with all necessary steps chained together as pieces of a URL.

12. So, I'm ready. How does the book work?

If you're an experienced surfer and you already know the name of the site you'd like to read about, or if your interest is limited to a specific topic, then just turn to the *NetStudy* index, where every site and subject covered in the book is listed alphabetically. If you prefer a more leisurely approach, you can simply browse through the book, which is divided into eleven parts:

• **Back to School**
• **English**
• **Mathematics**
• **Science**
• **Social Studies**
• **History**
• **Foreign Languages**
• **The Arts**
• **Electives**
• **Phys. Ed.**
• **School Library**

Back to School furnishes students, teachers, and parents with addresses and descriptions of the most general educational sites—everything from virtual classrooms in cyberspace to homeschooling home pages. **English** takes you into the world of grammar, composition, and literature. **Mathematics** collects resources on dozens of topics ranging from algebra formulas to geometric transformations. **Science** not only describes important concepts in biology, chemistry, and physics, but points net-surfers toward places online where they can find the very latest research. **Social Studies** describes the best of the Net's civics, economics, and human studies sites, addressing everything from ethnic identity to voter's rights. **History** reminds netsurfers that those who don't remember the past can look it up in cyberspace. **Foreign Languages** points out linguistic resources online, extracting the best translation references and tutorials on the Net. **The Arts** takes a closer look at dance, visual art, and music, both making and appreciating it. **Electives** shows the way to online authorities on home economics, industrial arts, and life skills like driving and typing. **Phys. Ed.** gathers resources on just about every sport played in school, from archery to weightlifting. And the **School Library** contains an exhaustive list of online libraries and general reference sites.

All entries in *NetStudy* have a name, description, and address. The site name appears first in boldface, followed by the description of the site. After the description, complete address information is provided. The name of the network appears first—**WEB** to designate the World Wide Web, **AMERICA ONLINE** to designate America Online, and so on. When you see an arrow (→), this means that you have another step ahead of you, such as typing a command, searching for a file, or subscribing to a mailing list. Bullets separate multiple addresses, which indicate that the site is accessible through other networks.

If the item is a Web site, FTP site, telnet, or gopher, it will be displayed in the form of a URL, which can be typed in the command line of your Web browser. FTP and gopher sites will be preceded by **URL**, while telnet sites, which cannot be launched directly through a browser, will be preceded by **TELNET**. If the item is a mailing list, the address will include an email address and instructions on how to subscribe (remember—the address given is usually the subscription address; in order to post to the mailing list, you will use another address that will be emailed to you upon subscribing). IRC addresses indicate what you must type to get to the channel you want once you've connected to the IRC server. Entries about newsgroups are always followed by the names of the newsgroups.

In an online service address, the name of the service is followed by the keyword (also called "go word"). Additional steps are listed where necessary.

In addition, there are a few special terms used in addresses. *Info* indicates a supplementary informational address. *Archives* is used to mark collections of past postings for newsgroups and mailings lists. And *FAQ* designates the location of a "frequently asked questions" file for a newsgroup.

13. When I'm done studying at cyberschool, where should I be looking to investigate other topics?

Try *NetChat, NetGames, NetSports, NetMusic, Fodor's NetTravel, NetVote, NetJobs, NetMarketing, NetTech, NetDoctor, NetCollege, NetSpy, NetSci-Fi, NetGuide, NetShopping, NetKids, NetLove,* and *NetMoney.*

PART 1

Back to School

HOMEROOM

I F IT WERE TRUE THAT ALL YOU need to know you learned in kindergarten, then you'd miss out on all the wonderful experiences that junior and senior high school have to offer. You'd never get to dissect a frog, write teenage poetry, weld a metal basket, or play field hockey. You'd miss out on your first crush, passing notes, and making fun of your substitute teachers. And where would you learn about sex, drugs, and coping with bullies? Besides, it's hard to imagine joining the work force at the age of four. Secondary school exists to let you grow into those adult clothes, and you may as well master reading, writing, and arithmetic while you're at it. It might seem like an endless chore now, but when you've reached the end of your high school career, you'll be happy to discover that you've got four years of college to go before you have to join the real world.

▶ STARTING POINTS

Ameritech Schoolhouse Disappointed to find that neither juggling nor model railroads are on the class schedule for this year? Don't despair—Ameritech's schoolhouse can help. The communications corporation's educational site is well-stocked with resources for students and teachers. Lesson plans can be found in the teacher's lounge. Interactive exhibits from "How Light Works" to "Aboriginal Trail" are linked through the Student Activities page. A What's New area keeps everyone up to date on newly constructed Web sites of interest.
WEB http://www.ameritech.com/products /education/schoolhouse

Classroom Connect This site's professional look and feel distinguish it from its homespun counterparts. Classroom Connect is clean and well-organized, which will no doubt come as a comfort to those who are intimidated by the daunting chaos of the Net. Search educational sites by subject—all the basics plus art, culture, writing, vo-tech, and early childhood. There are also databases for teacher contacts, conferences, and global school Web sites, as well as press releases from Classroom's multimedia publishing program.
WEB http://www.classroom.net

CPHS Resources for Teachers and Students College Park High School's contribution to electronic learning, direct from the utopian-sounding Pleasant Hill in California's techno-saturated Bay Area. If you happen to be in Contra Costa County and need to learn about its school system, you're in luck. For the rest of the world, there's also a good resource page with links to other wired schools, librarian guides, magazines, educational TV sites, and more.
WEB http://www.crl.com/~crcarter/CPHS /Ed-Resources.html

CyberSchool Magazine The monthly guide to edification on the Net. Departments include the Bionic Bard (literature and poetry), Time Machine (history), Nuclear Newton (science), and Electric Professor (modern educational issues). If you're not sure where to find what you're looking for, ask the Surfin' Librarian, who'll lead you to learning links and online books in your subject of choice.
WEB http://www.infoshare.ca/csm/index .htm

DeweyWeb John Dewey not only invented the Dewey Decimal System, he also founded the University of Michigan's School of Education, which has sponsored this Web site. DeweyWeb has designed a number of interactive learning projects for the online environment, including Monday Morning Games, which trains students to solve problems; and the Route 12 Project, which unites students from across the country.
WEB http://ics.soe.umich.edu

Education Picking classes, getting good grades, choosing a college, and teaching aren't easy, but deciding which online service to use for educational resources is a cinch. America Online has brought under a single menu an extensive pool of teachers, tutors, classes, counselors, educational publications, computer companies with educational software, reference tools, teaching organizations, and links to Internet educational resources. From the Teachers' Information Network to the Educational Software Libraries, from the Online Campus to the forum for the Library of Congress, from The Learning Channel forum to the full text of Smithsonian magazine, AOL is a powerhouse for learning.

AMERICA ONLINE *keyword* education

Education Forum Homeschooling parents, college professors, elementary teachers, and high school students are part of the community of people who use this forum to discuss a wide range of educational topics including teaching techniques, ongoing classroom projects, study abroad programs, grammar, and even teen pregnancy and vaccinations. In the libraries, CompuServe members can download a Mandarin dictionary, a molar mass calculator, a guide to punctuation, essays on the value of classical education and Montessori schools, and electronic student organizers.

COMPUSERVE *go* edforum

EdWeb Homeroom just isn't what it used to be. This site, sponsored by the Corporation of Public Broadcasting, explores educational reform and information technology in the twentieth century, sorting out what aspects of the hypermedia revolution will actually change classrooms and what are just plain "hype." EdWeb's homeroom contains such gems as a dictionary of technological terms from ASCII to WWW, a concise hypertext history of the information superhighway, and a clear rundown of educational trends. Teachers, administrators, and interested parties can also connect to other sites and discussion groups dealing with primary and secondary school education.

WEB http://edweb.cnidr.org

Explorer This is the University of Kansas's math and science site for k-12 students. Access in-depth reviews of hundreds of field trips—both virtual and brick-and-mortar varieties. Search for lesson plans to help with specific subjects, and learn how to order instructional aids. True to its mathematical roots, Explorer has an EduLette feature that randomly selects a teaching tool. The site's thorough methods of cataloguing resources—with information on availability, curriculum compatibility, and process skills—makes it a handy and comprehensive tool.

WEB http://unite2.tisl.ukans.edu/www home.html

Global Schoolhouse A pioneer in using the Internet for kids' education, the Global Schoolhouseproject was designed to explore the possibilities and potential of the Net in public schools. The Web site lets you in on the results, with reports from individual schools and projects, and links for contacting teachers.

WEB http://k12.cnidr.org/gsh/gshwelcome .html

Global SchoolNet What began a decade ago as a group of teachers in San Diego working at a grass-roots level has grown into an internationally recognized educational information infrastructure. The GSN Foundation now provides global Net-working opportunities for schools, students, and teachers everywhere. Features like the Global Schoolhouse, ThinkQuest, KidsPeak, Student Ambassadors, as well as links to newsgroups, articles, and Internet training, make this site a must-visit.

WEB http://www.gsn.org

GNN Education Center The center highlights the latest resources for the cyber-savvy k-12 teacher. The site includes information on how to get your kids involved in elections and politics online, interactive ideas for celebrating holidays, and a cybercourse to teach students about the stock market.

WEB http://www-e1c.gnn.com/edu

Integrating the Internet Arizona teacher Susan Hixson's educational resources include a monthly newsletter, the *Internet Travel Guide*, dedicated to helping educators harness the potential of the Net. Her Web site also provides links to classroom study units on a wide range of topics for specific grade levels: great impressionists like Monet, volcanoes, and fossils are just the beginning. Hixson's motto is "Save a tree—Read digitally," and there's no lack of reading material offered.
WEB http://www.indirect.com/www /dhixson/index.html

Janice's K-12 Cyberspace Outpost Janice is a super-dedicated teacher, and she's assembled a collection of links designed to make learning fun. Her Rave of the Month features new sites of interest—one month it was an online kids magazine, another month, a trip through the solar system. Links to libraries, schools, and museums round out her list.
WEB http://k12.cnidr.org/janice_k12 /k12menu.html

Jerome and Deborah's Big Page of Educational Sites This cozy site comes to you from Manitoba, Canada, where teachers at the Duck Bay School and the Oscar Blackburn School, have clearly put lots of love into its creation. Choose your areas of interest from student research, curriculum resources, special ed, ESL, counseling and guidance, and adult ed, to name just a few, then marvel at the vast selection of links. Student research will point you in the direction of folk and fairy tales from around the world, the comet Shoemaker-Levy, or Javanese mask collections, for starters.
WEB http://www.mts.net/~jgreenco/jerdeb .html

K-12 Education The National Lab for Computational Science and Engineering has goodies for students, teachers, and techno-wizards. Track down research opportunities, download curriculum development tools, or visit the Science Scholars Program, a computer-based

learning project for teenage girls. SSP features photos of kids who participated, as well as personal descriptions of their work—just one example of effective use of the Web to get students interested in learning about science and technology.
WEB http://www.sdsc.edu/education.html

K-12 Educational Resources SUNY Plattsburgh's exhaustive resource links include all the heavy-hitters like state departments of education and individual wired schools, but the site also delves a few steps deeper into the Net's educational vaults. Connect to libraries, including special exhibitions and offices at the Library of Congress; access a wide variety of Web search engines; or browse through kids' magazines, read electronically created stories, and check out invaluable gems such as an animal information database.
WEB http://137.142.42.95/K-12/K-12 EducationResources.html

Macintosh Education Forum A forum dedicated to using the Macintosh computer as an educational tool. There are interesting resources for parents, teachers, administrators, and students. The Weekly Update feature fills you in on the latest activities in the forum, including new uploads, live conferences, and updated information files. Education on the Internet is a searchable database containing articles, announcements, and information on educational happenings available on the Internet. The Electronic Books library includes literary classics like Shakespeare's plays and sonnets along with science-fiction and foreign-language texts. Several Special Interest Groups (SIGs) add to the resources, including Apple Classrooms of Tomorrow and Pictures of the World, which offer digital photographs of sites around the world that can be downloaded for classroom use.
AMERICA ONLINE *keyword* med

Middle of Nowhere If you taught courses called "Taming the Electronic Frontier" and "Using the Internet in the K12 Classroom," chances are your Web site

would be well-conceived, interesting, and useful. Brad Cox, a professor in the Program on Social and Organizational Learning at George Mason University, has built this ambitious site, which provides "broad and deep information to students of all ages." Middle of Nowhere is part marketing device for Cox and GMU and part beautifully constructed virtual learning community—chock full of layers of links, giving the impression that you could get stranded here for an endless length of time, probing and absorbing until your brain began to ache.
WEB http://www.virtualschool.edu/mon
• http://rembrandt.erols.com/mon

NCSA Education Program Teachers and students will find suggestions on how to get the most out of the Net through online tutorials, networking groups, and links to sites with both educational and entertainment value. Teachers will be delighted by the k-12 resource page which holds ideas for classroom fun on the Web.
WEB http://www.ncsa.uiuc.edu/Edu/Edu Home.html

UIUC's Learning Resources Server If you've got the inclination to muddle through a lengthy list of links on a rather dull-looking page, the University of Illinois's site offers access to federal, state, and local government educational bodies including the National Science Foundation and Illinois's wired school districts. Discover loads of useful networking projects, research sites, and virtual libraries, all in an extremely traditional and not-at-all high-tech looking environment.
WEB http://www.ed.uiuc.edu/Education -add.html

Virtual Schoolhouse All the amenities of traditional school, without the hall monitors or the scary cafeteria food. Visit the classrooms for educational links by subject, make a trip to the library if you're interested in cybercollections and online bookstores, stop in the art room to find museums and exhibits, or spend time on the playground for a little net recreation.

As always, stay away from the principal's office, unless you're interested in discipline and administration.
WEB http://sunsite.unc.edu/cisco /schoolhouse.html

World Education Exchange A global glimpse of the latest advancements in educational trends, policy, and infrastructure development. This Hamline University site covers technology in the classroom, research and grant sites, U.S. educational projects and school models from other countries, and scads of other school-related sites arranged by subject.
WEB http://www.hamline.edu/~kjmaier

World Wide Web Virtual Library: Education Library of links to hundreds of education-related sites around the globe. Scan the alphabetical listing or search by level (primary, secondary, tertiary, postgraduate), type of site (general, regional authority, clearinghouse, institution), resources offered, or country of origin.
WEB http://www.csu.edu.au/education /library.html

▶ **HOMEWORK HELP**

Academic Assistance Center For instant educational gratification, the Academic Assistance Center has no competition. Students can page teachers for help with their homework and expect answers within a few hours, join live nightly study sessions on subjects ranging from Algebra I to American History, post questions on more than a dozen message boards (Law and Medical Questions, Women's Studies, English & Literature Questions, Math Questions, etc.), or head to the Mini-Lesson Libraries for explanations and articles on hundreds of topics (Roosevelt and the Flappers, Polk and the War with Mexico, Logarithms and Statistics, Division, the Greek and Roman Gods, Sonnet 116, etc.). The Center also links to *Barron's Booknotes* (the quintessential cheat sheets), a reference desk with dictionaries and encyclopedias, and an

Exam Prep Center.
AMERICA ONLINE *keyword* homework

Cliffs Notes "So much to study, so little time." The familiar black-and-yellow stripes are here in full force with all the shortcuts to knowledge you have come to know and love. Aside from the hundreds of plain-language abbreviated versions of great works of literature, Cliffs Notes online has study guides and interactive software to help you prepare for standardized tests and review courses you never attended. Of course, wisdom has a price tag, but the Cliffs Notes home page gives you access to free stuff like a Cliffs Study Tips disk and a cool screen saver. ("Cool." As if.)
WEB http://www.cliffs.com

Teacher Pager Summoning academic help has never been easier. Type in the keyword and a form pops up on the screen. Input a topic or question, your grade level, and what time you want to meet a teacher for help. Click "send," and the mail is sent to the box of the Interactive Education Services Coordinator, who will inform you when and where you can meet a teacher. If you need help from a teacher ASAP, remain online for at least five minutes and someone will be with you shortly.
AMERICA ONLINE *keyword* teacher pager

TermPapers.on.Line If 15,000 papers isn't too many for you (and if you can deal with the guilt of not writing your paper yourself), check out what this company has to offer. The Web site offers a different essay every month—yours free for the plagiarizing—on such high-school favorites as "Breaking Free: An essay on self-rule in Alcott's 'Actress' and Emerson's 'Self Reliance.'" Email for a free catalog and then pay the piper.
WEB http://www.termpapersonline.com

> **COURSES**

CASO: The Internet University Trying to take an art class at Antioch, a history class at California State, and a religion class at the University of Florida in the same semester could make for a hell of a commute. But the Internet University makes it possible to find out about the 700 classes available nationwide that you can take by computer. Listings by course and college provider, along with related sites, articled on the values of Internet instruction, and information on each University's offerings, accreditation, and fees.
WEB http://www.caso.com/iuhome.html

College Courses Online Need help with Renaissance art history, macroeconomics, psychology 101, or the principles of physics? Look no further. There are complete courses here—with notes, illustrations, bibliographies, and sometimes even tests. Want to know the difference between a credit and a debit? Download a complete accounting course. If you hurry you can catch up with the weekly Spanish lesson—*vamos a la playa* means "let's go to the beach."
WEB http://www.yahoo.com/Education/Courses

Interactive Education Services Classes are offered regularly on topics ranging from creative writing to algebra to computer programming to music theory. Courses last from four to eight weeks and include real-time meetings with teachers and other students, support from teachers on the message boards, and resources archived in libraries. Cost of classes is usually less than $50.
AMERICA ONLINE *keyword* classes

Mindquest Going back for that high school diploma is getting easier. Mindquest, administered by the Bloomington public school system, is free to Minnesota residents and qualified out-of-state residents by tuition agreement with their local high school. Adults can earn a high school degree by taking online classes, as well as demonstrating what they've learned through work and life experiences and applying credit that they've earned in previously completed high school courses. Browse the FAQ to make sure you have all the right hardware and Mindquest will send you the

software needed to enter the virtual campus.
WEB http://www.mindquest.bloomington.k12.mn.us

Teaching and Learning on the World Wide Web A collection of cyberclasses, Internet-aware assignments, and online information and resources provided by the Maricopa Community Colleges in Arizona. The index of more than 300 sites is searchable by subject, from anthropology to zoology.
WEB http://www.mcli.dist.maricopa.edu/cgi-bin/index_tl

World Lecture Hall An attempt to use hypertext technology to create an online university, with pointers to information and educational Web sites in almost 50 disciplines. From accounting to virology, with plenty of stops in between—agricultural engineering, art history, cultural studies, marketing, mathematics, and pharmacology—these sites comprise university syllabi, articles, lecture notes, and even the occasional online exam.
WEB http://www.utexas.edu/world/lecture

SCHOOLS ONLINE

HotList of K-12 Internet School Sites Wondering what the Internet-active students at Mississippi's Moss Point High School are up to, or are you curious to see what school home pages look like in Hawaii? This site maintains links to elementary, middle and high schools nationwide that have some kind of Net presence (Web, FTP, gopher, telnet). Also noted are cybersavvy school districts, regional networks, and state departments of education as well as statistics on the number of schools known to be online by state, grade, and site type.
WEB http://www.sendit.nodak.edu/k12

KeyPals International Studying other countries and cultures becomes infinitely more interesting when you can visualize what your life would be like if you lived there. KeyPals is an impressive listing of email addresses for secondary schools on every continent. While it's tough to verify this, KeyPals claims to have listings for every secondary school in the world with a Web page. With friends in exotic countries all over the world, the possibilities for exploring are limitless.
WEB http://www.collegebound.com/keypals

School Districts For warm fuzzies about the future of education in the U.S. (and Canada), travel to Yahoo!'s ABCs of online school districts. From Alachua and Anne Arundel to Yupiit and Zeeland and every district in between.
WEB http://www.yahoo.com/Education/K_12/School_Districts

Web66: WWW School Registry Get your kicks on Web66, a collection of schools and kids exploring the Web. A school in Sholihull, England wants to know how many kids worldwide enjoy M&Ms. American Indian students in New Mexico offer recipes for Green Chile Chicken Enchiladas and other kids make cyberpals with students at the Bilkent University Prepatory School in Ankara, Turkey.
WEB http://hillside.coled.umn.edu/others.htm • http://web66.coled.umn.edu • http://hillside.coled.umn.edu

ON THE AIR

A&E Classroom A&E makes it easy for educators to plans lessons based on their shows. A&E biographies, mysteries, specials—it's all educational fodder. All the instructor has to do is tape the show and print out the classroom materials presented (including vocabulary words, discussion questions, class activities, and project suggestions). View a day or a week's worth of A&E programming on the TV listings page or search for your subject of choice.
WEB http://www.aetv.com/aeclassroom/classroom.html

The ABC Classroom ABC TV is online, with a variety of resources: guides to Afterschool Specials; a reference library with flags, atlases, and profiles of newsmakers; video clips of moments in television history; news releases; and an active message board for educators to share ideas about science fairs, gradebook software, and School House Rock.

AMERICA ONLINE *keyword* abc

CNN Newsroom An online companion to the fifteen-minute daily news program for school children, the forum is designed to help educators integrate news and current event discussions into their classrooms. What's on CNN? Daily classroom guides, tons of maps, an entire section devoted to adventure learning (Turner Broadcasting's term for electronic field trips to famous historical sites or natural wonders), live discussions about news events, and several areas where students and teachers can chat. What's not on CNN? James Earl Jones intoning, "Kids, do your homework, or else I will devour you!" But we can always dream.

AMERICA ONLINE *keyword* cnn

Discovery Channel School The folks at the Discovery Channel stick to what they do best—documentary television—and provide interesting ways for educators to integrate it into their lesson plans. Learning communities bring students and teachers together to explore a specific subject, like China or the African-American migration, placing a high priority on student contributions with the Student Showcase. The site also highlights a Discovery or Learning channel program teachers may want to videotape and contains a vault of clips they may have missed.

WEB http://school.discovery.com

History Channel Classroom Know who said, "I regret to say that we of the FBI are powerless to act in cases of oral-genital intimacy, unless it has in some way obstructed interstate commerce"? If you do, you could win a cap in the weekly History Channel quiz. This sister site to A&E makes integrating History Channel programs into the classroom, from "Who Built Stonehenge?" to "Churchill and the Cabinet War Rooms," as easy as point and click.

WEB http://www.historychannel.com /classroom/classroom.html

PBS Education Forum Learn to type or to program a multimedia presentation, memorize the names of prehistoric animals or conjugate Spanish verbs, communicate in sign language or understand the anatomy of the skull. The shareware libraries here don't require a library card just a registration fee if you decide to use what you downloaded. Class dismissed.

COMPUSERVE *go* pbseducation

STUDENT EXCHANGE

The Electronic Schoolhouse Teachers use the area to link classrooms to work on projects (recycling, the Underground Railroad, etc.); and schools link to help students find email pen pals, or to pool teaching resources and ideas. Teachers and classrooms can add their names to a "project partner" directory. The libraries are filled with the resources and project lessons used in hundreds of projects.

AMERICA ONLINE *keyword* esh

Intercultural E-Mail Classroom Connections Do your kids need help with their class project on Korea? Do they want to improve their Dutch? This site provides a scholastic matchmaking service for classrooms and individual students. Kids can post an intellectual personal ad and end up with a world of cyberpals.

WEB http://www.stolaf.edu/network/iecc
Info: **EMAIL** iecc-request@stolaf.edu

KIDINTRO Picture the first day of school, but everyone's new and the students come not just from across town, but across the globe. KIDINTRO is presented as a game, in which kids choose a partner in their class and post information about each other by way of introduction to the group.

EMAIL listserv@sjuvm.stjohns.edu
Type in message body: subscribe kidintro <your full name>

KidLink Since its inception in 1990, Kidlink's Global Youth Dialog has had more than 60,000 participants from 85 different countries. To join, participants must first answer "The Four Questions" at the organization's home page, and then choose from a number of mailing lists. KIDCAFE engages students in discussions about poetry, music, sports, the environment, and everything else on their minds. Hiroko, a 13-year-old Japanese student, recently expressed her concern over learning that shampoo pollutes water. KIDLINK is the organization's official news and information mailing list. There are also discussion groups in different languages, forums for special projects, and opportunities to help coordinate activities.
WEB http://www.kidlink.org

Kids & Teen Student Forum Let's talk about literature and geography. Not quite. The forum does have discussion topics and libraries of resources devoted to academic interests, but the more popular areas focus on extra-curricular interests (music, sports, and general chat among teens). Religious education is also a popular topic ("Was God created?" "I need advice!" "Any Jewish teens?").
COMPUSERVE *go* student

KIDSPHERE This international network for students and teachers has a dual objective: getting individual schools connected to the Net, class by class, and a "grand scheme" of linking the whole world. In the meantime, KIDSPHERE primarily consists of teachers trading information—on workshops, grants, books, Web tools, computers, and research projects, and everything in between.
EMAIL kidsphere@vms.cis.pitt.edu *Type in message body:* subscribe kidsphere <your full name>

PENPAL-L Suzie tells Mickey she's dyed her hair red. Mahmud tells the group about daily life in Saudi Arabia. Bilge tries to escape the Turkish draft. There's talk of *Star Trek*, health, the children's march in Washington, ham radio operat-

ing, and shopping in Boston. This active list is a virtual coffee klatch for conversation of all levels of seriousness, a penpal club where you seem to always get more penpals than you bargained for. While the intellectual stimulation is scattered, it does exist, and lengthy dissertations and debates on bizarre socio-cultural topics can spontaneously erupt. Most participants are American, but the international presence offers first-hand insight into other cultures for those willing to make small talk until the "conversation" heats up.
EMAIL listserv@unccvm.uncc.edu *Type in message body:* subscribe penpal-l <your full name>

Student Ambassadors Are you a student making exceptional contributions toward using the Internet in education? You may qualify to be elected a Student Ambassador. You must also be 6 to 18 years old, have daily email access, and must agree to be a "good global citizen." At this Web page, find out more about how to apply for the one-year position and check out the pictures, projects, and Web pages of current and past Student Ambassadors.
WEB http://www.gsn.org/gsn/sa/index.html

▶ SOFTWARE

Apple II Education Software Educational software for the Apple II series of computers is divided in this forum into categories, such as math, reading, and social studies. There are some useful tools for teachers in this library, such as computerized grade books and quizmakers. Click on the Special Interest Groups icon for live conferences and discussion boards.
AMERICA ONLINE *keyword* a2→Apple II Software Libraries→Education Software

The Children's Software Company Home Page An extensive catalog of educational software for children of all ages (preschool through high school) and all major platforms (Mac and PC).
WEB http://www.childsoft.com/childsoft

Cool Software for Kids Prove to Mom and Dad that the computer is an educational tool that benefits us all with this page, which includes reviews for kids by kids. The site is primarily a catalog of software.
web http://www.internet.net/Kidz/index.html

Education & Children's Multimedia Study the elements for chemistry class. Practice elementary Spanish. Use the multimedia aids in this library to help you learn quickly.
AMERICA ONLINE *keyword* mmw→Libraries →Education & Children's

Education/Reference You can learn the geography of Hungary or explore astrology with the shareware and freeware programs in this library. The collection includes language programs, math tutors, religious quizzes, and even music lessons.
COMPUSERVE *go* winshare→Libraries→ Education/Reference

SimTel DOS Education Software A directory of educational shareware for DOS users, including an animated addition and subtraction tutorial, a companion program to *The Diary of Anne Frank*, a coin recognition game, a spelling program, an interactive chemistry game, a beginning Spanish program, a typing training program, and a Russian-English dictionary.
web http://www.acs.oakland.edu/oak /SimTel/msdos/educatin.html
url ftp://oak.oakland.edu/SimTel/msdos /educatin • ftp://wuarchive.wustl.edu /systems/ibmpc/simtel/msdos/educatin

SimTel Windows Education Software A collection of Windows programs for educational purposes, including a student organizer and a multimedia flash-card system. Most programs are for a fairly young crowd.
web http://www.acs.oakland.edu/oak /SimTel/win3/educate.html
url ftp://oak.oakland.edu/SimTel/win3 /educate • ftp://wuarchive.wustl.edu /systems/ibmpc/simtel/win3/educate

Windows Educational Software Programs for both students and teachers, including a math tutor, a planetarium simulator, and grading organizers, all designed to run under Microsoft Windows. The collection of programs is diverse, with titles ranging from piano instruction to bible study. Unfortunately, the software has not been organized by category, so you'll have to browse through the listings or use the search engine.
AMERICA ONLINE *keyword* winforum→ Browse the Software Libraries→ Applications→Educational

TEACHERS' LOUNGE

WHOEVER SAID THAT TEACHING was a noble profession should be shot. What's so great about being an underpaid, overworked, underappreciated babysitter? Until the world puts that halo over your head where it rightfully belongs, the Internet can help you keep those snot-picking, note-passing, spitball-throwing brats (and if you're one of them, get out—this is the teachers' lounge!) under control and maybe even help you teach them a thing or two. Start with Learning on the Web to find out how to take cyberspace to task in the classroom. Swap lesson plans can help at The Academy One Curriculum Exchange. Then converge at the Teachers' Lounge on AOL for coffee, tea, and sympathy.

> STARTING POINTS

AskERIC This site is under development for use as an automated information outlet for AskERIC, a pilot project of the ERIC system and the Department of Education. The Educational Resources Information Center (ERIC) is a federally-funded national information system that provides access to an extensive body of education-related literature. AskERIC is an Internet-based question-answering service for teachers, library media specialists, and administrators. Anyone involved with k-12 education can send a message to AskERIC. Drawing on the extensive resources of the ERIC system, AskERIC staff will respond with an answer within 48 working hours.
WEB http://ericir.syr.edu

Choices Education Project The CEP is an educational program of the Thomas J. Watson Jr. Institute for International Studies at Brown University, whose self-proclaimed goal is "to engage the American Public in the consideration of international issues and strengthen the quality of public life in the United States." Through the Web site, educators can purchase daily lesson plans that coincide with the program's mission—a curriculum that focuses on global environmental problems, immigration issues, and the role of the U.S. in a changing world. Also, learn about professional development programs, or subscribe to the Choices newsletter.
WEB http://www.brown.edu/Research /Choices

Cisco Education Archive Cisco's Cearch engine provides access to a huge database of educational articles, with a special emphasis on the Internet's role in teaching and learning. This hefty site is always a good starting point for information on high technology and education.
WEB http://sunsite.unc.edu/cisco/edu -arch.html

Classroom Compass This online science and math magazine for educators is devoted to exploring the connections between specific classroom activities and broader ideas about learning. Each issue addresses a different theory such as constructivism or cooperative learning, and provides articles, reading lists, and links to educational associations.
WEB http://www.sedl.org/scimath /compass/cchp.html

Edlinks A West Virginia high school principal includes some of the Net's best education sites on his page. John Mullens covers the biggies like Educom, AskERIC, and the Library of Congress along with smaller sites like Kathy Schrock's Guide for Educators and Teacher Talk, an online conferencing system for k-12 instructors to share advice and anecdotes about their latest teaching triumph or struggle. Each site is succinctly described.
WEB http://webpages.marshall.edu /~jmullens/edlinks.html

Educational Links This site offers links to museums, government organizations, current events, and student sites, but gets its highest marks for the teachers' resources offered. This is the place for

quirky, enlightening, and fascinating information for use by educators. It'll even help you access primary source materials on the Web, like the "Letters from an Iowa Soldier in the Civil War," available through one linked site. The museum listings are a bit paltry: The current list includes only one art museum and the Lascaux cave paintings in France.
WEB http://wacky.ccit.arizona.edu/~susd/dvlinks.html

Eisenhower National Clearinghouse
Sponsored by the U.S. Department of Education, this clearinghouse provides info for k-12 math and science teachers. Curriculum resources, published articles, grant opportunities, classroom-ready materials—it's all here, as well as links to sites on topics as far-reaching as "phylum Mollusca, class Cephalopoda."
WEB http://www.enc.org

Electronic Learning You might think the new generation of teachers will be technology-trained, but a report shows that schools of education are barely keeping up on the information superhighway. "New Teachers: Unplugged" is one of the bi-monthly exclusive reports featured on this Scholastic site devoted to the exploration of technology in the classroom. Other digital departments include news and conferences, software-at-a-glance, grants update, and emerging technology.
WEB http://199.95.184.10/EL/index.html

K-12 Sources Hundreds of links (you'll lose count after 500) to resources for k-12 teachers are offered. Lesson plans, commercial and individually maintained sites, schools, training programs and materials, health and safety issues, publications, and a General Resources section which by itself has more than 200 links. Many of the sites are even annotated. All in all, a fantastic resource.
WEB http://execpc.com/~dboals/k-12.html

Learning on the Web An Internet instructor's manual authored by TeleEducation NB, a Canadian distance learning network centered in New Brunswick, the site takes would-be cyberteachers through the process of creating an online learning environment and links to net resources to aid in adapting and developing courses for Web delivery.
WEB http://cnet.unb.ca/lotw

Macintosh Educators Site Iowa's Hampton-Dumont Community School District has taken up the community-spirited task of providing links for fellow Mac users. It's got links to sites for math, science, music, technology, social studies, languages, arts, and—of course—Macs.
WEB http://www.hampton-dumont.k12.ia.us/web/mac

National Education Association The cyberarm of the NEA—America's oldest and largest organization committed to advancing the cause of public education—covers issues such as the latest in innovative approaches to restructuring school learning, how schools are faring under federal budget cuts, and public schools with a Web presence. For lighter fare, take a break on the recess page where teachers offer classroom anecdotes good for a chuckle or two, like the one about the kindergartener who announced that the octopus he was drawing needed more testicles, or this one from Nancy in Nebraska: "I called Kenny and Louie to my desk to explain that they had failed their test due to cheating. Kenny demanded, 'How do you know?' I told them that the tests were nearly identical. Kenny then said, 'That could be a coincidence.' I agreed except for number thirteen. Kenny had written, 'I don't know.' Louie wrote, 'I don't know either.'"
WEB http://www.nea.org

National PTA The 100-year-old National PTA has created what amounts to an online branch of its organization, a site where you can learn about joining any number of PTA projects, gather news and info, discuss pertinent issues and emerging initiatives, or join the real organization. The comprehensive site has clearly marked the hotlinks that lead to pages not contained on the organization's own server, so parents and teachers can stay alert as they surf the Net. The site has links to local PTA chapters, plus access to the organization's reference library, press releases, and calendar of events.

WEB http://www.pta.org

The School House Project If you believe that form follows function, then you'll love this virtual school that's designed just like the real thing. The Schoolhouse Project has classrooms, a library, and offices for the nurse, the principal, and the counselor—all that's missing is the charming smell of cafeteria food. Funded by the Department of Education, Funds for Innovation in Education, and the Teacher/Pathfinder Project, this site is a terrific treasure chest for teachers: lesson plans, teaching standards, special projects, field trips, papers, and periodicals are all at your fingertips. The Schoolhouse will also connect you to bulletin boards for collaborative projects or discussion groups.

WEB http://www.nwrel.org/school_house

Teachers' Information Network Teachers rarely get the support they need or deserve—but there's support aplenty on the Teachers' Information Network. TIN provides educators with links to forums for the largest teaching organizations in the country, including the American Federation of Teachers and the National Education Association; a large resource pavillion with links to CNN, C-Span, the Smithsonian, and dozens of other teaching resources; a searchable list of educational TV and radio programming; educational libraries with software (teaching state capitals, cataloging grades, or creating quizzes); lesson plans for all grade levels and subjects; and HyperCard learning stacks. In addition, there's a searchable database of information about hundreds of educational magazines, journals, and reports; support areas for dozens of education software providers; and AskERIC Online, a service that is partly a searchable database of education-related literature and reports

and partly a teacher hotline with help for educators.

AMERICA ONLINE *keyword* teachers

Teachers' Lounge A leisurely way to network with fellow teachers awaits at this AOL forum. In the Idea Exchange section, swap exams, lessons plans, and classroom techniques on every k-12 subject from art to English to science and social studies. The Express Yourself message boards let educators communicate informally on a range of topics from managing the classroom to preventing burnout. And in the Work Room, teachers chat with other educators in real time.

AMERICA ONLINE *keyword* teachers lounge

▶ EDUCATIONAL PUBLISHERS

Addison Wesley Longman The educational publisher's site functions as online catalog and effective communications tool. Educators can access details about books and software, submit materials for publishing consideration, and apply to become an Addison-Wesley reviewer. Learn about upcoming conferences, signings, and online chats, delve into the corporation's Media Lab, and order books to your heart's content—which is, obviously, the main point.

WEB http://www.aw.com

Projected Learning Programs, Inc. Online catalog for educational software and videos. Browse and order or request a hard copy of the catalog by mail. Projected Learning produces software on disk and CD-ROM for science and vo-tech courses, plus a smaller selection of math, social studies, language arts, and home economics subjects.

WEB http://www.pinsight.com/~plp

Saxon Publishers, Inc. Saxon's philosophy is that kids learn by doing, and the company's textbooks and curriculum materials for school and home study are geared toward teaching math "just as a foreign language or musical instrument is taught," which means incrementally and with continuous practice. Its Web

site is both marketing tool and missionary, and seeks to promote educational change through sales of the company's teaching materials, access to relevant articles, and contacts for local representatives. For the unitiated, the site's cult-like environment offers encouragement and reassurance at every turn.
web http://www.saxonpub.com

Scholastic This revered publisher has a lot more on its Web site than just ads for its books (e.g., *The Baby-Sitters Club*) and film productions (e.g., *The Indian in the Cupboard*). It also has information on innovative educational programs such as The Global Community Project and Team Nutrition, as well as access to Scholastic's online magazines for kids and teachers, and a preview of the Scholastic Network on the World Wide Web.
web http://www.scholastic.com

LESSON PLANS

The Academy One Curriculum Exchange While the initial page may look paltry and a bit confusing, each hotlink on the list calls up an interesting and unique lesson plan contributed by a participating teacher. Enhancement of a Model Rocket Unit, for example, is a lesson on motion and space exploration put together by an Ohio-based fifth grade teacher. Lessons are organized much like a science class lab report: overview, goals, general procedures, information on Internet resources that will add to the student's learning on the subject, and a conclusion. The Curriculum Exchange contains scores of "mini-lessons" on math, languages, science, and social studies, designed by teachers nationwide.
web http://www.nptn.org/cyber.serv/AOneP/academy_one/teacher/cec

Allegheny Schools Partnership: Lesson Plans Lesson plans for math from teachers in the Allegheny Schools Partnership. Currently the selection is rather slim, though presumably there are more links coming.

web http://woodstock.ccit.duq.edu/~brown/Partnership/LessonPlans.html

Teacher's Edition Online A teachers' guide to the Internet, produced by a teacher at Lawrence Elementary School in Wichita, Kans. Mini-courses on subjects like Class Decor and Management or P.R. and Organization present creative ideas for teachers on everything from newsletter publishing to sprucing up a classroom to cure the winter blues. Teacher's Edition provides a free weekly email newsletter of teaching tips and lesson plans, and manages a mailing list, both of which are supported financially by sales of the Education@Large calendar, filled with lesson ideas and "micro-activities" to occupy those moments when lessons finish earlier than planned.
web http://www.feist.com/~lshiney

FOR PARENTS ONLY

Family Involvement in Education Looking for some summer home learning recipes, not for apple pie and cookies, but for reading, writing, math, and science? The Department of Education's grassroots project Partnership for Family Involvement is designed to increase children's learning by actively involving family and community members. The partnership's site provides all the info you need on getting involved in local efforts to boost learning. Browse through research papers, download the Partners' Activity Guide, order books and brochures, connect with satellite town meetings, and start building your child's skills today.
web http://www.ed.gov/Family

FutureNet Education Site The Wichita school system is on the ball, with information about enrollment, remedial and enrichment programs, and a slew of other Wichita-specific details for parents of students from kindergarten through college. Track down phone numbers, check dates for school semesters, and keep up on news through this community-based site that's part of a local gener-

al-interest digizine.
WEB http://www.fn.net/education.html

Help Kids with Homework The National
Education Association's advice page for
parents helping kids with homework.
Aside from tips on ensuring a productive
learning environment for parents and
children, the site also has ideas for
enriching the "homework experience,"
with hot-linked examples. Reference
resources, educational TV, and family
field trips are among the suggestions, as
is exploring other online sites together.
WEB http://www.nea.org/resources
/homework.html

Home Education Resources Center
Home schooling doesn't have to be an
isolating experience anymore, thanks in
a large part to Internet advances. Home
educators can exchange experiences
they've had with educational products
and methods, contribute to the HERC
student reading list, and catch this
month's "Science Fun With the Backyard
Scientist." Also available are each state's
home schooling regulations and links to
other Net resources for stocking the
home school.
WEB http://www.cts.com/~netsales/herc

misc.education.home-school.christian
This well-attended newsgroup discusses
a range of popular topics from "home-
school apparel" to the effect of homeschooling on children. Predictably, a
thread titled "Compulsory Education"
has been receiving a lot of attention lately and has been crossposted to such
disparate groups as alt.fan.rush-lim-
baugh and alt.politics.libertarian.
USENET misc.education.home-school
.christian

misc.education.home-school.misc "I
have been considering home schooling
my children, but am distressed that
almost all the information has a heavy
Christian slant," writes Claire. "While I
am not against the religion, it conflicts
with my family's spiritual beliefs. Are
there any other homeschooling parents
reading this area that are not Christian?"

Another user responds that there's
"plenty of stuff out there" and provides a
helpful list of books for Claire to start
with. This hot spot for home-schoolers
receives plenty of crossposts with
misc.education.home-school.christian,
but occasionally the dissimilar topic of
interest will crop up.
USENET misc.education.home-school.misc

Parenting Home Page Tracy Mahan,
mother of two, has created this site to
share her discoveries of parenting
resources on the Web. The categories
are Books and Reading, Education, Gift
and Toy Suggestions, Health, Kid Links,
and Parenting. Because the lists are
compiled by a dedicated mom, concerned parents can be assured of the
relative safety of browsing through the
kids' links with their children: A good
place to start for those looking for ways
to use and benefit from the Internet as a
family.
WEB http://www.healthtrek.com/tracyhm
.htm

Parenting Info At-home parents will find
special lists of links just for them, but
everyone can find something of interest,
plus helpful descriptions of sites for parents. Child safety and health, the Internet
for kids, general parenting, home
schooling, and a dozen or so educational
initiatives, as well as resources for
women's issues, and for parents of children with special needs are all
addressed.
WEB http://iquest.com/~jsm/moms
/parenting.html

TEACHERS' DISCUSSION GROUPS

▶ K-12 EDUCATION

AERA The American Educational Research Association runs the following sublists at:
listserv@asu.edu ✍ *Type in message body:* subscribe aera <your full name>

AERA-B Curriculum Studies Forum.
listserv@asu.edu ✍ *Type in message body:* subscribe aera-b <your full name>

AERA-F History and Historiography.
listserv@asu.edu ✍ *Type in message body:* subscribe aera-f <your full name>

AERA-E Counseling and Human Development.
listserv@asu.edu ✍ *Type in message body:* subscribe aera-e <your full name>

AERA-G Social Context of Education.
listserv@asu.edu ✍ *Type in message body:* subscribe aera-g <your full name>

AERA-H School Evaluation and Program Development.
listserv@asu.edu ✍ *Type in message body:* subscribe aera-h <your full name>

AERA-I Education in the Professions.
listserv@asu.edu ✍ *Type in message body:* subscribe aera-i<your full name>

AERA-J Postsecondary Education.
listserv@asu.edu ✍ *Type in message body:* subscribe aera-j <your full name>

AERA-K Teaching and Teacher Education.
listserv@asu.edu ✍ *Type in message body:* subscribe aera-k <your full name>

DTS-L Dead Teacher's Society List, a general education discussion.
listserv@iubvm.ucs.indiana.edu ✍ *Type in message body:* subscribe dts-l <your full name>

EDRES-L Talk about online educational resources.
listserv@unbvm1.bitnet ✍ *Type in message body:* subscribe edres-l <your full name>

EDSTYLE Discuss educational styles.
listserv@sjuvm.stjohns.edu ✍ *Type in message body:* subscribe edstyle <your full name>

SCHOOL-L Discussion for both primary and secondary schools.
listserv@irlearn.ucd.ie ✍ *Type in message body:* subscribe school-l <your full name>

SHED Chat about secondary and higher education.
listserv@etsuadmn.etsu.edu ✍ *Type in message body:* subscribe shed <your full name>

▶ COMPUTERS IN CLASS

INCLASS Discuss using the Internet in the classroom.
istproc@schoolnet.carleton.ca ✍ *Type in message body:* subscribe inclass <your full name>

INFED-L Discuss computers in the classroom.
listserv@ccsun.unicamp.br ✍ *Type in message body:* subscribe infed-l <your full name>

WWWEDU Chat about the World Wide Web in education.
listproc@educom.unc.edu ✍ *Type in message body:* subscribe wwwedu <your full name>

▶ EDUCATION ISSUES

BULLY-L A mailing list about bullying and victimization in schools.
listserv@nic.surfnet.nl ✍ *Type in message body:* subscribe bully-l <your full name>

DRUGABUS Drug abuse education mailing list.
listserv@umab.bitnet ✍ *Type in mes-

sage body: subscribe drugabus <your full name>

EDLAW Discuss legal issues in education.
listserv@ukcc.uky.edu ✍ *Type in message body:* subscribe edlaw <your full name>

EDPOL Talk about educational policy.
listproc@wais.com ✍ *Type in message body:* subscribe edpol <your full name>

NLA The mailing list for National Literacy Advocacy.
majordomo@world.std.com ✍ *Type in message body:* subscribe nla <your full name>

PHILOSED Discuss the philosophy of education.
sued@syr.edu ✍ *Type in message body:* subscribe philosed <your full name>

STARNET Talk about students at risk.
listproc@services.dese.state.mo.us ✍ *Type in message body:* subscribe starnet <your full name>

▶ EDUCATION NEWS

CESNEWS Coalition of Essential Schools News.
listserv@brownvm.brown.edu ✍ *Type in message body:* subscribe cesnews <your full name>

EDINFO The U.S. Department of Education updates.
listproc@inet.ed.gov ✍ *Type in message body:* subscribe edinfo <your full name>

▶ ALTERNATIVE EDUCATION

AEELIST The mailing list of the Association for Experimental Education.
listserv@pucc.princeton.edu ✍ *Type in message body:* subscribe aeelist <your full name>

ALTLEARN Discussion about alternative approaches to learning.
listserv@sjuvm.stjohns.edu ✍ *Type in*

message body: subscribe altlearn <your full name>

NEWEDU-L Talk about new trends in education.
listserv@uhccvm.uhcc.hawaii.edu ✍ *Type in message body:* subscribe newedu-l <your full name>

▶ MULTICULTURAL

MULT-ED Mailing list about multicultural education list.
listproc@gmu.edu ✍ *Type in message body:* subscribe mult-ed <your full name>

MULTC-ED Discuss multicultural education.
listserv@umdd.umd.edu ✍ *Type in message body:* subscribe multc-ed <your full name>

MULTI-L Share thoughts on multilingual education.
listserv@barilvm.bitnet ✍ *Type in message body:* subscribe multi-l <your full name>

▶ NEWSGROUPS

k12.chat.teacher Informal discussion for k-12 teachers.

k12.ed.special Discussion about education for k-12 students with special needs.

misc.education Chat about the educational system.

misc.education.multimedia Talk about using multimedia for education.

schl.news.edupage Educom's *EDU-PAGE* Newsletter, posted three times a week.

schl.sig.ethics Discussion about how to teach kids ethics and morals.

sci.edu Discussion about the science of education.

EXTRA CREDIT

SAMPLE QUESTION #1: SAT : INTEL-ligence : : (A) Bill : Ted (B) Latoya : infomercials (C) Jordan : Bulls. The answer? None of the above, of course, but try telling that to your parents. They've taped vocabulary words to every surface in the house, hired a medium to channel dead MENSA members for last-minute tutoring, and bought out a near-by No. 2 pencil factory. One would think the draft is on for all their anxiety over your college admissions. Fortunately, there are low-key ways to study for the SAT online, and some of them are even free. You can register for the pesky test online, at the College Board Home Page. And you don't have to give up your weekends to take an online prep class. Kaplan, the Princeton Review, and Stanford Testing will help you kick ETS's butt in the name of higher education and familial harmony. If you've already got the SAT licked, make the most of your intelligence surplus at the Gifted Resources Home Page or start racking up points for your academic future at the College Board Online Advanced Placement Program.

ADVANCED PLACEMENT

College Board Online Advanced Placement Program The College Board's Advanced Placement page is all about information; when, where, and why to take the exams that strike terror into the hearts of teacher's pets and slackers alike. The page's FAQ answers such fear-based questions as "How difficult are AP courses?" and "Why should I take a more difficult course and risk getting a lower grade?" The College Board's responses are comically predictable ("more difficult than regular high school courses," "to learn a subject in greater depth"), encouraging students to experience the joy of an educational challenge. This transparent ploy to win registration fees should not go unpunished. **WEB** http://www.collegeboard.org /ap/math/html/indx001.html

COLLEGE ADMISSIONS

The College Board Online No, this isn't a clever trap, nor does entrance to the site require age-based knowledge of 1950s television trivia. The enemy really has rolled out the red carpet for its young, impending torture victims. The College Board Online welcomes high- and middle-schoolers with open arms in a vain attempt to curry favor with those for whom their very name is anathema. The sentiment is appreciated, but there are no secrets to be learned here; no cheat sheets or recipes for a Ritalin cocktail. However, along with the public relations gloss, visitors to the College Board Online can do the following: register for the SAT online, access test dates, and even try their hand at the Test Question of the Day. Practice! Practice! There is also specific information on Advanced Placement Exams and the PSAT. America Online's College Board service, like its Internet counterpart, allows students to register for the SAT, but also invites specific testing and college-related questions in its Ask the College Board section. **WEB** http://www.collegeboard.org **AMERICA ONLINE** *keyword* student center→College and Beyond→College Board Online

Collegeapps.com Shannon Barth and Sue Berescik, the two former English teachers behind Collegeapps.com, claim to be able to motivate you to get started on those college applications, take the fears out of the process, show you how to self-assess and find your unique qualities and experiences, and give you a sure-fire method of writing essays that leap off the page—IF you buy their book for $19.95. For $34.95, you can get their video, too, and for a mere $500 you get the deluxe package that includes school selection, financial assistance information, and essay and resume editing. But on their home page, all you can hope for is a free evaluation of your college essay

rough draft by email.
WEB http://www.collegeapps.com

Resource Pathways There's a glut of information on the market to help you make your college decisions, but how do you know which resources are right for you? Resource Pathways has gone down that road for you, reviewing books, CD-ROMs, videotapes, software, WWW sites, and other online resources. Provided are the one- to four-star ratings of each resource's breadth of content, added value, and ease of use, as well as an overall evaluation.
WEB http://www.sourcepath.com

soc.college.admissions As the school year winds down and anxiety over college admissions drives seniors to drink, this newsgroup experiences a remarkable surge of angst-ridden traffic. "I still haven't heard from U. Texas!" moans one fated hopeful, evoking sympathetic yet realistic responses from students who received their acceptance letters months back. One student requests help in her decision between Berkeley and Cornell (this is what is known as a "good problem"), prompting a heated debate between maniacally loyal students at the institutions in question.
USENET soc.college.admissions

▶ GIFTED & TALENTED

Gifted Resources Home Page Ostracized on the playground, gifted children grow up to run Fortune 500 companies and, in some cases, small countries. Yes, revenge is both lucrative and sweet. But why postpone happiness? Parents can help to allay the pain of the precocious in the here and now, through enrollment in summer programs, special classes, and enrichment programs that allow gifted kids to rub cerebral cortexes with fellow over-achievers. This collection of resources for the gifted and talented is incredibly thorough and current, with links to programs, publications, mailing lists and FAQ files.
WEB http://www.eskimo.com/~user/kids.html

Gifted Resources from ERIC The Educational Resources Information Center connects "virtually all educational information providers and educational information users." Daunting in sheer volume and scope, ERIC has thoughtfully culled its pertinent gifted and talented resources at this site.
WEB http://www.aspensys.com/eric/index.html

TAG-L Talented and gifted education discussion. Teachers and parents talk up their children's IQ points, voice pride in junior's four-move checkmate against a Russian octogenarian, and generally live vicariously through the glorious achievements of the fruits of their loins.
EMAIL listserv@vm1.nodak.edu ✍ *Type in message body:* subscribe tag-l <your full name>

▶ STUDY ABROAD

Worldwide Classroom You don't have to join the Navy to see the world. Worldwide Classroom has amassed a compilation of intercultural and educational programs available worldwide including university study, foreign language immersion, adult enrichment programs, internships, volunteer programs, and teen camps. Also included is a planning guide to make the passage from one country to another a bit easier with information on everything from dealing with culture shock to money matters to weather around the world.
WEB http://www.worldwide.edu

School Partners Abroad The program requires the presence of a chaperone teacher, but don't let that stop you. School Partners Abroad fosters relationships between students of countries such as Germany, France, Spain, Costa Rica, and Japan, through a reciprocal exchange program. Each exchange lasts three to four weeks, and provides participants with an opportunity to live with host families, attend classes, and participate in extracurricular and community activities. The average group size is 10 to 15 students, so if you hate con-

tinental breakfasts, you can yearn for steak and eggs with sympathetic peers.
WEB http://www.ciee.org/sep/spabroc.htm

▶ TEST PREP

One-on-One with the S.A.T. In yet another desperate move to negate the influence of those costly SAT classes, the College Board has designed its own brand of online SAT preparation software. And, of course, they do have one very real claim to fame: One-on-One "is the only program with hundreds of real SAT questions." This may seem akin to accepting aspirin from a flu bug, but there is something to be said for test verité. The program includes an advisor from the hallowed halls of the College Board, who promises to guide students through the painful process. The program requires an IBM-compatible personal computer and costs $49.
WEB http://www.collegeboard.org/library/html/oneonone.html

The Princeton Review Its name a nod to ETS territory, the Princeton Review debunks the SAT mystique through utter mockery of its writers, Jim and Pam, and all they represent. Process of elimination techniques focus on wiping out the worst answers rather than finding the best ones. A character named "Joe Bloggs" teaches students to avoid falling into pitfalls designed for average-scoring students. The company's Web site includes information on courses, books and software for the anxious college hopefuls. Learn about the course, browse message boards, or shop till you drop at the Princeton Review store. The company's AOL presence does not differ substantially from that of its Internet Web site.
WEB http://www.review.com
AMERICA ONLINE *keyword* princeton

Kaplan The Kaplan Web site is almost daunting in scope, offering a wide range of services, including the opportunity to take a sample SAT or GRE online, free of charge. Kaplan's services don't end with test preparation, however. The College

Simulator invites post-matriculators to tour a virtual campus and face day-to-day scenarios, while the Hot Seat simulates a nerve-racking job interview. A new package, SAT RoadTrip Multimedia, promises to prepare students for the test via an in-depth software package (the cost: $30). A visit to the test center of the virtual campus on AOL yields SAT FAQs that answer baffling questions like "What is the purpose of the PSAT?" An article sings the praises of the Kaplan course, and message boards act as a conduit through which college hopefuls can vent—and Kaplan workers can recruit.
WEB http://www.kaplan.com
AMERICA ONLINE *keyword* kaplan

Syndicate.com You can receive tutoring from Einstein's ghost and offer your little sister into paid servitude to the president of the College Board, but nothing's going to raise your SAT score if you don't study vocabulary. Twelve synonyms for "terse" and a billion ways to call someone a tightwad are required just to get a registration form. Fortunately, Syndicate .com is tapped into the needs of monosyllabic teens, with puzzles, contests, comic strips and other word play designed to make learning less excruciating, if not exactly good, extracurricular fun.
WEB http://syndicate.com

TestPrep.com The questions are culturally biased and the class fees are economically biased, but Stanford Testing Systems, Inc. negates the influence of the status quo with its absolutely free and complete online test preparation resources. Simply register by following the directions provided: The WebWare system will diagnose and work to improve your weak areas. The experts at Stanford Testing mean business. No cartoons or "fun SAT games" detract from the learning process. WebWare may be free, but it's no lightweight.
WEB http://www.testprep.com/wwmain .sat.html

PART 2

English

LITERATURE

IN A PERFECT WORLD, X-MEN COMIC books would replace the Scarlet Letter as required high school reading and vocabulary tests would give way to the rote memorization of Amanda's lovers on Melrose Place. Alas—it's not a perfect world but now it's a little easier to negotiate. Your test on Huck Finn is tomorrow morning and the local library's all checked out? No problem. There's sure to be a copy online, and it may even be annotated. Believe it or not, many people read Twain for the pure love of the prose. If you ask nicely, one of them will probably lend you a hand with the weightier symbolism. Check out the message boards over at English Help or post a message of your own at rec.arts.book. Who knows? With this kind of brain trust at your disposal, you may never have to crack a book again.

> STARTING POINTS

AmLit-L This mailing list attracts mostly academic users, a situation that has both benefits and drawbacks. On the plus side, academics generate a uniformly high level of discourse, with detailed and often fascinating meditations on American literature. How is beat poetry related to the projective verse of Charles Olson and the Black Mountain School? What were the factors involved in the rise and fall of African-American poet Melvin Tolson? But the same intellectual rigor that produces diligent investigations of these issues also gives rise to a self-importance that is sometimes stultifying. If you can overlook the arch tone and the pretension, you'll find that the heavier material is offset by a number of lighter entries—graduate students confessing their weaknesses for (gasp!) popular authors, professors relating humorous classroom anecdotes, and ordinary citizens celebrating the simple pleasure of reading good literature.
EMAIL listserv@mizzou1.missouri.edu ✍ Type in message body: subscribe amlit-l <your full name>

Author's Pen This virtual salon is the home base for literary lights past and present. The large collection of links will take you to sites dedicated to the lives and works of authors from Lewis Carroll to Douglas Adams. You can even vote for your favorite young American novelist—Chabon? Powers? Minot? Franzen? **WEB** http://www.books.com/scripts /authors.exe

Authors Links and Info Alphabetically arranged, this diverse collection of mostly modern links has something for even the most discerning reader. Herman Hesse isn't your cup of tea? How about Mamet, Kundera, or Martin Amis? Some of the more respected science fiction authors—Herbert, LeGuin and Brin, for example—are also included. There are links to general literature pages, an informative FAQ, and one laughably anomalous link, to the Society for Keanu Consciousness—shamelessly, and hopefully facetiously, devoted to the worship of the oft-miscast Hollywood celeb. **WEB** http://www.empirenet.com/~rdaeley /authors/authors.html

Literary If you are kept awake at night by apocalyptic visions of Shakespeare's bald pate overrun with circuitry, take heart in this mailing list, which proves not only that readers of fine literature are alive and well, but also that technology can aid their pursuits. Thanks to the synthetic community of mailing lists, bibliophiles can debate first editions of Saul Bellow's novels, recommend favorite plays, and even address more arcane matters. If you're interested in an extended conversation about the linguistic basis for sexual identity in Proust's *Recherche*, this mailing list—textured and thoughtful—is the place to go. **EMAIL** listserv@bitnic.cren.net ✍ Type in message body: subscribe literary <your full name>

The Literary Forum Gossipy and prone to drift wildly off topic, CompuServe's

Literary Forum will frustrate any serious reader of literature—for example, a thread titled "Literary market" contained advice on how to keep visiting in-laws from smoking indoors. The Romance/Historical section is ruled by ladies who have queened and duchessed themselves, in a sort of role-playing game called *The Keep*. In a topic about research methods, a writer struggling to perfect her leprechaun dialect was advised to learn Gaelic from an Enya CD. A rear guard of literary hardheads snap bitterly in a corner of the Poetry/Lyrics section. Surrounded by what they call "heartfelt quick-draw poetry," they veer in tone between curmudgeonly and virulent. "You want advice on how to fix your poem?" one beleaguered Net critic asked. "Burn it." After reading poems that rhyme "budgie" with "fudgie," you'll agree.
COMPUSERVE *go* literary

rec.arts.books This baggy newsgroup debates matters such as whether Yeats was an obscurantist, who belongs on a list of the top ten poets of this century, and the delicately inflected ambiguities in *Go, Dog, Go*. Amateurs post reviews on everything from sci-fi to Michael Ondaatje, although sometimes one suspects the handiwork of a publishing house's paid flunky. Several camps—sci-fi and fantasy, hermetic postmodern novels, poetry, and long, fat British books—coexist peacefully but fairly separately. On the evidence here, American readers are not as stick-in-the-muddish as the *New York Times Book Review*. If you rant about academic cabals, for instance, you will politely but firmly be advised to read Jonathan Culler and Terry Eagleton and then to try again.
USENET rec.arts.books

▶ 19TH CENTURY

Jane Austen Information Page Everybody's favorite posthumous Hollywood screenwriter, Jane Austen was—believe it or not—also a fairly well-known nineteenth-century writer. While some students may opt to wear out their Block-buster card when confronted with an Austen assignment, those who crack a book may be pleasantly surprised. Replete with irony, subtle humor, and even hints of feminism, her novels have inspired volumes of criticism, a great deal of which can be found at this site. The scope of the material is somewhat daunting. Along with the comprehensive set of links to e-texts (annotated and otherwise) of Austen's novels, minor work, and letters, there are notes on her period in history, images, and quotes, organized by category. Failed pick-up lines, for example, include such excerpts as Darcy's heavyhanded marriage proposal in *Pride and Prejudice*. From this site, one may also sign up for the Austen mailing list.
WEB http://uts.cc.utexas.edu/~churchh/janeinfo.html

Bronte-L Although they're hardly Harlequin types, this rarefied crew is a window onto the origin of the romance novel—the Brontë sisters clustered on the Yorkshire moors, indulging their own fevered imaginations as they created dark, mysterious heroes and passionate, headstrong heroines. On this list, seasoned world travelers meet Ph.D. candidates. Professors seek advice on college syllabuses. Subscribers share travel tips and book reviews. Modern Brontë readers argue over the ideal film cast for a film of *Jane Eyre*. No flames generally, but woe unto the subscriber who confuses Catherine, Heathcliff's inamorata, with Cathy, her daughter, in *Wuthering Heights*. This is exactly the sort of mistake that suggests that the poster is a fan of the vilified Olivier-Leigh film, which rendered the distinction moot.
EMAIL majordomo@world.std.com ✍
Type in message body: subscribe bronte-l <your full name>

The Dickens Page The prom queen is your life-long nemesis, the Beastie Boys show is 21 and over, and, of course, your parents just don't understand. Before you start bemoaning your plight, check out childhood à la Dickens. Overworked, underfed, and generally mis-

treated, the Oliver Twists, David Copperfields, and Pips of Dickensian London will put your problems in perspective before you can say, "child labor laws." Providing unparalleled insight into the author's bleak world, this site is the Dickens resource, with links, e-texts, and criticism. Please sir, may I have some more?
WEB http://lang.nagoya-u.ac.jp/~matsuoka/Dickens.html

Nathaniel Hawthorne A fan of the author garnered this fantastic collection of Hawthorne's writing, writings on Hawthorne, and other "Hawthorniana." If you prefer to learn visually, check out the site's collection of art, including portraits of the artist and illustrations from editions of his books. The lazy student may opt to order the audio book version of the *Scarlet Letter*. The ultra-lazy may even go for the comic book. Hey, it may not be Batman, but at least it's more accurate than the Demi Moore vehicle.
WEB http://www.tiac.net/users/eldred/nh/hawthorne.html

Herman Melville From his early days as a seafaring adventurer to his maturity as a writer—which produced some of the most vivid pieces about spiritual crisis in the history of American literature—Herman Melville was a compelling figure, and while the early 20th century forgot him almost entirely, F.O. Matthiessen and other critics returned him to prominence. Join the search for the white whale at this excellent Web site, and learn more about the creator of *Typee*, *Omoo*, *Pierre*, *The Confidence Man*, *Billy Budd*, *Benito Cereno*, and *Bartleby the Scrivener* (not to mention a piece of fluff called *Moby Dick*); there's a biography and a generous and diverse collection of links on everything from sailing to whales to French Polynesia.
WEB http://www.melville.org

Mark Twain Resources on the World Wide Web "Huckies" and Trekkies alike will appreciate the breadth of this Mark Twain clearinghouse, which includes analysis of his character's appearance on *Star Trek: The Next Generation*, along with other popular culture references. For those who don't live near the Mississippi River but are in search of a more traditional raft ride, e-text links and biography and criticism resources abound. Also included is a list of maxim's from Twain's writing, from the terse ("Tell the truth or trump—but get the trick.") to the convoluted and rambling.
WEB http://web.syr.edu/~fjzwick/twainwww.html

Twain-L "Clothes make the man. Naked people have little or no influence..." Mark Twain is America. Almost everyone knows Huck and Tom and can quote a pithy statement or two. On this active mailing list, academics and amateurs meet to interpret Twain's work and worship at his shrine. These people love Twain and want him on their side. Thus a recent thread about Twain's meeting another 19th-century wit, Oscar Wilde, sparked a long discussion about Twain and his probable opinion toward homosexuality. Those who saw Twain as liberal cited his acceptance of Walt Whitman (Twain was "a sexual libertarian"); the other side pointed toward his "moral" family life ("Twain was an honorable man"). Sometimes the list is academically trendy—how Huck's raft becomes a site of homoerotic friendship—sometimes it is just an exchange of favorite stories.
EMAIL listserv@vm1.yorku.ca ✍ *Type in message body:* subscribe twain-l <your full name>

▶ 20TH CENTURY

Ralph Ellison's Invisible Man This page, created by the University of Pennsylvania English Department, contains a chapter summary of the novel, as well as excerpts from various reviews and critical essays, including that of Saul Bellow.
WEB http://www.english.upenn.edu/~afilreis/50s/ellison-main.html

William Faulkner A guide to Yoknapatawpha County, with a bibliography of Faulkner's oeuvre (novels, short stories, and essays), maps of his fictional Mississippi landscape, and an essay on Faulkner's time in Hollywood.

WEB http://www.mcsr.olemiss.edu /~egjbp/faulkner/faulkner.html

F. Scott Fitzgerald The original preppy, F. Scott Fitzgerald once said that, "an author ought to write for the youth of his generation, the critics of the next, and the schoolmasters ever afterward." True to his aspiration, Fitzgerald's masterpiece of voyeurism, *The Great Gatsby*, is a canonical high school must-read, while *Tender Is the Night* often acts as an introduction to the wacky world of Freudian literary analysis. This site is essentially an extensive biography, with pictures of the author and his infamously unstable wife, Zelda, as well as summaries of each of Fitzgerald's novels. Anyone with an interest in literary death should be sure to check out the picture of Fitzgerald's resting place.

WEB http://acs.tamu.edu/~jtc5085/index .htm

FWake-L "And so they went on, the fourbottle men, the analists, unguam and nunguam and lunguam again, their anschluss about her whosebefore and his whereafters and how she was lost away." What is there to say about a group of people who spend time trying to figure out what was probably a big practical joke? Actually, FWake-L, which occasionally talks about Joyce's other works, is a very friendly list. In the spirit of Joyce, FWake-L welcomes all manner of enthusiasts and helps them "catch up." When they finally get down to business, members are fond of analyzing the novel one paragraph at a time. But that's not all—then they go through the "levels" of the text, which means constant speculation on Joyce's polyglot stew. ReJoyce.

EMAIL listserv@irlearn.ucd.ie ✍ *Type in message body:* subscribe fwake-l <your full name>

William Golding "Suck to your asthmar, Piggy!" Ah, the compassionate sensitivity of youth! If not for adult interference—not to mention that of society's facist infrastructure—kids could handle themselves just fine. And school? Who needs it! The classroom of life is the best learning institution, and life experience the wisest teacher. But even Utopia has its problems, as Ralph, Piggy and Jack learned. What did the pig's head symbolize, and why did Simon have to die? For the answers to these and other *Lord of the Flies* questions, check out this informative Golding site.

WEB http://www.empirenet.com/~rdaeley /authors/authors.html

Thomas Hardy Resource Library This site encompasses e-texts, criticism, and reviews of the author's work. If you're parched after all of the intellectual stimulation, follow the brewing instructions for Thomas Hardy's ale.

WEB http://pages.ripco.com:8080/~mws /hardy.html

Kazuo Ishiguro Who says post-modernism has to be messy? Ishiguro's novels, most famously *The Remains of the Day*, explore questions of identity with refreshingly simple, graceful prose. The Japanese-born British screenwriter and fiction writer achieved fame at the age of 25. His most recent novel, *The Unconsoled*, has been compared to Dostoevsky's masterpieces. This site includes a short biography of the writer, as well as links to other Ishiguro resources.

WEB http://www.speakeasy.org/sal /speaker/ki.html

James Joyce in Cyberspace Stately, plump Buck Mulligan would certainly have been a netsurfer, and might have stopped taunting unstately, unplump, Stephen Dedalus long enough to come to this page, which serves as a clearinghouse for Joyce resources, including links to Joyce discussion groups, mailing lists and information about the hypertext journal of Joyce criticism, Hypermedia Joyce Studies.

WEB http://www.2street.com/joyce

ModBrits These scholars of modern British literature (Joyce, Wilde, Woolf,

Conrad, etc.) are a tad hip and not overly cerebral. In addition to discussions of the subtext of *To the Lighthouse*, you will find information on how to run a *Ulysses* scavenger hunt ("a pin for her drawers"). A recent long thread sought opinions on texts that crack you up and times that you have trouble keeping a straight face while in class.

EMAIL listserv@kentvm.kent.edu ✍ *Type in message body:* subscribe modbrits <your full name>

The Papa Page The Papa in question is, of course, Ernest Hemingway, hard-drinking Floridian turned expatriate. Created by a Hemingway scholar/fan, the site was the first to post pictures of the author, inspiring others to follow. The site contains an extensive biography of the man, as well as images culled from books on Hemingway, including those by A.E. Hotchner and Anthony Burgess. There are numerous links, as well, allowing users to join mailing lists, access a timeline of Hemingway's life, or find out more about that ever-so-safe hobby, the running of the bulls.

WEB http://www.ee.mcgill.ca/~nverever /hem/pindex.html

Proust Said That Settle back with a plate of madeleines and start clicking through this online zine, which brings a dash of humor to the great Gallic obsessive. Did you know that the French choreographer Roland Petit once met with the members of Pink Floyd to discuss a ballet based on *Remembrance of Things Past*? Did you know that Proust lined his apartment walls with cork? And why do all the women in the novel have feminized versions of men's names? You can even download an account of preparing Nesselrode Pudding, a chestnut-flavored dessert favored by the narrator's dinner guests.

WEB http://www.well.com/user/vision /proust

Thomas Pynchon Thomas Pynchon probably loves the Net. Why wouldn't he? It assists polyphony, produces paranoia, and allows for the transmission of

information quicker than you can say "Trystero." And it also has a page devoted to Pynchon's works. Read two Pynchon FAQs, consult a brief biography, and marvel at impressionistic, rebus-like accounts of Pynchon's major works.

WEB http://www.pomona.edu/pynchon /index.html

J.D. Salinger The archetypal portrait of disenfranchised youth, *The Catcher in the Rye* has a cult following that even L. Ron Hubbard would envy. What is it about Holden Caufield that resonates with adolescents the world over? It's simple, really. The guy has a bad attitude, a really bad attitude. Salinger understood growing pains, just as this site can help the confused student understand Salinger. The truly inspired can follow a link to learn to bitch and moan, Salinger style.

WEB http://www.empirenet.com /~rdaeley/authors/salinger.html

Alice Walker A comprehenisve site detailing the Pulitzer Prize-winning author's varied life, with annotated works, an excerpted interview, and critical essays.

WEB http://thunder.ocis.temple.edu /~ajokinen/alicew_html

▶ BEATS

The William S. Burroughs InterNetWeb-Zone Burroughs may have proclaimed that "Language is a virus" but that hasn't stopped him from talking and writing for the past forty years. Come to this worshipful sight for a taste of Burroughs in graphics, sound files, online texts, and biographical sources. You can even connect to Net vendors of Burroughsiana.

WEB http://www.hyperreal.com/wsb

Jack Kerouac On the road and on the sauce, Jack Kerouac is the undisputed poster child of the Beat Generation. This site includes a short biography of the author (née Jean-Louis Lebris de Kerouac), excerpts from *On the Road*, as well as various critical essays and reviews. Want to listen to the author

ramble on? Follow the link to Kerouac audio files. In the mood to discuss disillusionment and wanderlust with fellow roadies? Access the Kerouac mailing list and moan away.
WEB http://www.empirenet.com /~rdaeley/authors/kerouac.html

Literary Kicks Leave the material world behind and enter a realm where beat poetry is still revered as the optimum in artistic expression. The site was created by fiction writer Levi Asher and in spite of his instructions to visitors—"turn your mind off, relax, and float downstream"—the site is a clearinghouse of pragmatic information. There are extensive bios on everyone for the well-knowns to the more obscure beats such as Gregory Corso.
WEB http://www.charm.net/~brooklyn /LitKicks.html

▶ MYTHOLOGY

Greek Mythology The Ancient Greeks liked their gods petty, vengeful, and angst-ridden; in other words, human. To learn about Zeus's thunderbolts, Athena's sagacity, and Aphrodite's libidinousness, explore this many-faceted reference work on the residents of Mount Olympus. Having trouble keeping up with Hera's fecundity? A family tree is provided to allay the confusion. A limited selection of myths is included, along with biographical rundowns of the gods, the heroes, and the creatures. Could Ares beat up Mars? A fact sheet explores the differences between Greek and Roman mythology. If studying mythology seems like a trip to Hades, let this site shed some light on the matter.
WEB http://www.intergate.net/uhtml/.jhunt /greek_myth/greek_myth.html

▶ WOMEN'S LITERATURE

19th Century American Women Writers Web Why were Louisa May Alcott's women so little? Was it the corsets? Malnutrition? Find the answers at this informative site, where etexts, critical journals and a message board are devot-

ed to the likes of Alcott, Emily Dickinson, and Harriet Beecher Stowe.
WEB http://www.clever.net/19cwww

A Celebration of Women Writers An online exhibit honoring women's prose and poetry. New texts are being added but there is already an impressive collection of works, including biographies of significant women. Don't miss the hypertext version of Austen's *Pride and Prejudice* or anarchist Emma Goldman's essay on patriotism. There are even illustrated mysteries by Mary Roberts Rinehart.
WEB http://www.cs.cmu.edu/Web /People/mmbt/women/writers.html

Women Writers in English 1330-1830 Brown University's Women Writers Project spans the years 1330 to 1830, the advent of the great Victorian women novelists. The project has collected works such as Elizabeth Carew's *The Tragedie of Mariam* (1613) and Hannah Cowley's 1780 description of a trip to Turkey. Unfortunately, you cannot retrieve the texts electronically, but a list of the universities that own them is included.
WEB http://www.stg.brown.edu/projects /wwp/wwp_home.html

▶ LISTS & BOOK REVIEWS

alt.book.reviews Is Stephen King a serious writer? What is a serious writer anyway? Inquiring bookworms want to know. Wandering consistently from the topic at hand, posters to this newsgroup concentrate less on reviewing than on discussing books. Unfortunately for the befuddled student, the pretentions are at an all-time high, as hapless homework help seekers are savagely censured by the snooty intellectual types. A thread entitled, "Why Do My Own Homework When People on the Net Can Do it for Me?" explores the issue, as students write in to defend their interests ("Why so anal??? How long ago was it that you were in high school?").
USENET alt.book.reviews

The Book Nook Left to their own reading devices, today's kids tend to bypass the classics in favor of a particularly gruesome brand of young adult horror fiction, prolifically populated by the likes of R.L. Stine and V.C. Andrews. The Book Nook invites kids to write about their favorites across a number of creepy genres, and to exchange suggestions via a message board. In light of the aforementioned trend, it should come as no surprise that the most commonly suggested books are those in which the protagonists are either locked in an attic by evil parents, get revenge at school, or asked to solve the mystery of the prom queen's decapitation.
WEB http://schoolnet2.carleton.ca /english/arts/lit/booknook

Young Adult Reading Contains reading lists and book reviews specifically for young adults. For 1995, Judy Blume has been usurped by *Cyberspace Cowboy*.
WEB http://www.docker.com/~whitehead m/yaread.html

▶ E-TEXT LIBRARIES

Alex: A Catalog of Electronic Texts on the Internet Alex likes to read. In fact, Alex is one of the largest clearinghouses of electronic-text links, with thousands of books ranging from classical Greek plays to 19th-century fiction to contemporary political philosophy.
WEB http://www.lib.ncsu.edu/stacks /alex-index.html

Banned Books Online Remember the guilty pleasure of reading *Lady Chatterley's Lover* for the first time, hunched under the blanket with a flashlight and a box of Kleenex? (Well, maybe the details of the memory are a bit too specific, but the sentiment is universal.) Now you can get all lathered up with Lawrence on the Net's collection of banned books. The taboo tomes aren't all lascivious—devotees of the suppressed press can page through Tom Paine's *The Rights of Man* and even fantasize about future evolutionary developments while poring over Darwin's *The Origin of Species*.
WEB http://www.cs.cmu.edu/Web /People/spok/banned-books.html

The Gutenberg Project Remember that moveable-type Bible that changed the world? If you do, go see a doctor. You should be dead by now. The online Gutenberg has nothing to do with moveable type, but it aspires to another paradigm shift in the reading world, this time to electronic texts. With a goal of 10,000 texts by the year 2001, Gutenberg has already started to amass the great works of English-language literature, from Conrad to Conan Doyle. Get wired to get Gutenberg, then get literary in a hurry.
WEB http://www.w3.org/pub/DataSources /bySubject/Literature/Gutenberg/

Project Bartleby Melville's Bartleby the scrivener, after a short and thwarted existence, died curled into a comma in the tombs, his negation absolute and mystifying. Columbia University's Project Bartleby, which bills itself as "The Public Library of the Internet," doesn't want that to happen to you, and the directors of the project have begun to assemble an extensive collection of English-language classics, including the works of Emily Dickinson, Herman Melville, Walt Whitman, and William Wordsworth.
WEB http://www.cc.columbia.edu /acis/bartleby/index.html

The WorldWideWeb Virtual Library: Literature One of the best places to begin exploring the virtual world of books. Before you do anything else, stop by the hypertext newsletter that tracks new Net literary sites and offers links to book-related topics. Online literary exhibits and a notable quote collection furnish a pleasant diversion; does A. F. F. von Kotzebue's "There is another and a better world" refer to the Internet? And then there are the directories of links, which range across the Web in search of authors, awards, booksellers, libraries, reference, poetry, publishers, and writing resources. If it's about the written word and it's out there, it's in here.
WEB http://sunsite.unc.edu/ibic/IBIC -homepage.html

BOOKS ONLINE

THE SELECTION OF ELECTRONIC texts on the Internet is so extensive that one would have to spend days endlessly browsing the choices, even longer to alphabetize them. So we've done just that for you. From Aeschylus to Aristotle, Jane Austen to Emily Brontë, Elizabeth Barrett Browning to Samuel Taylor Coleridge, Wilkie Collins to Joseph Conrad, the history of the world's literature is being stored for present use, and for posterity, at Web sites, gophers, and FTP directories across the Net. Follow Pip and his *Great Expectations*. Stock up on heroic epithets with the *Iliad*. Then, gallop away into the sunset with everybody's favorite equine, *Black Beauty*. Texts appear in both plaintext and hypertext, and formats are noted in the entries.

A

Agamemnon By Aeschylus. Hypertext format.
web http://the-tech.mit.edu/Classics /Aeschylus/agamemnon.txt.head.html

Complete (Existing) Plays By Aeschylus. Text only.
url gopher://gopher.vt.edu:10010 /11/34

Prometheus Bound By Aeschylus. Hypertext format.
web http://the-tech.mit.edu/Classics /Aeschylus/prometheus.txt.head.html

Aesop's Fables By Aesop. Text only.
web http://www.w3.org/hypertext /DataSources/bySubject/Literature /Gutenberg/etext92/aesopa10.txt

Little Women By Louisa May Alcott. Hypertext format.
web http://www.datatext.co.uk/library /alcott/littlew/chapters.htm

Ragged Dick By Horatio Alger. Text only.
web http://wiretap.spies.com/ftp.items /Library/Classic/ragged.txt

Complete (Existing) Plays By Aristophanes. Text only.
url gopher://gopher.vt.edu:10010/11/40

Metaphysics By Aristotle. Hypertext format.
web http://the-tech.mit.edu/Classics /Aristotle/Metaphysics.html

Poetics By Aristotle. Hypertext format.
web http://the-tech.mit.edu/Classics /Aristotle/Poetics.html

Emma By Jane Austen. Text only.
web http://www.w3.org/hypertext /DataSources/bySubject/Literature /Gutenberg/etext94/emma10.txt
• http://wiretap.spies.com/ftp.items /Library/Classic/emma.ja

Pride and Prejudice By Jane Austen. Hypertext format.
web http://uts.cc.utexas.edu/~churchh /pridprej.html

B

New Atlantis By Francis Bacon. Text only.
web http://wiretap.spies.com/ftp.items /Library/Classic/atlantis.txt

Peter Pan By James M. Barrie. Plain text only.
web http://www-cgi.cs.cmu.edu/afs /andrew.cmu.edu/acs/library/etexts /namedsubject/literature/Peter_Pan .txt.Z

Familiar Quotations By John Bartlett. Hypertext format.
web http://www.columbia.edu/~svl2 /bartlett

The Wonderful Wizard of Oz By Frank Baum. Hypertext format; text only.
web http://www.w3.org/hypertext /DataSources/bySubject/Literature /Gutenberg/etext93/wizoz10.txt
• http://www.cs.cmu.edu/Web/People /rgs/wizoz10.html

Jane Eyre By Charlotte Brontë. Text only.
URL gopher://gopher.vt.edu:10010
/02/50/1

Wuthering Heights By Emily Brontë.
Hypertext format.
URL gopher://ftp.std.com/00/obi/book
/Emily.Bronte/wuther.html.Z

Sonnets From the Portuguese By Eliza-
beth Barrett Browning. Text only.
WEB http://www.inform.umd.edu/EdRes
/Topic/WomensStudies/ReadingRoom
/Poetry/BarrettBrowning/SonnetsFrom
ThePortuguese

The Pilgrim's Progress By John Bunyan.
Hypertext format.
WEB http://www.cs.pitt.edu/~planting
/books/bunyan/pilgrims_progress/title.html

The Secret Garden By Frances Hodgson
Burnett. Text only.
WEB http://www.w3.org/hypertext/Data
Sources/bySubject/Literature/Gutenberg
/etext94/gardn10.txt • http://wiretap
.spies.com/ftp.items/Library/Classic
/garden.txt

Jungle Tales of Tarzan By Edgar Rice
Burroughs. Hypertext format; text only.
WEB http://www.wonderland.org/Works
/Edgar-Rice-Burroughs/jungle-tales-of
-tarzan • http://www.w3.org/hypertext
/DataSources/bySubject/Literature
/Gutenberg/etext94/tarz610.txt

The Arabian Nights Translated by Sir
Richard Burton. Text only.
URL gopher://gopher.vt.edu:10010/02
/56/1

Don Juan By George Byron. Text only.
URL gopher://gopher.vt.edu:10010
/02/58/1

C

Alice's Adventures in Wonderland By
Lewis Carroll. Hypertext format; text
only.
WEB http://www.cs.cmu.edu:8001/Web
/People/rgs/alice-table.html • http://www
.w3.org/hypertext/DataSources/by

Subject/Literature/Gutenberg/etext91
/alice30.txt

Through the Looking Glass By Lewis
Carroll. Hypertext format; text only.
WEB http://www.cs.indiana.edu/metastuff
/looking/lookingdir.html • http://www.w3
.org/hypertext/DataSources/bySubject
/Literature/Gutenberg/etext91/lglass18
.txt

O Pioneers! By Willa Cather. Text only;
plain text.
WEB http://www.w3.org/hypertext
/DataSources/bySubject/Literature
/Gutenberg/etext92/opion11.txt
• http://www-cgi.cs.cmu.edu/afs/andrew
.cmu.edu/acs/library/etexts/named
subject/literature/O_Pioneers.txt.Z

Everyman Edited by A.C. Cawley. Hypertext format.
WEB http://etext.lib.virginia.edu/cgibin
/browse-mixed?id=AnoEver&tag=public
&images=images/mideng&data=/lv1
/Archive/mideng-parsed

Don Quixote By Miguel de Cervantes.
Text only.
URL gopher://gopher.vt.edu:10010/02
/62/1

Canterbury Tales By Geoffrey Chaucer.
Text only.
URL gopher://ccat.sas.upenn.edu:3333/00
/Medieval/Chaucer
WEB http://wiretap.spies.com/ftp.items
/Library/Classic/canterbury.txt
The Awakening and Other Short Stories
By Kate Chopin. Text only.
WEB http://www.w3.org/hypertext/Data
Sources/bySubject/Literature/Gutenberg
/etext94/awakn10.tx
URL ftp://nptn.org/pub/e.texts/gutenberg
/etext94/awakn10.txt

Fanny Hill By John Cleland. Text only.
URL gopher://english-server.hss.cmu.edu
/00ftp%3aEnglish.Server%3aFiction%3a
Cleland-Fanny%20Hill

The Rime of the Ancient Mariner By
Samuel Taylor Coleridge. Text only.
WEB http://www.w3.org/hypertext/Data

Sources/bySubject/Literature/Gutenberg
/etext94/rime10.txt
URL ftp://nptn.org/pub/e.texts/gutenberg
/etext94/rime10.txt

The Moonstone By Wilkie Collins. Text
only.
WEB http://www.w3.org/hypertext/Data
Sources/bySubject/Literature/Gutenberg
/etext94/mston10.txt
URL ftp://nptn.org/pub/e.texts/gutenberg
/etext94/mston10.txt

The Woman In White By Wilkie Collins.
Text only.
URL ftp://ota.ox.ac.uk/pub/ota/public
/english/Collins/wwhite.1779

Heart of Darkness By Joseph Conrad.
Text only.
WEB http://www.w3.org/hypertext/Data
Sources/bySubject/Literature/Gutenberg
/etext95/hdark11.txt
URL gopher://ccat.sas.upenn.edu:3333/11
/Fiction/Joseph%20Conrad%3A%20
Heart%20of%20Darkness

The Secret Sharer By Joseph Conrad.
Text only.
WEB http://www.w3.org/hypertext/Data
Sources/bySubject/Literature/Gutenberg
/etext95/sshar11.txt • http://wiretap
.spies.com/ftp.items/Library/Classic
/sharer.txt

The Last of the Mohicans By James
Fenimore Cooper. Text only.
URL ftp://ota.ox.ac.uk/pub/ota/public
/english/Cooper/mohicans.1976

The Red Badge of Courage By Stephen
Crane. Hypertext formats.
WEB http://www.cs.cmu.edu:8001/Web
/People/rgs/badge-table.html

▶ **D**

Robinson Crusoe By Daniel Defoe.
Hypertext format.
WEB http://www.datatext.co.uk/library
/defoe/robin/chapters.html

**Discourse on the Method of Rightly
Conducting the Reason, and Seeking**

Truth in the Sciences By Rene
Descartes. Text only.
WEB http://www.cs.cmu.edu:8001/Web
/People/rgs/badge-table.html • http://
www.w3.org/hypertext/DataSources
/bySubject/Literature/Gutenberg/etext93
/dcart10.txt

A Christmas Carol By Charles Dickens.
Text only.
WEB http://www.w3.org/hypertext/Data
Sources/bySubject/Literature/Gutenberg
/etext92/carol10.txt
URL gopher://ccat.sas.upenn.edu:3333
/11/Fiction/ChristmasCarol

A Tale of Two Cities By Charles Dickens. Text only.
WEB http://www.w3.org/hypertext/Data
Sources/bySubject/Literature/Gutenberg
/etext94/2city11.txt • http://wiretap.spies
.com/ftp.items/Library/Classic/twocity.txt

Great Expectations By Charles Dickens.
Hypertext format.
WEB http://www.datatext.co.uk/library
/dickens/greatexp/chapters.html

The Brothers Karamazov By Fyodor
Dostoevsky. Text only.
URL gopher://gopher.vt.edu:10010/02
/72/1

My Bondage and My Freedom By Frederick Douglass. Text only.
WEB http://www.w3.org/hypertext/Data
Sources/bySubject/Literature/Gutenberg
/etext95/bfree10.txt
URL ftp://uiarchive.cso.uiuc.edu/pub/etext
/gutenberg/etext95/bfree10.txt

The Adventures of Sherlock Holmes By
Sir Arthur Conan Doyle. Text only.
WEB http://www-cgi.cs.cmu.edu/afs
/andrew.cmu.edu/acs/library/etexts
/namedsubject/literature/A.C.Doyle.dir
/holmes/The_Adventures_of_Sherlock
_Holmes.dir

The Return of Sherlock Holmes By Sir
Arthur Conan Doyle. Text only.
WEB http://www.w3.org/hypertext/Data
Sources/bySubject/Literature/Gutenberg
/etext94/rholm10.txt • http://www.w3

.org/hypertext/DataSources/bySubject
/Literature/Gutenberg/etext95/rholm11b
.txt

Sister Carrie By Theodore Dreiser. Text only.
URL gopher://gopher.vt.edu:10010/02/75/1

E

Sinners in the Hand of an Angry God By Johnathan Edwards. Text only.
URL ftp://ftp.mcs.com/mcsnet.users
/falcon/christian/sinners.txt

Middlemarch By George Eliot. Hypertext format; text only.
WEB http://etext.lib.virginia.edu/cgibin
/browse-mixed?id=EliMidd&tag=public
&images=images/modeng&data=/lv1
/Archive/eng-parsed • http://www.w3.org
/hypertext/DataSources/bySubject
/Literature/Gutenberg/etext94/mdmar
10.txt

The Mill on the Floss By George Eliot. Hypertext format.
WEB http://www.datatext.co.uk/library
/eliot/mill/chapters.htm

Essays By Ralph Waldo Emerson. Text only.
URL gopher://gopher.vt.edu:10010/02
/79/5

The Bacchantes By Euripides. Text only.
WEB http://altair.stmarys-ca.edu:70
/0/studwork/integral/bacchant.txt

Medea By Euripides. Hypertext format.
WEB http://the-tech.mit.edu/Classics
/Euripides/medea.txt.head.html

F

Buttered Side Down By Edna Ferber. Illustrated hypertext format.
WEB http://etext.lib.virginia.edu/cgibin
/browse-mixed?id=FerButt&tag=public
&images=images/modeng&data=/lv1
/Archive/eng-parsed

The History of Tom Jones, a Foundling By Henry Fielding. Text only.

URL gopher://gopher.vt.edu:10010
/02/82

G

The Beggars Opera By John Gay. Text only.
WEB http://wiretap.spies.com/ftp.items
/Library/Classic/beggars.txt

Herland By Charlotte Perkins Gilman. Plain text only.
WEB http://www-cgi.cs.cmu.edu/afs
/andrew.cmu.edu/acs/library/etexts
/namedsubject/literature/Herland.txt.Z

The Yellow Wallpaper By Charlotte Perkins Gilman. Hypertext format.
WEB http://www.en.utexas.edu/~daniel
/amlit/wallpaper/wallpapertext.html

Patriotism: A Menace To Liberty By Emma Goldman. Text only.
URL file:/etext.archive.umich.edu/pub
/Politics/Spunk/anarchy_texts/writers
/Goldman/Spunk064.tx

Grimm's Fairy Tales By Jacob Grimm. Text Only.
WEB http://www-cgi.cs.cmu.edu/afs
/andrew.cmu.edu/acs/library/etexts
/namedsubject/literature/grimm.dir

Rumpelstiltskin By the Grimm Brothers. Illustrated hypertext.
WEB http://128.172.170.24/Grimm
/rumpeng.html

Beowulf Translated by F.B. Gummere. Text only.
WEB http://wiretap.spies.com/ftp.items
/Library/Classic/beowulf.txt

H

King Solomon's Mines By H. Rider Haggard. Text only.
WEB http://wiretap.spies.com/ftp.items
/Library/Classic/solomon.hrh

Frances Waldeaux By Rebecca Harding. Hypertext format.
WEB http://etext.lib.virginia.edu/cgibin
/browse-mixed?id=DavFran&tag=public

&images=images/modeng&data=/lv1
/Archive/eng-parsed

Jude the Obscure By Thomas Hardy.
Text only.
WEB http://www.w3.org/hypertext/Data
Sources/bySubject/Literature/Gutenberg
/etext94/jude11.txt • http://wiretap.spies
.com/ftp.items/Library/Classic/jude.th

Mayor of Casterbridge By Thomas
Hardy. Hypertext format; text only.
WEB http://www.dircon.co.uk/datatext
/library/hardy/mayor/chapters.htm
• http://www.w3.org/hypertext/Data
Sources/bySubject/Literature/Gutenberg
/etext94/mayrc10.txt

Return of the Native By Thomas Hardy.
Text only.
WEB http://www.w3.org/hypertext/Data
Sources/bySubject/Literature/Gutenberg
/etext94/nativ10.txt • http://wiretap.spies
.com/ftp.items/Library/Classic/native.th

Tess of the D'Urbervilles By Thomas
Hardy. Hypertext format; text only.
WEB http://www.datatext.co.uk/library
/hardy/tess/chapters.html • http://www
.w3.org/hypertext/DataSources/by
Subject/Literature/Gutenberg/etext95
/snowy10.txt

The Scarlett Letter By Nathaniel
Hawthorne. Text only.
WEB http://www.w3.org/hypertext/Data
Sources/bySubject/Literature/Gutenberg
/etext92/scrlt11.txt
URL gopher://ccat.sas.upenn.edu:3333
/11/Fiction/Nathaniel%20Hawthorne%3A
%20The%20Scarlet%20Letter

Leviathan By Thomas Hobbes. Text only.
URL gopher://gopher.vt.edu:10010
/02/98/1

Iliad By Homer. Hypertext format.
WEB http://the-tech.mit.edu/Classics
/Homer/The_Iliad.html
URL gopher://ccat.sas.upenn.edu:3333
/11/Classical/Homeric/Iliad

Odyssey By Homer. Hypertext format;
text only.

WEB http://www.cc.columbia.edu/~svl2
/chapman/index.html
URL gopher://ccat.sas.upenn.edu:3333
/11/Classical/Homeric/Odyssey

Les Miserables (In English) By Victor
Hugo. Text only.
WEB http://www.w3.org/hypertext/Data
Sources/bySubject/Literature/Gutenberg
/etext94/lesms10.txt • http://wiretap
.spies.com/ftp.items/Library/Classic
/lesmis.vh

**An Enquiry Concerning Human Under-
standing** By David Hume. Text only.
URL gopher://english-server.hss.cmu
.edu/00ftp%3aEnglish.Server%3a
Philosophy%3aHume-Human%20
Understanding

I

The Wild Duck By Henrick Ibsen. Hypertext format.
WEB http://etext.lib.virginia.edu/cgibin
/toccer?id=IbsWild&tag=public&
images=images/modeng&data=/lv1
/Archive/eng-parsed&part=0

The Legend of Sleepy Hollow By Washington Irving. Hypertext format; text
only.
WEB http://auden.fac.utexas.edu/~daniel
/amlit/sleepy/sleepy.html
URL gopher://ccat.sas.upenn.edu:3333
/11/Fiction/SleepyHollow

J

Portrait of a Lady By Henry James. Text
only.
URL gopher://gopher.vt.edu:10010/02
/105/1

Turn of the Screw By Henry James. Text
only.
WEB http://www.w3.org/hypertext/Data
Sources/bySubject/Literature/Gutenberg
/etext95/tturn10.txt
URL ftp://uiarchive.cso.uiuc.edu/pub/etext
/gutenberg/etext95/tturn10.txt

A White Heron By Sarah Orne Jewett.
Hypertext format.

WEB http://auden.fac.utexas.edu/~daniel
/amlit/wh/wh.html

**The History of Rasselas, Prince of
Abissinia** By Samuel Johnson. Text only.
URL gopher://dept.english.upenn
.edu/00/E-Text/PEAL/Johnson
/rasselas

Bartholomew Fair By Ben Jonson. Text
only.
URL gopher://english-server.hss.cmu.edu
/00ftp%3aEnglish.Server%3aDrama%
3aJonson-Bartholomew%20Fair

Dubliners By James Joyce. Hypertext
format.
WEB http://www.datatext.co.uk/library
/joyce/dublin/chapters.html

Finnegans Wake By James Joyce. Text
only. (No U.S. Access)
WEB http://www.cs.cmu.edu/Web/book
-nonus.html

Portrait of the Artist as a Young Man
By James Joyce. Hypertext format.
WEB http://www.datatext.co.uk/library
/joyce/artist/chapters.htm

K

The Poetical Works of John Keats By
John Keats. Hypertext format.
WEB http://www.w3.org/hypertext/Data
Sources/bySubject/Literature/Gutenberg
/etext92/bible11.txt

The Rubaiyat of Omar Khayyam By
Omar Khayyam. Text only.
WEB http://wiretap.spies.com/ftp.items
/Library/Classic/rubaiyat.txt

King James Bible Text only.
WEB http://www.w3.org/hypertext/Data
Sources/bySubject/Literature/Gutenberg
/etext92/bible11.txt
URL gopher://ccat.sas.upenn.edu:3333
/11/Religious/Biblical/KJVBible

The Jungle Book By Rudyard Kipling.
Text only.
WEB http://wiretap.spies.com/ftp.items
/Library/Classic/jungle.rk

L

Lady Chatterley's Lover By D.H.
Lawrence. Hypertext format.
WEB http://www.cs.cmu.edu/Web/book
-nonus.html

Sons and Lovers By D.H. Lawrence.
Hypertext format.
WEB http://etext.lib.virginia.edu/cgibin
/toccer?id=LawSons&tag=public&
images=images/modeng&data=/lv1
/Archive/eng-parsed&part=0

The Phantom of the Opera By Gaston
Leroux. Illustrated hypertext format; text
only.
WEB http://etext.lib.virginia.edu/cgibin
/browse-mixed?id=LerPhan&tag=public
&images=images/modeng&data=/lv1
/Archive/eng-parsed • http://www.w3.org
/hypertext/DataSources/bySubject
/Literature/Gutenberg/etext94/phant10.txt

White Fang By Jack London. Text only.
URL gopher://gopher.vt.edu:10010/02
/117/6

The Song of Hiawatha By Henry W.
Longfellow. Text only.
WEB http://www.w3.org/hypertext/Data
Sources/bySubject/Literature/Gutenberg
/etext91/hisong12.txt • http://wiretap
.spies.com/ftp.items/Library/Classic
/hiawatha.txt

A Dome of Many-Coloured Glass By
Amy Lowell. Text only.
URL ftp://uiarchive.cso.uiuc.edu/pub
/etext/gutenberg/etext95/domcg10.tx

M

Le Morte D'Arthur (Volume I) By
Thomas Mallory. Text only.
WEB http://etext.lib.virginia.edu/cgibin
/browse-mixed?id=Mal1Mor&tag=public
&images=images/modeng&data=/lv1
/Archive/eng-parsed

Le Morte D'Arthur (Volume II) By
Thomas Mallory. Text only.
WEB http://etext.lib.virginia.edu/cgibin
/browse-mixed?id=Mal2Mor&tag=public

&images=images/modeng&data=/lv1
/Archive/eng-parsed

Miscellaneous Poems By Andrew Marvell. Hypertext format.
WEB http://etext.lib.virginia.edu/cgibin
/browse-mixed?id=MarPoem&tag=public
&images=images/modeng&data=/lv1
/Archive/eng-parsed

Moon and Sixpence By W.Somerset Maugham. Text only.
WEB http://www.w3.org/hypertext/Data
Sources/bySubject/Literature/Gutenberg
/etext95/moona10.txt
URL ftp:/uiarchive.cso.uiuc.edu/pub
/etext/gutenberg/etext95/moona10.txt

Of Human Bondage By W. Somerset Maugham, Text only.
WEB http://wiretap.spies.com/ftp.items
/Library/Classic/humbond.txt

Bartleby, the Scrivener By Herman Melville. Hypertext format.
WEB http://auden.fac.utexas.edu/~daniel
/amlit/bartleby/bartleby.html

Benito Cereno By Herman Melville. Text only.
URL gopher://gopher.vt.edu:10010/02
/121/1

Moby Dick By Herman Melville. Text only.
URL gopher://ccat.sas.upenn.edu:3333
/11/Fiction/MobyDick
WEB http://wiretap.spies.com/ftp.items
/Library/Classic/mobydick.txt

The Subjection of Women By John Stuart Mill. Text only.
WEB http://wiretap.spies.com/ftp.items
/Library/Classic/women.jsm

Renascence and Other Poems By Edna St. Vincent Millay. Text only.
WEB http://wiretap.spies.com/ftp.items
/Library/Classic/renasc.evm

Paradise Lost By John Milton. Hypertext format; text only.
WEB http://www.wonderland.org/Works
/John-Milton/paradise-lost • http://

www.w3.org/hypertext/DataSources
/bySubject/Literature/Gutenberg/etext92
/plrabn12.txt

Paradise Regained By John Milton. Hypertext format; text only.
WEB http://www.wonderland.org/Works
/John-Milton/paradise-regained • http://
www.w3.org/hypertext/DataSources/by
Subject/Literature/Gutenberg/etext93
/rgain10.txt

O

The Scarlett Pimpernel By Baroness Orczy. Hypertext format.
WEB http://www.cs.cmu.edu:8001/Web
/People/rgs/scarp-table.html

Metamorphoses By Ovid. Text only.
URL gopher://gopher.vt.edu:10010/02
/128/1

P

The Defense of Poesie By Sidney Phillip. Hypertext format.
WEB http://www-vms.uoregon.edu/~rbear
/defence.html

History of My Heart By Robert Pinksy. Text only.
URL gopher://marge.smith.edu/00/more
/capa/pinsky.robert.history.of.my.heart

The Rape of the Lock By Alexander Pope. Text only.
URL gopher://dept.english.upenn.edu/00
/E-Text/PEAL/Pope/rape

R

The Goblin Market By Christina Rossetti. Hypertext format.
WEB http://www.crocker.com/~lwm
/goblin.html

The Confessions of Jean-Jacques Rousseau By Jean-Jacques Rousseau. Text only.
URL gopher://gopher.vt.edu:10010/02
/137/1

Charlotte Temple By Susanna Rowson.

Text only.
URL ftp://uiarchive.cso.uiuc.edu
/pub/etext/gutenberg/etext94
/chtem10.txt

S

The Way of Perfection By Saint Teresa
of Avila. Hypertext format.
WEB http://www.cs.pitt.edu/~planting
/books/teresa/way/way.html

Ivanhoe By Sir Walter Scott. Text only.
WEB http://www.w3.org/hypertext/Data
Sources/bySubject/Literature/Gutenberg
/etext93/ivnho12.txt • http://wiretap
.spies.com/ftp.items/Library/Classic
/ivanhoe.ws

Black Beauty By Anna Sewell. Text only.
URL ftp://uiarchive.cso.uiuc.edu/pub
/etext/gutenberg/etext95/bbeau10.txt

A Midsummer Night's Dream By William
Shakespeare. Text only.
URL gopher://spinaltap.micro.umn.edu
/11/Ebooks/By%20Title/shake/Comedies
/Midsummer%20Night%27s%20Dream
%2c%20A

Antony and Cleopatra By William
Shakespeare. Text only.
URL gopher://spinaltap.micro.umn.edu
/11/Ebooks/By%20Title/shake/Tragedies
/Antony%20and%20Cleopatra

The Complete Works By William Shakespeare. Text only.
WEB http://www.w3.org/hypertext/Data
Sources/bySubject/Literature/Gutenberg
/etext94/shaks12.txt
URL gopher://ccat.sas.upenn.edu:70/77
/.index/Shakespeare

Hamlet By William Shakespeare. Text
only.
URL gopher://spinaltap.micro.umn.edu
/11/Ebooks/By%20Title/shake/Tragedies
/Hamlet

King Lear By William Shakespeare. Text
only.
URL gopher://spinaltap.micro.umn.edu
/11/Ebooks/By%20Title/shake/Tragedies

/King%20Lear

Macbeth By William Shakespeare. Text
only.
URL gopher://spinaltap.micro.umn.edu
/11/Ebooks/By%20Title/shake/Tragedies
/Macbeth

Much Ado About Nothing By William
Shakespeare. Text only.
URL gopher://spinaltap.micro.umn.edu/11
/Ebooks/By%20Title/shake/Comedies
/Much%20Ado%20About%20Nothing

Romeo and Juliet By William Shake-
speare. Text only.
URL gopher://spinaltap.micro.umn.edu/11
/Ebooks/By%20Title/shake/Tragedies
/Romeo%20and%20Juliet

The Tempest By William Shakespeare.
Text only.
URL gopher://spinaltap.micro.umn.edu
/11/Ebooks/By%20Title/shake/Comedies
/Tempest%2c%20The

Shakir Translated by M.H. Shakir. Text
files for each Surah.
WEB http://www-cgi.cs.cmu.edu/afs/cs
.cmu.edu/project/cmt/resources/Quran

Frankenstein By Mary Shelley. Hyper-
text format.
WEB http://electron.rutgers.edu/~keithf
/Frankenstein/contents.html

The Necessity of Atheism By Percy
Shelley. Hypertext format.
WEB http://freethought.tamu.edu/free
thought/percy_shelley/necessity_of
_atheism.html

The Jungle By Upton Sinclair. Text only.
WEB http://www.w3.org/hypertext/Data
Sources/bySubject/Literature/Gutenberg
/etext95/spyuk10.txtn
URL ftp://nptn.org/pub/e.texts/gutenberg
/etext94/jungl10.txt

Antigone By Sophocles. Text only.
WEB http://the-tech.mit.edu/Classics
/Sophocles/antigone.txt.head.html

The Oedipus Trilogy By Sophocles. Text

only.
WEB http://www.w3.org/hypertext/Data
Sources/bySubject/Literature/Gutenberg
/etext92/oedip10.txt • http://wiretap
.spies.com/ftp.items/Library/Classic
/oedipus.txt

Complete On-Line Works By Edmund
Spenser. Hypertext format.
WEB http://wiretap.spies.com/ftp.items
/Library/Classic/shepherd.txt

Kidnapped By Robert Louis Stevenson.
Text only.
WEB http://wiretap.spies.com/ftp.items
/Library/Classic/kidnap.rls

Treasure Island By Robert Louis Stevenson. Hypertext format; text only.
WEB http://www.dircon.co.uk/datatext
/library/stevensn/island/chapters.htm
• http://www.w3.org/hypertext/Data
Sources/bySubject/Literature/Gutenberg
/etext94/treas10.txt

Dracula By Bram Stoker. Hypertext format.
WEB http://www.cs.cmu.edu/Web/People
/rgs/drac-table.html

Uncle Tom's Cabin By Harriet Beecher
Stowe. Text only.
WEB http://www.w3.org/hypertext/Data
Sources/bySubject/Literature/Gutenberg
/etext95/utomc10.txt
URL ftp://uiarchive.cso.uiuc.edu/pub
/etext/gutenberg/etext95/utomc10.txt

Gulliver's Travels By Jonathan Swift.
Text only.
URL gopher://gopher.vt.edu:10010/02
/146/1

T

Gitanjali By Rabindranath Tagore.
Hypertext format.
WEB http://etext.lib.virginia.edu/cgibin
/browse-mixed?id=TagGita&tag=public&
images=images/modeng&data=/lv1
/Archive/eng-parsed

On the Duty of Civil Obedience By
Henry David Thoreau. Hypertext format;

text only.
WEB http://www.cs.indiana.edu/statecraft
/civ.dis.html • http://www.w3.org/hyper
text/DataSources/bySubject/Literature
/Gutenberg/etext93/civil10.txt

Walden By Henry David Thoreau. Text
only.
WEB http://www.w3.org/hypertext/Data
Sources/bySubject/Literature/Gutenberg
/etext95/waldn10.txt
URL gopher://gopher.vt.edu:10010/02
/149/5

Sir Gawain and the Green Knight Edited
by J. R. R. Tolkien and E. V. Gordon. Text
only.
WEB http://www.simons-rock.edu/~tevis
/gawain.html

Anna Karenina By Leo Tolstoy. Text only.
URL gopher://gopher.vt.edu:10010
/02/151/1

War and Peace By Leo Tolstoy. Text
only.
URL gopher://gopher.vt.edu:10010
/02/151/2

Ayala's Angel By Anthony Trollope. Text
only.
WEB http://wiretap.spies.com/ftp.items
/Library/Classic/ayala.txt

**A Connecticut Yankee in King Arthur's
Court** By Mark Twain. Text only.
WEB http://www.w3.org/hypertext/Data
Sources/bySubject/Literature/Gutenberg
/etext93/yanke11.tx • http://wiretap.spies
.com/ftp.items/Library/Classic/yankee.mt

The Adventures of Huckleberry Finn By
Mark Twain. Hypertext format; text only.
WEB http://www.lm.com/~joseph/finn
/finntitl.html • http://www.w3.org/hyper
text/DataSources/bySubject/Literature
/Gutenberg/etext93/hfinn10.txt

The Adventures of Tom Sawyer By Mark
Twain. Hypertext format; text only.
WEB http://www.cs.cmu.edu/Web/People
/rgs/sawyr-table.html • http://www.w3
.org/hypertext/DataSources/bySubject
/Literature/Gutenberg/etext93/sawyr10.txt

V

Around the World In Eighty Days By Jules Verne. Hypertext format; text only.
WEB http://www.datatext.co.uk/library/verne/world/chapters.html • http://www.w3.org/hypertext/DataSources/bySubject/Literature/Gutenberg/etext94/80day10.txt

20,000 Thousand Leagues Under the Sea By Jules Verne. Text only.
WEB http://www.w3.org/hypertext/DataSources/bySubject/Literature/Gutenberg/etext94/2000010.txt
URL ftp://nptn.org/pub/e.texts/gutenberg/etext94/200010.txt

Aeneid By Virgil. Hypertext format; text only.
WEB http://the-tech.mit.edu/Classics/Virgil/The_Aeneid.html
URL gopher://ccat.sas.upenn.edu:3333/1m/Classical/Aeneid

Candide By Voltaire. Text only.
URL gopher://gopher.vt.edu:10010/02/155/1

W

Ben-Hur : A Tale of the Christ By Lew Wallace. Text only.
URL gopher://gopher.vt.edu:10010/02/157/1

Up From Slavery By Booker T. Washington. Text only.
URL gopher://gopher.vt.edu:10010/02/157/1

Daddy-Long-Legs By Jean Webster. Text only.
WEB http://www.w3.org/hypertext/DataSources/bySubject/Literature/Gutenberg/etext94/dlleg10.txt
URL ftp://nptn.org/pub/e.texts/gutenberg/etext94/dlleg10.txt

The Invisible Man By H.G. Wells. Text only.
WEB http://wiretap.spies.com/ftp.items/Library/Classic/invisman.txt

The Time Machine By H.G. Wells. Text only.
WEB http://www.w3.org/hypertext/DataSources/bySubject/Literature/Gutenberg/etext92/timem10.txt • http://www-cgi.cs.cmu.edu/afs/andrew.cmu.edu/acs/library/etexts/namedsubject/literature/Time_Machine.txt.Z

The War of the Worlds By H.G. Wells. Hypertext format; text only.
WEB http://www.fourmilab.ch/etexts/www/warworlds/warw.html • http://www.w3.org/hypertext/DataSources/bySubject/Literature/Gutenberg/etext92/warw10.txt

The House of Mirth By Edith Wharton. Text only.
URL ftp://uiarchive.cso.uiuc.edu/pub/etext/gutenberg/etext95/hmirt10.txt

Leaves of Grass By Walt Whitman. Hypertext format.
WEB http://www.cc.columbia.edu/~svl2/whitman/index.html

The Picture of Dorian Gray By Oscar Wilde. Text only.
WEB http://www.w3.org/hypertext/DataSources/bySubject/Literature/Gutenberg/etext94/dgray10.txt • ftp://uiarchive.cso.uiuc.edu/pub/etext/gutenberg/etext94/dgray10.txt

A Vindication of the Rights of Woman By Mary Wollstonecraft. Text only.
WEB http://wiretap.spies.com/ftp.items/Library/Classic/woman.txt

The Voyage Out By Virginia Woolf. Text only.
WEB http://www.w3.org/hypertext/DataSources/bySubject/Literature/Gutenberg/etext94/voout10.txt • http://wiretap.spies.com/ftp.items/Library/Classic/voyage.vw

The Complete Poetical Works of William Wordsworth By William Wordsworth. Hypertext format.
WEB http://www.cc.columbia.edu/~svl2/wordsworth/index.html

POETRY

REMEMBER THE GOOD OLD DAYS of poetry, when "ham" rhymed with "Sam I am," and a poet's biggest worry was whether or not the stubborn Sarah Stout would ever take the garbage out? Then, someone—a teacher, maybe, or a cruel sibling—announced that poetry was more than just a good rhyme scheme and some clever illustrations. Stanzas and personification replaced Horton's egg and Dr. Seuss was expelled from the canon. In the face of this cruelly codified reality, everyone needs a helping hand. The Internet is a poetry-friendly resource, filled with uncomplicated analyses and online anthologies that help even hapless bards go from bad to verse.

▶ STARTING POINTS

A Procession of Poets This collection of works, reprinted without permission from the *Norton Anthology of Poetry*, is the lazy student's dream. Why lug your weighty books home when you can read, print, and study poems online? Maybe Donne, Marvell, and Pound wouldn't have approved of such labor-saving, but you will.
WEB http://mud.bsd.uchicago.edu/~mohanraj/Poets/favpoems.html

American Verse Project A collaboration of the Michigan Humanities Text Initiative and the University of Michigan Press, the American Verse Project is in the process of assembling an archive of American poetry prior to 1920. Already quite comprehensive, the archive allows users to search by a single word, words, or artist. From standbys like Emerson and Sandburg to lesser-known patriots (ever heard of Bliss Carman?), the poets are a prolific bunch, reflecting the diversity of the American landscape.
WEB http://www.hti.umich.edu/english/amverse

The Atlantic Monthly's Poetry Pages Take an informal, nostalgia-driven journey into the *Atlantic Monthly's* past, where the emphasis is less on critique and analysis than on the magazine's personal connection with artists of the past. The magazine prides itself on "a history of bringing new literary talents to light," and, indeed, a young Emily Dickinson was so inspired by an *Atlantic* article that she began writing to its author. In 1891, after Dickinson's death, these letters were published, and are included in their entirety. In a 1902 article, a journalist recalls his friendship with Walt Whitman. There are also articles on Frost, as well as a collection of poems by Emerson, Longfellow, and Lowell, which appeared in the magazine's first issue.
WEB http://www.theatlantic.com/atlantic/atlweb/poetry/poetpage.htm

British Poetry 1780-1910 "A hypertext archive of scholarly editions," this site includes illustrated, annotated texts by poets including Lewis Carroll, Coleridge, Dickinson, and Keats.
WEB http://etext.lib.virginia.edu/britpo.html

Directory of Ebooks/Poetry A poetry buffet for the gluttonous scholar, the site effortlessly guides users to works by poets from "Anonymous" to Zolynos.
URL ftp://ftp.books.com/eBooks/poetry

▶ PRE-18TH CENTURY

Resources for Studying Beowulf Without the likes of Freddy Krueger, or even the affable Casper, as imaginary fodder, what demons plagued the sleep of the tenth-century 12-year-old? For sheer nightmare-inducing value, there's no denying the potency of *Beowulf*'s Grendel. With a name that means "one who grinds and crushes," this is the last guy one would want to meet in a dark alley. Fortunately, even in the Old English, good balances evil, and our hero, Beowulf, has Grendel's number. Anonymously written and nearly impossible to

comprehend without the benefit of a trusty translation, *Beowulf* is presented at this site, along with a bibliography of studies and an Old English tutor.
WEB http://www.uky.edu/~kiernan/BL/kportico.html

ILTweb Digital Dante Project The project in question is an online, multimedia translation of Dante's *Divine Comedy*, developed by the Institute for Learning Technology at Columbia University. Each Longfellow-translated canto includes an illustration and notes. So, whether you choose to enter the Inferno, Purgatory, or Paradise, your trip to hell is bound to be a little easier. Thank the Lord!
WEB http://www.ilt.columbia.edu/projects/dante/index.html

The Milton-L Home Page If Beelzebub and his cohorts had had this kind of resource at their disposal, maybe their little rebellion would have met with more success. As it is, the perplexed student of *Paradise Lost* should check out the mailing list's home page before entering the inferno that is Milton's epic of good and evil. Of course, the zealous Milton fan can sign on for epistolary hell (i.e. the mailing list proper).
WEB http://www.urich.edu/~creamer/milton.html
EMAIL mailserv@urvax.urich.edu. ✍ *Type in message body:* subscribe milton-l

Some Information on Publius Ovidius Naso (Ovid) Sure, Latin is a dead language, but that's not going to stop sadistic teachers from forcing hapless students to study it in all of its exacting glory. Fortunately, this Ovid site contains the English translation of poems such as "Metamorphoses," as well as an interesting description of the poet's exile from Italy by Emperor Augustus for subversive writings and "an unknown act of folly."
WEB http://Cam031205.student.utwente.nl/Ovidius.html

Edmund Spenser Upon reading the Faerie Queene's first phallic line—"A Gentle Knight was pricking on the plaine"—it is clear that this is not the English language of the MTV generation. While Middle English may not be as incomprehensible as its precursor, some 50 cantos of the stuff doesn't exactly qualify as "a little light reading." But if one manages to wade through the mire of vowels, the rewards are numerous: dragons, knights, and jousts galore.
WEB http://darkwing.uoregon.edu/~rbear

► ROMANTICS

The Blake Multimedia Project As the site is quick to point out, William Blake would have been a bonafide Internet junkie. One of the most innovative multimedia artists, even without the benefit of hypertext, the early Romantic adorned his verse with trippy, codified illuminations. Sadly, his psychedelic visual artistry loses something in the translation to screen, but the Cal Poly students who authored this site use the technology admirably, inviting both detailed and general exploration of Blake's words and images.
WEB http://luigi.calpoly.edu/Marx/Blake/blakeproject.html

Selected Poetry by George Gordon, Lord Byron Who was "mad, bad, and dangerous to know?" Dylan McKay before rehab? Maybe, but the epithet was originally attached to the itinerant royal poet, Lord Byron, in all of his rabble-rousing glory. The artist responsible for Don Juan's immense popularity as cliché, Byron raised hell as a playboy/adventurer, had an affair with his half-sister, and generally embodied the cult of the Romantic artist.
WEB http://library.utoronto.ca/www/utel/rp/authors/byron.html

Coleridge Where is Xanadu? And what kind of sick mariner goes around killing seabirds? Reading Coleridge evokes many such questions, just as a visit to this site yields the answers.
WEB http://www.lib.virginia.edu/etext/stc/Coleridge/stc.html

The Poetical Works of John Keats It is

the rare high school student who escapes the English classroom un-Urned; that is, without decrypting, deciphering, and generally deconstructing Keats' "Ode on a Grecian Urn." The poem often acts as an introduction to the big league of literary criticism, a symbol that the playful puns of Nash and Silverstein are not entirely welcome in the adult world of metaphor and alliteration. But at least the Keatsian wake-up call is a gentle, lyrically beautiful one. The odes, the epics, and the dedications are included for perusal and appreciation.

WEB http://www.cc.columbia.edu/acis/bartleby/keats/index.html

Complete Works of Percy Bysshe Shelley The complete works of the moody Romantic are featured, along with a lengthy biographical sketch and an unflattering, bloated portrait.

WEB http://www.cc.columbia.edu/acis/bartleby/shelley/index.html

Completed Poetical Works by William Wordsworth Wordsworth's obsession with childhood memory and imagination—particularly his own—makes for some interesting reading. His twelfth book, *Prelude*, is a metaphorical bounty for the English scholar and the Freudian alike, replete with more imagery than a mirror factory, and spanning western Europe from Cambridge to the Alps. For those interested in exploring the Romantic fascination with the self, Wordsworth is the reigning king of introspection.

WEB http://www.cc.columbia.edu/acis/bartleby/wordsworth/index.html

19TH CENTURY

Elizabeth Barrett Browning Web How do I love thee? In case you forgot how to count the ways, visit this Web site, which furnishes the complete texts of *Sonnets from the Portuguese* and *Poems of 1844*.

WEB http://www.inform.umd.edu:8080/EdRes/Topic/WomensStudies/ReadingRoom/Poetry/BarrettBrowning

Emily Dickinson With links to more than 350 of her poems online, this Dickinson site, created by students at Brigham Young University, also includes a FAQ, a biography of the poet, and access to the Dickinson mailing list.

WEB http://lal.cs.byu.edu/people/black/dickinson.html

Rudyard Kipling: "The White Man's Burden" and Its Critics Crossing that hazy line between Manifest Destiny and outright imperialist racism, Kipling is one of the world's most insidious colonists, hiding aggressively eurocentric tendencies behind a façade of cute talking animals. This site explores one of Kipling's most patently imperialist efforts, "The White Man's Burden," and includes responses to the work upon its timely publication in 1899. The satirical "Brown Man's Burden," "The Poor Man's Burden," and "The Black Man's Burden" were all written within weeks of the Kipling poem. The site also includes cartoon responses and more recent criticism of the poem.

WEB http://web.syr.edu/~fjzwick/kipling/whiteman.html

Qriss's Poe Pages "Nevermore," quoth both the Raven and the fed-up student after forced memorization of the Master of Macabre's lengthy verse. But you've got to admire the guy's commitment to everything grisly. More than a century before Jason started slashing co-eds, Poe was scaring up proper society with his talking birds, disfiguring plagues, and morgue murders. It's no wonder that Poe appeals to today's Anne Rice-loving "goths." One of the black-clad youths has erected this impressive site in honor of his literary hero. E-texts, a message board inhabited by the likes of "Darth" and "VampuBro," and biographical pages are included at a site that is both comprehensive and suitably dark.

WEB http://www.cs.umu.se/~dpcnn/eapoe/ea_poe.html

Arthur Rimbaud "The precocious boy-poet of French symbolism," Rimbaud broke up a marriage, lived an infamously tortured life, and wrote an epic poem, *A Season in Hell*, all before the age of 20. Most of the poet's works online are in French, but the resourceful scholar can follow links to Rimbaud home pages, yielding biographical information and scholarly criticism.

WEB http://www.empirenet.com/~rdaeley/authors/rimbaud.html

The Tennyson Page One needn't be a card-carrying member of the Jousting Club to appreciate a good Arthurian legend. Everyone loves a vicarious search for the Holy Grail, as Alfred Lord Tennyson knew well. The "Idylls of the King" is his lengthiest work, but most of Tennyson's poems deal with some palatably heroic subject, from the journeys of Ulysses to the Arabian nights. The site also includes a timeline of the poet's life and a portrait of the bearded man.

WEB http://charon.sfsu.edu/TENNYSON/tennyson.html

Walt Whitman A guide to the premier American bard of the 19th century, including an autobiographical note, the full texts of *Leaves of Grass*, and an index of first lines.

WEB http://www.cc.columbia.edu/acis/bartleby/whitman/index.html

▶ 20TH CENTURY

Early Modernist Poets What is modernism? A word invented to perplex hapless students? A blanket term for any number of ghastly paintings? Visit this site for the dictionary definition of the word, a cogent explanatory essay, and a collection of works by six poets—Eliot, Pound, Moore, Stevens and Carlos Williams—who exemplify early modernist verse.

WEB http://ccwf.cc.utexas.edu/~trog/english.html

Dr. Maya Angelou Angelou may be the poet *du jour*, having read a rousing piece for the 50th anniversary of the U.N. and a triumphant verse for Clinton at his inauguration ceremony, but she also has staying power. *I Know Why the Caged Bird Sings* was published more than 25 years ago, and Angelou's not finished yet. Robert Daely's Angelou site contains a short biography, as well as links to related sites and online texts.

WEB http://web.msu.edu/lecture/angelou.html

e.e. cummings page the undisputed master of lowercase lettering and rampant punctuationlessness (cummings revolutionized the look and feel of poetry) this site includes a collection of the poet's works (as well as one isn't-it-lovely example of his painting prowess) the author promises to include a short bio of the poet (in the) future

WEB http://www.unc.edu/~jyandle/cummings

T.S. Eliot: What the Thunder Said "Like a patient etherised upon a table," the student of Eliot is often rendered catatonic with confusion. Sure, the guy is responsible for the decidedly anti-intellectual musical, *Cats*, but he also wrote "The Waste Land," "Gerontion," and many other cryptic stanzas. Fortunately, this excellent resource has tools for the student and casual reader alike, making it the ultimate Eliot site, "Now and Forever!"

WEB http://www.cacs.usl.edu/Departments/English/authors/eliot/index.html

The Robert Frost Web Page Why is Frost North America's most famous poet? Who among us has not stood at the proverbial crossroads, contemplating "the road less traveled" with a wistful, yearning eye? Frost's most famous poem captures the spirit of rebellious longing that is central to America's popularly touted identity. This Web page is a family affair, created by Jay and Sue M. and their Uncle Danny Clayton. Including a biography of the poet, a selection of poems, recordings of Frost reciting his own work, and papers and critiques, the site is an excellent place to begin exploring the life and times of America's poetic hero.

WEB http://pronews.pro-net.co.uk/home

/catalyst/RF/rfcover.html

Pablo Neruda Want to woo the person of your dreams? Sadly, there's no magic formula, but a working knowledge of one or two Neruda poems can't hurt. The Chilean poet turned socialist penned some of the most romantic verse this side of Barrett Browning, even as he devoted himself to the Republican cause during the Spanish Civil War. Already the subject of the award-winning *Il Postino*, Neruda is clearly slated for commercial rediscovery. The sage student would do well to check out this selection of poems—it could do wonders for your love life.
WEB http://www.cris.com/~Huntress/neruda.shtml

Sylvia Plath Making depression fashionable and artsy, Sylvia Plath was nevertheless genuine in her poetic laments, ripe as they are for psychoanalytic unpeeling ("Daddy, I have had to kill you..."). Many of Plath's poems are included in this site, giving the reader insight into one of the most creative depressed minds of the century.
WEB http://pandora.micro.umn.edu/~calypso/SPlath.html

Carl Sandburg The complete text of the Chicago Poems.
URL gopher://wiretap.spies.com/00/Library/Classic/chicago.txt

The Anne Sexton Archive Anne Sexton wrote nearly a dozen books of poetry in her too-brief career before dying by her own hand in 1974. The introduction to this selection of her poems is shamelessly maudlin ("Anne Sexton's life and work is an open wound of confession..."), but there's no tainting the brilliance of her work.
WEB http://www.crl.com/~miko/sexton.html

Renascence and Other Poems by Edna St. Vincent Millay E-texts of selected poems are featured.
WEB http://wiretap.spies.com/ftp.items/Library/Classic/renasc.evm

The Dylan Thomas Place "Do Not Go Gentle into that Good Night"—the hackneyed motif of uplifting films the world over, especially those having to do with inspirational teachers— is just one of Dylan Thomas's lachrymose poems. Many others can be found at this site, along with photographs and recordings of the alcoholic but beloved Welsh poet. Plenty of related links are here as well.
WEB http://pcug.org.au/~wwhatman/dylan_thomas.html

Yeats Home Page For information on Yeats, why not go right to the source— Sligo (Sligo, Ireland, that is)? The Yeats Society Sligo's aim is "to promote, celebrate and foster the works of W.B. Yeats and his family." Towards that end, it provides images and essays detailing the poet's numerous artistic achievements.
WEB http://www.rtc-sligo.ie/rtc_ug/yeats.html

DRAMA

TO STUDY OR NOT TO STUDY Shakespeare on the Internet? If the Web is pricked, does it not bleed? Are you there, Bard, it's me, perplexed high school student? The answer to these and many other Elizabethan questions can be found among the Net's numerous Shakespearean resources. There's just something about iambic pentameter that sets cyberhearts pattering. Of course, old Shakes isn't the only playwright in cyberspace. The downloadable complete works at the Drama Gopher allow aspiring thespians to wax histrionic in the comfort of their own homes. No applause, please.

▶ STARTING POINTS

American Plays What does the unicorn symbolize in the *Glass Menagerie*? What's a good thesis topic for a paper on the *Crucible*? Everyone has an opinion at America Online's Academic Assistance Center—and they're happy to share—so log on and prepare to be enlightened.

AMERICA ONLINE *keyword* aac→Assistance by Subject→English and Literature→ English and Literature Questions→ American Plays

Drama Gopher There is a center stage-seeking diva living inside of all of us. Come on, admit it! You know you've been dying to play all seven roles from Sophocles' *Electra* in the shower, to crank up the music and sing along with the *Beggar's Opera*. This gopher accesses a limited but varied selection of full scripts, aiding and abetting the inner thespian that, in many cases, might be better left alone.

URL gopher://eng.hss.cmu.edu:70/11ftp %3AEnglish.Server%3ADrama%3A

rec.arts.theatre FAQ Sadly, the rec.arts.theatre newsgroup has gone the way of the dodo, but nostalgic *Les Mis* junkies can relive the glory days at its FAQ. While some questions are only relevant to current and aspiring Broadway ticket holders (e.g. "What should I wear to <insert name of pricey musical>?"), others pertain to online resources, the location of drama-related bookstores from New York to the Netherlands, and how to access scripts.

WEB http://www.lib.ox.ac.uk/internet /news/faq/archive/theatre.part1.html

rec.arts.theatre.misc All the word's a stage and everyone wants the spotlight, yet this newsgroup is mercifully free from the pitiful moanings of unemployed actors. Instead, posters range from psychotic theatre zealots to the merely curious. Experts on all manner of theatre trivia respond to questions promptly, eager to display their esoteric expertise. A call for humorous theatre stories evokes replies from actors and audience members alike; the announcement of an upcoming flea circus, on the other hand, elicits no response whatsoever.

USENET rec.arts.theatre.misc

rec.arts.theatre.plays Due to an abundance of cross-posts with rec.arts.theatre.misc, a visit to this site may seem a bit redundant. It is, however, a good place to partake in debates on the literary and philosophical merits of specific plays.

USENET rec.arts.theatre.plays

Theatre and Drama From the recesses of the World Wide Web Virtual Library to your computer consul, let this well-stocked theatre and drama clearinghouse open your eyes to a world of costumes, divas and puppetry. With links to mailing lists, newsgroups, and electronic text archives, the site is an excellent first stop in your journey—behind the cyber-curtain.

WEB http://theatre.brookes.ac.uk/theatre .html

▶ CLASSIC

Greek Drama Page Links to etexts of the

plays of Aeschylus, Sophocles, Euripedes, and Aristophanes. Some are as hard to download as they are to read.
WEB http://www.lick.pvt.k12.ca.us/~ndurbin/html/gd.html

The Plays of Sophocles Project Gutenberg's etext of Freud's great inspiration, the *Oedipus Trilogy*.
WEB http://www.stud.his.no/~odd-arne/oedip10.txt

SHAKESPEARE & CO.

Commentary—*The Taming of the Shrew* This "literary overview" of the termagant's tale may strike just the right chord with high schoolers looking for a ready-made topic for that term paper. "The play contains three stories of deception," claims the thesis sentence, and the rest, as they say, is plagiarism history.
WEB http://www.penguin.com/usa/academic/summer95/classics/taming/comment.html

The Complete Works of William Shakespeare Everyone knows that *Macbeth* begins with chanting witches and funky lighting, and most Shakespeare buffs know that the mock trial scene in *King Lear* did not appear in the First Folio. But how many know that part of *Coriolanus* takes place in a Volsican camp, or that stage directions (including the infamous "Enter PERICLES, wet") have been vexing textual issues since the 17th century? Read or act along with this collection of the Bard's works, encoded in hypertext so readers can grasp the subtleties of sixteenth-century English. Readers solely interested in the clichés can check out Bartlett's list of famous Shakespeare quotations.
WEB http://the-tech.mit.edu/Shakespeare/works.html

Falcon Education Macbeth and Hamlet Page High school teacher Rodger Burnich created this page as "a resource for all students struggling with Shakespeare." The site contains links to other Shakespeare sites, as well as humorous, high school student-friendly summaries of the two featured plays. Wondering about all that "foul is fair" stuff? Burnich obliges curious minds with links to information on everything from the chanting of the witches to the role of "Fortune." With a resource like this one, the sage student would do well to pray for an assignment on these plays.
WEB http://www.falconedlink.com/falcon

humanities.lit.authors.shakespeare Amazing, isn't it, how contentious literary types can be in the comfort of their own esoteric newsgroup. "Hamlet's a wimp!" one poster exclaims, and others are quick to jump to their favorite procrastinator's defense. With all of the talk of term papers and study carrels, it is clear that the group is populated by college types, but anyone can get a question answered. Appeal to the superior knowledge of these bookworms, and they'll be sure to respond with helpful hint after hint.
USENET humanities.lit.authors.shakespeare

Thomas Middleton Middleton's *Women Beware Women* (1621) and *The Changeling* (1622) are among the bloodiest and best Jacobean tragedies, lacking the richness of Shakespeare's late work, but with a firm grasp of the conventions of the genre—sexual betrayal, double identity, and brutality. This page is part of an initiative to put all of Middleton's works online.
WEB http://dayhoff.med.virginia.edu/~ecc4g/middhome.html

A Midsummer Night's Dream: Annotated Hypertext Edition Poised precariously on the border of pretentious and helpful, this site contains the text of the oft-produced comedy, with critical notes by the site's author. Nary an iambically pentametered verse goes by without the site's author offering his none-too-pithy opinions on allegories, imagery and comic foreshadowing. After a full read, one may feel as if the play has been analyzed into the ground, but at least its better than notes à la Cliff.
WEB http://quarles.unbc.edu/midsummer

Shakespeare In the Shakespeare section of CompuServe's Living History message forum, literary experts and neophytes rub cyberelbows, exchange opinions, and clamor to answer trivia questions. Is the *Merchant of Venice* anti-Semitic—and if so, should it be included in the canon? Who has this week's trivia answer? Can anyone help Jeff with a particularly cryptic crossword question involving a Shakespearean jester? These are the questions that keep the Bard's most zealous fans awake at night.
COMPUSERVE *go* living history→
Shakespeare

Shakespeare's Astrology Macbeth must be an Aries. What's Hamlet's rising sign? Astrology was alive and well in Shakespeare's time—even without the on-staff experts at *Cosmo*—and the Bard himself was clearly influenced by the signs of the times. This article examines the relevance of astrology to Shakespeare's plays, with particular emphasis on *All's Well that Ends Well* and *King Lear*.
WEB http://www.idirect.com/oracle/library/wspr.html

Shakespeare Illustrated If you like your classes heavy on slides and light on lectures, this may very well be your gateway to Shakespeare nirvana. Exploring the relationship between the Bard and his visually artistic peers, the site wastes little time on verbose theorizing, and, instead, cuts right to the chase, displaying a selection of artwork influenced by various plays and sonnets. According to the introduction, "pictures from Shakespeare accounted for about one-fifth—some 2,300—of the total number of literary paintings recorded between 1760 and 1900." How did the painters, actors, directors, and critics of the Bard's era influence one another? Although the site focuses primarily on one author (Shakespeare, duh) it answers a number of more general questions about the relationships at work in the artistic world.
WEB http://www.cc.emory.edu/ENGLISH/classes/Shakespeare_Illustrated/Shakespeare.html

The Skinhead Hamlet Something of a misnomer, this site does not feature a racial invective-hurling, jackboot-wearing Ophelia; rather, it comes to the Internet straight from the Cliffs Notes Reform School for Boys. Translating the famous play into "modern English," in this case, means disrupting the iambic pentameter with more profanities than occur in an Eddie Murphy double feature.
WEB http://icarus.uic.edu/~blor1/hamlet.txt

The Sonnets of William Shakespeare Lo! All of the Bard's sonnets are here for your reading and reciting pleasure.
WEB http://www.sbbs.se/com/home/dabj/Poetry/sonnets.htm

William Shakespeare's Sonnets Homoerotic love poetry or overblown self-laudatory verse? Whatever your opinion of the Bard's sonnets, there's no denying their resonance within the literary and popular culture of the English-speaking world. What desperate Romeo has not attempted to woo the prom queen with a little, "Shall I compare thee to a summer's day?" Along with the hackneyed standards included in this site, some lesser known sonnets work the magic of poesy. The etymologically curious may be interested in the site's discussion of the word, "sonnet."
WEB http://www.eecs.uic.edu/~mocampo/sonnets.html

▶ 19TH CENTURY

Faust Never make a deal with the Devil, baby, 'cause the Devil always gets his due. And never, ever challenge God to a test of power. Why is it that mortals—from the builders of the Tower of Babel to Dr. Frankenstein—are pathologically incapable of learning this lesson? The vainglorious quest for omnipotence can only end in tragedy. Just ask Goethe's protagonist, Faust. Of course, one might have trouble finding him—he's in Hell.
URL gopher://eng.hss.cmu.edu/00ftp:english.server:drama:Goethe-Faust

Peer Gynt The script of Ibsen's play, spanning six years in the life of a Norwegian peasant boy, is presented in its drawn-out entirety.
URL gopher://eng.hss.cmu.edu/00ftp :english.server:drama:Ibsen Peer Gynt

Strindberg The eminently quotable, long-suffering, multi-talented bad boy from Sweden, August Strindberg wrote plays and novels, painted and drew, and raised hell around Europe with the likes of Munch and Gaugin. Late in his life, Strindburg developed an interest in the occult, and some of the most interesting pages of this site include excerpts from his *Occult Diary*, in which he describes nighttime visitations from the spirit of his remarried ex-wife ("Is she literally two persons? And do I possess one? The better one?").
WEB http://www.jmk.su.se// jmk/stud/H93-120/d-hedjon /index.html

Wild Wilde Web Oscar Wilde's plays revolutionized the art of conversation, paving the way for such repartee-driven popular culture standbys as *Seinfeld* and *Cheers*. His public life plagued with scandal and prejudice, the oft-maligned Wilde was nevertheless a sought after dinner guest (at a time when being a sought after dinner guest was the be-all and end-all in social eminency). This site educates, even as it encourages reverence of the multi-talented author in question.
WEB http://www.clients.anomtec.com /oscarwilde

▶ **20TH CENTURY**

The Children's Hour A database allowing users to search Lillian Hellman's play by a specific word or words.
WEB http://www.public.iastate.edu/~spires /child.html

English Contemporary Theatre 1950-1990's Learn about the lives, times and works of British playwrights like Orton, Pinter, and Churchill at this well-organized, somewhat limited site.

WEB http://weber.u.washington.edu /~redmama/barry/titlejm.html

Musical Lyrics Drive your friends and family to drink with non-stop acapella recitals of your favorite Broadway hits. Visit this site, and "Greased Lightning" can go, go, go at your house tonight!
URL gopher://gopher.etext.org/11/Quartz /theater/musicals

The Puppetry Home Page Not just for muppets anymore, puppetry has entered the cyber-realm with a vengeance. A visit to the Puppetry Home Page may still yield links to, for example, the Dilbert Sock Puppet Page, but these are few and far between, sandwiched between the likes of Motion Capture Technology and Avatar Zone Animatronics. Watch out, Grover! A robot is coming for your job.
WEB http://www-leland.stanford.edu /~rosesage/puppetry/puppetry.html

Samuel Beckett
Act I, scene I
A high school classroom, Anytown, USA.
Teacher: Bobby, where's your 6 billion word essay on *War and Peace*?
Student: I didn't do it.
Teacher: Why not?
Student: I was too busy waiting.
Teacher: Waiting? For what?
Student: For Godot.
Teacher: Oh. That's a good reason. You can have an extension.
Lights dim, and music rises (Van Halen's "Hot for Teacher")
WEB http://www.empirenet.com/~rdaeley /authors/beckett.html

Eugene Ionesco If you think the most interesting thing about the French playwright is that his most celebrated play is entitled *Rhinoceros*, think again. At the absurdist's home page, a short biography describes his self-titled antiplays, which "characteristically combine a dream or nightmare atmosphere with grotesque, bizarre, and whimsical humor." In a word, cool.
WEB http://www.empirenet.com/~rdaeley /authors/ionesco.html

Mamet A short biography of the brilliantly caustic American playwright, screenwriter, and director responsible for *Oleanna*, *American Buffalo*, and *Glengarry Glen Ross* is included, as well as links to interviews and reviews of his films.
WEB http://www.empirenet.com/~rdaeley/authors/mamet.html

Arthur Miller Although sitting through a production of *The Crucible* may seem like an inquisition, witch-hunt and persecution trial rolled into one, there is no denying Miller's resonance in the literary and popular culture of the United States. "Don't be such a Willy Loman!" is often heard over the counter at the local welfare office, just as *The Crucible* is synonymous with Salem. Of course, if that doesn't earn the guy respect, there's always the little matter of his marriage to Marilyn Monroe.
WEB http://www.empirenet.com/~rdaeley/authors/millera.html

Stoppard The great Tom Stoppard has been pushing the boundaries of theater for years. Just as Rosencrantz misuses free speech "to prove that exists" in *Rosencrantz and Guildenstern Are Dead*, Stoppard invokes the conventions of traditional theatre merely to flout them. For more information on the only playwright who dared to tangle with *Hamlet* (and won), check out the Stoppard home page.
WEB http://www.empirenet.com/~rdaeley/authors/stoppard.html

Thornton Wilder Be glad it's not your town, because nothing much ever seems to happen in *Our Town*. A funeral here, a lengthy monologue there, and you have the basic elements of the most frequently produced play in the history of student theater.
WEB http://www.sky.net/~emily/thornton.html

Internet Resources Pertaining to Tennessee Williams Get off the roof, and let Stanley in the house before he has your neurotic sister committed. Alcoholism, dysfunctional families and hints of incest abound in Williams' plays, and all before breakfast. This index of links to online resources is comprehensive.
WEB http://www.mps.net/mockups/playhouse

CREATIVE WRITING

YOU'RE THE NEXT SHAKESPEARE, but no one seems to care. Your parents stopped hanging your papers on the fridge years ago, and your older brother doesn't know a metaphor from a jockstrap. It's no better at school. Your friends believe you're insane when you spout verse during home room, and even your English teacher, while appreciative of your effort, thinks your short stories are a little "out there." What's an unappreciated writer to do? Thanks to the Internet, you don't have to suffer in silence, hoping for posthumous recognition of your genius. Send poetry and prose to the Quill Society, The Writing Fun Page, or Middlezine, and learn the meaning of support, respect, and erudite feedback. Need to vent about the angst-ridden "writer's life"? The self-absorbed constituents of misc.writing may not actually listen, but at least posting to the group provides another opportunity to practice your writing.

▶ STARTING POINTS

Middlezine (Showcasing Exceptional Middle School Writing) Middle school isn't just the gateway to puberty. Sure, movies, dating, and phone privileges are big issues, but preteens have even weightier concerns—and original thoughts, too. Devoted exclusively to middle school writing—in an array of genres—this incredible resource includes contributions from a diverse selection of young adults. As schools hit the Net in increasing number, *Middlezine* invites contributions from entire classes. The "Poets of Munsey Park," for example, showcases the talents of a class from Manhasset, N.Y.
WEB http://www.salamander.net/people /hnoden

misc.writing A forum for the discussion of writing, this newsgroup seems to attract bitter has-been (or never-been) writers, who spend their days obsessing over the semantics of terminology, liter-ary merit, and genre. Tiffs break out at every turn, and threads tend to be verbose, as the hyper-critical members censure even the quality of writing within postings to the group itself. The group's FAQ answers questions about manuscripts, agents, copyrights, and other topics of interest to the aspiring professional.
USENET misc.writing
FAQ: **WEB** http://www.cis.ohio-state.edu /hypertext/faq/usenet/writing/FAQ/faq .html

The Quill Society The exclusive gathering of online writers, ages 12 to 24, from around the world. Entrée into the group requires submission of a personal profile, whereupon one may present pieces of writing for inclusion in the Quill Library. At least two other members look at incoming work. Feedback is plentiful, with an emphasis on the positive.
WEB http://www.aimnet.com/~hyatt /quill/quilhome.html

Readers and Writers Between flirting shamelessly, exchanging vital statistics, and talking up their home towns, it's a wonder that the denizens of CompuServe's Teens Students Forum have time left over for intellectual pursuits. However, those who choose to forgo the bustling chat rooms in favor of the more staid Readers and Writers message section will find an active community of young would-be scribblers and avid readers. While some post original poems, inviting feedback from their peers, others discuss favorite authors or genres. The library section contains numerous resources, including essays, press releases, and biographies of famous writers.
COMPUSERVE *go* stufoa→Readers and Writers→Messages *and* Libraries

Resources for Young Writers An excellent set of links for young writers, including FAQs, online journals, and contests. The site also contains a section entitled, "Tips for Young Writers by Young Writers." There is also a listing of publications seeking stories by young writers.

WEB http://www.interlog.com/~ohi/inkspot/young.html

Writers Club Writers can be pretty zealous when it comes to their chosen craft. Witness the slew of regular visitors to America Online's Writers Club. One needn't don a black turtleneck to rub elbows with the literati in the Writer's Cafe, a populous chat room, replete with jargon-slinging regulars with a penchant for word-play. The message boards, divided by genre, are extremely active, as posters engage in a mixture of ego-stroking, literary analysis, and debate. While some may be turned off be the seemingly endless spate of self-important musings—not to mention the perfunctory analysis of works and the vainglorious quest for employment—others will be sure to enjoy the free flow of ideas, advice, and trivia.

AMERICA ONLINE *keyword* writers

Writers on the Net A group of published writers has formed this online resource center, where classes and individual tutoring sessions are available for a fee. Instruction is offered via email for $36 per hour.

WEB http://www.writers.com

▶ FICTION & PROSE

My-View A mailing list for young people interested in sharing their views of the world, as well as in reading the ideas and opinions of their peers.

EMAIL listserv@sjuvm.stjohns.edu ✍
Type in message body: subscribe my-view <your full name>

▶ POETRY WRITING

The Alien Flower Poetry Workshop Take part in a real-time poetry discussion, submit your work for group critique, or simply engage in a little haiku voyeurism.

WEB http://www.sonic.net/web/albany/workshop

Logos and Haiku
japanese verse form
students can contribute their
pictures and poems
WEB http://www.bekkoame.or.jp/~ryosuzu/index.html

Poetry Writing Tips A simple—possibly simplistic—document that doesn't claim to have all the answers. The site's author, offers 18 steps, many of which focus on what not to do (e.g., "Don't explain EVERYTHING"). Those interested in living a writer's lifestyle may be interested in some of his more general tips: "When you can't write, lie on the floor for a while."

WEB http://www.azstarnet.com/~poewar/writer/Poet's_Notes.html

THe UNstoppable DReamers (THUNDR) "Pixel by pixel our thoughts come together," boasts this mawkish poetry cyberslam. Anyone can submit poetry to the site, but so far, almost no one has, leaving the site's creator free to display his own brand of "language" poetry (hence the rebellious use of capitals to form the site's acronym). Fortunately, THUNDR is just one of many online forums where aspiring poets can submit their work for critique.

WEB http://www.uni.edu/pirill44/th

▶ PLAYWRITING

The Playwriting Seminar So, you say you want to be a playwright. Well, contrary to quixotic belief, writing isn't all innate talent and gritty life experience. There are rules, my friend, hard and fast ones; and, while they're certainly made to be broken, you have to know them before you can flout them. That's where this extensive site comes in. "An opinionated Web companion on the art and craft of playwriting," this online course by Richard Toscan may be beyond the scope of the average high school scribbler. However, the course has generated a lot of positive feedback among "those

who know." Indeed, every facet of the playwriting process is covered in extensive detail, from the basics of character and plot to the complexities of conflict and subtext.
WEB http://www.fpa.pdx.edu/depts/fpa/playwriting/seminar.html

Resources for Screenwriters and Playwrights A well-organized, diverse listing of links, resources, and publications for playwrights.
WEB http://www.interlog.com/~ohi/www/screen.html

Screenwriters and Playwrights Home Page An excellent resource for the aspiring playwright, including access to online scripts, tips from the pros, and a Voices of Experience section where the enlightened share their insights.
WEB http://www.teleport.com/~cdeemer/Playwrights.html

Suspense Plot Techniques Why visit this site? Because "the butler did it" just doesn't cut it in today's complex world. Because even your 2-year-old baby sister has seen all of the *Nightmare on Elm Street* movies, and *Psycho* is the Saturday morning feature on the Disney Channel. These are dire times for the budding suspense writer. With subheads such as Clarifying Suspense Plots and Physical Activity as Structure, this online course is obviously intended for the creative writing elder. The information is both comprehensive and well-organized.
WEB http://www.fpa.pdx.edu/depts/fpa/playwriting/suspensetech.html

▶ TEACHERS' LOUNGE

A Handbook of Terms for Discussing Poetry Compiled by a class at Emory University, this is an excellent basic resource for the teaching of poetry critique and writing. The explanations comprise basic definitions and examples of paradox, personification, ambiguity, different genres, meters, and verse forms.
WEB http://www.cc.emory.edu/ENGLISH/classes/Handbook/Handbook.html

The Alliance for Computers and Writing With a mission to facilitate the use of technology in the English classroom, the ACW provides a number of services and hosts meetings for members and other interested parties. The alliance's home page details its activities, provides a schedule of upcoming events, and includes links to related resources.
WEB http://english.ttu.edu/acw

Global SchoolNet Foundation Including a variety of projects for entire classes, this site links kids around the world, through newsgroups, online newspapers, special projects and contests, and mailing lists. In 1995, the Global Schoolhouse project allowed students worldwide to speak face to face through CU-SeeMe video conferencing software. Writing specific projects include the *Newsday* journalism exchange, in which students produce their own newspaper using information gathered from online correspondents around the world.
WEB http://www.gsn.org

Issues Related to Teaching Writing and Journalism A relatively new forum for the discussion of teaching writing at the high school and middle school levels. Although the site, created by the University of Massachusetts English department, has great potential, it's underutilized.
WEB http://www.radio.alma.unibo.it/SpecialPrograms/ISN/teaching.html

Journal Writing A detailed suggested assignment for creative writing teachers, the journal writing project asks students to comment on each other's work.
WEB http://www.csus.edu/journalw.html

Writing Labs on the Web Writing labs connect aspiring writers with experienced teachers for tutoring sessions and feedback via email. This site includes a collection of links to numerous writing labs, writing centers, and other instructional resources.
WEB http://owl.trc.purdue.edu/writing-labs.html

COMPOSITION & GRAMMAR

PROPER GRAMMAR ISN'T JUST A matter of a comma here, a well-placed prepositional phrase there. As any bell hooks fan knows, grammar has serious political implications, and objectivity is only a dream in the mind of the ruling hegemony. Even e.e. cummings mastered the rules in school before defying them in verse. The Internet houses many grammar resources, from the extremely dry Grammar and Style Guide to the playful Word Wizard to the disturbingly obsessed alt.usage .english. And feminist semioticians will delight in the Gender-free Pronouns FAQ, where he/she can explore the repercussions of "gendered" words.

STARTING POINTS

The Elementary Grammar Learn the fundamentals of the English language at this detailed site.
WEB http://www.hiway.co.uk/~ei/intro .html

School House Rock (unofficial) Home Page Conjunction Junction, what *is* your function? Remember the '70s? Probably not, but one needn't be a child of the disco generation to appreciate the wit of School House Rock. Teaching everything from grammar to politics through the clever use of animation, rock music, and catchy lyrics, David McCall revolutionized television, proving that public channels don't have the monopoly on education. Now, thanks to an unnamed School House Rock zealot who knows how to build Web pages, a whole new generation can get acquainted with the talking teeth and singing kangaroos that were the erudite rock stars of a previous era. The Web site carries lyrics to the complete set of catchy tunes as well as audio clips.
WEB http://hera.life.uiuc.edu/rock.html

The Virtual Writing Laboratory Purdue University's writing lab contains a number of documents on scintillating subjects such as comma usage, formats for citing sources, and non-sexist language.
WEB http://owl.english.purdue.edu

WORD USAGE

alt.usage.english Some people play sports. Others collect comic books or baseball cards. Still others play with words. While there may not be a grammar club at the average high school, the Internet—that bastion of the disenfranchised and esoteric—has an entire newsgroup devoted to the discussion of words, punctuation, and more. Wondering about the origin of your favorite cliché? These experts will gladly bring you "up to speed." You may not have patience for the excruciating detail, but questions are answered promptly, and with mind-numbing exactitude. The newsgroup's voluminous FAQ includes word and phrase origins, discussions of usage disputes, "words frequently sought," and spelling information.
USENET alt.usage.english
FAQ: **WEB** http://www.cis.ohio-state.edu /hypertext/faq/usenet/alt-usage-english -faq/faq.html

Collective Nouns A massive (and maybe even obsessive) list of collective nouns (e.g. "a bevy of quail," "a colony of ants" or "a wealth of information").
WEB http://www.lrcs.com/collectives

Usage Experts Change Their Minds, Too Deceptively cut and dried, the *American Heritage Dictionary* is actually anything but, with a panel of word experts debating the minutiae of usage at every turn. One can read the notes explaining how the panel voted on particularly controversial topics. The contraction *impact on*, for example was censured as utterly crass, as was the adverb *arguably*, but the usage of *disinterested* to mean *uninterested* is gaining increasing acceptance.
WEB http://www.eei-alex.com/eye /usage.html

The VOCONs Family Meet Dick Shinary, Cinny Nym, Al Literation, and Sam Manatics. Together, they comprise the VOCON family. Teaching vocabulary through a fun-filled comic strip, the VOCONs know that visual learning is good learning. Visit the comic strip, or follow the links to a variety of word puzzles.
web http://syndicate.com/comicstrip.html

The Word Detective The Word Detective is the online version of "Words, Wit and Wisdom," a newspaper column that has been answering readers' questions about words and language since 1953. Lately, the most common queries have come from people desperate to track down the last of the "-gry" words. There are apparently three of them, but most people only know "angry" and "hungry." The column's author is, sadly, unable to shed light on the issue, offering "aggry," meaning a type of prehistoric bead. On other subjects, however, he is extremely knowledgeable, and happy to respond to queries of any kind.
web http://www.users.interport.net/~words1

Word Traps Amend vs. emend, all right, not alright, and much more. This site confronts and rectifies common vocabulary usage and spelling errors.
web http://granite.cyg.net/~stampact/edit/ind_edit.html

The Word Wizard The Word Wizard is fascinated by "anything to do with words," and he wants to share his hobby with like-minded wordsmiths. Membership is free, and club members can take part in contests, contribute to the Wizard's slang lexicon, and attend online Fancy Word Parties (come dressed up in a specific style/vocabulary). The Public Scribe function allows a member to enlist the eloquence of the rest of the club. Simply submit a rough draft of a problematic letter or essay, and other members will redraft it. Quotes, insults, and journal entries of the day make this site a highly entertaining foray into the wild world of language.

web http://www.wordwizard.com

▶ COMPOSITION

A Guide for Writing Research Papers The Modern Language Association's in-depth, dryly written guide to the research, writing, and proper citation of research papers.
web http://webster.commnet.edu/Library/mla.htm

▶ GRAMMAR & STYLE

The 11 Rules of Grammar Explore correct and incorrect examples of the most common grammatical errors, and heading the list is the ubiquitous joining of two independent clauses with a conjunction.
web http://ucsu.colorado.edu/~giaquint/grammar.htm

A Study of Proper Grammar William Safire's "Rules for Writers," including objective grammar rules ("the adverb always follows the verb") and more subjective, somewhat stylistic pointers ("a writer must shift your point of view" and "take the bull by the hand and avoid mixing metaphors").
web http://www.kcilink.com/brc/other/v3n6.html

Capitalization This treatise on proper capitalization is extracted from the book *Grammar, Punctuation, and Capitals*. The information is applicable universally and should therefore be revered as an authority on the big letters.
web http://sti.larc.nasa.gov/html/Chapt4/Chapt4_TOC.html

The Elements of Style The full text of Strunk and White's grammar and composition bible.
web http://www.columbia.edu/acis/bartleby/strunk

Gender-Free Pronouns FAQ Feminism's campaign against the phallocentricity of the English language reaches absurd new heights in this gender-free FAQ. If those sexist pronoun pigs have been

getting you down, why not utilize this site's suggested alternatives? Here's a little example: "If the person from the insurance company calls, tell him I'll call him back tomorrow" becomes "If the person from the insurance company calls, tell em I'll call em back tomorrow." Note that "em" is not a contraction for "them," but a whole new verbal creation altogether. Avoid defaulting to the male pronoun, get hints on how to do it here, and jump on the gender-free boat!
WEB http://www.eecis.udel.edu/~chao/gfp

Grammar and Style Guide An all-too-familiar scenario: Your bus is coming in ten minutes and you have one more paragraph to write for your final English paper. Suddenly, your brain freezes in a rare moment of grammatical retardation—"i before e except after..." What's a ninth-grade procrastinator to do? Assuming you're hooked up to the Net, Jack Lynch's guide may very well be your ticket to salvation. Simply click on the letter that corresponds to your question, and read the cogent, answer-filled paragraph.
WEB http://www.english.upenn.edu/~jlynch/grammar.html

Grammar Checker Type some words, any words, into the space provided, and the grammar checker will let you know if you've formed a proper sentence.
WEB http://edservices.testcorp.com/Forms/grammar_checker.html

Grammar Hotline at MSU Do you need to know the difference between "farther" and "further"? Befuddled about whether it should be "the staff is" or "the staff are"? If so, contact Michigan State University's Writing Center Grammar and Usage Hotline, by telephone or email.
WEB http://atl46.atl.msu.edu/Words/ghotline.html

The Homograph Page Homographs are words that have identical spellings, but different pronunciations and meanings. Not surprisingly, someone out there is batty for the things, and has compiled a list that is both mind-boggling and slightly disturbing in its magnitude. The sheer number could make you even number.
WEB http://members.aol.com/jonv0/homograph/homograph.html

"It's" vs. "Its" Nary a language complicates its pronouns and contractions the way English does. It's mayhem, but finally, there's help. Admirably pithy, the site restores order to chaos with a few well-chosen sentences.
WEB http://www.rain.org/~gshapiro/its.html

The King's English Eradicating ignorance the English-speaking world over, H.W. Fowler's book not only covers the ins and outs of grammar basics, but also explores ambiguity, style, and euphony. An "Airs and Graces" chapter takes aim at trite phrases, cheap originality, and repetition. Not for the jingoist, the book sneers at the "Americanisms" which have corrupted the language. Still, this longwinded tome has a certain entertainment value in its archaism.
WEB http://www.columbia.edu/acis/bartleby/fowler

On-Line English Grammar At this site, one can search for answers to pressing grammatical questions by using the table of contents, a keyword search, or emailing the experts at the Lydbury English Centre.
WEB http://www.edunet.com/english/grammar/index.html

Punctuation Need help with punctuation?! Visit this site!!
WEB http://sti.larc.nasa.gov/html/Chapt3/Chapt3-TOC.html

PART 3

Mathematics

BASIC MATH

ALBERT EINSTEIN ONCE SAID, "The search for truth is more precious than its possession," but your math teacher probably won't accept that as an excuse for not doing your homework. Instead, you might quote Blake, who exclaimed, "God forbid that Truth should be confined to Mathematical Demonstration!" If the teacher still won't let you off the hook, try the Internet for help. First, find the answer to basic questions like "What are numbers?" at the Mathematics FAQ. Learn shortcuts to math problems at Math Tips & Tricks. If you still can't get the answers to your problems, send them to Ask Dr. Math! If all this Netsurfing makes you hungry, get your slice of the pi at the Ridiculously Enhanced Pi Page.

▶ STARTING POINTS

CTC Math/Science Gateway: Mathematics A fine site from a group of math education gurus, this collection of resources and links is a good starting point for further explorations. Nicely organized, detailed and friendly, CTC is neither chatty nor minimalist—it's just right.
WEB http://www.tc.cornell.edu/Edu/Math SciGateway/math.html

Dave Rusin's Miscellaneous Math Articles This laid-back site compiles assorted math articles for advanced research, but also provides links to high-school level resources, such as the Cornell Secondary School Math Site. The page's author sounds like a fairly interactive individual, and he offers links to his own home page, as well as abstract games, and other math-related activities.
WEB http://www.math.niu.edu/~rusin /known-math

David Eppstein's Articles and Links Describing himself as someone who gets paid to "just sit around and think," this associate professor of computer science at the University of California,

Irvine, has some highly technical data on his home page,as well as some neat Recreational Math resources. Links include "fun" math puzzles and the geometry junkyard, which is "a bunch of recreational geometry along with some research material such as open problem lists, lecture notes, usenet postings, and brief blurbs from my own papers."
WEB http://www.ics.uci.edu/~eppstein

The E-Database of Student Research: Math There's no frivolity at this site, which opens with a table of contents and proceeds through a no-frills archive of mathematical research prepared by middle-school students on topics such as "The Frequency of Occurrence of Different Colored Skittles."
URL gopher://hub.terc.edu/11/hub/owner /other/NSRC/math.d.b

E-mail Math As an online history of a worldwide exercise in information gathering and problem solving, this site reproduces the questions, answers, and methods used by some of the international participants. It's fascinating to see what the elementary school participants did. To describe the weather in Newfoundland, they gathered data from the Web, called the weather office, and were able to provide information about the total snowfall, the difference between the amount of snow still on the ground and the annual snowfall, etc. Find out how they did it—and how you can, too.
WEB http://calvin.stemnet.nf.ca /~elmurphy/emurphy/math.html

Eric's Treasure Trove of Mathematics A fine site for alphabetically accessing concise info on math topics and concepts. The site also has archives of astronomy, physics and planetary science topics. As a bonus, Eric posts a feedback button at the end of each query—you might as well use it.
WEB http://www.gps.caltech.edu/~eww /math/letters.html

Family Math Family Math programs are based on the idea that the family that computes together does everything better together—especially if the kids doing the computing are the mathematically underepresented, i.e. girls and minority students. As part of the EQUALS project at the University of California at Berkeley, Family Math is a six-week tutoring program generally sponsored by schools, community groups, or clubs, but individuals can use this site, too. Girls will be especially interested in getting a copy of *Math for Girls and Other Problem Solvers*. Back issues of the *Family Math* newsletter are also available, as are numerous math-related links.
WEB http://theory.lcs.mit.edu/~emjordan/famMath.html

Genesee Area Mathematics / Science / Technology Center Known as GAMSTC for short, the Genesee Area Mathematics/Science/Technology Center promotes the education and fun of thinking symbolically—and this site is a decent introduction to its efforts.
WEB http://gamstcweb.gisd.k12.mi.us

Glenn T. Seaborg Center for Teaching and Learning Science and Mathematics Named for the 1951 Nobel Prize-winner in chemistry, this teaching and learning center for science and math has a Web site that proclaims its goal of making its innovations and resources and traveling science programs available for teachers and students everywhere. Based in Michigan, the center claims partnership with far-flung colleagues—and could take an interest in your school, too, if you contact them. The site could be stronger, but the center it promotes is intriguing enough to warrant a visit.
WEB http://seaborg.nmu.edu

Math Archives Another site that is teacher focused but has some useful links for kids, the Math Archives has links to software databases, archived articles, online mailings lists, discussion groups and more. It's easy to use and offers lesson plans and teaching tools that can be quite educational without the suggested intermediary adult interface.
WEB http://archives.math.utk.edu

Math Pages Sort of like a specialized online library, this site holds more than 300 articles on topics ranging from algebra to the history of mathematics. The detail is immense—click on the math history link and up comes a menu of choices from Archimedes and the square root of 3 to Zeno and special relativity. Check out the Mayan Math entry—it's a head squeezer.
WEB http://www.seanet.com/~ksbrown

Math Teaching Assistant Although this site pretty much addresses teachers and parents, there's no reason why students can't take advantage of its special offerings. The math teaching assistant package is useful for "encouraging independent achievement opportunity"—what's more independent than getting the stuff instead of waiting for someone to hand it to you? The program covers basic math through algebra, calculus, geometry, and world problems. The package provides assignments, progress tests, and challenge problems—all self-administered.
WEB http://www.csun.edu/~vcact00g/math.html

Mathematics "The history of proportion in art and architecture has been a search for the key to beauty" is just one of the quotes of the day at the CompuServe math forum. In the Libraries section, you can download a file on prime factorization or a pictorial proof of the binomial theorem. In the Messages section, converse on such popular topics as matrix operations, famous mathematicians, and Pascal's triangle.
COMPUSERVE *go* science→mathematics→ Messages *and* Libraries

Mathematics Kids Web's basic links to student math resources, including the Mathematics FAQ and Ask Dr. Math, plus sites on the ever-trendy topics of chaos, complexity, and fractals.
WEB http://www.npac.syr.edu/textbook

/kidsweb/math.html

Mathematics FAQ Compiled by sci.math, this FAQ seems to have an answer for everything, from "What are numbers?" to "Why is there no Nobel Prize in mathematics?"
web http://daisy.uwaterloo.ca/~alopez-o /math-faq

Mathematics Information Servers Comprehensive, exhaustive, deep, vast—this functions as the simplest of simple hubsites. The selections go on for pages on mathematical topics. The list of Mathematics Department Web Servers is international, running from Argentina's Universidad Nacional de Cordoba to Youngstown State University.
web http://www.math.psu.edu/OtherMath .html

Mathematics Topics Many, many links free of annotations, leaving you to guess which sites might be most useful, interesting or diverting. In general, the offerings run toward math department links at U.S. universities, with some occasional detours to off-the-beaten path URLs such as a Swedish page or a network for young mathematicians.
web http://ucunix.san.uc.edu/~niehofp /math.html

Online Mathematics Dictionary An online dictionary for all things mathematical. The definitions are concise: "Chord: the line joining two points on a curve is called a chord." More complex subjects get more complex treatment: "Farey sequence: the sequence obtained by arranging in numerical order all the proper fractions having denominators not greater than a given integer." A handy resource for times when you have no idea what your math teacher is talking about.
web http://www.mathpro.com/math /glossary/glossary.html

PBS Mathline An interactive service aimed at students, teachers and parents. For students, there's a helpline for dial-up homework assistance. For teachers

and parents, there are resource guides including classroom programs and video conferences. For everyone, there's a schedule of math-related courses that will be broadcast on PBS and supplemented by online activity Topics include PSAT and SAT prep, accelerated learning in the lower grades, and remedial work for older students.
web http://www.pbs.org/mathline/math line.html

sci.math An active newsgroup for everyone with numbers on the brain. Topics run the gamut from the gamma function to the Golden Mean. Confused math students can post urgent questions like "Why Least Squares???" and "Why 10 dimensions?" and fear neither ridicule nor recrimination.
usenet sci.math

▶ ONLINE MATH HELP

Ask Dr. Math! The introductory page for the Dr. Math! project sponsored by Swarthmore College, this site links to the archive of math questions and answers students have submitted in the past. You may want to check it out in case you're tempted to ask the same question that someone else has already asked.
web http://forum.swarthmore.edu /dr.math/dr-math.html
email dr.math@forum.swarthmore .edu

Ask Dr. Math, 6-8 Middle-school teachers and students submit questions to math experts. Part of a multi-grade project, this is the middle-school level Dr. Math! site. It offers both archived Q&As on math-related issues, as well as the promise of individualized attention to your specific math needs. The Why Divide Fractions section alone could save you hours of woe or, for the advanced student, it might answer some questions your teacher pretends don't really matter.
web http://forum.swarthmore.edu /dr.math/drmath.middle.html

Ask Dr. Math, 9-12 High school teachers and students submit questions to math experts. One student wrote, "I need to know examples of where the Fibonacci sequence is found in nature, and how that relates to the Golden Mean." Click here if you need to know, too.

web http://forum.swarthmore.edu /dr.math/drmath.high.html

Ask Mr. Math The work of a lone, dedicated teacher (who apparently isn't as educated as Dr. Math), this site is set up as an online classroom and it is rich in ask-me links, which are scattered like electronic gumdrops throughout the text. There's a handy FAQ, a useful glossary filled with definitions, and the promise of personal attention to emailed questions within 24 hours.

web http://www.localnet.com/~rseiden /mr_math/ask_mr_math.html
FAQ: web http://www.localnet.com /~rseiden/mr_math/faq.html

Meet the Swat Team! If you're curious about the people whose brains are at the disposal of online Dr. Math! users, visit this site, which contains the list of the Swarthmore College affiliates involved with the project, some of whom have home pages. Ken Williams is one of the Math Doctors who isn't shy about revealing his true nature—he likes to knit, he has mold growing in his room as a self-contained experiment, and he notes that "If you add up all the numbers from 1 to 1789, you probably should have been doing something else."

web http://forum.swarthmore.edu /dr.math/staff/staff.html

> **NUMBER THEORY**

Favorite Math Constants All the math constants you know and love, from the Golden Mean to functional iteration, beloved for generations because they just make math a little easier. "Just as physical constants provide 'boundary conditions' for the physical universe, mathematical constants somehow characterize the structure of mathematics,"

writes this page's author.

web http://www.mathsoft.com/asolve /constant/constant.html

Fuzzy Logic Overview "Fuzzy logic is a superset of conventional (Boolean) logic that has been extended to handle the concept of partial truth—truth values between 'completely true' and 'completely false.' It was introduced by Dr. Lotfi Zadeh of U.C. Berkeley in the 1960s." One of the math world's trendier topics, fuzzy logic is popular with people who can't balance their checkbooks. Dealing both in concepts and equations, this site gives a decent introduction to the notion.

web http://www.quadralay.com/www /Fuzzy/overview.html

Mathematics Archives: Numbers From a slice of pi to a date with "amicable and sociable" numbers, this frequently updated site offers instructive, witty and helpful definitions of mathematical concepts, with links to more expanded discussions. Try it—it's a really painless way of learning new concepts or an amusing take on things you already know.

web http://archives.math.utk.edu/subjects /numbers.html

Number Theory Web Minimalist in its packaging but focused on number theory, this site skips any fussing over layout or design and goes directly to the lists and information links that people who crave contact with the world of number theory need.

web http://www.maths.uq.oz.au/~krm /web.html

The Prime Page As the self-described "prime source for information about prime numbers," this frequently updated page takes its responsibilities seriously, but still has fun. Begin your tour with the amusing table of contents, foray into the land of the special types of primes, explore the helpful FAQ, or take a detour to the section on proving primality.

web http://www.utm.edu/research/primes

Ridiculously Enhanced Pi Page "If a bil-

lion decimals of pi were printed in ordinary type, they would stretch from New York City to the middle of Kansas." If your browser can handle the extreme version, you'll see the many decimal places of pi scrolling across the top of your screen. Then you can read about all the exploratorium museum's fun pi activities. Take a look at pi to the 1,600th decimal place represented by resistor colored beads. Listen to pi music. Or bake a pie for National Pi Day (March 14th).
WEB http://www.exploratorium.edu /learning_studio/pi

Things of Interest to Number Theorists A list of links that are of interest to people who are fascinated with number theory. About as no-frills, simple and direct as a site can be, this is the place to come for all your number theory needs, from computational number theory centers to conference information.
WEB http://www.maths.uq.oz.au/~krm /number_theory.html

▶ PRACTICE PROBLEMS

21st Century Problem Solving The idea here is that problem solving is a skill that can be learned, and this site promises to sell you the educational materials to do just that. There's some explanation of general problem solving approaches, some soul searching about spreading "problem-solving literacy," and a free software preview.
WEB http://www2.hawaii.edu/suremath /home.shtml

Erdos 4 Kids Featuring the input of noted mathematician Paul Erdos and offering prizes for solutions to problems is this site's way of extending math wisdom to students everywhere. The slickly designed interface has a Gallery of Open Problems and a Museum of Solved Problems, plus a Kid Zone and a Mathematician Zone. Whimsically charming and with possibilities.
WEB http://csr.uvic.ca/~mmania

Math Tips & Tricks Where was this site

during last year's math final? Math Tips & Tricks sets out to prove that if something is worth figuring out, it's worth doing the old-fashioned way. At the moment, there are about 30 tips and tricks, from squaring a two-digit number beginning with five to multiplying a multi-digit number by eight and adding the last digit. The site also has links to other materials, including software, math projects, mailing lists, and newsgroups.
WEB http://forum.swarthmore.edu/k12 /mathtips/index.html

Mathematical Mayhem A five-times-yearly math journal online covering articles and math problem sets rated at the High School, Advanced and Challenge Board levels. Though the subscription has a price, problem sets from back issues are available free online.
WEB http://www.toronto.edu/math /mayhem.html

Mathematics Problem Solving Task Centres "Task: Eric the sheep is lining up to be shorn before the hot summer ahead. There are 50 sheep in front of him. Eric can't be bothered waiting in the queue properly, so he decides to sneak toward the front. Every time Eric passes two sheep, one sheep from the front of the line is taken to be shorn. How many sheep will be shorn before Eric?" Just another problem of the month at this math site that hails from Australia (hence the preoccupation with sheep). Problems are archived, along with strategies to solve them. Updates are provided through the mailing list.
WEB http://www.srl.rmit.edu.au/mav /PSTC/index.html

MathMagic! Breaking away from the "me" approach that sometimes dominates life at the high-achieving end of the grade-point average spectrum, this site encourages—no, requires—people to work together. Students register in teams and pair up with other teams to cooperatively solve math problems. The system mainly attracts teachers and their classes, but individual math scholars and their friends can sign up, too. Home schoolers

or students whose schools aren't wired, can contact the site to make special arrangements for participation.
WEB http://forum.swarthmore.edu/mathmagic

ProMath The online companion to a Lexington, Ky., math course for high school students, ProMath offers access to its past and current problem sets. New and old competition problems and their solutions are also posted.
WEB http://www.ms.uky.edu/~promath

▶ PUZZLES & GAMES

American Mathematics Competitions Described as a series of "friendly mathematics competitions for junior/middle and senior high school students," the contests cataloged are under the umbrella of the Mathematics Association of America. The site includes exam dates and contest listings, and offers—for purchase—the problem books that competitors use as study guides. The site is compact, easy to use, and includes an email link.
WEB http://www.unl.edu/amc

Brain Teasers Divided by grade level, and presented with the idea that puzzles should not be impossible to solve, the brain teasers in this site strike a balance between being challenging and fun. There are current puzzles, last week's puzzles and an archive of puzzles, for hours of brain-teasing fun.
WEB http://www.hmco.com/hmco/school/math/brain

Clever Games for Clever People "If you play these games enough, you will become so completely clever at them that you can always have a strategy that will win." Promising perfection with practice, this site by math fan John Conway provides first-rate problems and graphics for students at the elementary to college level.
WEB http://www.cs.uidaho.edu/~casey931/conway/games.html

Internet Mathematics Contest Open to anyone under the age of 21 with a degree in math or anyone else without one, this site's math contest is scored using slightly offbeat criteria—one point for each problem, one point for a solid generalization, and one point for a generalization on the level of original research. As the author says, "The level of proof is that you need to convince me that you can make the argument rigorous." If only math teachers everywhere worked the same way.
WEB http://thoth.stetson • http://www.cco.caltech.edu/~zare/contest.html

The Island Puzzler "We want you to think of the *Island Puzzler* newsletter as the voice of a great puzzle club that spans the globe," this site says. The puzzles are presented in the form of black-and-white cartoons and are not so hard that you weep with frustration but not so easy that your younger sibs won't respect you.
WEB http://deck.com/puzzler/sampler.html

Make That Number: Puzzle Archive All puzzles, all the time, claims this site, but it's been a while since the last update. The archives are still up and active though, and they have a solid eight months of daily mind benders to offer. No word is offered on when the daily publishing will resume, but there's quite a bit to cruise through in the meantime.
WEB http://www.wwa.com/math/puzzles/digitEquations/archive.html

Math Magic Activities The magic tricks described are all based on math, but—"To those who do not understand mathematics, they seem magical." They're fascinating, and the site recommends books that extend the illusion.
WEB http://www.scri.fsu.edu/~dennisl/topics/math_magic.html

Mathematics and Modern Art Totally rad sites for its combination of whimsy and science, art and philosophy plus logic and visual poetry, this site is simultaneously a theoretical discourse on the artistic applications of math and actual proof of the foregoing, in the shape of

some beautiful, interesting and strange pieces of art. And you can do this, too.
WEB http://thoth.stetson.edu/mama /index.html

Project Watch Aimed at elementary school students, but easily adapted to the interests of older kids, this site documents the naturalist efforts of a group of kids determined to count every living thing they saw during a given period. The kids posted their request for worldwide data, added a mailing list, and waited to see what would happen next. In the meantime, they made their own local observations. Find out how to join the fun.
WEB http://www.hmco.com/hmco/school /projects/mathproj.html

Puzzle Archive A vast collection of puzzles, this no-frills site gives you what you need in straight text. There are some excruciatingly difficult problems and some easy ones ones. If the question "How many times a day do the hour and minute hands of a clock form a right angle?" is too easy, try this one: "You go and visit a friend whose clock loses 7 minutes every hour; it's exactly 3 minutes slow at the moment you happen to be there. Later the same month, the friend visits again and notices that the clock has the exact right time—but it hasn't been adjusted. What day is it?"
WEB http://www.nova.edu/Inter-Links /puzzles.html

Puzzle Corner With a new puzzle section every month and an online archive going halfway through the previous year, there's a lot to select. A recent posting offered a "linear disappearing puzzle," similar in style to those common a century ago: "A crew of astronauts surrounding a planet mysteriously shrinks by one member when the planet and the crew are spun in a circular motion—why?"
WEB http://204.161.33.100/Puzzle /puzzleList.html

Puzzle of the Week "We all know that February is the shortest month—which

is the longest?" asks one archived puzzle. "October," is the answer. "Due to the time change in October (in the U.S.), the clocks are set back 1 hour, so October is 341 days and 1 hour—1 hour longer than the other months with 31 days." Links include a Riddle du Jour, a contest page, and a weekly riddle page.
WEB http://www.wam.umd.edu /~panthera/pow.html

Puzzle Page Talk about interactivity— the answers to some of the riddles posted can only be obtained by sending in a puzzle with the answer. The puzzles are fairly interesting and reasonably difficult: correctly labeling a shipment of tennis balls or planning a voyage to the lost city of Zine with the optimal crew and supply load.
WEB http://www.ditell.com/~ericward /puzzle.html

Puzzles and Mind Teasers A homemade collection of brain ticklers of various levels of difficulty. Problems involve light bulbs and switches, toothpicks and squares, patterns of letters… you get the idea. Answers to current puzzles are posted the following month. An archive of problems and solutions is available. Email participation is encouraged.
WEB http://www.folkart.com/puzzle /puzzle.htm

Refrigerator Math Aimed at parents, this collection of elementary school puzzles runs through the sixth-grade level, and is also suitable for older kids who are math tutors and need new information to jazz up their lessons. Refrigerator Math offers many clear, fun and useful ideas.
WEB http://www.hmco.com/hmco/school /math/res/parentbk/phs5.html

Quick and Easy Math Games Although this is aimed at parents—with suggestions for presenting kids with intellectually challenging math games—there's no reason why kids can't do these things themselves. The game suggestions are mostly along the lines of brain teasers and puzzles, from divining the pattern in a

series of numbers to teaching young children the early equivalent of algebra using pennies, nickels, dimes and quarters.
WEB http://www.hmco.com/hmco/school/math/res/parentbk/phs3.html

▶ MATH HISTORY

Biographies of Women in Mathematics A good resource to learn about women in math. This Web site, put up by students at Agnes Scott College in Atlanta, Ga., intends to "illustrate the numerous achievements of women in the field of mathematics." The students are doing a fine job. Bios and essays from other contributors are welcome. The index of women discussed is lengthy, and the information is generally excellent. The brilliant and unconventional Ada Byron Lovelace, who is today credited as the founder of modern computer programming, has an interesting page detailing her triumphs and struggles.
WEB http://www.scottlan.edu/lriddle/women/women.html

Blaise Pascal As a large contributor to the field of math and philosophy, Blaise Pascal deserves his own Web page at least as much as other folks so immortalized. The page houses an interesting biography with enough tidbits to supplement and enrich any term paper, plus links to Pascal's own writings.
WEB http://www.nd.edu/StudentLinks/akoehl/Pascal.html

Furman's Mathematical Quotations Server Use either the keyword search or the alphabetical index to find a quote by a famous mathematician. A mix of the technical and the silly, offering math-related quotes from people ranging from Aristotle to Woody Allen, this site is worth visiting for both its educational and entertainment value. If you're looking for a slick quote to top off a paper, you can probably find one easily.
WEB http://math.furman.edu/~mwoodard/mquot.html

Hypatia of Alexandria She was a mathemician and a philosopher, best known for her work on the idea of conic sections. She was also one of the most controversial women of her time. When it comes to discussions of Hypatia of Alexandria, the only certainty is that sparks will fly. This hubsite, created by someone dedicated to researching the life and times of Hypatia, contains a good mix of historical information, transcripts of rare texts, and screaming arguments.
WEB http://www.hal.com/~landman/Hypatia

Ludolph Van Ceulen "He spent most of his life approximating 35 decimal places of pi using polygons of size 262 sides." And for that, he got the number named after him (in Germany, anyway, where it was known as the Ludolphine). According to this page devoted to one of the math world's stars, Van Ceulen had this engraved on his tombstone when he died: 3.14159265358979323846 264338327950288. Links lead to more sites on "that most irrational of irrational numbers."
WEB http://sac.uky.edu/~ksmcke0/Van_Ceulen

MacTutor History of Mathematics An archive of historical material, including biographies, chronologies, and an index of math history topics. Special features include a map of the birthplaces of famous mathematicians and a Famous Curves Index, where you can read about such well-known sinuous lines as the Kampyle of Eudoxus.
WEB http://www-groups.dcs.st-and.ac.uk/~history

Mathematicians throughout the Year Pick any month and day of the year and receive a list of mathematicians who died or were born on that day. Click on the mathematician's name for biographical information.
WEB http://www-groups.dcs.st-and.ac.uk/~history/Day_files/Year.html

▶ TEACHERS' LOUNGE

Activities Integrating Mathematics and

Science (AIMS) A site with a mission, AIMS hopes "to enrich the education of students in k-9 through hands-on activities that integrate mathematics, science, and other disciplines," and the idea here is to make some related tools available. One of the most useful is the *AIMS* magazine, which keeps subscribers current on developments, supplies puzzles, problem-solving methodologies and more.
web http://204.161.33.100

Allegheny Schools Partnership The online gathering place for the members of a coalition whose aim is to improve and enhance the way communities and schools relate, this is a fairly small site that nonetheless contains some useful ideas and information. One project, a study of math used in today's workplace, explores how math happens in the real world. There's a list of email addresses of the project's members in case you want to ask them about it.
web http://woodstock.ccit.duq.edu/~brown /Partnership/Partnership.html

Appetizers and Lessons for Math and Reason A cybercafe of lesson plans for teaching math and reason, plus lengthy discussions on related topics. The ideas and summaries are lively and bright, the topics are useful and interesting,and there's a great deal of information. One subject areas include general reasoning skills and logic. There are also some fine links to other sites.
web http://www.cam.org/~aselby /lesson.html

Balanced Assessment in Mathematics Project Instead of judging a child's mathematical progress with multiple choice tests that screen more for guessing ability than for creative thought, a new approach called balanced assessment is being born. This site chronicles the effort and makes available sample versions of testing programs that ask students to demonstrate competency by creating a problem-solving plan, implementing it, and then explaining what they did. The documents download as

Microsoft Word files, but converter tools are included. There's also a catalog of publications and an order form, which, unfortunately, has to be printed out and snail-mailed.
web http://edetc1.harvard.edu/ba/default .html

Calculus & Mathematica Distance Education Program This site's logo of a radio tower and a spider's net spanning the globe is an apt description of its mission, which is "to form a human electronic community devoted to learning mathematics." In conjunction with the University of Illinois at Urbana-Champaign, the site makes available to smart math students everywhere the advanced mathematics work that was once limited to an elite few. The quotes compiled from satisfied students generally say that the course was hard, but well worth taking.
web http://www-cm.math.uiuc.edu/dep

CONNECT CONNECT is the acronym for the Colorado state initiative whose guiding principle is that "everyone can do math and science." One of the more ambitious statewide approaches to education reform, the program attempts to develop k-12 state model content standards in math and science. The fruits of that effort are gathered at this site, which has a certain randomness to it but contains interesting and useful information, much of which transcends the stated curriculum goals and deals with various aspects of cultural literacy, equity issues and politics.
web http://bcn.boulder.co.us/connect

Cornell Theory Center Math and Science Gateway The information is so nicely arranged and carefully presented that just reading the descriptions of the links makes you feel smarter. Not only are these people math wizards, but they can write, too. The computer section hooks you up with everything from a description of the National Cryptologic Museum to on-line programming courses. Along with some excellent links to various math and science resources, this

site offers access to some first-rate, advanced mathematics programs for pre-college students.
WEB http://www.tc.cornell.edu/Edu /MathSciGateway

Dynamical Systems and Technology Project An exemplary collection of information and resources, this site celebrates the pure beauty of math—the equations and the images. Focusing primarily on fractals and chaos but making forays into other areas as well, the site is sophisticated, smart, and a pleasure to visit. The resources include classroom lessons and games, that can be presented with or without hi-tech machinery. A simple chaos game requires only a pair of dice, a felt-tip marker, a little time, and a poet's sense of awe at the beauty of the deep structures of the universe.
WEB http://math.bu.edu/DYSYS/dysys .html

Educational Resources for K-12 Mathematics Teachers Some lists of links and resources are longer, but few more thoroughly deal with what this site contains, including visual media, curriculum materials, games, toys, and software. The items are concisely and sharply reviewed, after an official disclaimer that praise does not constitute an endorsement. There's also a collection of discussion groups—for both students and teachers.
WEB http://www.math.utah.edu/ed /resources/resources.html

Electronic Sources for Mathematics A user-friendly site that is more than just a list of links; there's an excellent guide to preprint collections that tend to be on the theoretical side. The other information is a good mix of classroom resources and assorted math-related topics. The international links are a nice variation on the basic theme.
WEB http://www.math.upenn.edu/Math Sources.html

Freudenthal Institute Part of Utrecht University, the Freudenthal Institute makes its carefully documented resources available in English, and includes the work of the Center for Science and Mathematics Education, which takes a partly theoretical and partly hands-on approach to scientific literacy. There are interesting ideas, and the research seems to be aimed in several useful and interesting directions. After you read it, you can click on the Meet the Staff page to learn about the personalities behind the projects.
WEB http://www.fi.ruu.nl

Honest Open Logical Debate (HOLD) Highly politicized, and occasionally fiery in its rhetoric, this is a local California effort to block changes in how math is taught in Palo Alto schools. The right-leaning, text-heavy contents tend more toward ideological salvos than calm considerations. The site's dominant opinion is buttressed with a long list of links to op-ed pieces, news stories and musings from rightwing posterboy Chester E. Finn, Jr.
WEB http://www.rahul.net/dehnbase/hold

Houghton Mifflin Mathematics Center A cheery page stuffed with links to brain teasers, activities and other resources, this site has plenty to offer teachers, parents, and teachers who are parents. The Project Watch area, which offers suggestions such as documenting the histories of the people who are at rest in your town's cemetery, allows classes to cooperate on research adventures online, with the promise that all participants will be included along the way.
WEB http://www.hmco.com/hmco/school /math/index.html

The Hub Math, science and technology teachers interested in new ideas will find a lot to think about at this site, which supports reform plans in teaching these subjects, from k-12. The page is a clearinghouse for information, and it is arranged coherently and comprehensively. In addition to program summaries and contacts, there are rich resources available for teachers who are especially interested in addressing equity, gender, and ethnicity issues in the classroom.

WEB http://hub.terc.edu

Image Processing for Teaching Program The idea here is that students can enchance their knowledge and thinking skills in many areas of science, math and technology by using the latest and greatest in Image Processing for Teaching. If that sounds interesting to you—and if your school has the equipment to launch a digital imaging program—find out more by reading the informative newsletters stored, connecting with other interested people through the discussion links, or checking out the Image of the Month.
WEB http://ipt.lpl.arizona.edu

Institute for Technology in Mathematics Part of the educational research sponsored by the New Jersey Department of Higher Education, the Institute for Technology in Mathematics is a pilot program with two major objectives—to transform secondary schools by using technology and to prepare teachers who are ready to serve as technology leaders for their colleagues. That said, it doesn't hurt to add that "technology forces new ways of thinking about and doing mathematics, and it is an exciting and challenging medium for all of us."
WEB http://pioneer.wilpaterson.edu /wpcpages/icip/itm/vision.html

Internet Resources for Science and Mathematics Education A handy collection of links, with a largely academic and theoretical bent, this site divides the world into two kingdoms—online and paper—and offers in each various keys to their mailing lists, FTP sites, journals and newsletters, books, activities, videos, and, as a special bonus, info about Internet Service Providers.
WEB http://www.inform.umd.edu:8080 /UofMd-System_and_State_of_Maryland /UMD-

Journal for Research in Mathematics Education Densely academic but interesting once you discover that you don't have to be familiar with the jargon to catch the drift of the archived articles, this site offers online access to back issues of the official research journal of the National Council of Teachers of Mathematics. People engaged in research are invited to contribute their papers, philosophical studies, and book critiques.
WEB http://www.indiana.edu/~jrme

k12.ed.math Math teachers of all specialties can discuss their esoteric concerns, from grading policy to the old new math. The thread on "What's wrong with education and what is being done to change it?" is popular as well.
USENET k12.ed.math

LabNet Set up as an electronic faculty lounge for teachers who want to hang out and discuss their ideas about teaching, this easy-to-use site functions on several levels: a Web chat station, a library of publications and papers, and a somewhat self-referential adventure that is doing research on how people do online research. If you're inclined towards concepts and theories, by all means stop and cross-pollinate.
WEB http://hub.terc.edu/terc/LabNet /LabNet.html

Lawrence Hall of Science—Mathematics Education Group Dedicated to creating "exciting learning environments where people can succeed in problem solving, work cooperatively and enjoy the beauty of mathematics," the LHS Mathematics Education Group Web page presents information about workshops, courses, creative play, and field trips to the UC Berkeley campus. Teachers are encouraged to make learning and thinking about math and science an adventure for their students—and there are tools here to help them do that.
WEB http://www.lhs.berkeley.edu /MEG.html

Learning through Collaborative Visualization A resource for teachers and students who are interested in geoscience, which has numerous and complex connections with math, this chatty and well-organized site is a departure point for

entering a whole universe of specialized programs and services, including software and support. There's also a handy search utility, plus links to more.
WEB http://www.covis.nwu.edu

Math Not the biggest site, but certainly one of the best things around, this is a swell place to visit for games, projects, online activities, and email addresses of math teachers who want to talk about teaching math. Impressed? According to the credits, this site is the handiwork of one Jonathan K., a seventh grader at the Marshall Middle School, in Olympia, Wa.
WEB http://mh.osd.wednet.edu/Homepage /Math.html

The Math Forum Featuring a useful What's New section for frequent visitors, this is an ambitious effort by people with a somewhat academic bent who also keep an eye out for practical, hands-on classroom tips and resources. The descriptions accompanying the links are detailed enough to be useful.
WEB http://forum.swarthmore.edu

Math Resources This site offers a little bit of everything, from interactive online geometry and a math art gallery to an online math dictionary. Efficiently presented, experiencing this site is not unlike going to a math convention party and spending time randomly eavesdropping on other people's conversations just to see what's on their minds.
WEB http://www.teleport.com/~vincer /math.html#math

Math & Science Pavilion of Virginia An example of how the Web allows people to simultaneously act locally and globally, this friendly site compiled by math, science and technology teachers in Virginia offers math resources that are useful everywhere. Although it's targeted to teachers in their classrooms, there's also data of interest to kids doing their homework and to parents interested in learning about the educational process. The contents include projects that encourage students to see math as part of life and a well-edited selection of math links.

WEB http://pen.k12.va.us/Anthology /Pav/MathSc

Mathematical Resources on the Web Divided into rough categories such as journals, math departments gopher servers, history and software, this very long list of links has little or no descriptive information.
WEB http://www.math.ufl.edu/math /math-web.html

Mathematically Correct Heavily political, with polemics and opinion pieces, this site is dedicated to the notion that mathematics is under siege and someone has to do something to save it. See what forces are fomenting across this great nation.
WEB http://ourworld.compuserve.com /homepages/mathman

Mathematics Archives Organized into four basic categories—Lesson Plans, Schools, Software and Other—this site gathers a vast amount of material and presents it with generously descriptive subheads that, which can give you the sense you're in a little over your head. One approach is to simply print the site's very detailed link descriptions and read them later.
WEB http://archives.math.utk.edu/k12.html

Mathematics Experiences Through Image Processing (METIP) A nice site on the pluses of conceptual thinking over rote memorization, plus a small but gemlike collection of software for making that happen in your classroom. There are also links for people who want to participate in the continued development of this group's efforts, and links to related projects. This site is definitely cutting edge.
WEB http://www.cs.washington.edu /research/metip

Mathematics Gophers Short, sweet and simple, this site at the moment links to ten math gophers at locations mostly in the U.S. and the U.K. As with most gophers, the existence of a link is not always enough to get you in the door—

some of the connections allow you to knock but answer by telling you to go away. That said, this site provides lots of interesting pathways to the great, wide world of data.

WEB http://euclid.math.fsu.edu/Science/Gophers.html

Mathematics Hot Links Paying tribute to sci-fi scribe Ray Bradbury and *Fahrenheit 451*—named for the temperature at which book paper burns—this site opens with a cool graphic of blazing hot links. The page offers a large collection of topics and sites, and a search function to get you to where you think you want to go.

WEB http://hakatai.mcli.dist.maricopa.edu/links/math.html

Mathematics in Education An eclectic collection of links that, alas, does not describe them, leaving you pretty much on your own to figure it out. This site does contain some excellent material, grouped into areas of interest including k-12, undergraduate, periodicals and communication technology.

WEB http://camel.cecm.sfu.ca/Education/education.html

The Mathematics Learning Forums The Bank Street College of Education has long been honored with a reputation for creative thinking, and this site is an invitation to join its online seminars. The site is clean and easy to use. With enough information about Bank Street's courses and forums, you'll feel smarter just for having visited.

WEB http://www.edc.org/CCT/mlf/MLF.html

Michigan Gateways Michigan Gateways is a television series for math and science teachers working in k-12 classrooms, and this straightforward site supports the broadcasts with schedule information, discussions of series highlights, and a video catalog. Feedback is encouraged: An email address as well as a phone number is included.

WEB http://web.msu.edu/comptech/gateways

National Council of Teachers of Mathematics Part networking site, part educational resources collection and part search engine for locating specific information, this page is a powerful yet easy-to-use tool for teachers who want to find about NCTM meeting dates and involvement opportunities, curriculum-enhancing materials, and more.

WEB http://www.nctm.org

Natural Sciences and Mathematics A gopher-based site with all the strengths and weaknesses of that particular animal, this locale can get you deep into some ecology, science and math databases. Check it out if you're doing hardcore research; skip it otherwise.

WEB http://www.provo.lib.ut.us/natscie.html

The Nebraska Mathematics and Science Coalition From information summer work internships for teachers to links with other state coalition pages, this straightforward but info-packed site is a fine example of how people in education use the Web disseminate and gather information about programs, ideas and approaches that make teaching rewarding and make learning fun.

WEB http://nde4.nde.state.ne.us/NMSI/NMSIhome.html

Networking Infrastructure for Education Take the National Science Foundation, add the Networking Infrastructure for Education, combine them with the Education Group of the National Center for Supercomputing Applications, and you get some high-intensity discussions of how to support and introduce computational science in the k-12 classroom. The only hitch is that the introductory screens seem to go on forever before you actually get to the information.

WEB http://www.ncsa.uiuc.edu/edu/nie

The New Jersey Mathematics Coalition Home Page A combination think tank, discussion group and general resource, this site is the work of a broad-based group whose constituency extends from the schoolhouse to the statehouse. Dis-

cover a good overview of what can happen when adults decide that education really is important.
web http://dimacs.rutgers.edu/nj_math _coalition/index.html

Office for Mathematics, Science and Technology Education An outstanding collection of well-organized resources for teachers—for their own intellectual enrichment and for the direct benefit of their students—this site offers everything from information about a high-tech summer program for teachers to a collection of Web-related lessons.
web http://www.mste.uiuc.edu

OSU Math Ed Center Designed mostly as a resource for teachers who want to upgrade their theoretical knowledge and mix in some classroom activities at the same time, this site offers a nicely abridged collection of well-annotated links. Although most are the hardy perennials that seem to pop up on everyone's list, the brevity of this collection makes it one of the more streamlined and useful reference points.
web http://www.math.okstate.edu /archives/k-12.html

Presidential Awardees for Excellence in Science and Mathematics Teaching Sponsored by the National Science Foundation, this awards program identifies outstanding teachers in k-12 classrooms across the U.S. The program "seeks to enhance the status and visibility of the teaching profession and to demonstrate the importance of good teaching,"—posting news and information about these honors is certainly one way of achieving that. This site includes information about the winners, projects, and program guidelines.
web http://k12.cnidr.org/pa/pa.html

Project MATHEMATICS! If teaching math with a chalkboard, textbook and workbook seems boring, consider these videotape/workbook packages, which cover everything from the Pythagorean Theorem to Sines and Cosines. Produced with a National Science Founda-

tion grant, the modules are billed as an innovative way to introduce excitement and understanding into the math curriculum.
web http://www.projmath.caltech.edu

Project Skymath An example of how teachers and students are creatively using the Web, this site describes a detailed educational project: Using math concepts, kids gather and study real-life weather data and document their efforts.
web http://www.unidata.ucar.edu/staff /blynds/Skymath.html

Science, Mathematics, and Environment Education There's a bonanza of information at this site, which is the ERIC clearinghouse for Science, Mathematics and Environment Education. One thing that separates ERIC from other similarly rich information sites is that "special attention is given to the needs of minorities, females and people who are differently abled." The well-organized information comes with a handy little search function, and a link is available for people who want further contact via snail mail.
web http://www.ericse.org

South-Western's Math Mailing List An online catalog, a subscription mailing list, and various leads and links to educational products are offered. The subscription form couldn't be simpler—just type your name—there's no fussy code—and prompt service is promised.
email majordomo@list.thomson.com ✍
Type in message body: subscribe south -western-math <your email address>
Info: **web** http://www.thomson.com /swpco/sub_ma.html

ALGEBRA

AS YOU SIT IN YOUR DREAM-LIKE stupor during algebra class, numbly copying formula after formula into your spiral-bound notebook, one thought niggles persistently in the back of your brain: "If Tom has three times as many apples as Susan, and Susan has one-fourth as many as Joe, who has four, how many does Mary have if she has two more than Tom?" Only after you graduate from high school will you realize that in the real world, algebra is completely useless. Tom, Susan, Mary, and Joe will have become faded memories and their bodies will rot under piles of algebraic apples. Until then, you can get by with a little help from the Internet. After mastering Algebra I, begin Algebra Quest, and share what you learned at alt.algebra.help.

▶ ALGEBRA 101

21st Century Problem Solving "What is a problem? A problem is a request for an outcome subject to a number of conditions that must be simultaneously satisfied. In the typical end-of-chapter problems the outcome requested and the conditions are well defined. In so-called real life problems the conditions are usually a mixture of well defined and poorly defined conditions." This Web site explains not only what is a problem but why students should learn to solve them, and how they can solve them faster using a symbolic algebra program called Suremath. Designed to help solve word problems reliably whether in algebra, physics, or real life, Suremath features word problems submitted by others using the techniques.
web http://www2.hawaii.edu/suremath/home.html

Algebra Problem of the Week Kevin Eagan and Carl Detzel at Shaler Area School District in Pittsburgh pose weekly algebra problems in a creative manner. One week, for example, they pre-

sented students with an artistically rendered Mexican/English menu and asked Net students to write a function expressing the exchange rate. Visitors are invited to submit solutions, the most unique of which are published the following week.
web http://sasd.k12.pa.us/homepages/AlgebraPOW

Algebra Quest A multimedia way to learn algebra in eight chapters, including multiplying polynomials and solving equations. No downloads and no examples are available; the whole nine yards will cost about $40—but hey, there's no such thing as a free lunch.
web http://www.algebraquest.com

alt.algebra.help A newsgroup for algebra students and lifelong math fans. Participants try to stump each other with posts entitled "Challenge: See if you can solve this!" Threads typically follow such subjects as the distance formula, converting gallons to cubic feet, and the ever-intriguing slide rule.
usenet alt.algebra.help

AMATH—Basic Math Skills—Pre-algebra A good learning tool for those interested in mastering pre-algebra skills. Created by the Woodruff Consulting group in Dublin, Ohio, the site contains 97 AMATH modules with over a billion problems. Students can click onto different "file drawers," ranging from algebra to arithmetic measurement, and receive problems to solve. Wrong answers are written out step-by-step so students can learn the correct way to solve problems. Proficiency is measured by the student answering 10 problems correctly. But, the price of knowledge is high: AMATH charges $80 per student for the computer download.
web http://www.amath.com/index.html

Carl Miller's Math Problem of the Day For the student looking for extra homework problems in algebra, Carl Miller

has obliged wonderfully. The only complication is that the most recent math problem posted ("Determine if there exists a continuous function defined for -1<x<1, which intersects every non-vertical line in an infinite number of points") dates back to 1995. No solutions are given for that particular brainteaser, so visitors to this Web site are left hanging. There are solutions for 16 other algebra problems, however, each with its own difficulty rating.
WEB http://mmm.mbhs.edu/~cmiller /MPOTD

ADVANCED ALGEBRA

Advanced Algebra Beginning with a brief review of basic algebra concepts, this interactive fee-based course covers advanced algebra topics intended to facilitate a smooth transition to more advanced math topics such as geometry, trigonometry, and calculus. At the end of the course, the instructor will present "an algebra problem of atrocious proportions." The first student to solve it wins a prize. The course costs $40.
AMERICA ONLINE *keyword* courses→ Mathematics→Advanced Algebra

Algebra Research Group Those who didn't know there was still research left to be done on the topic of algebra will find enlightening information at this Belgian Web site authored by the mathematician Michel Van den Bergh. Algebra fanatics who simply aren't satisfied with solving problems involving bushels of fruit and colliding trains can browse through some of the papers on invariant theory, graded rings, and enveloping algebras. The truly obsessed (if paper with titles like "Central extensions of 3-dimensional Artin-Schelter regular algebras" ring your bell, you probably qualify) can then contact the people who wrote them via a list of links to the home pages of present-day mathematicians.
WEB http://www.luc.ac.be/Research /Algebra/AlgebraHome.html

REDUCE The Reduce Computer Algebra System is an interactive program

designed for general algebraic computations—an algebraic calculator, so to speak. Mainly of interest to mathematicians, scientists, and engineers, algebra students may find some utility in the program's efficient method of factoring those killer polynomials. Information about the system is also available.
WEB http://www.rrz.uni-koeln.de /REDUCE

LINEAR ALGEBRA

Elementary Linear Algebra High school students studying linear algebra may believe there's nothing elementary about it. This Web site provides lecture notes on the basic course given by Keith R. Matthews, a math professor at the University of Queensland. Dedicated math students can learn about linear equations, matrices, and determinants, then try their hand at scores of linear algebra problems.
WEB http://www.maths.uq.oz.au/~krm /ela.html

Linear Algebra WebNotes Have you ever wanted to audit a linear algebra course? Dr. Mark V. Sapir at the University of Nebraska at Lincoln has provided an undergraduate linear algebra course including the text of lectures, homework assignments, and pretests with solutions. Sorry, no grades or college credit given.
WEB http://www.math.unl.edu/~msapir /cgi-bin/visit

MTHSC 311—Linear algebra This "Extra Credit Project of Tripp (Martin) & Clay (Moody)" is dedicated to the further enhancement of the education of students around the globe on the subject of Linear Algebra. The site features great outlines by Dr. Beth Novick, which illuminate the shadowy world of linear, vector, and matrix equations. For pure giggles, link to the Top 10 Suggestions on Teaching Linear Algebra, which includes frequent use of bad puns—"Vector? I don't even know her…"
WEB http://www.clemson.edu/~gangsta /linear

MULTIMEDIA

An Audio Glance at Algebra An interesting advancement for teaching algebra to blind students. Algebra notation relies heavily on the use of pencil and paper. Without the ability to use them, mathematics becomes inaccessible to the blind. Dr. Robert Stevens at the University of York has developed Mathtalk, a program which articulates standard algebra notation using a speech synthesiser, thus giving blind people the opportunity to learn algebra actively. Sample recordings are available.
WEB http://dcpu1.cs.york.ac.uk:6666 /hci/aig/robert/glance.html

Computer Algebra Kit Software Effectively an ad for the Computer Algebra Kit by Stepstone. Some files can be downloaded, but you first need to install the Stepstone software onto your computer.
WEB http://www.can.nl/~stes/software _stpstn.html

FUNdamentally Math Chip Publications' directory of FUNdamentally Math software contains teachers' aids for a variety of math topics from addition to matrix algebra. The Web site includes a list of available software on just about everything in the k-12 math curriculum, except calculus.
WEB http://pages.prodigy.com/FL/Miami /chippub/chippub.html

Groups, Algorithms and Programming (GAP) This Web site provides info about a British system for computational discrete algebra, which was developed with particular emphasis on computational group theory, but has already proved useful in other areas. The program is free and can be downloaded anonymously.
WEB http://www-gap.dcs.st-andrews .ac.uk/~gap

The MAGMA System for Algebra From the computational algebra group at the University of Sydney. The MAGMA computer language system is a radically new system designed to solve difficult problems in algebra, number theory, geometry, and combinatorics. Many examples of MAGMA code are illustrated as well.
WEB http://www.maths.usyd.edu.au:8000 /comp/magma/Overview.html

MathMedia Teachers can access MathMedia software at this Web site. Algebra programs include Exponents, Roots, and Radicals which teaches and reviews multiplication, division, power of a power, negative and fractional exponents, solving exponential equations, imaginary/complex numbers, and logarithms. Other algebra titles include Functions and Relations and Pre-Algebra.
WEB http://www.interaccess.com/mmel /MathMedia

TEACHERS' LOUNGE

Algebra Video Tapes A variety of different approaches to teaching algebra is captured on the Etmitt videotapes described at this Web site. In *Pattern Trains: From Manipulation to Formula and Back*, seventh-grade teacher Steve Barkin demonstrates techniques enabling students to grasp algebra concepts. Other videos demonstrate classrooms in which inquiry learning takes place.
WEB http://copernicus.bbn.com/WWW /ETMITT_/algebra_list.html

PUMP—Pittsburgh Urban Mathematics Project The PUMP (Pittsburgh Urban Mathematics Project) is an excellent reaction to the National Council of Teachers of Mathematics statement that "first-year algebra in its present form is not the algebra for everyone. In fact, it is not the algebra for most high school graduates today." A collaborative effort between Anderson Research Group and a group of teachers in the Pittsburgh Public School system, this Web site shows an attempt to make high school algebra more accessible to all students through the use of situational curriculum materials and an intelligent computer-based tutoring system.
WEB http://sands.psy.cmu.edu/ACT/awpt /pump-home.html

GEOMETRY

IF YOU DIDN'T HAVE TO MEMORIZE formulas and postulates, geometry would be fun—after all, what other subject lets you recreate the shapes found in a box of Lucky Charms? The Internet can help you recapture the excitement of geometry by capitalizing on its inherently graphic nature. Get inspired by tessellations at The World of Escher. Use the sketch pad at the Geometry Forum to build a simple fractal tree, then visit the Mandelbrot Exhibition to see fractals taken to the extreme. If these sites set your mind spinning, try the Geometry Tutorial, which promises to make scalene triangles and obtuse angles simple, or visit the Room 8 Geometry Book, where you'll find yourself nostalgic for the time when circles and squares were still new concepts to you.

▶ GEOMETRY 101

A Gallery of Interactive On-Line Geometry Elaborate curves have never been so easy to draw with the WebPisces algorithms at this cybergallery for interactive geometry. You can build your own rainbow by firing different rays of light into a prism, use Kali to unlock the secrets of M.C. Escher, or even play pinball in negative space. If you think seeing something in 3-D is neat, try 13 dimensions. An understanding of intermediate geometry is recommended.
WEB http://www.geom.umn.edu/apps/gallery.html

Center for Geometry Analysis Numerics and Graphics (GANG) What word rhymes with orange? Oorange, for one, which is the name of the geometry visualization project developed by the GANG at the University of Massachusetts. Its archive features fun multimedia activities on topics ranging from surface geometry to 3-D knots, plus a library of software for making shapes. Fans of the movie *Toy Story* will want to download the QuickTime animation features.
WEB http://www.gang.umass.edu

Geometry and the Imagination in Minneapolis Can you tell which direction a bicycle is going just by looking at its tracks? This site explains how and provides an overview of many other geometry concepts. Try to learn the technical explanation of the Distance Recipe, and the difference between algebraic and geometric proofs. And if flat geometry isn't enough for you, try sphere geometry. For hands-on math, use the paper cutting patterns or construct a Moebius strip. And if you like to give credit where it's due, Gauss, Descartes, Euler, and each of their famous contributions to gepmetry are all listed here.
WEB http://www.geom.umn.edu/docs/doyle/mpls/handouts/handouts.html

Geometry Center Interactivity is the key at this geometry resource sponsored by the Center for the Computation and Visualization of Geometric Structures. Its Web page links to a full range of Web and Java applications, multimedia documents, software, and videos, all about geometry. Geometric proofs? Check out the student resources and you'll be taking the converse and applying modus ponens in no time. What's not a knot? Find out in KnotNot. Feeling skeptical about *USA Today* polls? Try the Chance Database, which uses mathematical methods to test validity of surveys in newspapers. You can also view the 6-foot high icosahedron built entirely out of paper, or turn spheres inside out in 3-D. This is math you can manipulate.
WEB http://www.geom.umn.edu

Geometry Forum High schoolers can win a free t-shirt by entering the Geometry Problem of the Week at this forum which also features a Geometer's Sketchpad for building fractal trees and practice sets on probability, plus a section on Mathematics in Poetry. Math maniacs can download the mad math screen savers. The site also features math problems for all levels of learning, and for those times when it just does

not compute, there's an email form to Ask Dr. Math.
WEB http://forum.swarthmore.edu

geometry.pre-college All shapes and sizes of students and teachers converge at this newsgroup to discuss high school geometry. Topics range from an inquiry about Stewart's Theorem to the benefits of project-based learning. The Geometry Forum also posts its Problem of the Week here.
USENET geometry.pre-college

geometry.puzzles "If the perimeter of a right triangle is 10 units, and one of the legs times the hypotenuse equals the other leg squared, what are the measurements of the three sides?" Polyhedron problems such as these are regularly submitted by the knowledgeable, but sometimes contemptuous, participants of this newsgroup, where even a simple circle rhyme can turn into a snub-fest.
USENET geometry.puzzles

MathMagic Pythagoras and Euclid cheered in their graves when this Web site was created. Why? It challenges students to discover the secrets of Pascal's triangle, find two prime numbers whose product is a prime number, or calculate the length of a stripe on a barber pole. Grades k-12 can compete to solve all sorts of problems, which are updated regularly. MathMagic, which will soon have connections to international sites, also accepts submissions from students who want to stump fellow math-heads worldwide.
WEB http://forum.swarthmore.edu /mathmagic

Peek: For Visualizing 3-Dimensional Objects Bored with the third dimension? Perhaps you'd like to see a four-dimensional hypercube? View this object and more by using Peek, the software that brings N-dimensional polytopes into the third dimension. How is this possible? Picture the way a sphere looks like a circle in the second dimension, then watch the demo of a hypercube as it is "dragged" in and out of 3-D.
WEB http://www.graphics.cornell.edu /~gordon/peek/peek.html

Room 8 Geometry Book "A circle looks like a ball. It has no corners. Pennies are circles."Review basic geometry concepts at this Web site featuring crayon drawings of squares, triangles, octagons, and other shapes by such (soon-to-be) famous artists as Heidelinde and Saba. Although the drawings might be more suitable for a refrigerator door than for a museum, each provides valuable insight into each geometric shape, describing its defining characteristics and even its emotional state ("The hexagon is a closed shape"). Concepts such as symmetry, perimeter, and area are also illustrated and explained, along with words of wisdom, such as "don't ever mistake angles with corners because this is very easy to do."
WEB http://192.152.5.115/room8 geometry/intro.html

Symmetry and the Shape of Space Travel from the Mississippi River to Zaire to see symmetry patterns in nature and in ancient artifacts. The secrets of symmetry are revealed at this Web site, which provides full explanations of basic geometry concepts. Delve into the gallery to identify isometries and repeating motifs in various illustrations, including beautiful drawings from Escher and Chaim Goodman-Strauss, then test your knowledge by answering a list of critical questions. Download geometry software and try your hand at some of the homework assignments. Translate, reflect, and rotate to your heart's content.
WEB http://www.geom.umn.edu/~strauss /symmetry.unit

Visual Dictionary of Special Plane Curves Webster's got nothing on Zah, the editor of this online dictionary. You can read about the history of astroids, cardioids, deltoids, and other "oids". Other features let you download software to realize geometrical images using equations and plotting points, even in 3-D. All images include equations, their

analysis, and an explanation of their relation to other geometries.
web http://www.best.com/~xah/Special PlaneCurves_dir/specialPlaneCurves.html

Wallpaper Groups Find exactly the right color wallpaper to match your Escher original. This Web site provides 17 different patterns and explanations of how each is created by means of translations and reflections. Plaid will seem boring after seeing these full-color patterns. Also included are explanations of the International Union of Crystallography.
web http://aleph0.clarku.edu/~djoyce/wallpaper

▶ EUCLID

Euclid's elements This Java-enhances version of all 13 parts of Euclid's geometry classic really brings the subject alive. But even the Java-deprived can benefit from hypertext links to such essential axioms as "A point is that which has no part." In case even basic definitions elude you, yet another hypertext link provides further explanation: "The description of a point, 'that which has no part,' indicates that Euclid will be treating a point as having no width, length, or breadth, but as an indivisible location."
web http://aleph0.clarku.edu/~djoyce/java/elements/elements.html

On Euclid's Fifth Postulate Can a mathematical statement be both true and false? Yes, if it is Euclid's fifth postulate: "If a straight line falling on two straight lines make the interior angles on the same side less than two right angles, if produced infinitely, meet on that side on which are the angles less than the two right angles." This one-page proof without hypertext is provided by mathematician al-Haytham. His buddy Omar Khayyam provides commentary on its validity.
web http://sunset.backbone.olemiss.edu/~rpagejr/euclid.html

▶ FRACTALS

Exploring Fractals Fractal geometry.

What is it and what does it mean to you? Mary Ann Connors will explain all the basics including where the heck the funny name comes from. Learn about the Sierpiniski Triangle (no, ships do not mysteriously disappear there) and how it is generated. Also, study such mind-boggling puzzles as the Koch Snowflake and its Higher Dimension Analog, all with many neat pictures.
web http://www.math.umass.edu//fractal/fractal.html

Fract-Ed Iterate, bifurcate, and recurse fractal images (and also learn what these terms mean) with the lessons provided at this site. Study population growth using the works of Malthus. Learn about seed parameters (you won't find them in a greenhouse) and strange attractors (not Jim Carrey) and how they can be used to make fractals. Worlds within worlds, self similarity, and chaos are all detailed here.
web http://www.ealnet.com/ealsoft/fracted.htm

Fractal Microscope This educational page solves the problem of reproducing fractal images in the classroom by linking up a supercomputer to participating school networks (normally the equations would take hours or even days to process). This Web site explains the practical use of fractals for studying soil erosion, coastlines, and seismic patterns. Visit the French archive and see loads of animations and pictures.
web http://www.ncsa.uiuc.edu/Edu/Fractal/Fractal_Home.html

FRACTINT, A Program for Generating Fractal Images Popcorn, Newton, Spider, and Chip. Commonly used cat names? Sure, but also nicknames given to different fractal types at this Web site, which provides a freeware fractal generator program. Flipping through some of the sample images is like watching an unedited cut of the last half hour of *2001: A Space Odyssey*. Who needs acid when this software gives you "Deep Zooming" capability? The program uses basic mathematical skills to generate

patterns that resemble the funky rainbow-colored swirls on the surface of a hot cup of coffee. For PC users only.
WEB http://spanky.triumf.ca/www/fractint/fractint.html

Mandelbrot Exhibition Mandelbrot (b. 1924) popularized fractal geometry through his work with computer graphics. Links to several different galleries of fractal images from all over the world are gathered at this Web site. After you've spent a few hours gaping at them, read about the "Geometry of the Mandelbrot Set," then test your knowledge with an animated quiz. You can even hear the Mandelbrot Set, with sound files that assign notes to mathematical numbers corresponding to portions of Mandelbrot images (sounds like the opening credit sequence to *Dr. Who*). At the Screening Room, animation excerpts let you see fractals in action. Is it the inside of a black hole? How about the inside of a nerve cell firing? A Rorschach test? Household pets and kids of all ages will gaze in awe as the images change, morph, and overlap, producing millions of colors.
WEB http://www.comlab.ox.ac.uk/archive/other/museums/computing/mandelbrot.html

Sprott's Fractal Gallery Serves up the Fractal of the Day with a side order of isometric geometry, a dash of higher level algebra, and a Coke to go. The daily image lets you zoom in, see the fractal move, and feel its power. Full mathematical explanations are provided. If you feel that life's too simple, too ordered, try the Chaos Demonstration. If you're fascinated by aerial ocean views, the Quadratic Map Basins will give you plenty to view.
WEB http://sprott.physics.wisc.edu/fractals.htm

▶ GEOMETRY & ART

Geometry Through Art Teacher/artist Norman Shapiro promotes the use of art in teaching geometry at this Web site. Some of his lessons include new uses for used coffee cans and information on

the geodesic circle illusion. So whip out the straight edge, compass, rope, and pencil and go to it.
WEB http://forum.swarthmore.edu/~sarah/shapiro/shapiro.html

Logical Art and the Art of Logic After visiting Logical Art and the Art of Logic, geometry students will understand Escher's infinite regress tessellation, figure out the puzzle of pentominoes (flat shapes formed from five unit squares), and hopefully learn to see art a bit more logically. Budding mathematicians and woodmakers will want to check out the wood mosaics made of pentominoes.
WEB http://pubweb.acns.nwu.edu/~gbuehler/index.html

Synergetics on the Web: 3-D Geometry and the Visual Arts Explore the realm of geometry where points occupy volume in space. Concepts such as Isotropic Vector Matrix, Concentric Hierarchy of Polyhedra, and Sphere are all explained with full-color illustrations. Homebuilders looking for something unusual can contact manufacturers of pre-fab geodesic domes. Find out why the United Nations selected Peter's Projections to represent the world.
WEB http://www.teleport.com/~pdx4d/synhome.html

▶ MOEBIUS STRIP

The Moebius Strip Paper, pencil, scissors, tape, and time to kill are all you need to make a Moebius strip—a two-dimensional object with only one surface discovered by a nineteenth-century German mathematician. The Web site also features things to do with the darn one-sided objects. Links let you view the famous Escher rendering of ants meeting each other on a Moebius strip, and learn what Moebius said when he was drafted into the Prussian army during his thesis (it wasn't pretty) as well as other historical details.
WEB http://forum.swarthmore.edu/sum95/math_and/moebius/moebius.html

Polyhedra Can Platonic solids truly be

just friends or is the possibility of sex always an issue? Isocahedrons, dodecahedrons, and many other shapes ending in "hedron" are pictured in all their multi-faceted glory at this Web site that teaches the basics of polyhedra. Mac-users can download the Kaleidotile software to make suggested shapes and create original ones. Try the Triangular Face exercise (no, it does not turn your head into a pyramid). Need to do something with that cardboard box the computer came in? Convert it into a regular polyhedron and watch the salespeople laugh hysterically when you return it.

web http://forum.swarthmore.edu/sum95 /math_and/poly/polyhedra.html

Polyhedral Solids Platonic solids should be familiar to fans of Dungeons and Dragons or any game that has weird-shaped dice. This site includes full-color illustrations of these and other polyhedral solids. Get out the cardboard and glue and make some of these shapes. You'll find ways of putting together pentagrams that even a Satanist wouldn't know.

web http://www.teleport.com/~tpgettys /poly.shtml

PYTHAGOREAN THEOREM

Interactive Proof of Pythagoras' Theorem This nifty little program demonstrates that "the square of the hypotenuse of a right angle triangle is equal to the sum of the squares of the other two sides," which is otherwise known as the Pythagorean Theorem. Your browser must have Java to interact with the page.

web http://www.math.ubc.ca/javamath /pythagoras.html

TESSELLATIONS

Highland Tessellations Art meets science at Highland Tessellations. You can compare tessellations with other students (and it's completely legal). If you don't know what a tessellation is, you can find out and learn how to do one with only a straight-edge and a com-

pass. In case you don't have a straight-edge and a compass, the page provides a link to tessellation software; download template patterns for hours of enjoyment.

web http://www.elk-grove.k12.il.us /schoolweb/highland/highland.tess.html

The World of Escher Everything Escher. The Gallery features such mind-bending classics as "Drawing Hands" and "House of Stairs." The Reading Room contains a chronology of his life, the artist's own reflections on his work, plus stories and essays, including one on how he might feel about the distribution of his drawings on the Web. The Escher Store sells t-shirts and stuff, all imprinted with Escher's distinctive geometric art. You can also enter your own Escher-inspired drawing in a competition to win a place in the Escher hall of fame.

web http://www.texas.net/escher

TEACHERS' LOUNGE

ArtMath Transformations The definitive page for incorporating art into a geometry curriculum. Includes plenty of worksheets and even a grid for transferring illustrations onto transparencies. Learn how to teach students to classify different Escher drawings, identify the transformations within them, and render the actual drawings. Take note of the Escher thumbnail sketches in which horsemen pounce on each other or reptiles slither in and out of themselves. Links to other Escher pages are provided.

web http://www.ucs.mun.ca/~mathed /Connections/ArtMathTransTeacher.html

Connected Geometry Project Funded by the National Science Foundation, the Web site of this curriculum development project contains information on and sample problems from its five geometry textbooks which offer an integrated approach to math. A full description of the project and a bibliography of research papers by the project's staff are also included.

web http://www.edc.org/LTT/ConnGeo

CALCULUS

IF MATH IS A LEFT-BRAIN ACTIVITY, then calculus must be performed by the most radical brain cells in your head. You can actually feel them organizing into troops as they prepare to go off on tangents and cosines. Learning calculus may seem like an uphill battle, but for anyone considering a future in engineering, chemistry, biology, or even political science, the subject is vital. Calculus provides the basic tools that enable one to make accurate predictions and extrapolations based on an indefinite number of variables. Does President Clinton know calculus? No, but his campaign manager probably does. Do you need to know calculus? Yes, if you want to get through high school. Students who take the initiative can try the Mathematica Self-Tutor for Calculus. Those gunning for early college credit should make a point to visit Alvirne's AP Calculus Problem of the Week. If you just can't live without pocket mechanical aids, you can learn how to use your calculator more effectively at TI-85 Examples and Programs Related to Calculus.

▶ CALCULUS 101

C&M Remote This Ohio State University site offers a Calculus & Mathematica course via the Web, written in Mathematica notebooks—for Ohio State credit. C&M Remote, according to the site, is designed to mimic the interactive nature of calculus instruction on campus by allowing students to work on the lessons, and connect via the Internet to mentors who help them with problems and/or concepts. Lessons can be downloaded. C&M Remote is an idea whose time has come.
WEB http://www.math.ohio-state.edu
/~davis/cmremote.html

Interactive Learning in Calculus and Differential Equations with Applications If you're looking for flashy graphics or a fun calculus student connection, the home page of Indiana University's

Mathematics department is not the place for you. It does have, though, various helpful test differential equations and their applications, as well as links to helper resources, mathematics software sites, teacher tutorials, and a textbook search. There's also a mirror site for students "down under," making this a calculus resource for educators and students worldwide.
WEB http://www.ma.iup.edu/MathDept
/Projects/CalcDEMma/Summary.html
● http://www.opennet.net.au/resources
/CalcDEmma

The Calculus of Origami Use math to unlock the secrets of origami. It sounds like it should be the other way around, but sure, why not? This site lays the ground rules for paper-folding and then provides challenges for understanding the calculus behind the creases. Start with the basic constructions (e.g. "fold paper so it occupies half its area"), then progress to some of the real toughies. Learn the difference between a natural, made, and exposed edge and how they can all learn to live in peace and harmony.
WEB http://www.eden.com/~joshk
/thought/origami.html

Graphics for the Calculus Classroom Now here's a calculus teacher who's got his stuff together. This is mainly a resource for other calculus instructors but it's worth a look from anyone interested in this mathematical genre. Stocked with charts, graphs and .GIFs, links to MPEG simple animations and instructions on how to recreate them all, the page includes instructions and accompanying diagrams for Archimedes' calculation of pi, secant and tangents, How the Ball Bounces, and other classic calculus dilemmas.
WEB http://www.math.psu.edu/dna
/graphics.html

InterQuest Calculus Scared off by the phrase "pedagogic imperatives?" No? Then here's something for you to con-

sider. InterQuest Calculus is a Web-based type of differential calculus designed to meet "pedagogic imperatives" enhanced by electronic teaching. Its founders are interested in addressing an array of calculus students by forcing them into proactive learning, providing individual access to instructors and assessing students on work done in context.
web http://www.orst.edu/~robsonr/IQ

Mathematica Self-Tutor for Calculus
Mathematica Self-Tutor for Calculus is just what you might expect it to be. Designed by professors at the University of Toronto, this Web site's got everything from an overview of mathematica to the history of the beginnings of calculus. There's an introduction to "The Derivative," as well as information on calculus projects, work in basic statistics, derivative calculations, and vector calculus. Check out the "read me" file first for detailed instruction on how to make best use of this site.
url ftp://ftp.utirc.utoronto.ca/pub /instruction/readmethis

TI-85 Examples and Programs Related to Calculus
Having trouble getting to know your TI-85 graphics calculator, the lifeline for any serious student of calculus? Fear not. This page is devoted to the TI-85, with programs and test equations written to show you how to get the most use out of your TI-85, as well as links to official and unofficial TI-85 home pages, and an FAQ list. Wondering about those little white flakes embedded beneath the screen on your calculator? Check here for answers to such mind-bending dilemmas—you'll even find out how to remove them (no, they're not supposed to be there.)
web http://www.math.uoknor.edu /~amiller/ti85/calc.htm

▶ ADVANCED PLACEMENT

Alvirne's AP Calculus Problem of the Week
For students preparing for the AP Calculus exam, Alvirne's AP Calculus Problem of the Week is a fun (well, "fun" may be too strong a word) practice forum featuring word problems created by high school calculus students. Test your skills on problems categorized by question orientation (e.g. volume, area, velocity). Follow answer icons and send your answer to the question's creator. A teacher reference station offers a variety of calculus resources including some decent graphics for the classroom.
web http://www.seresc.k12.nh.us/www /alvirne.html

▶ CALCULUS REFORM

Calculus, Concepts, Computers, and Cooperative Learning (C4L)
This page completed by Purdue University's math department exists solely to answer questions about its calculus reform project, C4L. Never heard of it? It's a way of teaching calculus, "a decomposition of each mathematical concept into developmental steps following a Piagetian theory of knowledge based on observation of, and interviews with, students as they attempt to learn a concept." Translation: Get student's heads out of books and get them interacting with faculty to discern their needs. Sounds like a strategy that could almost be universally applied.
web http://www.math.purdue.edu /~ccc

Calculus Reform Archive
Hmmm... who would have thought calculus instruction could spark such intense debate? Actually, it's not surprising given that teachers and students of calculus tend to have the most analytical minds. But the passion... the passion was a surprise. Messages on this gopher list of the now-defunct Calculus Reform mailing list contain emphatic rhetoric about how traditional modes of teaching calculus can damage a student. The more mild-mannered student, however, will find interesting tips, thoughts and exchanges on the AP Calculus exam and some valuable insight from past and future test takers.
url gopher://gopher.maths.soton.ac.uk /11/newsletters/Calculus%20Reform %20Discussion%20List

▶ SOFTWARE & TEXTBOOKS

Calculus Modules OnLine Authored by PWS publishing, a division of Thomson International Publishing, Calculus Modules OnLine is meant to create awareness and generate need for PWS calculus coursebooks. The Web site contains a wealth of case studies and demonstrating .GIFs act as insights into the complexity of the calculus genre. It also has a comprehensive glossary and intuitive FAQ/guided-tour.
WEB http://zelda.thomson.com/pws/math/modules.html

SimCalc Project: Simulations for Calculus Learning SimCalc takes its calculus seriously. Hardly just another form of mathematics, according to SimCalc, The Mathematics of Change is centrally important to living and working in a rapidly evolving democratic society. Developed by the National Science Foundation, this site is home to The SimCalc software. The program was designed to help students develop full understanding and practical skill with basic concepts of the mathematics of change in meaningful contexts, through a combination of advanced technology and curriculum reform. The page has some color—almost refreshing in the often gray world of calculus.
WEB http://tango.mth.umassd.edu

▶ TEACHERS' LOUNGE

Calculus & Mathematica You'd think it odd that the penetration of computers into mainstream society has made little difference in professorial strategies/tactics surrounding calculus. The maintainers of Calculus & Mathematica are trying to change that. This page, geared toward instructors, recognizes they are overburdened and may not have time to figure out how to implement machinery into instruction, so they're pushing C&M as the quick and efficient alternative—a computer-based course an instructor can purportedly use immediately. You'll find a broad introduction to the theory and practice of computerized calculus

instruction, as well as the ability to download test tutorials.
WEB http://www-cm.math.uiuc.edu

Focus on Calculus All things, all thoughts, all theory on calculus. If you eat, drink, sleep, and breathe calculus, you'll be in good company here. Check out the back archive of calculus newsletters for such spell-binding theories as "The Rule of Three," a form of instruction that presumably encourages understanding, while giving students with "weak manipulative skills" a chance to grasp the concepts behind calculus. Charts and graphs clarify the more complicated concepts.
WEB http://www.math.arizona.edu/focus/calc.html

Instructional Media and Calculus Courses If you're a student of Dr. Gregory Holdan at Duquesne University in Pittsburgh, look here to get an insight into the man. If you're a teacherlooking for some pointers from a pro, bookmark this page. Don't let the Bugs Bunny cartoon on the opening page fool you, though: Holdan has thoroughly researched the science of teaching calculus to students. Benefit from his hard work. He's got theories on how to get students more involved, and how to get them to work with and get drive from their peers. He also breaks down the fundamentals. You'll find precisely what kind of foundation a student must have before he or she can master calculus.
WEB http://www.mathcs.duq.edu/~holdan

PART 4

Science

BASIC SCIENCE

SOMETIMES BASIC SCIENCE CAN seem anything but basic. There is, ironically, one tried and tested way to simplify a problem—the scientific method. First, identify the problem. You need a little inspiration in time for the science fair. You just don't get how the water cycle works in nature. Or maybe you're having trouble getting excited about science at all. Next, gather all the relevant data. You've already got that covered by using this book. Science fair stimuli? Try Science Fair Research or the Virtual Science and Mathematics Fair. Explanations of the water cycle? Ask someone at Compuserve's General Science forum or AOL's National Academy of Sciences or post your problem on Discovery Channel Online. Bored with science? Dr. Bob's Interesting Science Stuff fascinates with facts. Now, formulate your hypothesis, perhaps something like, "I will be able to deal with general science by using the Net as my guide." Finally, go ahead and test that hypothesis.

▶ STARTING POINTS

Cyberspace Middle School Activities Guide The space shuttle photo that greets visitors to this site should be an instant clue to the treasures that lurk just beyond the home page. Designed for sixth through ninth graders, CMS covers most sciences you can name off the top of your head, including oceanography and astronomy. These are not just your run-of-the-mill links, either. CMS will take you to "Liza's notes on the Care of Reptiles," where you can learn about herpetology, or "Bugs, Bugs and More Bugs," which is more or less self-explanatory. View the online Periodic Table of the Elements or learn about space colonization.
WEB http://www.scri.fsu.edu/~dennisl /topics/topics.html

Discovery Channel Online Why not learn while you lounge in front of the television? Here you'll find a TV guide devoted to programming on the Discovery and Learning Channels. Also available—information on Discovery CD-ROMs, videos, and collectibles; a place to register for Discovery Channel School (a commercial-free area devoted to k-12 educational resources and experiences); the Discovery search engine that remembers what you were looking for and notifies you when new listings appear; and a bulletin board devoted strictly to science.
WEB http://www.discovery.com

Franklin Institute Virtual Science Museum The science museum that never closes and doesn't charge admission. View such virtual exhibits as "The Heart: An Online Exploration," "An Inquirer's Guide To The Universe," and "Benjamin Franklin: Glimpses of The Man." The Institute also spotlights stories each month like "Web Gardens" (some beautification projects on the information superhighway), "Science Fairs: Love Them or Hate Them" (start-to-finish help with your experimental endeavors), and "The North Pole" (what it's really like to be on top of the world.)
WEB http://sln.fi.edu

General Science Plants and magnetism, metric measurements, how water is made, and misused science terms. Just a few of the popular topics of discussion at this basic science forum. Put your two cents in at the Messages section or browse the Libraries to find a primer on virtual reality or a downloadable files to test your brain dominance.
COMPUSERVE *go* science→General Science →Messages and Libraries

InQuiry Almanack What's new at the Franklin Institute? InQuiring minds want to know. The Almanack not only offers the scoop on the Institute's latest offerings but also includes a monthly Spotlight story; Fistful of Favorites, FI's five featured links; Caught in the Web, the

online school of the month; and Science News.
WEB http://sln.fi.edu/qanda/qanda11.html

National Academy of Sciences Offers a range of information on scientific topics from agriculture to space. The biology section, for example, has articles such as "Biologic Markers Show Pollution Effects on the Immune System." The earth sciences folder informs the visitor on subjects like "Radioactive Waste Issues." The site also houses the NAS archives, a bookstore, a lecture hall, and a chat forum. A search engine simplifies research.
AMERICA ONLINE *keyword* nas

Science/Math Education Forum A full range of science and math education topics is available at this CompuServe forum. In the Messages and Libraries sections, information can be found on everything from brainwaves to geology to weather. The Teachers Only Area provides info on videos, software, and lesson plans. The Student Area stores interesting picture files and tidbits submitted by students.
COMPUSERVE *go* science

ScienceWeb Find out what our neighbors to the north are accomplishing science-wise. Science Web presents the spectrum of science and technology activities going on in Canada, in an attempt to expose its thriving science culture to the rest of the world. There's plenty in it for you—links to the coolest Canadian science sites, cybertours, the latest news, and scholastic resources.
WEB http://scienceweb.dao.nrc.ca/can /can.html

UT Science Bytes Each installment of this cybercommunique synopsizes the latest work being done by scientists at the University of Tennessee. Find out if Dr. James Wu and Dr. Ahmad Vakili were able to figure out a way to design a fighter plane that can change directions as quickly and easily as the dragonfly can ("On the Wings of a Dragonfly"), what Dr. Suzette Tardif found out about

the marmoset after spending some quality time with the mysterious mammal ("Mad About Marmosets!"), and what a day is like for Will Fontanez in the Cartographic Services Laboratory ("Mapmaker, Mapmaker, Make Me a Map").
WEB http://loki.ur.utk.edu/ut2kids/science .html

▶ RESEARCH

The Empiricist An online peer-reviewed journal for the high school scientist, featuring research articles from all fields. Should you be inspired to start some empirical examinations of your own, stop by Brainstorm Central for guidance.
WEB http://javaman.biol.vt.edu

MendelWeb Mendel meets hypermedia. This site, modeled around Gregor Mendel's 1865 paper, "Experiments in Plant Hybridization," integrates elementary biology, discrete mathematics, and the history of science. An English translation of Mendel's paper, which is considered to mark the birth of classical and evolutionary genetics, is presented in hypertext, with links to traditional reference material (glossaries, biographies, and the original German text) as well as images, tutorials, active commentaries, notes, homework sets, related Web sites, and animation. Cyberstudents will learn about more than genetics and nineteenth century botany though— Mendel's paper presents a context for learning more about techniques of data analysis, the rhetorical strategies of scientific literature, and a variety of topics in the history and philosophy of science.
WEB http://www-hpcc.astro.washington .edu/mirrors/MendelWeb

▶ SCIENCE FAIR

Science Fair Research Remember when your entry in a science fair was as easy as building a miniature volcano or discovering the reasons why a plant grows remarkably better when it receives ample water and sunlight than when it's left a

dark closet? Well, you're not in third grade anymore. Science fairs are getting sophisticated, and so should your research methods. Get an online head start here, where you can find some good starting points on sundry scientific subjects—from botany to zoology.
WEB http://spacelink.msfc.nasa.gov/html/scifairt.html

Virtual Science and Mathematics Fair
Washington State University's cybergym can show off 100 student projects each year, submitted by students from kindergarten to college. All projects must be original work, conceived and executed specifically for this forum and conducted live during the fall of that year, and all students must actively work with their assigned mentors. High school experiments from the '95 virtual exhibition ranged from finding the best type of soap to use when taking a bubble bath so the bubbles won't dissolve (apparently Boraxo is the best) to studying the effects of music on animal learning patterns (it turns out mice actually learn best in silence).
WEB http://www.educ.wsu.edu/fair_95/index.html

▶ TRIVIA

Dr. Bob's Interesting Science Stuff
Weird Science. Did you know that in the distant future the sun that lights our solar system will die a violent death? Were you aware that the ears of a cricket are located on its front legs, just below the knee? Or that the most powerful laser in the world, the Nova laser, generates a pulse of energy equal to 100,000,000,000,000 watts of power for .000000001 second to a target the size of a grain of sand? You would if you made regular appointments to see Dr. Bob. The only thing that ties together the tidbits of trivia found here is the fact that Dr. Bob, a chemist by trade, finds them fascinating. But random as they are, they're guaranteed to get the scientific side of your brain whirring.
WEB http://ny.frontiercomm.net/~bjenkin/science.htm

▶ TEACHERS' LOUNGE

American Association for the Advancement of Science (AAAS) Project 2061
Project 2061 is a long-term initiative by the AAAS to reform k-12 education nationwide so that all high-school graduates are science literate. Sounds like a plan. But you won't find the specifics on their strategies here—just information on how to buy the books and disks that contain all the details.
WEB http://www.aaas.org/project2061/2061main.htm

Atlantic Science Curriculum Project/SciencePlus Teachers Network The ASCP is a grassroots curriculum project seeking to change the way science is taught in middle school by linking teaching, research, and development. Here you can find out about their SciencePlus textbooks, the SciencePlus Teachers Network, and the ASCP newsletter, *Interactions*.
WEB http://www.ccn.cs.dal.ca/Education/SPTN/ascphmpg.html

Center of Excellence for Science and Mathematics Education (CESME) A starting point for cybersavvy educators looking to improve their science teaching. The University of Tennessee Center has provided an activity manual for physical science teachers to download, science spreadsheet templates, and information on how recreational freeware or shareware can be used to meet learning objectives. Interested teachers can also register to receive the CESME newsletter or check out some related Web resources.
WEB http://cesme.utm.edu

For Science Teachers and Students
Cyber-resources for science teachers, sorted into six discipline areas—biology, chemistry, physics, environmental studies, health studies, and earth sciences—as well as more general science education support links.
WEB http://www.webcom.com/~pjgrant

k12.ed.science

misc.education.science sci.edu

You've seen one science educators' newsgroup, you've seen them all. Or so it seems. There's a lot of overlap, but they are still the best places to go for discussion and debate on a wide range of topics in science and education with teaching colleagues from kindergarten to college.

USENET k12.ed.science • misc .education.science • sci.edu

Knowledge Integration Environment (KIE)

The aim of the KIE project is to pioneer educational uses of the Internet and World Wide Web for K-12 science instruction by creating a curriculum that is student project-based and focused around scientific evidence. Its Web site has information on getting involved in a KIE project, ready-to-use KIE curriculum, networked evidence databases (or NEDs) of scientific evidence directly appropriate for student projects, and downloadable software.

WEB http://www.kie.berkeley.edu/KIE.html

Lawrence Berkeley Laboratory's ELSI Project

The Ethical, Legal, and Social Issues in Science Project is a pilot program designed to stimulate discussion on the ramifications of scientific research. ELSI provides teachers with the tools to start significant classroom debate on such controversial subjects as who should pay for scientific research, genetic patents and intellectual property, indoor and outdoor air pollution, personal privacy and medical databases, and genetic testing for cancer. Links to current activities at the Berkeley lab, as well.

WEB http://www.lbl.gov/Education/ELSI /ELSI.html

National Science Teachers Association (NSTA)

For the more than 50,000 science teachers, administrators, scientists, and business and industry leaders who are already members of NSTA, this site provides access to the association's publications, programs, and online resources. Those thinking about joining can find out about the NSTA's strategies for respond-

ing to new standards in science education, the explosion of cyberspace education, a decline in federal funding, and the ever-increasing challenge of classroom teaching. Info on services for science educators like awards and scholarships, teacher training workshops, educational tours, and an employment registry is also accessible.

WEB http://www.nsta.org

NSTA Scope, Sequence, and Coordination Project

The NSTA's Scope, Sequence, and Coordination of Secondary School Science is more than just a tricky tongue twister. The SS&C program covers the scope of physics, chemistry, biology, and the earth and space sciences; emphasizes appropriate sequencing of learning, taking into account the students' prior knowledge and preferred mode of learning; and encourages coordination among the science disciplines leading students to an awareness of the interdependence of the sciences and their place in the larger body of human knowledge. Since 1990, the project has been implemented in middle schools across the country and it is now being introduced at the secondary level. At the SS&C site you can preview the individual science Micro-Units arranged by grade level, designed to achieve the National Science Education Standards.

WEB http://www.gsh.org/NSTA_SSandC

The Science Educator's Jump Page

From aquariums to zoological parks, astronomy to volcanology, this jump page houses an encyclopedic listing of science education related sites. Each site is given a rating from one to five stars (one star indicates nothing at all for teachers, but still has good information that can be used, five stars indicates especially for teachers, usually including complete lesson plans and activities.) So go ahead and jump.

WEB http://ftphome1.gte.net/jwagner /edujump.htm

The Science Teacher's Homepage

Home to the journal for secondary sci-

ence education published by the NSTA. Preview the current issue, enter contests, answer calls for manuscripts, use the index of articles going back to 1990, and find out how to receive a hard copy of *The Science Teacher.*
WEB http://www.nsta.org/pubs/tst

UCI—Science Education Programs (SEP) Encyclopedic and then some, UCI—Science Education Programs contains some 2,000 science links appropriate for the classroom in the areas of physical, earth, life, and health sciences. This page is updated weekly.
WEB http://www-sci.lib.uci.edu/SEP/SEP .html

Wright Center for Innovative Science Education From posters for the classroom wall to QuickTime movies, this Tufts University Center wants to provide secondary school teachers with all the Wright stuff to stimulate interest in science and encourage more students to pursue scientific careers. The center's site also provides information on upcoming teacher workshops, educational conferences, fellowship opportunities, and science lectures, as well as links to the Wright Fellows' favorite Web pages.
WEB http://www.tufts.edu/as/wright _center/index.html

SCIENCE MUSEUMS

Academy of Natural Sciences (Philadelphia, Pa.)
WEB http://www.acnatsci.org

Academy of Sciences (Chicago, Ill.)
WEB http://www.chias.org

Carnegie Science Center (Pittsburgh, Pa.)
WEB http://www.gsia.cmu.edu/bb26 /45-853/projects/csc/csc.html

The Computer Museum (Boston, Mass.)
WEB http://www.net.org/index.html

Discovery Centre (Halifax, Nova Scotia, Canada)
WEB http://www.cfn.cs.dal.ca/Science /DiscCentre/DC_Home.html

The Exploratorium (San Francisco, Calif.)
WEB http://www.exploratorium.edu

Franklin Institute (Philadelphia, Pa.)
WEB http://sln.fi.edu

Hands On Children's Science Museum (Olympia, Wash.)
WEB http://www.wln.com/~deltapac /hocm.html

Lederman Science Education Center (Batavia, Ill.)
WEB http://www.fnal.gov/ed_lsc.html

Liberty Science Center (New Jersey)
WEB http://www.lsc.org

Montshire Museum (Norwich, Vt.)
WEB http://www.valley.net/~mms

Museum of History of Science in Florence, Italy
WEB http://galileo.imss.firenze.it

Museum of Life and Science (Durham, N.C.)
WEB http://ils.unc.edu/NCMLS/ncmls.html

Museum of Physics (University of Naples, Italy)
WEB http://www.na.infn.it/Museum /Museum.html

Museum of Science (Boston, Mass.)
WEB http://www.mos.org

National Museum of Science (Israel)
WEB http://www.elron.net/n_sci _museum

Ontario Science Center WEB http://www.osc.on.ca

Oregon Museum of Science and Industry
WEB http://www.omsi.edu

Physics Museum (Queensland, Australia)

WEB http://www.physics.uq.oz.au:8001/physics_museum/homepage.html

Science Museum (London, England)
WEB http://www.nmsi.ac.uk

Science Museum of Minn. (St. Paul, Minn.)
WEB http://www.ties.k12.mn.us/~smm

The Sciencenter (Ithaca, N.Y.)
WEB http://edison.scictr.cornell.edu

Smithsonian Institution
WEB http://www.si.edu

St. Louis Science Center
WEB http://atg1.wustl.edu/~slsc/slschome.htm

The Tech Museum of Innovation (San Jose, Calif.)
WEB http://whyanext.com/thetech.html

NATURAL HISTORY MUSEUMS

Canadian Museum of Civilization (Hull, Quebec)
WEB http://www.cmcc.muse.digital.ca/cmc/cmceng/welcmeng.html

Cleveland Museum of Natural History
WEB http://www.cmnh.org

Dinosaur Museum (Honolulu Community College)
WEB http://www.hcc.hawaii.edu/dinos/dinos.1.html

Field Museum of Natural History (Chicago, Ill.)
WEB http://www.bvis.uic.edu/museum

Florida Museum of Natural History (University of Florida, Gainesville)
WEB http://www.flmnh.ufl.edu

Houston Museum of Natural Science
WEB http://www.hmns.mus.tx.us

Kelsey Museum of Archeology (University of Michigan)
WEB http://classics.lsa.umich.edu/Kelsey/Outreach.html

Los Angeles County Natural History Museum
WEB http://www.lam.mus.ca.us/lacmnh

Museum of Natural History and Science (New Mexico)
WEB http://www.aps.edu/htmlpages/nmmnh.html

Museum of Natural History (Santa Barbara, Calif.)
WEB http://www.rain.org/~inverts

Museum of Natural History (Sweden)
WEB http://www.nrm.se/default.html

Museum of Paleontology (Berkeley, Calif.)
WEB http://ucmp1.berkeley.edu/welcome.html

Natural History Museum (London, England)
WEB http://www.nhm.ac.uk

Oriental Institute (University of Chicago)
WEB http://www-oi.uchicago.edu/OI/PROJ/NUB/NUBX/NUBX_brochure.html

Peabody Museum of Natural History (Yale University, Conn.)
URL gopher://gopher.peabody.yale.edu

Public Museum of Grand Rapids (Michigan)
WEB http://www.iserv.net/~grmuseum/index.htm

Royal British Columbia Museum (Victoria, Canada)
WEB http://rbcm1.rbcm.gov.bc.ca

Smithsonian Gem & Mineral Collection (Washington, D.C.)
WEB http://galaxy.einet.net/images/gems/gems-icons.html

ASTRONOMY & SPACE

STAR LIGHT, STAR BRIGHT, FIRST star I see tonight—I wish I may, I wish I might, find the best astronomy and space Web sites. Your wish is our command. To find your way through the universe, let AstroWeb or The Star*s Family of Astronomy and Related Resources be your guide. Amateur stargazers and professional astrologers can find useful information at Star Facts, the History of Astronomy, and AOL's Astronomy Club. Outer space meets cyberspace at Youth Enhancing Space, Liftoff to Space Exploration, and A Guide to the Nine Planets. You'll also find plenty of information about cosmic quirks like quasars and black holes, space travel, and space telescopes.

▶ ASTRONOMY

Amazing Facts About Black Holes What would happen to an astronaut if he or she tripped and fell into a black hole? How much would a feather weigh on the surface of a black hole? Will black holes devour the universe? This FAQ answers all types of questions on these theoretical objects, from the paranoid to the purely inquisitive.
WEB http://twsuvm.uc.twsu.edu /~obswww/o34.html

The Astronomy Club The sky's the limit for amateur astronomers. The Sky At a Glance and Planet Roundup tell you what to look for in the skies each week, an FAQ covers everything from "What's the Best Telescope?" to "How do I buy a star?" A discussion board contains active debates on everything from the Big Bang Theory to black holes.
AMERICA ONLINE keyword astronomy

Astronomy Hypertext Textbook With documents on inverse square law and planetary motion, this isn't the most basic of sites, but it is a useful resource. In addition to its general resources, this site includes problem sets, syllabi, and reading lists for astronomy classes at the University of Oregon.
WEB http://zebu.uoregon.edu/text.html

Astronomy Picture of the Day Master the universe one day at a time. Every 24 hours, a different facet of our fascinating cosmos is featured, along with a brief explanation written by a professional astronomer.
WEB http://antwrp.gsfc.nasa.gov/apod /astropix.html

AstroWeb When you wish upon a star, it makes no difference where you are. But when you're wishing upon astronomy Net sites, it makes all the difference in (or out of) the world. Weave your way through AstroWeb, which links to Internet astronomy resources of all types— Web sites, gophers, telnet sites, FTP sites, and Usenet newsgroups.
WEB http://marvel.stsci.edu/net-resources .html

Comets and Meteor Showers The latest on comets and meteors, introductions to the celestial bodies for the astro-beginner, and related links. If you think a coma is what you fall into when your substitute teacher drones on about astronomy, you might want to visit the glossary. It explains everything from an anti-tail (a comet's tail that points toward the sun) to zenithal hourly rate (the rate a meteor shower would produce if seen by an observer with a clear, dark sky, and with the radiant at the zenith). And no, there's no such thing as a meteor shower curtain.
WEB http://wums.wustl.edu/~kronk /index.html

Cybersky Planetarium Through the magic of shareware, transform your computer screen into a planetarium. This desktop version of the real thing goes it one better though, allowing you to compress days, weeks, and months into minutes, enabling the studious stargazer to learn things about astronomy that would normally require days or weeks of stargazing or repeat trips to a planetarium to observe.

web http://www.astro.ucla.edu/staff/stephen/cybersky.html

Frequently Seen Acronyms FYI, you should learn these ASAP, from ASIS to FOS to FWHM to MECO to NASM to SOHO to SPAN to SSPS to XVV to YSO. OK?

web http://www.cis.ohio-state.edu/hypertext/faq/usenet/space/acronyms/faq.html

General Astronomy Information What is a star? Why do we have summer? What about leap years, pulsars, supernovae, sundials, and space shuttles? Get answers to basic questions of astronomy, including a list of the 25 brightest stars and the 30 stars closest to the Earth.

web http://cast0.ast.cam.ac.uk/RGO/leaflets

Hands-on Astronomy Activities The activities proposed—"A Walking Tour of the Solar System" and "Lift the Planets" seem like physical impossibilities. But by making a few minor adjustments they're not, and you may begin to fathom the actual size of our solar system. If you set up a scale model of the solar system, you can walk from the sun to Pluto and get some idea of the relative distances involved. And by using, say one penny to represent Earth, a paper clip for Mercury, and a feather for Pluto, you can lift the planets and begin to comprehend their relative sizes.

web http://www.scri.fsu.edu/~dennisl/topics/astro.html

The History of Astronomy If your knowledge of the history of astronomy is limited to the invention of the telescope by Galileo, you may want to become more enlightened. Brief biographies are available on every major influence in astronomy from Ernst Abbe (a clockmaker and private astronomical observer) to Fritz Zwicky (an eccentric Swiss-American astronomer fond of referring to people as "spherical bastards"). This online archive of astronomy also includes a general history of this branch of science

as well as information on observatories, museums, societies, publications, and historians.

web http://aibn55.astro.uni-bonn.de:8000/~pbrosche/astoria.html

List of Astronomical Observatories A list of world observatories, from Hungary's Konkoly Observatory to the Mt. Wilson Observatory to the Gemini 8m telescope.

web http://www.cfht.hawaii.edu/html/astro_observ.html

Quasars Quasars are quizzical things. They may be the most distant and brightest objects in the universe. Then again, they may not be. This is the place to learn more about the controversy surrounding these relatively small, starlike, extragalactic objects.

web http://twsuvm.uc.twsu.edu/~obswww/o38.html

sci.astro.amateur What's the best beginner's book on astronomy? Where can I find good shareware? What kind of telescope should I buy? This is a user-friendly source of starting points for beginning amateur astronomers, as well as a thriving cybercommunity of more seasoned star gazers.

usenet sci.astro.amateur

Star Facts Pete Harris brings astronomy information down to earth for us. His monthly *Electronic Journal About the Universe* ponders such fascinating questions as "If the Earth Were a Grape, How Far Would the Stars Be?", "Big Dipper? Or Big Spatula?" and "Is It Possible to Stand Still?" Astro-Jewels from the Net also highlights some of the best online astronomy articles.

web http://www.ccnet.com/odyssey

The Star*s Family of Astronomy and Related Resources What if you woke up one morning and found that the Web was constellated with astronomy links? Make your fantasy reality with the Star*s family, a set of links to astronomy organizations, institutes, and projects across the globe.

WEB http://cdsweb.u-strasbg.fr/~heck/sf.htm

The Web Nebulae If you look at the sky with the naked eye all you see is a black void interspersed with stars, but with the aid of a telescope the gas and dust clouds known as nebulae appear. Those without access to such expensive equipment can view the spectacular interstellar sights here. Although the study of the physics of many of these objects is of considerable scientific importance, their simple beauty can be enjoyed by all.
WEB http://seds.lpl.arizona.edu/billa/twn

▶ SOLAR SYSTEM

A Guide to the Nine Planets The site should actually be titled The Nine Planets and 61 Known Moons, Described and Presented With Multimedia Tools and Including Chapters on Spacecraft, Terminology, and Space Science. From Mercury to Pluto (and Chiron), the entire solar system is addressed.
WEB http://seds.lpl.arizona.edu/nineplanets/nineplanets/nineplanets.html

Earth and Universe Billed as a comprehensive multimedia guide to our universe, this site links to educational programs about the origin of the universe, the life cycle of stars, the sun, the galaxy, nebulae, planets, and other remarkable sites. Proceed through the program with or without audio—either way, you'll come out of this experience knowing more about the stars then Carl Sagan, Jack Horkheimer, and Spock combined.
WEB http://www.eia.brad.ac.uk/btl

Mars Exploration Complete information on upcoming missions to Mars, access to the *Martian Chronicle*, and links to related sites like the Daily Martian Weather Report and *Mars Today*.
WEB http://www.jpl.nasa.gov/mars

Planetary Fact Sheet Just the facts on all the planets, as well as the moon, Chiron, asteroids, and comets. If you're looking for titillating trivia, you've come to the wrong place. The information here is purely technical data on bulk parameters, orbital parameters, magnetospheres, and atmospheres.
WEB http://nssdc.gsfc.nasa.gov/planetary/planetfact.html

Views of The Solar System Space travel made possible through hypertext. Click on your planet, asteroid, comet, meteor, or astronomer of choice and discover related information and images.
WEB http://bang.lanl.gov/solarsys

Welcome To The Planets Some of the best images of the solar system we call home from NASA's planetary exploration program, from Earth to Uranus. Heh, heh… we said "Uranus." Seriously, there are some startlingly sharp photos of the planets nine, as well as portraits of such spacecraft as Mariner, Viking, Voyager, Galileo, and the space shuttles.
WEB http://stardust.jpl.nasa.gov/planets

▶ SPACE TELESCOPES

Bradford Robotic Telescope This is a prototype of a robotic telescope that can decide when conditions are good enough to make observations of the sky by itself so an astronomer does not need to wait for clear weather. Anyone can access images of the moon, galaxies, stars, nebulae, and more from this telescope located high on the moors of West Yorkshire, England. Or you can submit a job to have it return requested images.
WEB http://www.eia.brad.ac.uk/rti

Earth Viewer Need a change of perspective? You can look at terra firma from the Sun, the Moon, the night side of the earth, above any location on the planet specified by latitude, longitude, and altitude, or from a satellite in earth orbit. And the images can be generated based on a topographical map of the earth, up-to-date weather satellite imagery, or a composite image of cloud cover superimposed on a map of the earth.
WEB http://www.fourmilab.ch/earthview/vplanet.html

Hubble Space Telescope Greatest Hits
The Best of HST: 1990-1995. The Hubble has been around the universe and has brought back a slideshow that would put your Uncle Phil's trip to Phoenix to shame. Some of the impressive images on display include a supernova explosion, newborn stars, and a galaxy so far away that the Hubble saw it as it appeared about the time dinosaurs roamed the earth.
WEB http://www.stsci.edu/pubinfo /BestOfHST95.html

THE SPACE PROGRAM

Friends & Partners in Space What's the real thermometer of The Cold War? Friends & Partners in Space might be. It's a page devoted to the U.S. and Russian space programs, full of historic information on each. Interested in who the Cosmonauts were in 1966 or an overview of the mission of the Salyut 6 Space Station? This site reveals inside information that would not have been accessible to the general public more than 20 years ago.
WEB http://solar.rtd.utk.edu/~jgreen /fpspace.html

How to Become an Astronaut Being an astronaut requires a lot more than being comfortable sans gravity and enduring the taste of freeze-dried food. You'll need to get a Ph.D., be conservative and conformist in appearance and actions, practice public speaking, and be able to pass a security clearance. And we haven't even touched on the physical requirements. If you're still interested, pay a visit to this site for more details on preparing for this cosmic career or to join a mailing list for future candidates.
WEB http://www.ksc.nasa.gov/facts /faq12.html

Liftoff to Space Exploration They may not be giving away any state secrets, but the NASA-employed creators of Liftoff to Space Exploration certainly provide enough information to whet the aeronautically intrigued appetite and even pique the curiosity of those with only a pass-

ing fancy. Here you'll get news on flight missions and the latest developments taking place in the space academies. Choose the "cool" button on the control panel for links to NASA's hottest projects.
WEB http://liftoff.msfc.nasa.gov

NASA INSPIRE Program If you're in high school and really into space (as in outer, not as in "I need my...") this site is calling you home. Run by NASA, the INSPIRE program was founded to aid students in observing natural and manmade radio waves in the audio region. It wants to involve you in its current analysis of the response of the ionosphere to electron and plasma injections from devices on the Russian Space Station, MIR. But don't let such challenges scare you. The program is designed to stimulate students on all levels with science and technology. Check it out for information on volunteering or setting up a "listening program" at your school.
WEB http://www.gsfc.nasa.gov/education /inspire/inspire_home.html

Space FAQs Questions and answers on everything from mission schedules to planetary probes, from astronomical mnemonics to astronaut training.
WEB http://www.cis.ohio-state.edu/hyper text/faq/usenet/space/top.html

Space Movies If you can't get enough of flicks like *Apollo 13* or *2001: A Space Odyssey*, this is the virtual viewing room for you. This site has clips from every space movie imaginable from pure science fiction fare like *Star Trek* and *Tron* to reality-based animations of Apollo missions, satellites, space probes, and celestial bodies.
WEB http://www.univ-rennes1.fr/ASTRO /anim-e.html

Space Shuttle Launches Usable information about the Space Shuttle program, from the first launch in 1981 to future missions in the works. Read the latest shuttle manifest, get information on orbiter vehicles, access the image library, browse astronaut biographies, or

search the server.
WEB http://www.ksc.nasa.gov/shuttle/missions/missions.html

Students for the Exploration & Development Space The pioneering spirit behind SEDS comes through in their site dedicated to that final frontier. You'll find an electronic petition pushing for continuing support for the space station, the latest space exploration news, a space tourism survey, an archive of space images, chat rooms, and links to information on space, astronomy, and rocket science.
WEB http://seds.lpl.arizona.edu

US Space Camp If you're interested in an astronomical alternative to the typical summer experience, Space Academy Level II may be for you. An eight-day adventure could include training as a technician, engineer or pilot, participating in a 12-hour space shuttle mission, scuba diving in the Underwater Astronaut Trainer, spinning in the two-person centrifuge, capturing and repairing a satellite, and flying a single-engine airplane. The Space Camp site outlines all the programs as well as the attractions available at The U.S. Space and Rocket Center.
WEB http://www.spacecamp.com

Youth Enhancing Space KidSat is a set of Earth-viewing cameras and instruments that will eventually be based on the International Space Station, currently controlled by students. The hundreds of eye-popping images of the earth, from the moon and beyond alone make this worth the trip. But NASA, Johns Hopkins University, and others have made this an information destination full of MPEG movies of shuttle launches, links to space-related publications, computer images tracking the course of the most recent Space Shuttle endeavor, and explanations of just what the nation's space programs are all about.
WEB http://www.jpl.nasa.gov/kidsat

▶ **TEACHERS' LOUNGE**

Activities and Resources for the Classroom The lesson plans using the World Wide Web outlined here were developed by teachers in the classroom and cover subjects like What is Your Sign: The Science Behind the Zodiac, The Great Satellite Search, and Auroras: Paintings in the Sky. Should inspiration strike during your stay here, there's a toolkit to aid you in creating your own cyberlesson.
WEB http://www.cea.berkeley.edu/Education/ed_resourcelist.html

AstroEd: Astronomy Education Resources Links to curriculum resources, newsletters, hypertext articles, images, animations, astronomy history, and views of the sky for the k-12 teachers' astronomy and space science lessons.
WEB http://www-hpcc.astro.washington.edu/scied/astro/astroindex.html

Astronomy Resources for Teachers A star is born. The life story of a celestial body is only one of the virtual lessons offered. Also included are an online exploration of the Milky Way and links to astronomy activities, video tapes, observing programs, and learning programs.
WEB http://twsuvm.uc.twsu.edu/~obswww

Challenger Center for Space Science Education The families of the Challenger 51-L crew founded this center to continue their loved ones' educational mission. One way the Challenger Center accomplishes that is by using the theme of space exploration to create positive learning experiences, foster interest in math, science and technology, and motivate students to explore. Interested educators can learn how to integrate such ideals in their classrooms with information on teaching training programs, classroom simulations, and educational resources.
WEB http://www.challenger.org

Educational Space Simulations Project Everything the Net-savvy educator needs to bring telecommunicated space simulation into the classroom. Links to a

long-term international project simulating a journey to Mars, Microsoft's Space Simulator, and step-by-step instructions for involving students in a space simulation are brought to you by none other than the National Association of Space Simulating Educators.
WEB http://chico.rice.edu/armadillo /Simulations/simserver.html

Exploration in Education Download electronic picture books, tutorials , and reports like "Gems of Hubble," "Apollo 11 at Twenty-Five," and "Space Science for the 21st Century" courtesy of the NASA-supported ExInEd program.
WEB http://www.stsci.edu/exined-html /exined.home.html

NASA Teaching From Space Who better than NASA to educate students on outer space through videoconferencing? If you're an educator wondering how to implement the latest technology and rig your classroom for live broadcasts, interactive telephone Q&A sessions, and curriculum materials—NASA has made it easy for you to get started. Specific broadcast schedules and direct email links allow you to register for broadcasts (for free) and exchange thoughts and ideas with the pros from both the space exploration and teaching disciplines. Schools must have either a C-band or Ku-band satellite receiving system, but alternative arrangements to receive the signal through the local cable TV system can be made.
WEB http://www.okstate.edu/aesp/VC.html

National Education Simulations Project Using Telecommunications If you're afraid your students aren't getting enough "real life" experience NESPUT will squelch those fears. It wants to simulate space shuttle launches in your classroom. But before you rush out for the virtual reality goggles, you should know that the only visual involved may be a single still-life picture from past shuttle launches. What NESPUT is really pushing here are instructions on how students can control their own shuttle launches, solar observatories, and space

stations. Tips for the educator on creating a realistic and controlled environment are plentiful, as well as a guide to building an inexpensive space simulator.
WEB http://www.nptn.org/cyber.serv /AOneP/academy_one/science/nesput .html

Project LINK at the Exploratorium Not only did some huge names (Eureka Scientific Inc., The Exploratorium, NASA/Ames Research Center) get together recently to conduct an air-to-ground, point-to-point Internet video conference between the Exploratorium and NASA's Kuiper Airborne Observatory (KAO), they got kids involved. Students participated in science experiments at the same time as the airborne scientists and exchanged results and questions via the Internet. Two teachers and one student flew aboard KAO to answer student questions, demonstrate experiments, and interview scientists. This site is a valuable chronicle of the whole project.
WEB http://www.exploratorium.edu /learning_studio/link

Quest! NASA's K-12 Internet Initiative Houston, we have Internet access. Put your students in touch with NASA professionals through online interactive projects, a four-step plan for getting and using the Internet in the classroom, and information on other online with which schools you may want to collaborate.
WEB http://quest.arc.nasa.gov

Space Educator's Handbook "One small click for all mankind…" These excerpts from NASA's hypertext handbook for teachers includes information on using science fiction to teach about real-life space technology, astronomy, math problems required to explore space, and links to random facts like what comic book character traveled to the moon and what science fiction character talked about orbiting the earth three years before it happened.
WEB http://tommy.jsc.nasa.gov/~woodfill /SPACEED/SEHTML/seh.html

BIOLOGY

WHAT IS BIOLOGY? IT'S THE study of life. What is life? Good question. Philosophers and scientists have debated the question for centuries. Perhaps it's safe to say that life is merely the interval between birth and death, but even that may be begging the question. Fortunately, one doesn't need to know what something is in order to study it (just as one doesn't need to know what the Internet is in order to use it). Discover "life" before humans even existed at The World's First Dinosaur Skeleton. Then learn about contemporary animal life at The Zooary. Find out what makes you tick at The Heart: An Online Exploration. After that, have some good holesome fun with The Nostril.

Cells Alive! and watch phagocytosis in action by a human macrophage cell or take a photographic Greenhouse Tour of the University of Georgia's Botany Department and discover the relationships among some major land plant groups. For the frog lover, there's the Interactive Frog Dissection which includes an actual lab manual and step-by-step photos of the frog. If insects are your thing, there's a collection of images and movies on beetles, mosquitos, and ticks. For an excellent explanation of how the brain deduces what we should see, click onto Blind Spots: The Eye and the Brain.
WEB http://www.tc.cornell.edu/Edu/Math SciGateway/biology.html

▶ BIOLOGY 101

The ABCs of DNA The University of California at San Francisco knows how difficult science can be, which is why they've developed a series of Web sites under the rubric of "Science Made Easy." This reader-friendly page on DNA is simple enough even for those who plan to major in English in college.
WEB http://www.ucsf.edu/research /science_made/abc_dna.html

Biology "I need information on whether or not there are no snakes in Ireland," began one earnest poster, who probably should have stopped at alt.grammar.help first. A thread of helpful responses followed, both serious and sarcastic. Other equally slippery topics of discussion include evolution, osmosis, and the difference between the left and the right halves of the brain. The Libraries section holds picture files, enticing the biology-lover with such neo-classics as "Grizzly bear feeding" and "Protozoa drawing."
COMPUSERVE go science→Libraries or Messages→biology

CTC Math/SciGateway: Biology Cornell Theory Center has collected a trim set of links to basic bio resources. Click onto

Evolution: Theory and History Everything you would ever want to know about evolution and then some. Learn about the theory behind systematics (study of the evolutionary interrelationships between living things) and taxonomy (scientific naming system). Click onto the history of vertebrate flight and learn how evolution has perfected the act of flying. The Web Lift will transport you to any Taxon, Period, Topic, or just the glossary. Links to notable naturalists and scientists are also provided.
WEB http://ucmp1.berkeley.edu/exhibit text/evolution.html

HUMEVO You might not feel it personally (and tabloid headlines may run to the contrary), but humans are constantly evolving. This mailing list on human evolutionary research examines the details, including adaptation, variation, and evolutionary medicine.
EMAIL listserv@gwuvm.gwu.edu ✍ *Type in message body:* subscribe humevo <your full name>

The Origin of Species by Charles Darwin The classic of evolutionary theory in its entirety online.
WEB http://www.wonderland.org/Works /Charles-Darwin/origin

World's First Dinosaur Skeleton. A complete history of Hadrosaurus foulkii, the world's first nearly complete dinosaur skeleton found in 1858 in Haddonfield, N.J., by Victorian gentleman and fossil hobbyist William Parker Foulke. Learn how he found the site while attending a dinner party at the house of his friend, John E. Hopkins. A map of Haddonfield lets you see where the actual site was located.
WEB http://www.levins.com/hadrosaurus.html

DISSECTION

Cow's Eye Dissection Veteran cow's-eye dissectors have put together this Web site to enhance your own personal cow's eye dissection experience. Witness an actual step-by-step cow's eye dissection prefaced by an audio introduction. Then download the Cow's Eye Primer, an interactive program, to learn about the parts of the eye. But before you attempt your own dissection, the first order of business is obtaining the cow's eyes: "You can order cow's eyes at a butcher shop or purchase them directly from a slaughterhouse. Try to get eyes with the muscles and fat still attached. If possible pick up the cow's eyes the day of the dissection, eyes are easier to cut when they are fresh."
WEB http://www.exploratorium.edu/learning_studio/cow_eye

The Interactive Frog Dissection This online tutorial from the Curry School of Education at the University of Virginia is like a lab manual except with nicer pictures. Full-color photos illustrate step-by-step instructions on the dissection of a frog, from making skin and muscle incisions to poking around the internal organs. Video clips of the actual dissection are available for downloading.
WEB http://curry.edschool.Virginia.EDU/go/frog

Whole Frog Project It's here—virtual frog dissection with rotating frog movies, a 3-D reconstruction of a frog's anatomy, and a frog dissection kit available in seven languages. After you've taken the frog apart, play the virtual frog builder game to see if you can put him back together.
WEB http://www-itg.lbl.gov/ITG.hm.pg.docs/Whole.Frog/Whole.Frog.html

MICROSCOPY

Electron Microscopy Gallery Think butterfles are pretty? Maybe not, after viewing the butterfly's proboscis as captured by the scanning electron micrograph. Tons of SEM pictures are on view, but after checking out some of the organisms that live on human skin, you'll probably feel like taking a long, hot bath. In fact, you may never want to pet a dog again after seeing the portraits of fleas found on animal hair. Biology students can witness the microscopic war that goes on inside the immune system as alveolar (lung) macrophage attacks *E. coli*. The pictures of dandelion pollen, ragweed pollen, and dust are nothing to sneeze at. Both black-and-white and digitally colorized photos are included.
WEB http://www.pbrc.hawaii.edu/%7Ekunkel/gallery/electron.shtml

Microscopy UK Netsurfers who've got a pair of blue-and-red 3-D glasses handy can check out pictures of fossils, insects, and even the tip of a syringe as they appear to jump off the screen at this site, which calls itself the "home of amateur microscopy on the Web." This truly comprehensive and innovative site has microscopic resources for everyone from the mildly curious student to the professional microscopist. Students can go "scoping" and examine the teeth of a snail, or take advantage of more onsite features, like the SEM (scanning electron microscopy) pictures of mildew, leaves, and other perennial favorites. You'll never feel the same about swimming in a pond after seeing what lives in one.
WEB http://www.microscopy-uk.org.uk

ANATOMY

The Amazing Body Pavilion This virtual tour of Houston's Museum of Health &

Medical Science walks visitors through the human body. The page only features photographic simulation of real museum visitors enjoying such attractions as the 27-foot intestine, the 10-foot brain, and the skeleton riding a bicycle, but those with active imaginations may glean some form of vicarious pleasure.

WEB http://www.mhms.org/amazing.html

Anatomy Pick a body part, any body part, and connect to close-up images of the part in anatomical splendor. You have a choice of six highlighted areas to select on the human figure, which is not anatomically correct. Each highlighted area leads to more choices. Click on the brain, for example, and find juicy pictorials of the left, right, anterior, superior, and inferior regions. Then you'll understand the term "grey matter."

WEB http://rpisun1.mda.uth.tmc.edu/se/anatomy

The Heart: An On-Line Exploration A comprehensive report on the heart by Reggie, a sixth-grader at Hillside School (which explains why disease is spelled "dease"). But even older students will be impressed by his descriptions of the structures of the circulatory system and their functions, history of heart science, tips on keeping the heart healthy, and explanation of how doctors examine the heart. At the end of each section, Reggie plays teacher by providing activities for testing what you've learned.

WEB http://sln2.fi.edu/biosci/heart.html

Interactive Knee You may not understand the terminology at this interactive radiology Web site (it was designed for medical students at the University of Pennsylvania), but you'll probably enjoy the graphic anatomical views of the knee, courtesy of the Visible Human Project.

WEB http://www.rad.upenn.edu/rundle/InteractiveKnee.html

The Nostril "Ladies and gentlemen... I'd like to dedicate this Web site to... the Nostril." A parody on the importance of the nostril by nasal fan Kwan Yeoh at the University of Sydney, the page highlights some interesting facts—did you know that the aperture of the nostril can be controlled by facial muscles such as the levator *labii superioris alaque nasi* and the depressor *septi nasi*? Learning about the nostril can be good holesome fun.

WEB http://www.usyd.edu.au/~kyeoh/nostril.html

The Visible Human Project The Visible Human Project creates 3-D digital models of a human male and female from radiographic and photographic images. The models can then be rotated a full 360 degrees and viewed on any plane, making them powerful tools for scientific, educational or simply recreational purposes. The project is intended for medical professionals, but high school bio students might find it a fun way to spend a Saturday afternoon.

WEB http://www.nlm.nih.gov/research/visible/visible_human.html

▶ ENTOMOLOGY

B-EYE An expert in bee vision illustrates what he thinks the world looks like to a honey bee.

WEB http://www.infomall.org/kidsWeb/biology.html

Entomology for Beginners This Web site provides concise information on insect anatomy and metamorphosis. Click on the different body parts of an insect diagram to get a brief description. Color diagrams of both complete and incomplete insect growth are included.

WEB http://www.bos.nl/homes/bijlmakers/ento.html

Entomology Index of Internet Resources If you're wondering whether the Gypsy Moth has a home page—it does.

WEB http://www.ent.iastate.edu/List/complete.html

Insect Biology and Ecology: A Primer If your only exposure to the ecology of

insects was Kafka's *Metamorphosis*, this Web page will provide enough concise background information to give you a leg (or six) up in the entomological world. The diagrams of insect growth and development are particularly charming.
WEB http://www.nysaes.cornell.edu/ent/biocontrol/info/primer.html

Insects & Human Society An engaging virtual lecture on how insects have changed major battles, altered governments, and generally proved influential in shaping human history.
WEB http://www.ento.vt.edu/IHS

Steve's Ant Farm Steve is the Uncle Milton of cyberspace. Every day, from 11 a.m. to 5 p.m. EST, see his live ants going about their anty business. Take a look at *Ant Farm, The Movie* in MPEG format. If you want to know more about the lives and times of ants, read the FAQ.
WEB http://sec.dgsys.com/AntFarm.html

▶ MARINE BIOLOGY

FISH-JUNIOR Correspond with a real marine scientist. This mailing list provides a forum for high school students to interact with marine biologists on topics such as fisheries ecology.
EMAIL listserv@searn.sunet.se ✍ *Type in message body:* subscribe fish-junior <your full name>

Marine Biology Database Did you know that flatworms are the most primitive animals to have bilateral symmetry? Useful facts such as this are at your fingertips at this excellent cybersource of information on the major marine animal classes. Find out about the flatworm's other invertebrate friends, as well as arthropods, birds, enchinoderms, fishes, mammals, mollusks, plants, and reptiles.
WEB http://www.calpoly.edu:8010/cgi-bin/db/db/marine-biology/:/templates/index

▶ MICROBIOLOGY

Bugs in the News! Jack Brown titled his Web page after the catch phrase he used to pique the interest of his students of his "Fundamentals of Microbiology" course at the University of Kansas. Basic microbiology questions are addressed ("What the heck is an *E. coli*?" "What is microbiology?") with great humor and enthusiasm. Truly refreshing for those who are tired of dry textbooks.
WEB http://falcon.cc.ukans.edu/~jbrown/bugs.html

Microbe Zoo The Digital Learning Center for Microbial Ecology from Michigan State University has created pictorial images and descriptions of microscopic organisms and the habitats in which they live. Click on a variety of environments: Dirtland, Animal Pavillion, Snack Bar, Space Adventure, or Water World. The last one yields information about the ever-popular amoebas. The latest additions to the Microbe Zoo's specimen collection is presented in Microbe of the Week.
WEB http://commtechlab.msu.edu/dlc-me.html

Primer on Molecular Genetics A basic brief apparently intended for U.S. Department of Energy bureaucrats involved in the Human Genome Project, but students will find the information here helpful. The site provides plain-language definitions of DNA, genes, chromosomes, and explains the mapping and sequencing of the human genome.
WEB http://www.gdb.org/Dan/DOE/intro.html

▶ NEUROSCIENCE

Neuroscience for Kids This home page was created by Eric Chudler of University of Washington for k-12 students and teachers who would like to learn more about the nervous system. A variety of activities and experiments are provided to learn more about the brain and spinal cord. Learn about the anatomy of the nervous system by modeling a brain from recycled materials, or discover which part of your tongue is most sensitive to salty foods. Links to interesting neuro-related sites like Bill Nye the Sci-

ence Guy, Newton's Apple, and Brain Poke.
WEB http://weber.u.washington.edu/~chudler/neurok.html

ORNITHOLOGY

Birding on the Web A bird enthusiast's heaven. Want to know what rare birds were spotted in a certain part of the country? Click on Hot Lists and find out. Then download a shareware copy of *North American Wild Birds*, which contains descriptions of birds' plumage, habitat, and nesting patterns, along with 30 color images and 9 songs. Links include the searchable Fuertes Collection from Cornell University library's collection of rare books and manuscripts.
WEB http://compstat.wharton.upenn.edu:8001/~siler/birding.html

Rainforest Birds The toucan and the macaw are just two of the hundreds of species of birds in the Amazon region. This page contains images and information on these and several other exotic species such as the White-Necked Puffbird, the Red-crowned Woodpecker, and the Blue Cotinga.
WEB http://mh.osd.wednet.edu/Homepage/Birds.html

ZOOLOGY

African Primates at Home Seven different African primates are featured in their natural habitats at this Web page. Sound files let you listen to the scream of the Pan troglodytes schweinfurthii, otherwise known as the common chimpanzee, and learn about its habitat, its eating patterns, and how it moves. Links to more East African information and other zoological sites are provided.
WEB http://www.indiana.edu/~primate/primates.html

Amphibians of the Rainforest The frog is the star of the show. Links to The Froggy Page for even more information on the most common amphibian in the world. Frog photos are accompanied by specific information on the marine toad, the leaf toad, and the poison arrow frog.
WEB http://mh.osd.wednet.edu/Homepage/Amphibians.html

Animal Information Database Extensive links connect you to the wild world of animals. Animal Bytes holds quick information and fun facts about terrestrial and aquatic animals. The Sea World/Busch Gardens Education Series teaches students about killer whales. Watch a Shamu TV movie clip and then learn about animal training at Sea World. Didn't you always want to know how dolphins do those tricks?
WEB http://www.bev.net/education/SeaWorld/infobook.html

Animals Around the World This project designed for seventh graders contains links to animal information from alligators to whales. Browsers are invited to submit their favorite animal sites.
WEB http://www.chicojr.chico.k12.ca.us/staff/gray/animals.html

The Cephalopod Page Octopii, squid, and the like are the stars of this page. Many interesting links are featured at this page. Go "In Search of Giant Squid" at the link to the Smithsonian's exhibit (the scary underwater photos of gigantic octopii might confine you to the wading pool for the summer). Or participate in a Eurosquid discussion group and find out if they're really as trendy as Americans say they are.
WEB http://is.dal.ca/~wood/www.html

Cyber Zoomobile Learn about distribution, individual characteristics, life cycles, reproduction and sex, endangered species status, and many other interesting aspects about animals. The section on Unusual Alliances explains how leopards and tigers can share a habitat that's not big enough for both of 'em. The worldwide links include search engines, zoos and wildlife parks, animal-related educational materials, and federal and state agencies.
WEB http://www.primenet.com/~brendel/index.html

Mammals of the Rainforest Feel like you're being watched? In the rainforest, you'd have cause for paranoia. Mammals are difficult to see in the Amazon, but this Web site's captured them in cyberspace. Learn all sorts of things about land-dwelling mammals, including anteaters, capibara, monkey, tapir, and the margay, with fun activities and games. Also includes links to information about other mammals of the rainforest.
WEB http://mh.osd.wednet.edu/Home page/Mammals.html

Zooary An online zoo aimed at educating people in the area of zoology. Choose from five animal categories: Amphibians, Arthropods, Birds & Mammals, Reptiles, and Miscellaneous. Click onto Birds & Mammals, for example, and find a color image of a guinea pig. Read about its habitat, breeding habits, and gestation period.
WEB http://www.poly.edu/~duane/zoo /mission.html

Zoological Information by Animal Group A comprehensive database of animal groups from mollusca to mammals. A list of links to other Internet sources on each one is included.
WEB http://www.york.biosis.org/zrdocs /zoolinfo/gp_index.htm

> **ENDANGERED SPECIES**

Endangered Species Saving wild salmon is just one of the Econet causes at this Web site. Find out why dams and wild salmon don't mix and then get involved by contacting endangered species organizations and emailing key politicos. The Datalink contains documents such as the U.S. Endangered Species Act or the Kempthorne ESA Bill of 1995. Links to more conservation resources make this a great starting point for conscientious bio students.
WEB http://www.econet.apc.org /endangered

Endangered Species Want to know what's endangered in your part of the country? The regional map at this Web

site shows which species are threatened and endangered in each state and lists fact sheets for some of those species. The page also links to international conservation sites and WWF's Ten Most Endangered Species of 1994.
WEB http://www.nceet.snre.umich.edu /EndSpp/Endangered.html

Global Show-n-Tell If the Global Show-n-Tell Museum were merely a great rainy-day reprieve, it would still be one of the best sites on the Web. But this five-winged virtual gallery of art by kids ages 10–17 is also an instructive example of how the Internet can be used to promote creativity, community, and activism through effective execution of one fairly simple idea. The museum's wings, which display original artwork cataloged by age group, are each named after a different endangered species of bird. Parents and children work together to post the child's drawing or painting— either created directly on a computer or scanned in later, and each exhibit includes the child's name and age and any other info they wish to share. The site also supports first amendment rights, and offers links to relevant sites.
WEB http://www.manymedia.com /show-n-tell

Twenty of the Most Endangered Animals The numbat, the golden bamboo lemur, the woolly spider monkey. Not the "Top 20" most threatened animals in the world but the ones "which are of popular interest," as chosen by the World Conservation Monitoring Centre. Judging criteria probably had a lot to do with their cute-sounding names. Those who don't think animal conservation is a popularity contest can link to the 1994 IUCN Red List of Threatened Animals, which lists all 6,000 threatened species, of which 1,184 are endangered.
WEB http://www.wcmc.org.uk/infoserv /species/sp_top20.html

> **TEACHERS' LOUNGE**

Instructional Resources in Biology The WWW Virtual Library's basic links

designed with the bio educator in mind. Connect to journals, organizations, and software.
web http://golgi.harvard.edu/biopages/edures.html

Teacher's Guides for Animal Units
Developed at Sea World, this series of k-12 lesson plans offer an active, hands-on way of learning how humans interact with the ocean environment and steps they can take to preserve it. For example, the Manatee Mansion unit challenges students to create a captive habitat where manatee's will thrive. Sample activities from each Teacher's Guide and ordering information are included.
web http://www.bev.net/education/SeaWorld/teacherguides.html

ANIMAL WEB SITES

American Alligators
web http://www.bev.net/education/SeaWorld/animal_bytes/alligatorab.html

Bat Conservation International
web http://www.batcon.org

The Bear Den
web http://www2.portage.net/~dmiddlet/bears/index.html

Bears
web http://www.ladue.k12.mo.us/Wildwatch/bear/bear.html

Dromedary Camel
web http://www.bev.net/education/SeaWorld/animal_bytes/dromedary_camelab.html

Chimpanzee
web http://www.bev.net/education/SeaWorld/animal_bytes/chimpanzeeab.html

California Condor
web http://www.fws.gov/bio-cond.html

Dolphin Page
web http://mingus.loni.ucla.edu:1028/FURMANSKI/dolphin2.html

Bottlenose Dolphins
web http://www.bev.net/education/SeaWorld/bottlenose_dolphin/bottlenose_dolphins.html

Bald Eagle
web http://www.fws.gov/bio-eagl.html

Eagle Page
web http://www.sky.net/~emily/eagle.html

Elephant
web http://www.fws.gov/bio-elep.html

Black-footed Ferret
web http://www.fws.gov/bio-ferr.html

Ferrets
web http://www.optics.rochester.edu:8080/users/pgreene/central.html

The Fox Box
web http://tavi.acomp.usf.edu/foxbox

Frogs
web http://www.cs.yale.edu/HTML/YALE/CS/HyPlans/loosemore-sandra/froggy.html

Gorillas
web http://www.bev.net/education/SeaWorld/gorilla/gorillas.html

Hippopotamus
web http://www.bev.net/education/SeaWorld/animal_bytes/hippopotamusab.html

Spotted Hyena
web http://www.csulb.edu/~persepha/hyena.html

Lemur
web http://www.bev.net/education/SeaWorld/animal_bytes/lemurab.html

Lion
web http://www.frontiertech.com/gall.html

African Lion
web http://www.bev.net/education/SeaWorld/animal_bytes/lionab.html

Manatee Club
web http://www.satelnet.org/manatee

Manatees
WEB http://www.bev.net/education/Sea World/manatee/manatees.html

Otter Page
WEB http://www.zoom.com/personal /aberno/otters.html

Giant Panda
WEB http://www.fws.gov/bio-pand.html

Brown Pelican
WEB http://www.fws.gov/bio-plcn.html

Penguins on the Web
WEB http://www.sas.upenn.edu/~kwelch /penguin.html

Carpet Python
WEB http://www.bev.net/education/Sea World/animal_bytes/carpet_pythonab .html

Raccoons
WEB http://www.loomcom.com/raccoons

Rhinoceros
WEB http://www.fws.gov/bio-rhin.html

Black Rhinoceros
WEB http://www.bev.net/education/Sea World/animal_bytes/black_rhinocerosab .html

The Salmon Page
WEB http://www.riverdale.k12.or.us /salmon.htm

California Sea Lion
WEB http://www.bev.net/education/Sea World/animal_bytes/sea_lionab .html

Sea Otter
WEB http://www.bev.net/education/Sea World/animal_bytes/sea_otterab.html

Great White Shark
WEB http://ucmp1.berkeley.edu/Doug /shark.html

Shark Museum
WEB http://turnpike.net/emporium/C /celestial/epsm.html

Sharks
WEB http://www.io.org/~gwshark/sharks .html

Skunk and Opossum
WEB http://elvis.neep.wisc.edu/~firmiss /mephitis-didelphis.html

Corn (Red Rat Snake) Snake
WEB http://www.bev.net/education/Sea World/animal_bytes/rat_snakeab.html

Tiger
WEB http://www.fws.gov/bio-tige.html

Bengal Tiger
WEB http://www.bev.net/education/Sea World/animal_bytes/tigerab.html

Walrus
WEB http://www.fws.gov/bio-walr.html

Warthog
WEB http://www.bev.net/education/Sea World/animal_bytes/warthogab.html

Whale Information Network
WEB http://www.macmedia.com.au/whales

Whaletimes
WEB http://lsnt5.lightspeed.net/~whaletimes

Whooping Crane
WEB http://www.fws.gov/bio-whoo.html

Wolf Haven International
WEB http://www.teleport.com/~wnorton /wolf.html

Wombats
WEB http://py2.genetics.uga.edu/PFfolder /wombats.html

Red-cockaded Woodpecker
WEB http://www.fws.gov/bio-rcw.html

Grevy's Zebra
WEB http://www.bev.net/education/Sea World/animal_bytes/grevysab.html

CHEMISTRY

EVER SINCE YOU COMBINED THE substances in your chemistry set and found that all it did was ruin your bedroom carpet (to the consternation of your mother who learned her lesson about buying "educational" toys), you've been fascinated by the stuff of which things are made. The Internet has an abundance of elements to help you on your chemical quest. Begin with an Introduction to Chemistry, then apply its theories to help you in Understanding Our Planet Through Chemistry. Once enlightened, you can talk the talk with other budding chemists at sci.chem.

▶ CHEMISTRY 101

Analytical Chemistry I and II Bored with those chemistry Web pages that only give you static models of molecules? Jaded Net students can jumpstart their chemical learnings with QuickTime animations of such favorites as the LC pumping system or the Ni-DMG complex. Can't find natural log on your calculator? Click on the scientific calculator. Got a burette handy? Study overviews of acid-base reactions, gravimetric methods, chemical equilibrium, chromatography, and spectroscopy. All subjects are presented as slides in lecture format. Introductory problems with solutions are also provided.
WEB http://odin.chemistry.uakron.edu /analytical/

Center for Polymer Studies What does lightning have in common with shattering plastic? Lichtenberg patterns. Watch movies of this and other fingering-and-branching patterns in the Dance of Chance Exhibit Hall at this Web site put together by Boston University and the Boston Museum of Science. Is composed music based on the rhythm of the heartbeat? Download MIDI files by Zack Goldberger and find out. More advanced budding scientists can see simulations of molecular networking, including Wasser and Lehnhard-Jones models.

WEB http://cps-www.bu.edu

Chemistry Your science project's due and you have the brilliant idea of making a fake volcano. If you didn't learn anything from *The Brady Bunch* reruns, you might want to check this forum's message board. A thread has erupted that covers fake volcanoes, plus other incendiary topics like Avogadro's Number, alkane reactions, and buckyballs. In case you're still stuck on the basics, the forum's library section houses downloadable software to make your own flashcards and a program to "Learn the Chemical Elements Fast!"
COMPUSERVE *go* science→Chemistry →Messages and Libraries

Chemistry Activities Can't make it to the drugstore to buy toothpaste? Make your own. Sponsored by Vancouver's Association for the Promotion and Advancement of Science Education, this general science site has several fun activities for young experimenters. In addition to engineering toothpaste, students can learn how to make recycled paper. A hands-on lesson explains what salt trucks and ice cream have in common (chemical reactions which cause supercooling or the reverse). Full instructions, including learning objectives and teaching tips, guide both student and teacher through each activity.
WEB http://www.etc.bc.ca/apase/unmixed /chemistry.html

Dimensional Analysis The problem: How long does a drop of water take to evaporate? The answer involves understanding the concept of moles—no, not the kind that dig tunnels in the backyard, but the "large number" that is used to measure the numbers of atoms and molecules in matter. This cyberdemo in dimensional analysis (courtesy of a teacher in Kooskia, Idaho) covers concepts such as Avogadro's Number and "proveable estimates."
WEB http://www.classroom.net/mole.htm

Internet Chemistry Resources Does wondering what a molecule of aspirin looks like give you a headache? Does your idea of a fun experiment involve an exploding can of methane (kaboom!) or a nuclear reactor (bigger kaboom!)? If your answer to either of these questions is yes, this site has resources suitable for you. Students will find links to online chemistry courses (including all the AP chemistry exams from 1970 to 1995) and a section on images that links to many 3-D models, such as one illustrating the origami of folding proteins. If your lungs hurt just thinking about the effect of the chemical industry on the ozone layer, vent your frustrations by linking up to corporate Web pages like those of Shell, Ciba, Dow, and Mobil. **WEB** http://rampages.onramp.net/~jaldr/item03.html

Introduction to Chemistry Before you take high school chemistry, you may want to take this online introduction to the subject. The focus of this fee-based course is the theory of chemistry, not the mathematics behind it. In eight short weeks, you will receive an answer to the question "What is science?" and learn about such chemistry basics as the properties and classification of matter, the structure of the atom, periodic law, the elements, bonding, and reactions. To sign up for the course, all you need is basic math (addition, subtraction, multiplication, division), $40, and a lot of free time over the summer. **AMERICA ONLINE** *keyword* courses→ Science & Nature→Introduction to Chemistry

MATHMOL—K-12 Mathematics and Molecules Turning green from studying photosynthesis? View 3-D images of chlorophyll, carotene, and other pigments. Drinking coffee to stay up late for an exam? Why not examine the 3-D structure of caffeine. Trying to figure out the cure for AIDS? Match the protein to the active site in the HIV-1 protease using links to NIH molecular modeling system. This Web site features many online activities and a library of 3-D molecules you can rotate and zoom in on. The database on water and ice dares to ask the question: Why does an ice cube float in water? **WEB** http://cwis.nyu.edu/pages/mathmol/K_12.html

Microworlds, Exploring the Structure of Materials Operated by the Lawrence Berkeley National Laboratory, this Web site solves a few mysteries of the world of materials. Students can read about the Advanced Light Source Building in San Francisco and find out how it revealed the inner strength of Kevlar, discovered in 1960, using a technology similar to the way a dentist uses X-rays to see inside teeth. Other articles explain the usefulness of polymers and how scientists make micromachines that can fit through the eye of a needle. **WEB** http://www.lbl.gov/MicroWorlds

sci.chem A newsgroup for those who "truly love science" in general, and chemistry in particular. Hot topics have included the chemical composition of diesel, how to dissolve compressed polystyrene, and whether a hotter or colder ping-pong ball will bounce higher. Advanced high school chemistry students will find much to pique their interest. **USENET** sci.chem

Understanding Our Planet Through Chemistry How old is the earth? Is a Jurassic Park really possible? What caused dinosaurs to become extinct? This Web site offers a collection of documents organized into a "book," which explains how chemical analysis can tell us many things about our world. Students can take a look at the current research on amber (tree sap) and fossils, learn how to predict volcanic eruptions, and read about the destructive effects of acid rain. The information ranges from the contemporary (see how robots perform many of the repetitive tasks of the analytical chemist) to the historical (did you know that in the early 1900s, horse-drawn carriages were used to determine elements in the field?). Per-

haps this was the original meaning of the term "mobile laboratory."
WEB http://helios.cr.usgs.gov/gips /aii-home.htm

The World of Materials What exactly are semiconductors? Are the ceramic tiles on a space shuttle the same as the ones in your bathroom? What about ceramic superconductors? In simple jargon, this site defines four classes of materials—metals, ceramics, semiconductors, and polymers. Three-dimensional molecular diagrams illustrate how the variable stiffness of polyester makes it suitable for everything from fabric to 2-liter Coke bottles. Students can examine the chemical structure of pantyhose (nylon) and see how it compares to the Kevlar (aromatic nylon) found in tires and bullet-proof glass. After you learn about Teflon, you'll never feel the same about frying an egg.
WEB http://tantalum.mit.edu/struc_mater /material_structures.html

▶ PERIODIC TABLE

Chemicool Periodic Table Superman might be interested to know that 1.653 log is the relative abundance of krypton in the solar system. Teens might be interested to find out that yes, lithium is a Nirvana tune—and the name of the lightest solid, with an atomic mass of 6.94. Who would be interested to discover that the going rate for pure mercury is $5 for every 100 grams? Maybe a thermometer company. Loads of elemental facts can be unearthed at the searchable database at this Web site. Does magnesium react with air? The simple answer is here, alongside the deeper complexities of the periodic table, including ionization energies, electronegativities, heats of fusion, heats of vaporization, electron affinity, specific heat, conductivity, and heat atomization.
WEB http://the-tech.mit.edu/~davhsu /chemicool.html

Periodic Table of the Elements Did you know that polonium was named after Poland by Pierre and Marie Curie in

1898? Or that strontium is used in fireworks? Did you know that there is such a thing as krypton and it's a gas used in lighting? If not, get up to speed at this Web page put together by an eighth-grader named Yinon Bentor. The "element-ary" information covers each element's melting point, boiling point, crystal structure, use, location, discoverer, and Bohr model. The old standbys like carbon and oxygen are featured along with the Periodic Table's most recent addition, ununbium, discovered on Feb 6, 1996 (try not to confuse it with ununnilium, which was discovered almost a decade earlier).
WEB http://www.cetlink.net/~yinon/index .html

▶ TEACHERS' LOUNGE

Chemistry Teaching Resources A comprehensive collection of links for teachers of chemistry, as well as other sciences. Resources include newsgroups, mailing lists, software companies, and lesson plans.
WEB http://www.rpi.edu/dept/chem /cheminfo/chemres/chemres_13.html

NCSA Chemistry Visualization High school teachers and their students can use the software developed by NCSA to visualize atomic and molecular structures. This home page provides the necessary information on obtaining the software and features previews of images created by ChemViz, including quantum mechanically accurate images of chemical compounds such as penicillin or formic acid.
WEB http://www.ncsa.uiuc.edu/Edu /ChemViz

PHYSICS

WANT TO KNOW WHAT HOLDS the universe together? Learn physics. Want to know what keeps your feet on the ground? Learn physics. Want to know why peanut butter sticks to the roof of your mouth? Get a life. Physics is the science that deals with matter, energy, motion, and force. Learn the basics at PhysicsEd. Visit sci.physics and match wits with armchair physicists. Any questions? Ask Dr. Neutrino. You don't have to be a rocket scientist to understand physics, but you can become one with Rocketry Projects.

▶ PHYSICS 101

Contemporary Physics Education Project Those looking for a solution to an infinite source of energy should visit this site. Plenty of deluxe full-color charts, software, classroom booklets, and more can be downloaded. Ever wonder what makes the universe stay together or how atoms were discovered? This site has the answer. Learn how to win the Nobel Prize at the small particle section which details the discovery of the neutrino and the lepton.
WEB http://www-pdg.lbl.gov/cpep.html

Physics Science project help is just one of the many topics students can find information on in the messages section of this forum. Other frequently discussed message topics include Planck's constant, the Meyer device, and atoms. The library holds even more for the physics student, including a glossary for quantum mechanics or announcements for high school physics competitions.
COMPUSERVE *go* science→Messages *and* Libraries→Physics

Physics Around the World Whether your interests involve chaos theory or firing a cannonball accurately, this site provides an abundance of resources. Sick of fiddling with those textbooks to find some heat of enthalpy? Try the section on constants and equations. Solve the problem

of the month to find out if others are smarter than you. Dig up mailing lists, physics societies and space agencies. Justify the decision to go into science by reviewing the "Value of Science." You'll be glad you did.
WEB http://www.physics.mcgill.ca /deptdocs/physics_services.html

PhysicsEd Numerous begining and advanced software topics are available at PhysicsEd, including time travel and flatlands. Learn about online courses from Perdue to Pennsylvania. Those in search of an adequate textbook on physics can try the PhysicsEd library. Histories, biographies, references and organizations are all at your fingertips.
WEB http://www-hpcc.astro.washington .edu/scied/physics.htm

sci.physics In the world of sci.physics, the question "Does light have mass?" exists side by side "Does tapping Coke can keep fizz from exploding?" But as in high school, this newsgroup's participants self-segregate into cliques. The "brains" confine themselves to such topics as hypersurfaces, infinite subdivisibility, and wave-particle duality, while the recreational-minded are more interested in how to use practical physics to subvert police radar or cool their bedrooms.
USENET sci.physics

▶ ENERGY

Department of Energy This branch of the U.S. government informs the public about coal, nuclear, solar, electric, petroleum, natural gas, and other types of fuel. Those afraid of the day when gas runs out can refer to the section on fuel efficiency, which explains the short- and long-term effects of depleting the Earth's resources. For people who want the bottom line on what effect energy depletion will have on the economy, a page has been devoted to the topic. Informed citizens can help the community by participating in one of the outreach programs

outlined.
WEB http://www.eia.doe.gov/energy

Energy Quest What on earth is bio-mass? Is it safe? Find out at this site for young scientists. Percy, a dinosaur with an AC outlet for a tail, will teach you the basics. Learn about geothermal, nuclear, wind, and solar energy, and what the future has in store. Learn ways to save energy with the Energy Patrol. Find out neat alternatives to gas-powered cars. If you still have questions about photo-voltaics or fossil fuels, basic answers are provided. The site also provides links to pages about dinosaurs, fish, frogs and other creatures.
WEB http://www.energy.ca.gov/energy/education/eduhome.html

Hydro Power Find out more about the nature of Hoover Dam by visiting this site, which provides basic explanations of alternative ways of obtaining power from nature. Small and large hydroelec-tric systems are explained as well as geothermal, wind, and solar. Plenty of pictures illustrate the no-nonsense overview of each alternative form of energy, including its applications, theory, case studies, and even economics.
WEB http://solstice.crest.org/renewables/re-kiosk/hydro/index.shtml

Mr. Solar Home Page Mr. Solar and his wife have been working for 18 years on letting the sun shine in. Ways to obtain environmentally friendly equipment for the solar age are available at their trilin-gual (English, Spanish and French) Web site. Browse the library of articles about progressive forms of energy, culled from the "Ask Mr. Solar" columns. Connect to other "enlightened sites" all over the globe and learn the specifics of configur-ing a home solar system. Inverters, pumps and batteries can also be bought online.
WEB http://www.netins.net/showcase/solarcatalog

Nuclear Energy If you've discovered uranium in the backyard and are won-dering what to do with it, visit the Nuclear Energy Web site. Learn facts about nuclear fusion. Study the advan-tages of nuclear energy (no air pollution, it's abundant in all countries). Find out about the magnetic fields in a tokamak (the plasma confiner) and other recent research in the field. The China Syn-drome was once just a possibility, but can be a reality.
WEB http://www.pppl.gov/oview/pages/fusion_energy.html

The Speed of Light: A Limit on Princi-ple Find out if the speed of light can be exceeded and if so, what would happen if you turned on the headlights? Are *12 Monkeys* and the *Terminator* scenarios actually possible or is there too much conflict with simultaneity? Use clocks and mirrors to shed some light on the problem. Physicist Laro Schatzer pro-vides diagrams and arguments covering all these questions and more in one "easy treatise." It will make the old Minkowskian versus Galilean space-time controversy seem as challenging as the "tastes great, less filling" debate.
WEB http://monet.physik.unibas.ch/~schatzer/space-time.html

▶ RELATIVITY

Theory of Relativity In four short weeks, any student with a grasp of ordi-nary algebra can learn Einstein's Theory of Relativity, which revolutionized physics about a century ago. Topics cov-ered include inertial reference frames, four-dimensional space-time, length contraction, time dilation, accelerating frames, general relativity, and gravitation through the Equivalence Principle. Sound incomprehensible? According to the course description, the relativity the-ory is quite "straightforward," but per-haps its author was speaking "relatively."
AMERICA ONLINE *keyword* courses→ Science & Nature→Theory of Relativity

▶ PARTICLE PHYSICS

Continuous Electron Beam Accelerator Facility Students can explore the atom online or go on a mission to Jupiter at

this site, which sponsors a program called BEAMS ("Being Enthusiastic About Math and Science"). Teachers can read about what's happening at CEBAF's SITE (Summer Institute for Teacher Enhancement). But the most useful resources for the classroom are the CEBAF Science Series videotapes. Physics topics include "The Nature of the Nucleus" and "What IS the Speed of Light, Anyway?" CEBAF videos are free and available on a first-come, first-served basis.
WEB http://www.cebaf.gov/services/pced

Fermilab Home Page Fermilab is a high-energy physics laboratory where scientists visit from around the world to test their theories on particle physics. Take a virtual tour of the home of the Tevatron, the world's most powerful particle accelerator. Discover the Feynman computing center and all the neat sites where ultra-microscopic colisions take place. For those with the gumption to cart themselves to Chicago, information on real-life tours is provided.
WEB http://fnnews.fnal.gov

Stanford Linear Accelerator Center SLAC has a lot to offer with its programs for the pre-college, college, and graduate level. This site describes them all, and provides answers to such burning questions as "What is synchotron radiation?" and "Why do we need a stream of high energy particles to study linear acceleration?" Also, information about equipment donations, online access to programs, and collaboration with Bay Area research are included.
WEB http://www.slac.stanford.edu /winters/pub/www/education /education.html

▶ **EXPERIMENTS**

Hands-on Activites from the Franklin Institute Hands-on activities to foster the young science mind. Use a toilet paper roll to listen to a heartbeat or conduct an experiment with puzzles that actually watch the brain learning. Budding Sally Rides can find out about aeronautic basics with the paper airplane experiment. Kids can become environmentally conscious by studing how our actions affect the environment. Learn about the forces that keep satellites in orbit.
WEB http://sln.fi.edu/tfi/activity /act-summ.html

Little Shop of Physics Find out what a laser bongo is. See if the phantom light bulb can be spotted. Execute an experiment that involves spitting at your computer, and then email your questions to the Colorado University faculty members who put up the site. If you like what you see, you can invite them to give a demonstration at your school. Cartoons and pictures make this an animated visit.
WEB http://129.82.166.181/default.html

Physical Science Activity Manual Newton would chop down his apple tree if he could see this site, which offers hands-on information relating to the physical sciences. Seeing a movie soon? Determine the percentage of water in the popcorn and save money. Use Tinker Toys to study the principle of definite proportions, then find out what dominoes have to do with calculating average speed. Have fun by dropping washers from the balcony to learn about gravity. Aspiring Dr. Frankensteins can build monster flesh to learn various chemical properties—and conquer the world.
WEB http://192.239.146.18/PSAM.html

Rocketry Projects Delve into the mind of McGyver by constructing a rocket out of matches and alumminum foil. Get out the soda cans and the antacid tablets and prepare to race. A brief historical account of rockets is provided, along with plenty of ways to make rockets.
WEB http://www.lerc.nasa.gov/Other _Groups/K-12/TRC_activities.html

Wonders of Physics Copperfield the magician meets Einstein—as Professor Clint Sprott (bizarre picture included) entertains and delights audiences for a mere $400 (to cover the cost of pyrotechnics). This Web site documents

Sprott's activities for free. Download sound files to hear the Wisconsin Capital Band perform "Clint," the Wonders of Physics Theme Song. See the Power Rangers battle the professor and challenge the scientific intellect. Check out this site's catalog of videotaped physics performances given by University of Wisconsin faculty to stir interest in Physics. The instructions for many of these experiments are also available to download (disclaimer included in case of explosions).
WEB http://sprott.physics.wisc.edu/wop.htm

PROBLEM SOLVING

Ask Dr. Neutrino Mr. Wizard and Beakman better hold on to their scientific calculators—Dr. Neutrino has arrived. This site has an open forum to answer physics-related questions. Pull up the home page to see the Far Side rendering of physicist humor. Learn how to build a medieval catapult for the next science fair. Find out who invented the thermometer or what makes water spin a certain direction down a drain. An archive of these questions and their answers are provided.
WEB http://nike.phy.bris.ac.uk/dr/ask.html

The Interactive Physics Problem Set At this site, discover more than 100 problems dealing with physics. It starts with an brief review of calculus and then proceeds to the hardcore stuff. Expend energy and work by reviewing this data set. Experience rotation and torsion when learning about these concepts. Enough material to make even a devoted physics fan want to turn their desktop into a projectile and calculate its velocity.
WEB http://128.32.163.55/Vol1/Contents.html

Quantum It is time to exercise the mind with an assortment of brain teasers and puzzles. The competitive types who solve the puzzle contest can have their names posted on the Internet. This online version of the magazine, Quantum (which originated in Russia and was

called Kvant), connects to other sites such as Discovery, the Geometry Page and Hot Air all of which might be of some help in solving the problems.
WEB http://www.nsta.org/quantum/index.htm

TEACHERS' LOUNGE

Introductory Physics Library Choose from a variety of introductory physics teaching links from colleges nationwide. Tempt the local fire marshal by performing some of the demonstrations created at North Carolina University. Pore over scores of physics lecture notes or the online electronic textbook from the University of Pennsylvania. Need something to challenge your students? Access the hundreds of problems from the University of California at Berkeley.
WEB http://www.phys.ufl.edu/~selman/IntroPhysLib.html

PEN The American Institute of Physics Bulletin of Physics Education News has provided archives for all sorts of teacher-related material, including links to employment opportunities and information on grants and outreach programs. Subscriptions are free. For those in search of a blast from the past, try the PEN archive.
WEB http://www.aip.org/pinet/listserver/PEN.info.html

Physics Around the World: Education From Budapest to Hawaii to Kansas, research facilities and educational resources are linked at this site for teachers. Bounce to British Columbia to try the electronic games for teaching math and physical sciences. Find fractals in France. Hey, the Web was created by physicists, so why not link up to some of their resources online?
WEB http://www.physics.mcgill.ca/physics-services/physics_education.html

EARTH SCIENCE

WELCOME TO THE CYBERLITHIC Era, a new age in which earth science information roams the Internet. Start out slowly with some basic earth science indexes. The environmentally minded can then head to the Ecology Channel or EnviroLink. To find out what's shaking in seismology, visit the National Earthquake Information Center or check out the ongoing discussions at sci.geo.earthquakes. Equally volatile are Volcano World and MTU's Volcanoes Page. If you need help understanding science under the sea, take a trip to Ocean Planet or Underwater World. Or explore the meaning of cliffhangers at Rockhounds Information Page and the Smithsonian Gem & Mineral Collection. Whether you fancy yourself the next Willard Scott, need to weather your meteorology unit in science, or just want to know whether it will rain tomorrow, you'll find a range of resources at The Weather Channel, The Daily Planet, and AOL's Weather News. If all this cybersurfing has you longing for a life in a simpler time, take a trip in the Web Geologic Time Machine.

EARTH SCIENCES 101

Earth Pages Who's better qualified to help you out with navigation than NASA? NASA's Earth Pages contain a search tool that allows users to delve into its database of earth science Web sites using keywords, returning a list of matching URLs with a short description of each site.
WEB http://epserver.gsfc.nasa.gov/earth /earth.html

Earth Science Site of the Week
Canada's Geological Survey Commission highlights a different hotbed of earth science activity each week, from atmospheric studies to volcanology, museums to universities, geology to hydrology.
WEB http://agcwww.bio.ns.ca/misc /geores/sotw/sotw.html

Earth Sciences The WWW Virtual Library houses hundreds of links to earth science organizations around the globe, current events, resources, software, and reference materials.
WEB http://www.geo.ucalgary.ca/VL -EarthSciences.html

ECOLOGY

EcoLogic: A Student Pugwash Project
This is the Web home of the Rensselaer Polytechnic Institute chapter of Student Pugwash USA, a national non-profit organization dedicated to building a commitment among students to solve global problems through the responsible use of science and technology. Take the Pugwash pledge, keep up to date on the latest national activities, or link to the newest related Web resources. In case you were wondering, the name comes from Pugwash, Nova Scotia, the location of the first Conference on Science and World Affairs which was held in 1957.
WEB http://www.rpi.edu/dept/union /pugwash

Ecology Channel Only here would a fabled frog make the front page. One of the recent lead stories on the Ecology Channel's Greenwire Eco Update was news that the California red-legged frog was listed as threatened under the Endangered Species Act. The legendary leaper in question is believed to be Mark Twain's infamous Celebrated Jumping Frog of Calaveras County. The Ecology Channel not only keeps on top of the latest environmental news, but also offers such features as Eco Travel and Eco Business.
WEB http://www.ecology.com

EnviroLink Every aspect of EnviroLink hints at man's innate connection to the earth, right down to the icons—they're actually ancient artwork from indigenous cultures worldwide, reflecting the rich and diverse heritage of our link to the earth. Get in touch with your own inter-

dependence with the planet by visiting the EnviroLink Library, reading EnviroNews, shopping at the Internet Green Marketplace, taking in some EnviroArts, or talking with other tree huggers in the online forum. Envirolink also rates other ecosites and online events in What Soars, What Snores (And What Bites).
WEB http://www.envirolink.org

Environet Think globally, act locally—words the maintainers of this Santa Clarita, Calif., site take seriously. Environet disseminates information to prevent two possibly destructive propositions: the Ahmanson project, designed to develop a mini-city at the expense of the area running from the Santa Monica Mountains through the Simi Hills; and the plan to turn Elsmere, a pristine canyon situated in the Angeles National Forest, into a garbage dump. Explore maps of the areas and read about the latest developments.
WEB http://www.aspenlinx.com/environet

Planet Keepers "The frog does not drink up the pond in which he lives." So goes a Native American proverb. These pages also provide the eco-minded with featured readings, upcoming events, things to do, and other enviro-links on everything from human overpopulation to wildlife preservation.
WEB http://galaxy.einet.net/galaxy /Community/Environment/Environmental -Activism/wayne-pendley/plankeep.html

▶ GEOLOGY

Ask-A-Geologist Need help with your geology homework? Don't call your classmates; they'll just expect something in return. Go to the experts—ask a geologist. Don't wait until the last minute though. Answers may take a few days.
WEB http://walrus.wr.usgs.gov/docs /ask-a-ge.html

Ask A Geology Question ...and you'll get a geology answer. What cataclysmic event killed off the dinosaurs? Why do beaches change from year to year? What can scratch a diamond? Scientists, engi-

neers, and support staff who study the geology of eastern Canada are standing by to satisfy your every earth science curiosity. But they specifically request you not send them your class assignments to complete.
WEB http://agcwww.bio.ns.ca/schools /classrm.html

A Decade of Notable California Earthquakes "I'm going back to Cali..." raps LL Cool J, but he may change his mind after reading about the foreshocks, mainshocks, and aftershocks that have occurred in the Golden State in the last ten years. This page also includes a map of probable future earthquakes in Southern California through the year 2004
WEB http://www.westworld.com/~shorose /califneq.html

Living in the Learning Web Learn about terrestrial topics that may actually concern you. Like how weather affects the streams in your state. Or what you can do to prepare for a volcanic eruption. The Learning Web comes courtesy of the U.S. Geological Survey.
WEB http://www.usgs.gov/education /living/index.html

National Earthquake Information Center What important establishment is located in Golden, Colo.? Not the Coors Brewing Company, but the National Earthquake Information Center—the national data center and archive for all seismic information. Cyberseismologists can access current worldwide seismic maps, earthquake facts and statistics, explanations of plate tectonics and the Richter Magnitude Scale, and a glossary of quake terminology.
WEB http://gldss7.cr.usgs.gov

National Geophysical Data Center Uncle Sam's center for geophysical data in the fields of marine geology and geophysics, paleoclimatology, solar-terrestrial physics, solid earth geophysics, and glaciology. If you're a hard-core geo-head, you can investigate the NGDC's activities, databases, images, and products.
WEB http://www.ngdc.noaa.gov

Rockhounds Information Page Members of the rockhounds mailing list have set up shop on the Web with links to images and pictures, rock shops and galleries, books and magazines, software and mailing list archives, general earth science info, and geology clubs and societies. Something for everyone, from the amateur rock collector to the professional geologist.
WEB http://www.rahul.net/infodyn /rockhounds/rockhounds.html
EMAIL rockhands-requests@infodyne.com
✍ *Type in subject line:* subscribe

sci.geo.earthquakes Do you feel the earth move under your feet? Experts talk shop and newbies come for elementary earthquake lessons. Some topics up for discussion—quake mapping, aftershocks, predictions, and safety.
USENET sci.geo.earthquakes

sci.geo.geology This newsgroup tends toward the technical, but you may find some helpful insights. However, be careful about posting elementary questions—things may get a little rocky. One innocent inquired about information on the layers of the earth and received this response: "It's called the library. I'd bet they have many excellent books on geology. If you are too lazy to walk there, and insist on trying to get answers to high school geology questions on the Web, then try any of the common search engines… But please don't clutter the newsgroups with simple-minded questions just because you are too lazy to look up the answers yourself."
USENET sci.geo.geology

Smithsonian Gem & Mineral Collection For the hard-core geologist, a trip to see the precious stones here is better than breakfast at Tiffany's. Some of the more remarkable rocks include a 98.6 carat Bismark Sapphire, one of the world's largest; an uncut corundum crystal, second only to diamond in hardness; and a spectacular and rare "Canary" diamond.
WEB http://galaxy.einet.net/images /gems/gems-icons.html
A Trip Through The Grand Canyon Your journey begins with the statement, "No trip through cyberspace can begin to communicate the thrill of actually running the Colorado River through the Grand Canyon." But if you're still willing to settle for the electronic version, you'll enjoy a tour through such geological wonders as Marble Canyon, the Palisades, Upper Granite, Elves Chasm, Lava Falls, and Lake Mead, complete with maps and photos.
WEB http://river.ihs.gov/GrandCanyon /GCrt.html

Volcanic Homepage This page can be as volatile as the volcanoes it explores, but that's not necessarily a bad thing. Since it's part of an ongoing project to model volcanic eruptions using a computer, the Volcanic Homepage is constantly undergoing changes. Explore some of the more stable aspects of the site, like photos, animations, current eruption news, and reference materials.
WEB http://www.aist.go.jp/GSJ/~jdehn /v-home.htm

Volcano World So you want to be a volcanologist. Be warned, it involves more than living in Hawaii. Volcano World describes the details of this consequential career choice. The site is expansive and explosive, containing data on volcanoes in the form of news, facts, volcanic parks and monuments, contests, links, and the ask-a-volcanologist pages.
WEB http://volcano.und.nodak.edu

Worldwide Earthquake Locator More than 800,000 earthquakes occur each year. But before you get too shaken up, realize that most are small and not felt by humans. A severe earthquake, with a magnitude of greater than 8.0 on the Richter Scale, can be expected every 8 to 10 years. But a significant number of smaller earthquakes, which are still capable of destruction, occur yearly. This University of Edinburgh Department of Geography site keeps track of the locations of all the latest seismic activity around the world.
WEB http://geovax.ed.ac.uk/quakes /quakes.html

▶ METEOROLOGY

The Daily Planet Not to be confused with a certain fictional newspaper of the same name, this Daily Planet is a product of the University of Illinois Department of Atmospheric Sciences. The Online Guide to Meteorology is a virtual textbook in weather. For those who master that and see forecasting in their future, the Weather Visualizer allows you to customize your own current weather maps and images and the Weather Machine offers satellite products.
WEB http://wx3.atmos.uiuc.edu

Explores! Basic Skills and Activities Although Aristotle didn't coin the word "meteorology" until 340 B.C., the first meteorologists were probably prehistoric farmers and hunters, who were dependent upon atmospheric conditions for their existence. Although they couldn't adequately explain many atmospheric phenomena (a problem even the best weather forecasters have today), a collection of weather "signs" were accumulated and handed down from generation to generation. This Florida State site explores the history of weather science and provides activities that assist in understanding atmospheric composition, the hydrologic cycle, thermometers, and that
dynamic duo—latitude and longitude.
WEB http://thunder.met.fsu.edu/explores /skillmenu.html

sci.geo.meteorology The most technical of the weather news groups (a frightening concept), sci.geo.meteorology is visited primarily by 'ologists (geologists, meteorologists, etc.). A recent thread concerning dew points drew upwards of 50 posts.
USENET sci.geo.meteorology

The Weather Channel A perfect site for the weather neophyte, The Weather Channel allows you to check out current conditions and the forecast for your favorite U.S. city and to view nifty national weather maps of the same. Submit your weather-related question to the site's Met on the Net, follow weather links across the Web in search of answers by yourself, or, best of all, fulfill your secret dream of becoming a meteorologist and explore TWC's Meteorologist's toolbox. You'll also find a short history of TWC, bios of your favorite forecasters, a monthly programming guide, and a list of TWC contacts.
WEB http://www.weather.com

▶ OCEANOGRAPHY

Aquatic Network A virtual clearinghouse of underwater wisdom, covering all the subjects of the sea—aquaculture, conservation, fisheries, marine science, oceanography, maritime heritage, ocean engineering, and seafood. The Aquatic Network covers news and events, contains information on related publications, and houses the AquaStore.
WEB http://www.aquanet.com/aquanet

Ocean Planet More than 99 percent of living space on Earth is ocean, all habitable by plants and animals. This traveling Smithsonian exhibition plumbs the workings of our watery planet. The culmination of a four-year effort to study and understand environmental issues affecting the health of the world's oceans, the exhibit will be touring from 1996-1999, but is available for private viewing in cyberspace.
WEB http://seawifs.gsfc.nasa.gov/ocean _planet.html

Oceanography When you hold a shell up to your ear, why does it sound like the ocean? The answer to that question and more will be taught at this four-week course. "Prof. Steve," as the course instructor likes to be called, "has a deep love of the sea" and a lot of experience chasing and tagging whales off Cape Cod. His oceanography course will enlighten and entertain on such seaworthy topics as the Bermuda Triangle, hurricanes, and tropical storms, as well as stories of mermaids and dolphins that save humans.
AMERICA ONLINE *keyword* courses→ Science & Nature→Oceanography

Underwater World Landlubbers beware. This site is located entirely underwater. Join deep sea explorer Jack Stein Grove on a diving adventure. Flip through the freaky fishes family album. Explore the Monterey Bay Aquarium. And more.
WEB http://pathfinder.com /pathfinder/kidstuff/underwater /index.html

World Data Center—Marine Geology & Geophysics "The ocean floor is a natural archive of information on how Earth works and has worked for millions of years." The World Data Center is an archive of that archive. The experts at the National Geophysical Data Center site study the composition and structure of sea floor sediment and underlying basement crust looking for clues to the evolution of life, ocean-atmosphere dynamics, and the tectonic processes that shaped Earth's continents and ocean basins as we know them today. You can search the center for clues to your oceanography queries.
WEB http://www.ngdc.noaa.gov/mgg /aboutmgg/wdcamgg.html

▶ **PALEONTOLOGY**

Dino Russ's Lair: The Earthnet Info Server Dino Russ (otherwise known as Russ Jacobson) provides a virtual view of dinosaur and vertebrate paleontology. No, his lair doesn't include food, fire, and water. Instead, it contains links, facts, images, and information on how you can participate in some cool dinosaur digs.
WEB http://128.174.172.76:/isgsroot /dinos/dinos_home.html

The Electronic Prehistoric Shark Museum Because sharks have no bones, only cartilage—which tends to disintegrate before fossilizing—the only records left behind by prehistoric ones are their lovely teeth. This site is devoted to displaying the "business end" of ancient sharks and contains teeth dating back some 25 million years.
WEB http://207.67.198.22/C/celestial /epsm.htm

Geologic Time Scale Was it 4,600 million years ago or 460 million years ago? It makes a difference. A handy reference when you just need to check an ancient geological occurrence—like when the earth's crust was formed or when dinosaurs disappeared from the earth.
URL gopher://wiretap.spies.com/00 /Library/Document/geologic.tbl

Ice Ages During most of the last billion years the globe had no permanent ice. However, at times large areas of the globe have been covered with vast ice sheets. These times are known as ice ages and this Illinois State Museum site covers the whens, wheres, and whys of those chilly eras. If all these glacial facts leave you cold, warm up by viewing a video showing the retreat of the ice sheet that once covered most of North America.
WEB http://www.museum.state.il.us /exhibits/ice_ages

The Midwest US at 16,000 Years Ago Imagine the Midwest with no shopping malls, suburban neighborhoods, or 7-11s. If you're having trouble, visit this site, which recreates the heartland of 16,000 years ago. Mastodons feeding in wetlands. Parklands dominated by spruce and poplar. An osprey hunting for fish over the marsh. And not a TCBY in sight.
WEB http://www.museum.state.il.us /exhibits/larson

Prem's Fossil Gallery Prem is an amateur fossil collector living in Tallahassee, Fla., and he's put together his own virtual collection of trilobites, graptolites, and Pennsylvanian plants for your petrified viewing pleasure.
WEB http://dev.uol.com/~prem/fossil.html

sci.bio.paleontology The discussion can range from serious debate on the possible discovery of a dinosaur larger than the T. Rex to more whimsical writing about why it's probably not a good idea to eat the meat of the komodo dragon. Their meat is very fatty, they're endangered and fully protected, and they just might have similar thoughts about you.

USENET sci.bio.paleontology

Stewart Wright's Paleo Page Stewart Wright's dinoriffic site features dinosaur art, pictures from the Royal Tyrrell Museum's Field Experience Program, and links to a different paleontology page each month.

WEB http://www.GEB.com/net/sw.html

University of California Museum of Paleontology Most people think paleontology is strictly the study of fossils. In fact, it incorporates many kinds of data from diverse fields. This University of California Museum enlightens about paleontology's facets beyond fossils with three online exhibits: a family tree connecting all organisms that ever lived, explanations of evolutionary topics and scientists from Darwin to da Vinci in their historical context, and "Geology and Geologic Time." A multi-volume, multimedia virtual glossary is available to help you with any new words.

WEB http://ucmp1.berkeley.edu/exhibit text/entrance.html

Web Geologic Time Machine Take a trip back (way back) in time. Visit the Paleozoic Era when there were only six major continental land masses, California ran east to west along the equator, and Africa was at the South Pole. Jump back to the Mesozoic Era when dinosaurs were the most popular creatures on the planet (for obvious reasons).

WEB http://ucmp1.berkeley.edu/timeform .html

Web Lift to Any Taxon Pick a taxon, any taxon. Explore age-old organisms from bacteria and viruses, to molds and mushrooms, to duck-billed dinosaurs and carnosaurs.

WEB http://ucmp1.berkeley.edu/taxaform .html

World of Amber Damselflies in distress. Bees in mid-buzz. Prehistoric plants frozen in their prime. Such are the fossils found in amber. Read about amber's

physical properties, uses, types, care, recovery methods, and myths. When you're done, take the amber quiz.

WEB http://www.emporia.edu/S/www /earthsci/amber/amber.htm

TEACHERS' LOUNGE

Explores! Teacher's Resource Guide For teachers who want to talk about the weather. The meteorological material here includes historical summaries of each meteorological satellite launched by the U.S., links to outreach programs offering weather curricula for the classroom, and assorted lesson plans and teaching guides.

WEB http://thunder.met.fsu.edu/explores /resources.html

Teaching in the Learning Web Complete units devoted to the topics of Earth Science, Global Change, and Working With Maps, including introductions, activities, images, and teachers' guides. The lessons were developed by the U.S. Geological Survey to meet national Earth Science curriculum standards and have been tested and reviewed by teachers and students.

WEB http://www.usgs.gov/education /learnweb/index.html

Volcano Lesson Plans Explosive lesson plans centered around Mt. St. Helens and the volcanoes of Hawaii.

WEB http://volcano.und.nodak.edu /vwdocs/vwlessons/lesson.html

The Weather Channel Weather Classroom Teachers, set those VCRs. The Weather Channel is offering on-air schedules for The Weather Classroom, their daily 10-minute live program featuring weather in action. The mavens of meteorology also offer an accompanying textbook and several video documentaries for sale.

WEB http://www.weather.com/weather _whys/wx_wonders/wx_classroom.html

COMPUTER SCIENCE

COMPUTER SCIENCE AS WE KNOW it began sometime in the mid-1920s when Dr. Julius Edgar Lilienfield of New York filed for a patent on his "Method and Apparatus for Controlling Electric Current," otherwise known as a transistor. Nearly half a century later, in 1971, Intel introduced the first microprocessor, and a decade after that, the notion of the home computer became a reality. The explosion of cyberspace, of course, has been the latest development, and the Internet is where you'll find all you need to know about computers. If the new Microsoft Word 6.0 has you tearing your hair out, consult the Microsoft Knowledge Base to get things under control. Brush up your programming skills with the resources at the WWW Virtual Library's Computer Programming Languages. Once you feel duly informed, learn to speak like a computer geek at the Hacker's Dictionary Jargon File.

▶ COMPUTING 101

Computer Library Online Part of the Ziff-Davis Publishing Group's extensive CompuServe database, this useful site is an information retrieval service designed to provide a complete reference and assistance resource for computer users. It consists of the three following searchable databases: *Computer Database Plus*, for magazine and newspaper articles related to computers; *Computer's Buyer's Guide*, for those in the market to buy computer hardware, software or peripherals; and Support on Site, a searchable database for technical support. All of these databases specialize in Macintosh and IBM-compatible products and the search engines are amazing.
COMPUSERVE *go* complib

Indiana University UCS Knowledge Base What is a microchip? How does the Internet work? Will computers ever be able to think like humans? This archive contains more than 3,000 ques-

tions and answers on the computer world, ranging from the most basic to the most advanced. Spend some time here, and your PC will bask in the glow of self-knowledge.
WEB http://sckb.ucssc.indiana.edu/kb/expsearch.html

The Microsoft Knowledge Base Don't risk being put on hold as your Word document disintegrates. Why wait until the next morning to find out how to fix an Excel report that appears to be corrupted? Microsoft has put several thousand technical articles online with answers and troubleshooting advice for questions about all their products. (On CompuServe, the articles also sometimes refer to software updates and programming aids that can be downloaded from the Microsoft Software Library.) The articles, which CompuServe members can easily search by topic and date and AOL members can search by topic, are the same documents used by Microsoft technical support staff to answer calls—and chances are high that if you've owned a PC for more than a few weeks, you've made one of those calls.
AMERICA ONLINE *keyword* knowledgebase
COMPUSERVE *go* mskb

▶ THE INTERNET

alt.newbie
alt.newbies
news.newusers.questions
comp.unix.questions Newsgroups created especially for Internet novices to post questions. The FAQ directory includes guides about email, FTP, Internet access providers, creating a signature file, and reading newsgroups.
USENET alt.newbie • alt.newbies • news.newusers.questions • comp.unix.questions
FAQ: **WEB** http://www.cis.ohio-state.edu/hypertext/faq/bngusenet/news/newusers/questions/top.html

EFF's (extended) guide to the internet

A basic primer on the Internet. This guide covers Internet providers, email programs and email addresses, Usenet culture and newsreaders, mailing lists, telnet instructions and sites, FTP instructions and sites, gophers and sites, IRC and MUDs, netiquette, the EFF, and much more.

WEB http://www.eff.org/papers/eegtti/eegttitop.html • http://www.eff.org/pub/Net_info/EFF_Net_Guide/netguide.eff

URL ftp://ftp.lib.ncsu.edu/pub/stacks/guides/big-dummy/bdg_toc.html

COMPUSERVE *go* inetforum→Libraries→ *Search by file name:* ntgd31.zip

The Internet Connection "Can I play MUDs through AOL?" "Can anyone help me find a mailing list for people who have an interest in Shakespeare?" "Hi all—I'm trying to find a program called MacPing. Any help would be greatly appreciated." Questions from AOLers about a wide range of topics flood the Internet Message Board. And while fellow AOLers share a fair amount of informaiton about the Internet with each other, AOL itself has spent extra effort to arm its members with information. Next to the newsgroup reader, for instance, are instructions and guidelines for reading and posting to newsgroups. AOL has also tried to make the Internet more user friendly with searchable databases of mailing lists, FTP sites, and gophers. Currently, AOLers can telnet, FTP, send email, read newsgroups, use gopher and WAIS clients, and, with a special AOL browser, access the Web.

AMERICA ONLINE *keyword* internet

Internet Services From within CompuServe, members can telnet, FTP, and read newsgroups. The main Internet menu also links to a trio of active Internet forums where netters discuss all facets of the Internet. In the New Users Forum (*go* inetforum) novices are introduced to Internet Web browsers, email, telnet programs, IRC channels, FTP, and CompuServe via PPP connections. They can ask questions on the boards or turn to the libraries to download Internet

guides, tutorials, and software. More experienced surfers should head straight to the Internet Resources Forum (*go* inetresource) for more technical discussions of Internet software and navigational tools. The strength of the Resources Forum lies with its libraries which are packed with FAQs on Net topics such as TCP/IP, firewalls, and cryptography as well as lists of mailing lists, Web browsers and HTML editors, telnet and gopher clients, and much more. The third forum, the Internet Publishing Forum (*go* inetpub), is exclusively for CompuServe members interested in Web design and creating home pages.

COMPUSERVE *go* internet

Netsurfer Tools A hypertext guide to new Net tools and software. Each listing in the guide includes a product description and a URL linking to a Web site for the product.

WEB http://www.netsurf.com/nst

EMAIL nstools-request@netsurf.com ✍ *Type in message body:* subscribe nstools-html

The Online World A guide to the online world that's revised every two months. It covers the Internet extensively and also offers information about commercial services such as CompuServe and BBS networks like FidoNet. It offers both how-to explanations and Net site recommendations. Not tremendously well written.

WEB http://login.eunet.no/~presno/index.html

ThinkQuest Internet Contest Yearly competition for students in grades 7-12. Students must use the Internet as a collaborative, interactive teaching and learning tool. Prizes may total more than $1 million.

WEB http://www.advanced.org/ThinkQuest/index.html

Zen and the Art of the Internet This guide is often considered the granddaddy of all Internet manuals. Generations of Internet users started with this compact reference that covers topics ranging from Archie file searching to the Internet domain name system.

WEB http://www.cs.indiana.edu/doc project/zen/zen-1.0_toc.html

URL ftp://ftp.internic.net/pub/internet-doc /zen.txt

AMERICA ONLINE *keyword* internet→Zen & the Art of Internet

▶ HISTORY OF COMPUTING

Chronology of Events in the History of Microcomputers From the early years (1926-1970) of transistors, integrated circuits, and programmable memory, to the post-1994 era of company mergers, PowerMac clones, and Pentium competitors, the long and tumultuous history of computers is outlined for your leisurely perusal.

WEB http://www.islandnet.com/~kpolsson /comphist.htm

comp.lang.misc Discussion about and help with any computer language, from C+ to JAVA.

USENET comp.lang.misc

comp.os.ms-windows.programmer .misc A newsgroup for amateur Microsoft Windows programmers, with suggestions for books and other sources of information.

USENET comp.os.ms-windows .programmer.misc

Computers: From the Past to the Present You wouldn't ordinarily think of computing as a science with a history— things happen so fast that a new technology is likely to appear in the time it takes you to down your morning bowl of Cheerios. But this site proves that your thinking machine has a deep past, beginning with counting and shamanistic tradition; working through primitive calendars, abacuses, Pascal, Babbage, Hollerith, and Turing; and then moving on to ENIAC, EDVAC, and John von Neumann's famous Stored Program Concept. Microsoft bigshot Bill Gates even gets a chapter for his role in the birth of BASIC programming. And the beautiful color slides that illustrate the narrative

make learning a pleasure.

WEB http://calypso.cs.uregina.ca/Lecture

The History of Computing Links to a variety of materials that could prove highly useful to your research on the history of computing. The site also archives biographies of people who were or are somehow influential in developing "the machine that changed the world."

WEB http://ei.cs.vt.edu/~history

Past Notable Women of Computing Sure, you know who Bill Gates is, but do the names Alice Burks, Grace Hopper, or Margaret R. Fox ring a bell? Didn't think so. Enlighten yourself at this expansive Web site dedicated to the female pioneers of the computing field.

WEB http://www.cs.yale.edu/HTML/YALE /CS/HyPlans/tap/past-women.html

Smithsonian Computer History If you don't have time for a quick trip to Washington D.C., take the short-cut to the Smithsonian Institution's computer exhibit. A slide tour will take you through images and descriptions of the more than 900 original artifacts in the exhibit, which includes everything from Bell's original phones to the latest in high-definition TV. To make your multimedia visit more complete, sample some sound and video clips from the Oral History area. We've come a long way from the abacus.

WEB http://www.si.edu/perspect/comphist /computer.htm

▶ PROGRAMMING

Conlang List for discussing constructed (a.k.a artificial) languages.

EMAIL listserv@diku.dk ✍ *Type in message body:* subscribe conlang <your full name>

The Language List A searchable list of more than 2,300 published computer languages. Successful searches return brief explanations of the languages, reference works written about the languages, and online resources related to them.

WEB http://cuiwww.unige.ch/langlist

PC MagNet Programming Forum Oriented toward PC users, this forum is a rich resource for programmers and programming students. In the library, there are hypertext tutorials for C++, FAQs for BASIC, Pascal source code, tools for Visual Basic, and a wide range of other programming files.
COMPUSERVE *go* program

Programmer University Folks who hate computer labs might try these self-paced, introductory, intermediate or advanced online courses for those interested in learning C or Pascal programming. The courses consist of a weekly online conferences with the instructor and regular programming assignments.
AMERICA ONLINE *keyword* programmer university

WWW Virtual Library's Computer Programming Languages An A-Z hypertext index to programming resources online. The site includes links to an introduction to the ABC programming language, FAQs about Perl, LISP, Dylan, and other languages, source code for C++ programs, and other programming indexes.
WEB http://src.doc.ic.ac.uk/bySubject /Computing/Languages.htm

> **TERMINOLOGY**

The Free On-Line Dictionary of Computing With more than 300 contributors and thousands of entries, this is the most comprehensive computer dictionary available online. Just remember—comprehensive doesn't always mean convenient, and you may find yourself baffled at the fact that the dictionary includes separate entries for the singular and plural versions of terms, as well as the occasional misspelling. Still, there's no better place to look when you need to find out the proper usage of "nagware" (shareware that reminds you incessantly to register), "My Favorite Toy Language" (the hobbyhorse of an overzealous programmer), or "zigamorph" (Hex FF when used as a delimiter or fence character).

WEB http://wombat.doc.ic.ac.uk

Hacker's Dictionary Jargon File Located in Austria, this dictionary lets you speak like a hacker, which is sort of like speaking like a surfer, except that there's no surf. Example: "Hey, dude, be careful that your case and paste doesn't lead to software bloat." Another example: "That magic cookie is one hell of an opaque identifier… or should I say capability ticket." Study this dictionary for a few hours, and you'll never scream at your computer in the same way again.
WEB http://www.tu-graz.ac.at/Cjargon;sk =CA12161C

Webster's Dictionary of Computer Terms Need to learn more about abbreviated addressing? Confused about the history of Arpanet? Just jump right into *Webster's Dictionary of Computer Terms*, available in an easy-to-search format on America Online. From arrival rate to ascending order, from daisy-wheel printer to data diddling, Webster's offers clear and concise definitions of thousands of computer words, phrases, and acronyms. And those AOLers on the leading edge of technolinguistics can supplement the dictionary with the special Add-a-Definition function. The area includes a message board for sharing definitions of new and familiar computer terms with America Online members and other newbies.
AMERICA ONLINE *keyword* computerterms

k12.ed.comp.literacy "Science research is what the Internet was originally designed for. Aside from all of the science education Web sites that have cropped up, there are real scientists posting real data all over the Web. If you pick a topic and have your students research it on search engines, you'll be amazed at what they find and who they can talk to!" At this newsgroup, teachers encourage each other on the possibilities of using computers in the classroom and use it as a forum to trade ideas, articles, and lesson plans.
USENET k12.ed.comp.literacy

PART 5

Social Studies

GEOGRAPHY

YOUR FIFTH GRADE TEACHER ruined your love of geography by making you memorize the state capitals and the world's six longest rivers. Now the thought of trying to read a map (let alone fold it back up) makes you wheeze uncontrollably. Fortunately, the Internet helps make geography less of a burden. The Hall of Geography will get you started, and the GIS FAQ will answer everything you need to know. It's still important to know where you are and whether Canada is a state or a country, so take a trip to the GeoNet game, or CompuServe's Social Studies Help for some fun skill builders. Tour the world from the Arctic to the Antarctic Map-Quest or the Great Globe Gallery, then browse the world dreamily with online galleries like The Connected Traveler.

▶ STARTING POINTS

Geography Ready Reference The Internet Public Library has an enormous—but searchable—collection of geography links and provides a nice introduction to some of the geographic possibilities on the Web. The glossaries and FAQs are invaluable, and a section on atlases leads to places where mankind has definitely gone before.
WEB http://www.ipl.org/ref/RR/GEN /geography-rr.html

The GIS FAQ Before you start investigating the enormous number of cartography resources online, a little background about what makes it all possible will serve as an amiable tour guide. GIS stands for Geographic Information Systems, and as geography fields go, it is red hot. These Q&As range from the trite ("What is a 'GIS'?") to the techno ("Will GRASS run under LINUS OS on my PC?") The list of resources is long, and there are mailing lists and newsgroups, where you can dish about the places you'll go.
WEB http://www.census.gov/geo/www /faq-index.html

The Hall of Geography Not Arsenio Hall, not Hall's Mentholatum, but the Hall of Geography. The links at this worldwide Web site run the gamut from Cape Cod to Portugal, from Rwanda to Wilmington, and provide great midnight inspirations for that in-depth regional studies paper that your ridiculous teacher—where's he from?—says is due tomorrow.
WEB http://www.tenet.edu/academia /geog.html

The World Factbook 1995 Country profiles, compiled by the CIA, for every nation on the planet. The site includes geographical, political, economic, and social information about countries ranging from Afghanistan (its infant mortality rate for the year 1995 was 152.8 deaths per 1,000 live births) to Zimbabwe (its government is a parliamentary democracy). A map is linked to each profile, and the site also maintains information on weights and measures conversion, international organizations, the United Nations, and environmental agreements.
WEB http://www.odci.gov/cia/publications /95fact/index.html

▶ SKILL BUILDERS

Do You Know Your State Capitals? Well, do you? If you're like many Americans, you may not even know the states, never mind the seats of their governments. This game has a clunky interface and sometimes doesn't seem to work right, but the answers are offered—if you can face the shame.
WEB http://www.cyberdesic.com/~joe /capitals

Finding Your Way With Map and Compass For those who didn't join the Boy or Girl Scouts because the uniforms were too geeky, the U.S. Geological Survey gives you another shot at honing your navigation skills. This online pamphlet is actually quite readable, and the kind of thing that your mother would say

"may come in handy some day," especially if you need to find your way out of the mess in your room.
WEB http://info.er.usgs.gov/fact-sheets/finding-your-way/finding-your-way.html

GeoNet Game If you ignore the goofy premise of this geographical trivia game (something about the Grunddargh, a group of aliens that wants to take over Earth—a gimmick that wouldn't reel in a 5-year-old—then you may find a genuine challenge. As with the game of Tetris, you choose the difficulty level, so once you know all the answers you can move on to higher ground. The game encompasses several categories from physical to political geography.
WEB http://www.hmco.com/hmco/school/geo/indexhi.html

How Far Is It? Plug in two locations in the U.S. or the world and this site calculates the distance between them. How far is it from Springfield, Mass., to Manhattan, NY? 116 miles. Mountain View, Calif., to Palo Alto, Calif.? Well, 335 miles if you're heading to the Palo Alto in San Bernardino County, but only 5.04 miles if you're visiting the one in Santa Clara.
WEB http://www.indo.com/distance

Social Studies Help The library of Compuserve's Teen Forum contains stacks of downloadable maps and globes, but especially useful are the skill building games which help with memorization. Try filling in a world map without country names, and then see whether you need to increase your global awareness.
COMPUSERVE *go* stufoa→Browse Libraries →Social Studies Help

ZipZapMap! "Tokyo is tumbling!" enthuses Promark Software about its cutely named geography game. The challenge is to put the Tetris-like pieces of the world (capitals, major topographical features) in their places as they fall from the top of the screen. Download a demo version of the USA game, and get ordering information on the Canada and World versions.

WEB http://vanbc.wimsey.com/~promark/index.html

▶ ATLASES AND MAPS

Country Maps from W3 Servers in Europe This is very simple: Pick a country from the list, click on the country's icon, and go to a place where there's a map of the country. There may even be other goodies, such as the photos and info on the Bosnia Home Page.
WEB http://www.tue.nl/europe

The Great Globe Gallery They're not kidding. There are hundreds of views of the whole world here. Click on Projection (just one of a dozen choices) and receive a menu of available globes from Albers Equal Area Conic to Transverse Mercator. Too complicated? Then select The Most Popular View to receive the famous photo shot from the moon. This site is guaranteed to fill all your global needs.
WEB http://hum.amu.edu.pl/~zbzw/glob/glob1.htm

Magellan Basic Maps Put the world into perspective with this collection of maps showing 500 different regions worldwide. You need to read and accept a formidable license agreement before accessing the maps, but once that's done, you have the whole world at hand.
COMPUSERVE *go* magellan

The Map Room The parent company of the MapQuest site, GeoSystems Global, brings you this helpful site. More than just a collection of maps (although it has that too, with featured maps available from around the world), this is a place to sharpen your knowledge of cartography with MapSkills, or download the MapGame.
WEB http://www.geosys.com/cgi-bin/genobject/library/tig544b

MapQuest Whether you're planning a road trip, hunting for the perfect map to illustrate your term paper, or merely trying to figure out on what street that cutie in your art class lives, you will never want to leave this entertaining site. It

features an interactive atlas: Just type in your street address and watch your neighborhood pop up in full color. Then, back up to see the region, the state, or the world, with your house marked for posterity. Try TripQuest, which will provide driving instructions from place to place. Are we there yet?
WEB http://www.mapquest.com

Perry-Castenada Library Map Collection One of the largest map collections on the Net, with everything from the maps in national park brochures to satellite maps of the planet. The site offers an interesting style of organization—categories include Islands, Oceans, Poles, Maps of Current Interest: Bosnia, Zaire, Gaza, Chechnya, and Maps of U.S. City Halls and Monuments.
WEB http://www.lib.utexas.edu/Libs/PCL /Map_collection/Map_collection.html

TIGER Mapping Service & the US Gazetteer This incredible public resource will take the name of any town, county, city or river in the United States, determine its longitude/latitude, and generate a high-quality, detailed map of the queried location and its surrounding terrain. The maps are downloadable, but be prepared to wait—the graphics files are very large.
WEB http://tiger.census.gov

USA CityLink Project Detailed maps of America's cities and towns. Information about local municipal services (police stations, government offices) are noted on each.
WEB http://banzai.neosoft.com/citylink

Xerox PARC Map Viewer High-resolution world and continent maps available for downloading. They take time, but are some of the best you can get. This is the site that all other mapping sites quote and envy.
WEB http://mapweb.parc.xerox.com/map

▶ **PICTURES OF THE WORLD**

City.Net Combining tourism and cultural information on cities worldwide, City.Net is a mandatory stop for armchair travelers. You can explore the world by region or by site name (listed alphabetically). A jaunt to Paris rewards you with street and subway maps, an insider's guide to the city, subway navigators, and hotel and restaurant recommendations. For a less urban trek, visit the Grampian Highlands of Scotland through online pictures and narrative, including a visit to a twelfth-century cathedral and a trip down the Malt Whiskey Trail.
WEB http://www.city.net

Condé Nast Photo Gallery Another gorgeous place to see the world from the comfort of your desk chair. This gallery is part of *Condé Nast Traveler* online, and for budding geographers, it is the best part. Click on an area of the world like the Arctic or the South Pacific, and be rewarded with *CN Traveler's* brand of eye candy. If you like the picture (which tends to be a close-up shot of blue sky and happy native folks), click on the text beneath it for a map and detailed information about the region. Then, book your flight. (Ah, don't you wish?)
WEB http://travel.epicurious.com/traveler /photo_gallery/photo_gallery.html

The Connected Traveler A view of the bold and the beautiful in world photography is waiting at this magazine. Russell Johnson, who does with travel what J. Peterman does with clothes and Martha Stewart does with housework, narrates his journeys with lush and enviable photos. Other notables such as Arthur C. Clarke of sci-fi fame contribute (if you're wondering, he now lives in Sri Lanka pondering this and other worlds). One of the best things about the Connected Traveler is that while it does paint the world in pastel hues, it is packed with information about the respective countries. Of particular note is the online guide to the Mekong countries. A restful place to contemplate geography.
WEB http://www.well.com/user/wldtrvlr

Corbis Media Image Gallery This is a stock photo company which has placed a part of its large collection on AOL for perusal. There are dozens of categories of photos from which you can choose, but World Travel and Culture is the place to go for really pretty pictures of geographical landmarks, cities from Paris to Istanbul, peoples of the world, and just about any country. The downside is that you view only tiny thumbnails before committing to the downlaod, but this is a great place to go if you know what you want.

AMERICA ONLINE *keyword* Corbis

Images and Photographs for Geographers A small index of links contained in the much bigger Internet Resources for Geographers, this set of images is both specific (Photographs of Russia) and very general (Satellite Images). All are useful, especially GeoImages, a lovely collection of photos from everywhere in the world.

WEB http://www.utexas.edu/depts/grg /virtdept/resources/contents.html #images

▶ TEACHERS' LOUNGE

GEOGED A mailing list for geography educators, this is another great way to support, and be supported by your peers. It's international and geared to secondary and higher education.

EMAIL listserv@ukcc.uky.edu ✍ *Type in message body:* subscribe geoged <your full name>

Geography and GIS Resources A collection of links for teachers, maintained by a teacher, featuring very detailed descriptions of what you will find at each site. No time will be wasted by a cyberstop here. Covers everything from GIS to Earth Sciences and back.

WEB http://www.clark.net/pub/lschank /web/geo.html

Geography Teacher's Lounge Whether you have a great geography resource you'd like to share, or you need help for a class that starts next period, this is where your peers are hanging out. There are exams, lesson plans, maps, and lots of other things to download. You can

also post questions and answers on the forum's message board.

AMERICA ONLINE *keyword* teachers lounge→ geography

Geography/Economics Part of the comprehensive History/Social Studies Web site for K-12 Teachers, this page points to lesson plans and maps galore. If you look nowhere else for geography or economics, visit this page.

WEB http://www.execpc.com/~dboals /geog.html

FEDERAL GOVERNMENT

"POLITICS," AS THEY SING IN *Evita*, "is the art of the possible." Everything about our government is subject to revision, at least in theory. The Constitution was designed to accommodate changes, because flexibility, in the view of the so-called founding fathers, is the basis for stability. But a government so huge, with hundreds of agencies, doesn't seem prone to change. Of course, that was part of the design, too, to keep changes from happening too quickly. Pretty nifty, don't you think? On the Internet, you can visit the Constitution yourself, Find Out How Congress Voted, have tea at The White House Home Page, then decide if you're an elephant or a donkey at The World's Smallest Political Quiz. After you've taken sides, join the Republican or Democratic Forum, where everything's political in this world. If you don't fit in there, try the Libertarian Web, where they're looking for a few good freedoms. Just don't end up on Teen Court TV.

▶ THE CONSTITUTION

Foreword and Notes to the Constitution Written by Jack Brooks, chairman of the House Judiciary Committee, this helpful introduction provides a little bit of history and contextual background for America's most vital government document.
WEB http://www.house.gov/Constitution /Foreword.html

Left Justified Homepage Here's a source for even more complete versions of the Constitution and related documents. LeftJustified Publiks is a shareware company devoted to constitutional education. Its downloadable (for Windows only) interactive book versions of the Constitution, the *Federalist Papers*, and other documents, are excellent ways to gain a greater understanding of how our political system has evolved.
WEB http://www.leftjustified.com/leftjust /leftjust.htm

The U.S. Constitution Dozens of people and organizations have thought our fundamental document important enough to place on the Web. The wording of the Constitution itself is full of enigmas, subject to continual interpretation, which is exactly how the founding fathers wanted it. Links to hypertext show exactly where the original was amended. All sites include the Bill of Rights and Amendments, too.
WEB http://www.law.cornell.edu /constitution/constitution.overview.html • http://Constitution.by.net/Constitution .html • http://www.house.gov/Constitution /Constitution.html

▶ LEGISLATIVE BRANCH

CapWeb A gold mine of basic information on Congress, including the whos, whats, and hows of current legislation. Many people don't even know who their representatives are—find out here with a quick ZIP code search. Need an email address so you can make your voice heard? You'll find links to many Congress members' home pages and their snail mail addresses, plus gazillions of links to and facts about government agencies. It's all brought to the American people courtesy of some congressional staff members who stay up very late at night to keep CapWeb both updated and refreshingly unofficial.
WEB http://policy.net/capweb/congress .html

Electronic Activist Check out the FAQ for guidelines for writing letters to congresspeople. Electronic Activist is also an excellent source for email addresses of congress members, state government officials, and local media.
WEB http://www.berkshire.net/~ifas /activist

Find Out How Congress Voted Type in your ZIP code and quicker than you can say "Bob Packwood," this site, hosted by *Congressional Quarterly*, generates a

list of votes by your area's representatives, keyed to hyperlinked bill numbers. If you want more information about the bill, clicking on the number will transport you to the corresponding article written by CQ. You can see how members of Congress voted on any bill, ranging from the Balanced-Budget Amendment to a farm bill on sugar. It's an easy way to hold your officials accountable, or to simply find out what Congress does all day long.
WEB http://www.timeinc.com/cgi-bin/congress-votes

House of Representatives A mother lode of information about the lower house, including facts on the legislative process, schedules for legislators, a member directory, committee profiles, legislative data, and even tourist information for those visiting Capitol Hill.
WEB http://www.house.gov

Legislative Information on the Internet A list of all available legislative information online, from full texts of bills to email addresses to C-SPAN.
WEB http://thomas.loc.gov

Library of Congress The Library of Congress isn't just a gigantic collection of books; it's also a legislative agency, entrusted with maintaining the documents that bear the nation's laws. Find out all about the library—its holdings, its exhibits, and even its electronic card catalog, which is a lot more complicated than the Dewey Decimal system.
WEB http://www.loc.gov

List of Congressional Email Addresses Various lists of email addresses for members of the 104th Congress.
WEB http://www.webcom.com/~leavitt/cong.html • http://www.geocities.com/CapitolHill/1007 • http://www.zoom.com/personal/biohzrd/USC_addr.html

The United States Senate The official Senate Web site contains well-organized guides to all sorts of historical and current legislative information. The tour begins with a senatorial directory, and

covers the usual topics such as committees and the legislative process. Visitors can also view a virtual art gallery from the Capitol Building's art collection or investigate a bibliography of Senate-related publications.
WEB http://www.senate.gov

> **EXECUTIVE BRANCH**

Federal Government Agencies Divided into executive, legislative, judicial, independent, and "quasi-official," this list of federal agencies collects links to more than 200 government sites.
WEB http://www.lib.lsu.edu/gov/fedgov.html

Federal Web Locator Billed as "one-stop shopping for the Federal Government," this site collects links for virtually every branch and agency, from the CIA (Central Intelligence Agency) to the FAA (Federal Aviation Administration) to the SEC (Securities and Exchange Commission). Agencies are listed in an easy-to-read short list, as well as a long-form outline.
WEB http://www.law.vill.edu/Fed-Agency/fedwebloc.html

FedWorld FedWorld serves as a searchable gateway to hundreds of U.S. Government bulletin boards and Web sites. Visit the Food and Drug Administration. Enjoy the friendly confines of the Small Business Administration. Drop by the Consumer Product Safety Commission. Let your government know that you exist.
WEB http://www.fedworld.gov

Government Agency Web Servers An alphabetical and linked list of government agencies online.
WEB http://www.seattleu.edu/~enricod/dwugovt.htm

President Devoted to online collection and display of material from presidential libraries, President also includes an exhibit on the First Ladies of the United States and a comprehensive list of additional sites that focus on the presidency.

WEB http://sunsite.unc.edu/lia/president

Texas A&M's White House Archives

One of the true benefits of electronic democracy, this site collects a wealth of information on the White House and the presidency, ranging from transcripts of informal remarks made by the Chief Executive during photo ops to detailed accounts of progress in health care lobbying to lists of awards and ceremonies held on the White House lawn. The archives can be searched and date back to 1992.
WEB http://www.tamu.edu/whitehouse

The White House Our president's online home has been completely updated for 1996 and now, like Clinton himself, seems a bit more grown-up. No longer does poor Socks Clinton have his own home page (although a cartoon version of the First Kitty does host the tour of the new White House for Kids.) Chelsea, too, despite her recent successful public appearances, is almost nowhere to be found. But there are recorded greetings from the president, vice president (that's Bill and Al to you), Hillary, and Tipper, plus candy-coated biographies of all four; a tour of the grounds; a history of the building; and even an Interactive Citizen's Guide to the federal government. A visit here is a lot less crowded than Pennsylvania Avenue.
WEB http://www2.whitehouse.gov/WH /Welcome-nt.html

▶ JUDICIAL BRANCH

Criminal Justice A forbidding picture of the Rock (Alcatraz) greets you at this Bay Area Web site, which offers an impressive collection of links to criminal-justice sites across the Web.
WEB http://www.stpt.usf.edu/~greek /cj.html

Federal Court Locator A home page for all federal courts, including the Supreme Court, the Third, Fifth, and Eleventh Circuit appellate courts, and links to related executive agencies, such as the Department of Justice.

WEB http://www.law.vill.edu/Fed-Ct /fedcourt.html

Federal Courts A tutorial on the operation of the federal court system, selected articles from *The Third Branch* (the newsletter of the Federal Courts), and a link to the Directory of Electronic Public Access, which permits citizens to retrieve federal court information.
WEB http://www.uscourts.gov

The National Center for State Courts

Founded in 1971 at the urging of Chief Justice Warren Burger, this organization seeks to strengthen communication among state courts in the hope of improving the efficiency and accuracy of justice nationwide. This page includes a mission statement, a history of the NCSC, and links to descriptions of most of the center's programs.
WEB http://www.ncsc.dni.us/about.htm

Supreme Court Decisions Few historic decisions of the Court are in the principal archives of the Legal Information Institute—justice has been on patrol since the 18th century, and this Cornell database didn't begin until 1990. However, the organization has also collected a few of the prominent pre-1990 decisions, including *Roe v. Wade* (reproductive rights) and *Engel v. Vitale* (school prayer).
WEB http://www.law.cornell.edu/supct

Supreme Court Justices A group picture of the justices, underexposed—much like the Court itself (Clarence Thomas excepted).
WEB http://www.law.cornell.edu/supct /justices/fullcourt.html

U.S. Supreme Court A database of cases argued before the Supreme Court, arranged by year. Files are available in a number of formats.
URL ftp://ftp.cwru.edu/U.S.Supreme.Court

▶ POLITICAL PARTIES

alt.philosophy.objectivism While objectivism has existed in some form since the mid-19th century, most adherents to this political philosophy trace the term to the influential 20th-century novelist Ayn Rand. But even if you don't have your dog-eared copies of *Atlas Shrugged* and *The Fountainhead* on hand, there's plenty to occupy you, including specific applications of objectivist thought to social matters such as health care, redistribution of wealth, and the rendering of legal opinion.

USENET alt.philosophy.objectivism

alt.politics.usa.republican Republicans convene in this newsgroup to debate the pros and cons of candidates, to comment on Republican policy initiative, and to sound off on topics ranging from morality to foreign policy. A typical day in the newsgroup might include discussions on subjects like "Bubba's speech on affirmative action," "Libertarians should join the Republican Party," and "Abortion IS murder." You'll find some off-topic posts, along with quite a few intended to get the extremists riled ("Republicans Stick It to the Constitution"), but generally the discussion is vigorous and varied, with opinions spanning the political spectrum.

USENET alt.politics.usa.republican

AOL Politics With links to the *Congressional Quarterly*, the ACLU, and the NRA, this large nonpartisan site contains a ton of information for the politically aware. Track the 1996 Presidential Campaign. Read about the Heritage Foundation. Email the President. Drop by the message boards to weigh in on everything from health care to crime, or visit the libraries and download a transcript of Congress' balanced-budget debate.

AMERICA ONLINE *keyword* politics

Conservative Corner A collection of files described as "non-mainstream conservative" and gleaned from the Birch Bark BBS. Many of the files come from conservative organizations, such as Accuracy in Media, the Future of Freedom Foundation, and the Lincoln Heritage Institute. Topics include the Vincent Foster case, government regulation, and the

failure of socialism.

WEB http://www.execpc.com/~jfish

Democratic Party Online The Democratic National Committee's site serves as an excellent spot if you're looking for information about the Democratic Party, whether on the national, state, or county level. The What's Hot section includes press releases and talking points from the DNC, while Connecting with America offers audio clips from the President and the DNC's chairman. Sensibly arranged, with lots of info.

WEB http://www.democrats.org

Democratic Party Platform "We call for a revolution in government—to take power away from entrenched bureaucracies and narrow interests in Washington and put it back in the hands of ordinary people." Yep, straight from the Democratic Party, the entire platform is available in hypertext format.

WEB http://www.global1.net/democrats /party/platform.html

Digital Democrats With sections for Democratic Party clubs, state and county party organizations, and government officials of all types, Digital Democrats makes it easy to find info about the party, its leaders, and politics in general. Lots of links, whether you're looking for college Democrat clubs or members of Congress.

WEB http://www.digitals.org/digitals

GOP-L GOP-L proclaims itself dedicated to discussion of all things Republican and Conservative. (Hint: the capital letters rule out less formal signs of conservatism, such as a love for Ayn Rand and wing tips.) This list is as divided as the party, with old-fashioned anti-government conservatives grumbling at the Christian Right, and the Christian Right grumbling at the Limbaugh brigades. As a result, while there is a fair amount of liberal bashing, feminist fearing, and grab-a-gun rightspeak, there is also real debate. What is one to think when a card-carrying ACLU member sides with a conservative against "lifestyle regula-

tion" while a third party insists on society's right to "legislate morals"?
EMAIL listserv@pccvm.bitnet ✍ *Type in message body:* subscribe gop-l <your full name>

Liberal Information Page The motto says it all: "When you know heading right is a dead end… turn left." Billed as "the home of liberalism on the Web," the Liberal Information Page offers sections on liberalism basics, social issues, government and politics, foreign policy issues, President Clinton, and civil liberties. Especially interesting is a section on Fighting Conservatism, with advice on debunking the Reagan myth, refuting "the Fat Man's lies" ("Anti-Rush Limbaugh stuff"), and "taking on and beating the radical religious right." Certainly one of the best sites for those interested in the left end of the political spectrum.
WEB http://www.cjnetworks.com /~cubsfan/liberal.html

Liberalism Described as a "quasi-FAQ," this site presents readers with the basic tenets of liberalism. Admittedly oversimplified in its answers, the document responds to such questions as "How do liberals differ from 'socialists' and 'communists'?" and "What is the liberal position on gun control?" Highly readable and well organized.
WEB http://www.cs.ncl.ac.uk/people/chris .holt/home.informal/lounge/politics /liberalism.html

Libertarian Web A well-ordered selection of libertarian resources includes the Libertarian Party program, an article titled "Understanding the Libertarian Philosophy," and a variety of leaflets and press releases. The site provides links to Web pages for a diverse selection of political groups, nonpartisan organizations, student clubs, and publications.
WEB http://w3.ag.uiuc.edu:8001/Liberty /libweb.html

The Republican National Committee "Welcome to Republican Main Street!" exclaims this cheerful site, with graphics depicting an "all-American" small town.

Visitors will find email addresses and links to relevant sites at the Post Office, coffee and conservative chat in the Cafe, and of course that treasure trove of elephant pens, mugs, and baseball caps at the Gift Shop. Download video and sound clips at the GOP-TV station, or visit the biggest building in town: naturally, the Rebublican Headquarters.
WEB http://www.rnc.org

The Right Side of the Web You know you've arrived at "the right side" when you think the far right isn't far enough for saying that all liberals are "greedy, sloth-like, and lying." The site includes an astonishing amount of info, links, and interactive features. Highlights include a Question of the Week, solicitations for ideas on casting "Whitewater: the Mini-Series," and the Right Side Message Wall, where you'll see items like the following "scrawled" on the screen of your Web browser: "These liberals are at it again. Now they want African-American English to be taught in our schools. I guess we need to teach color coding for gang recognition. What the hell is African-American English?"
WEB http://www.clark.net/pub/jeffd/index .html

talk.politics.libertarian If you're interested in talk of free markets, government regulation, and taxes, here's your discussion. Lurk for a while, getting a feel for the tenor of the group's lengthy, argumentative discussions on topics such as "The Liberal Lapdog Press" and "The First Amendment, the Flag, and Matches." Wildly active and flame-friendly.
USENET talk.politics.libertarian

World's Smallest Political Quiz Finally, a way to gauge your political leanings in five minutes or less! Just agree with five statements about personal issues, e.g. "Military service should be voluntary," and five on economic issues, e.g. "End taxes. Pay for services with user fees." (Note to wafflers: you can also answer "Maybe.") Submit the answers, and find out where you would stand if you happened to be a little red dot on a political map. Of those who've weighed in so far, 26.6 percent have been Centrist—how about you?

WEB http://www.self-gov.org/quiz.html

The Yankee Citizen Joe DiMaggio was the Yankee Clipper. Mark Twain wrote *A Connecticut Yankee in King Arthur's Court*. And the Yankee Citizen is a no-nonsense Web guide to American politics, with links for information on both major parties and a variety of guides to American government. Other categories include the 1996 elections, U.S. government agencies, and the executive, legislative, and judicial branches.

WEB http://www.tiac.net/users/macgyver/pols.html

▶ THE ELECTION PROCESS

alt.politics.clinton Like them or hate them, the first baby-boomer president and his wife have forever altered the face of American politics. For the first time ever, we have had a president not shaped primarily by the Good War, a powerful, active first lady, and a White House redecorated with the conflicts of late 20th-century America—antiwar activism, drug use, and shady financial and sexual dealings. On alt.politics.clinton, the FOBs (Friends of Bill) and SEOBs (Sworn Enemies of Bill) dig in and fire off, and the close quarters generate the kind of unyoked rhetoric that spices up the best political newsgroups. Those posting are mostly young adults, and the tone of messages ranges from juicy ("I have great respect for the Office of the President of the U.S., which is why I have no respect for the lying, incompetent excuse for a President who currently occupies that office") to clever ("This Halloween, Clinton is planning to wear a really outrageous costume—he's going as a two-term President") to flat-out cruel (Robert Reich is described as "a troll" and "a Marxist midget"). All in all, a crash course in how Bill became a target.

USENET alt.politics.clinton

alt.politics.elections It's the great American ritual, the behavior that repeatedly affirms and shapes our national identity. It's election time. Newsgroup members seem to enjoy examining the election process and the theory of representation almost as much as they enjoy speculating on current races. There's something elegant about purely theoretical arguments for proportional representation or term limits, and the intellectual marrow of the matter inspires some truly innovative proposals—one man suggests that officeholders be reimbursed for their service based on approval ratings. The newsgroup's strongest asset is its ability to collect the opinions of election watchers, who are almost like sports fans in their devotion to unbridled rhetoric and their belief in themselves as armchair Nostradamuses.

USENET alt.politics.elections

Clinton Yes! Despite his recent upswing, Bill Clinton has received a tremendous amount of flak during his presidency. He's been called everything from a philanderer to a killer, but this page has always championed Baby-Boomer Bill, pointing to an administration that has made tremendous strides in social policy, environmental policy, and crime prevention, and done it despite a Republican Congress. Decorated with news stories about the Clintons, this page links to a wide range of political resources online, from an archive of pro-Clinton jokes called the "Clickable Despicables," to an account of Hillary Rodham Clinton's spiritual beliefs.

WEB http://www.av.qnet.com/~yes

CyberCaucus Since the early seventies, the Iowa Caucus has been one of the most important parts of the presidential nomination process. This site includes a history of the caucus from 1846 to the present, a list of past election outcomes, and an explanation of the caucus process.

WEB http://www.drake.edu/public/caucus.html

CIVICS & CURRENT AFFAIRS

PRIVILEGES AND OBLIGATIONS. That's what civics is about. U.S. citizens have many privileges, we just happen to call them rights: the right to free speech; the right to free assembly; the right to bear arms; the right to life, liberty, and the pursuit of happiness. But these rights aren't always clearly defined. What if the right to free expression takes the form of flag burning? Who defines when life begins? What if your idea of liberty and happiness conflicts with someone else's? Cyberspace is a new home to old debates at newsgroups like talk.abortion and soc.human.rights. The Electronic Frontier Foundation has emerged as the leading advocate for speech in new media. Young, civic-minded netizens can plug their causes online, too, and reach millions. Get fired up at alt.activism.d, channel your energy with The Green Party, or simply Rock the Vote. It's the electronic equivalent of waving a sign or marching on a government building. Consider it your obligation.

unpremeditated killing? What does the Ehrlich study say about deterrence? Who is being executed soon? Dominated by foes of capital punishment, this newsgroup sometimes veers into tangential topics and is not as active as it once was, a much-lamented topic among its devotees.
USENET alt.activism.death-penalty

Teledemocracy Action News Network A voice for the Global Democracy Movement, "dedicated to the creative use of electronic media in all forms to directly empower citizens to have meaningful input into the political system," TANN is a Web zine with insightful articles and news on research projects. For example, an apparently successful experimental mailing in Oregon allowed folks to vote by mail for Bob Packwood's replacement. This Web site has more great ideas for the politically conscious who loathe leaving home, but still want to make a contribution to society.
WEB http://www.duc.auburn.edu/~tann

ACTIVISM

alt.activism.d A gathering place for activists of all stripes, there are plenty of discussions that seem to be parties of one. In addition to these lone voices, there are plenty of topics that blossom into interesting discussions such as a long and compelling explanation of the ins and outs of Vietnam draft dodging, or the debate over a daunting report, complete with "actual statistics," that claims that capitalism does not benefit the American worker ("The U.S. is becoming a polarized society—the rich are getting richer; the workers are getting less and less of what they produce.")
USENET alt.activism.d

alt.activism.death-penalty When is homicide justifiable? How do other nations treat their criminals? When does the statute of limitations expire on an

CIVIL RIGHTS

alt.discrimination Along with the usual common sense exposure of injustice ("Mistreatment is wrong"), there's a tremendous amount of new idiocy—complaints by male victims of affirmative action, a revisionist complaint that "*Schindler's List* falsifies history!", and a posting that tries to give new teeth to the old saw that girls can't do math. In other words, this site may not be the best forum for Anita Hill discussions.
USENET alt.discrimination

alt.society.civil-liberties Much of this newsgroup revolves around civil liberties in cyberspace, particularly the on-again, off-again Communications Decency Act. Occasionally, though, Usenet's civil libertarians look beyond the scope of their monitor and mouse to address three-dimensional issues, such as America's celebrated political prisoner (and jour-

nalist), Mumia Abu-Jamal.
USENET alt.society.civil-liberties

American Civil Liberties Union This forum sits uncomfortably between the ACLU's free-speech-at-any-cost ideology and America Online's reputation for regulating the content of its online partners. Visit Constitution Hall, the headquarters of online civil liberties chat, to discuss topics such as whether militias should be declared illegal and whether the government has any right to sweep the homeless off the streets.
AMERICA ONLINE *keyword* aclu

Birmingham Civil Rights Institute A promotional page for the CRI, which is devoted to recording the African-American struggle for social and political equality.
WEB http://www.the-matrix.com/bcri/bcri.html

Civil Liberties and Human Rights Links to national and international resources for the preservation of civil liberties.
WEB http://www.ping.be/~ping0044/civlib.html

▶ CURRENT AFFAIRS

Hotspot: USA Are our cities hurtling toward civil war? Should Cuban immigrants in the post–Cold War era be granted the status of political refugees? And what is the government doing for the American farmer? On CompuServe's Hotspot: USA message board, Americans of all races, creeds, colors, classes, ages, and regions sound off about the issues that stick in their craw. Whether it's a young woman writing to complain about the blocking of RU-486 ("Reproductive freedom is not and will never be a threat to good government, and it is owed unconditionally to the women of any intelligent nation"), or a middle-aged man criticizing government disease-control policy ("FDA inaction is increasing the spread of antibiotic-resistant bacteria"), the bulletin board accommodates a wide spectrum of political views. The true hot spots, however, seem to be

health care and abortion rights; one man even goes so far as to suggest that abortion-clinic bombings are not the work of anti-abortion activists but rather arson scams, or pranks—"'Innocent until proven guilty' is supposed to be the doctrine followed, but it doesn't seem to apply for right-wing Christians." Never a dull moment.
COMPUSERVE *go* crisis→Messages→Hotspot: USA

NewsLink One-stop shopping for news junkies. This site has links to more than 3,000 online newspapers, magazines, news services, and radio and TV stations. All are searchable and well-indexed, so you'll never get stuck without enough information for an informed debate.
WEB http://www.newslink.org

Talk of the Nation Simulchat The afternoon chat in the Talk of the Nation Forum's Control Room starts off with the same topic as that day's radio program (Should you own a gun at home? Should the U.S. government invade?), but the 45 participants online are soon barreling along on their own separate track. You don't really need to be listening to the radio to participate in this open marriage of online and on-air. Only when the radio show takes a break for a news update and returns with a new topic does the online chat downshift for the switch to the second hour's subject.
AMERICA ONLINE *keyword* npr→Talk of the Nation→The Control Room

▶ ENVIRONMENTAL

Environmental Forum The forum divides environmental issues into national and global topics. The former helps explain what ordinary citizens like Donna ("I try to recycle but sometimes my neighborhood doesn't help me with regular pickups") and Saul ("Are there any environmental harms to email?") can do to improve their environment. As for the latter, the Global Action and Information Network uses this forum as a base, publishing regular news releases and updates on environmental break-throughs, and encouraging all kinds of green activism. Live conferencing takes place in the Environmental Chat room. **AMERICA ONLINE** *keyword* eforum

talk.environment "I want to be green / recycle my mail / I'm hoping to be / a friend to the whale." It's just a song, of course, but it accurately summarizes the dominant sentiment on this newsgroup, which speculates on both the small (recycling your newspapers) and the large (nuclear power) things that we can do to clarify our responsibility to the earth. Subscribers are the usual sus-pects—younger activists who worry that the world will not bear their weight, as well as older activists who want to pro-vide for the future. Online conferences are ecologically airtight (except for the electricity use, the radiation from your monitor, and all the electromagnetic fields generated by the get-together). **USENET** talk.environment

GRASSROOTS POLITICS

Green Party USA With official policy on every topic from Economics to Indige-nous People, the Green Party often doesn't seem as decidedly green as its name implies, although the environmen-tal perspective has influenced the party's activity since 1984. It now claims alle-giance by more than 50 elected officials, but it has become less "grassroots" with every election. However, you'll still find the party at work in your neighborhood, and this site will tell you where. The site also links to similar environmental orga-nizations, and even other independent parties. **WEB** http://www.greens.org/usa

The New Party If you're "fed up with politics as usual" and are extraordinarily progressive (i.e., liberal), this may be the party for you. It's a new one (hence the name) and if you haven't heard of it, per-haps it's because it focuses on local elections. The New Party believes in sup-porting a viable candidate rather than fractionalizing the vote, so don't be sur-

prised when it promotes the Democrats, at least the "non-reactionary" ones. Its Web site is mostly a platform for its plat-form, which is full of high-minded ideal-ism. Definitely worth a look. **WEB** http://www.newparty.org

HUMAN RIGHTS

Human Rights Organizations The site serves as a clearinghouse for informa-tion from a variety of non-governmental organizations involved in human rights issues, including Physicians for Human Rights, the Committee to Protect Jour-nalists, and Human Rights in China. The materials from these groups include action alerts, newsletters, press releases, and other documents. **URL** gopher://gopher.humanrights.org :5000

Human Rights Web The site opens with a quote from poet W.H. Auden ("Acts of injustice done/ between the setting and the rising sun / In history lie like bones / each one"), setting the tone for the resources gathered. The materials include biographies of prisoners of con-science, a short history of the human rights movement, and a variety of docu-ments related to legal and political issues, debates, and discussions. The Human Rights Resource Page provides a great set of links and info. **WEB** http://www.traveller.com/~hrweb /hrweb.html

soc.rights.human The group discusses human-rights abuse throughout the world, and the topics range far and wide as the threads progress. A debate about Mumia Abu-Jamal may segue into a let-ter from a prisoner in Cuba. Debate is intelligent and only slightly impolite. **USENET** soc.rights.human

ISSUES DU JOUR

Abortion and Reproduction Rights Internet Resources Links to resources on both sides of the abortion debate, including the *ChoiceNet Report* and *The ProLife News*. You can also re-read the

pronouncements of the Supreme Court in *Roe v. Wade*, and of the Pope in *Humanae Vitae*.
WEB http://www.caral.org/abortion.html

Abortion Rights Web A collection of articles, Supreme Court decisions, and newsgroup postings related to abortion. The site takes a pro-choice stance.
WEB http://worcester.lm.com/women /resources/abortion.html

Health Care Postings in this forum cover a fairly narrow spectrum of issues: What do Americans want? Is universal coverage socialist? What can government afford? But in navigating the Sargasso Sea of risks and rewards, participants sometimes sound like amateur debaters, engaging in mental calisthenics that transcend common sense: "Should we outlaw cigarettes? Then why not beer? Then why not anything with cholesterol? Where does it stop?" Not here, apparently.
COMPUSERVE *go* politics→Messages →Health Care

Homeless Home Page The cruel (and apparently unintentional) irony of the title notwithstanding, this is an excellent collection of resources about homelessness, with statistics, fund raising ideas, and articles and reports such as "The Criminalization of Poverty" and "Non-Recreational Campers: Homeless People Who Use Public Lands." If you're interested in discussions of homelessness, check out the information and archives of the "homeless" mailing list. The site also includes a varied set of links to information about homelessness elsewhere on the Net.
WEB http://csf.colorado.edu/homeless /index.html

Lifelinks The right-to-life movement is online making its case against abortion. The site links to the *Feminists for Life* publication ("Abortion does not Liberate Women") and statements from public personalities such as *Village Voice* writer Nat Hentoff on third-trimester abortions, and Mother Teresa on abortion and peace. Statistics linked to this site suggest a relationship between legalized abortion with welfare mothers, juvenile violent crime, teen pregnancy, and child abuse.
WEB http://www.nebula.net/~maeve /lifelink.html

Overview of 54 Ways You Can Help the Homeless Written by Rabbi Charles A. Kroloff, this list aims to answer the question, "What can I do to help the homeless?" It provides practical tips on volunteering, giving to the homeless, and getting others involved in the cause. The specific suggestions include volunteering at a soup kitchen, playing with children in a shelter, and joining Habitat for Humanity.
WEB http://ecosys.drdr.virginia.edu /ways/54.html

Roe v. Wade, 410 U.S. 113 (1973) "A pregnant single woman (Roe) brought a class action challenging the constitutionality of the Texas criminal abortion laws…" So begins the most controversial Supreme Court ruling of our lifetime. Refresh your memory with the complete hypertext of the ruling opinion and dissensions.
WEB http://www.law.cornell.edu/supct /classics/410us113.ovr.html

talk.abortion "We've been subjected to 21 years of being told that a woman has a right to do with her body as she wishes," writes one exasperated man. "Can you present any compelling reasons why she should not be allowed to control her own body?" queries an equally annoyed man. Count on it. The abortion debate is not pretty, and some of it is quite volatile and—at times—humorous. Why shouldn't a woman be allowed control of her body, for instance? Well, you know, "in the U.S. no one controls his/her own body totally. You can be called to jury duty."
USENET talk.abortion

Terrorist Profile Weekly Described as "an electronic newsletter dedicated to the spread of information about war's

younger sibling, terrorism," this page maintains a list of terorrist groups worldwide—Abu Nidal to Nestor Paz Zamora Commission—and links to a brief FAQ about the publication (Stupidest question: "Can I get in touch with a terrorist group through you?").
WEB http://www.site.gmu.edu/~cdibona

▶ RIGHT TO BEAR ARMS

Citizens Committee for the Right to Keep and Bear Arms Keep on top of legislation and other issues affecting the civil rights of firearms owners by subscribing to this mailing list that receives action notices from the NRA, GOA, Neal Knox, and other activist groups. The archives include articles from *Gun Week* and civil rights activists, back issues of the *Gottlieb-Tartaro Report*, and a Congressional address book.
EMAIL listproc@saf.org ✍ *Type in message body:* subscribe rkba-alert <your full name>

▶ RIGHT TO FREE SPEECH

alt.censorship Discussion in this newsgroup is about censorship in all its manifestations. Should tabloid media be restrained? Should newspapers be prohibited from printing the names of rape victims? What about employers who monitor personal email on company systems? Or race hate spread by computer mail? One of the most compelling issues discussed here is the role of moderators. As one participant wrote, "If I believe my message is such that it merits placement in front of every Usenet reader, why should someone else's opinion that my belief is wrong take precedence?"
USENET alt.censorship

Electronic Frontier Foundation "Free Speech Online!" proclaims that ubiquitous blue ribbon. In addition to an extensive archive of material on First Amendment rights in the electronic age, the page links to EFF's Action Alert page, which serves as a sort of hotline to the ACLU of cyberspace. What is electronic crime? How can it be punished? Who

enforces? Who suffers? Find resources, if not exactly answers.
WEB http://www.eff.org

Electronic Frontier Foundation Forum The "digital revolution" is transforming our lives, traditions, and institutions. We may need an entirely new way of thinking regarding law, medicine, advertising, even personal identity. That's precisely the ambitious mission of the Electronic Frontier Foundation—not only to catalog these new concepts but to exert some critical control over them. This forum functions as an EFF storefront. For instance, after one woman complained that a new policy at her husband's company violated his electronic privacy— "The company may audit, access, and, if necessary, disclose any transaction such as phone usage, voice mail, and email messages, using corporate resources"— forum members responded, explaining that the company has not only the right but the obligation to manage its electronic resources.
COMPUSERVE *go* effsig

Sex, Censorship, and the Internet Huge site with a large number of case studies and countless links related to sex and censorship on the Internet. "Should the university carry the newsgroup alt.sex? Should students be punished for using vulgarities on the Net? Should Free-Nets such as PrairieNet label material as 'not suitable for children'?" The site tries to answer these and similar questions by looking to the experience of public libraries, student newspapers, and the computer facilities at several universities.
WEB http://www.eff.org/CAF/cafuiuc.html

Virtual Flag-Burning Page One of the best illustrations of symbolic speech available in cyberspace, this page chronicles the history of flag burning and traces the fate of current anti-flag-burning legislation. But the political wallop of this site resides in the virtual flag-burning link, which loads an image of Old Glory and then torches it with the help of Web animation.

WEB http://www.indirect.com/user/warren/flag.html

RIGHT TO PRIVACY

comp.society.privacy Governments, businesses, even fellow citizens want information about you. The average American fills out 45 forms a year that are monitored by some 25 businesses and institutions. The bulk of that information ends up in computer data banks. Who has access to these databases? Could a hacker enter your records? Could your credit report fall into the wrong hands? These concerns and many more (Net users worry that other Netters can trace them; a man rigs his ex-wife's answering machine so that he receives copies of her messages) are discussed here. True, sometimes the stories leave you hungry for a how-to guide.
USENET comp.society.privacy

RIGHT TO VOTE

League of Conservation Voters Rather than chaining themselves to trees or torching power plants, members of the League of Conservation Voters promote environmental issues by taking themselves to the polls. At its home page, read the league's annual National Environmental Scorecard, which rates how Congress members vote on the issues. Accountability is key, and the Web site provides plenty of tools for you to hold your elected representatives to their environmental word.
WEB http://www.lcv.org

League of Women Voters This uniquely nonpartisan although predominantly liberal advocacy and education organization celebrated its 75th anniversary in 1995. The Web site contains an FAQ and outline of its national platform and links to other sites pertaining to voting and public policy, voter registration, and making your voice heard.
WEB http://www.lwv.org/~lwvus

MTV's Rock the Vote Who says MTV rots the brain? This site has a positively

parental mission: to promote freedoms, educate young people about relevant issues, and motivate them to get out the vote. All this and a pretty interface, too. Speak your mind—the government might still be listening.
WEB http://www.rockthevote.org

NetVote '96 Too busy browsing the Web on your 18th birthday to be bothered with such a milestone of maturity? Well, now there's no excuse for not registering to vote. Just fill out the form here for the state you live in and with one click the nice people at this site will do the rest. Sponsored by several voter advocacy groups, NetVote '96 takes voting one step closer to effortless. And yes, it's legal. Just remember to sign the card and return it when it comes to your mailbox. (The one that has paper in it, remember?)
WEB http://netvote96.mci.com/register.html

TEACHERS' LOUNGE

Civnet "Why Do We Need a Government?" "What Responsibilities Accompany our Rights?" "How Can Citizens Participate?" These are just a few of the civics themes ready for teachers to plug in to the classroom at this international gateway to civics education. But Civnet provides much more than just lesson plans. Teachers can access a range of educational resources, including a bibliography on the methodology and pedagogy of civics-teaching; links to recent writings and speeches on civic education and civic journalism; and a cyberlibrary of important historical documents on such topics as democracy, toleration, human rights, liberty, and justice. Teachers interested in improving their classroom skills can refer to a directory of organizations that promote civic education and a calendar of their events and conferences. Civnet even provides educators and researchers with the CivTalk mailing list, a global forum to discuss civics topics (registration at this site is required to receive subscription info).
WEB http://civnet.org

ECONOMICS

GOING TO THE MALL TO BUY CK One and Gap jeans is one way to study economics. After all, in our capitalistic culture, the consumer reigns supreme. But before you exercise your rights, don't forget to pay homage to the Net's many shrines to the almighty dollar. Bri's Economics Page will start the hurried on their way to market wizardry. The more sedentary spender might want to first consume a few pages of The Wealth of Nations, commit the Investment Glossary to memory, or join the Dead Economists Society. Wealthy wannabes can at least make a fake fortune with the E*Trade Stock Market Game and then tour The New York Stock Exchange. Still feel like buying into the system? Then go hit the stores, but don't forget your mom's VISA card on your way out. She'll probably be reading The Daily Digital, written by her best friends at the IRS.

▶ STARTING POINTS

Bri's Economics Page A high school social studies teacher in Pennsylvania put up this index page to help his economics students. Lucky them, but lucky for students who don't go to Westmont Hilltop High, too. The index is a concise and well-organized list of places economics buffs will want to visit, from PC Quote to the FDIC.
WEB http://westy.jtwn.k12.pa.us/~brm /briecon.html

Economic Democracy Information Network An invaluable source of "alternative" economics and business information, EDIN is devoted to delivering information that has an impact on economics and business, but doesn't often show up in the business pages. The Web site offers documents on human rights, education and training, political organization, labor organization, health care, race, and the environment.
WEB http://garnet.berkeley.edu :3333

Gophers Devoted to Economics Notifies list subscribers of new or changing economic and financial sites on the Internet.
EMAIL listserv@shsu.edu ✍ *Type in message body:* subscribe egopher <your full name>

Resources for Economists on the Internet An extensive collection of links to economic resources gathered by a Mississippi college professor. The emphasis is on academic research, but there's something for everyone, from online journals to newsgroups to economic societies.
WEB http://econwpa.wustl.edu/EconFAQ /EconFAQ.html

sci.econ Home to debates and discussions about the economy, particularly the political economy. Discussion can get heated, but the quality stays unusually high.
USENET sci.econ

▶ APPLIED ECONOMICS

A Citizen's Guide to the Federal Budget In the first three years of its existence, the U.S. Government spent only $4 million. We spend just a little—well, maybe a lot—more than that now, as this simple guide indicates. The information applies not only to our ever-so-large budget, but to econ in general. For a government pamphlet, it's a pretty good read.
URL gopher://sunny.stat-usa.gov:70/00 /BudgetFY96/bud96g.txt

Accounting Resources on the Internet You wouldn't think an "Accounting Web" could be so graphically interesting, but you know what they say about assumptions. Hosted by Rutgers University, the site is heavily academic but complete—if it's a link to anything accounting, it's here under such headings as Journals, Big Six, and Finance.
WEB http://www.rutgers.edu/Accounting /raw/internet/internet.htm

The Digital Daily: the IRS "Faster than a speeding 1040-EZ" comes this IRS infosite posing as an online newspaper. High school students may have a few years before they join the taxpaying ranks of society, but it's never too soon to learn how to prepare.
WEB http://www.irs.ustreas.gov/prod/cover.html

FinWEB This collection of links is heavily weighted towards the academic side of the economics world, but there's a healthy selection of links to more general-interest sites, including stock quote services, economic databases, and investment houses on the Web.
WEB http://www.finweb.com

Investment FAQ This mammoth document offers a concise introduction to investment in the electronic age, answering questions on stocks, bonds, options, mutuals, brokers, and markets.
URL ftp://rtfm.mit.edu/pub/usenet-by-group/misc.answers/investment-faq/general
WEB http://www.cis.ohio-state.edu/hypertext/faq/usenet/investment-faq/general/top.html

Investment Glossary Basic vocabulary for economics and its application to general investment, investment instruments, mutual funds, stock analysis, bonds, and trading.
AMERICA ONLINE aaii→Reference Library→Investment Glossary

SCHOOLS OF THOUGHT

Adam Smith's Wealth of Nations Smith is the old-fashioned capitalist's guru. He coined the terms "division of labor" and "natural progress" in his 1776 master work available at this site. It's dry as dust to read, but if you haven't been assigned it yet, you will be someday. So dig in, as the economy grows and grows infinitely.
WEB http://www.duke.edu/~atm2/SMITH

Capitalism FAQ The no-frills text housed at this site provides an accurate portray-al of capitalist concerns, beginning with "What is capitalism?" and winding up at "How do I get my piece of the pie?" In between are academic questions explained in a digestible fashion by a professor at the University of California at Berkeley. A suggested reading list is also available.
WEB http://www.ocf.berkeley.edu/~shadab

Collected Works of Marx and Engels The socialist forefathers' key economic writings are available here for your perusal. A lovely rainbow-colored picture of Marx is on view, should the budding student of socialist thought require visual inspiration.
WEB http://english-www.hss.cmu.edu/marx

Dead Economists Society The society is very much in favor of free market capitalism, hence its choice of Adam Smith's face on a penny as its emblem. Promoting "classical liberal economists" is the ultimate goal of this page featuring pretty portraits and biographies for every economist from Smith to H.L. Mencken, along with text excerpts and links to relevant Web sites.
WEB http://cac.psu.edu/~jdm114

Post-Keynesian Thought Is unemployment a public policy problem? Paul doesn't think so, but Randy does. So leave the peacemaking to Steve, who steps in to opine that "both Paul and Randy seem to agree that inflation is mismeasured to some degree." This mailing list, devoted to post-Keynesian economic theories and thoughts, is populated mostly by academic economists.
EMAIL listproc@csf.colorado.edu ✍ *Type in message body:* subscribe pkt <your full name>

STOCK EXCHANGES

American Stock Exchange This competitor to the New York Stock Exchange provides a summary of market activity every trading day at about 6 p.m., including most active issues and greatest advancers and decliners. Also check out a graph of the Inter@ctive Week Internet Index, tracking a cross-section of companies involved in building cyberspace. Like other exchange sites, this one doesn't provide real-time stock quotes, since the exchange makes money selling quote feeds to other information distributors.

WEB http://www.amex.com

E*Trade Stock Market Game How to become a billionaire. E*Trade hosts a new stock market competition every month, and the names of the players with the ten largest pseudo-portfolios are posted daily.

WEB http://www.etrade.com/html/visitor_center/game.htm

Nasdaq Stock Market By far the slickest and most useful Web site of the three major U.S. stock exchanges, as befits the only one of the three that's fully electronic. The site is about data, data, and more data, with live graphs of major market indexes and delayed price quotes for stocks. The list of active issues includes corporate logos and links to—guess what?—more quote data. Even first-time users can find what they're looking for in seconds. The only background information on the exchange itself is buried in the investment glossary.

WEB http://www.nasdaq.com

New York Stock Exchange Home Page In this increasingly decentralized world it would be hard to choose any one place as the locus of the global financial system, but the venerable NYSE ranks at the top of the list of candidates. Its Web site provides a detailed analysis of the mechanics of stock trading in an informative, albeit dry format, along with a history of the exchange.

WEB http://www.nyse.com

▶ TEACHERS' LOUNGE

EcEdWeb: Economics Resources for K-12 Teachers A lifesaver for the desperate economics educator. Lesson plans, interactive games, and networking opportunities.

WEB http://ecedweb.unomaha.edu/teach.htm

Economics A great starter list for teachers who don't know where to start. Links to everything from tax forms to *The Economist*.

WEB http://www.execpc.com/~dboals/geog.html#ECONOMICS

Taking Stock Up to 50 schools, grades 5 through 12, take part in this online stock market simulation every season. The Web site's developers provide the lesson plans and activities on such topics as "Understanding the Stock Page," "Profit and Loss," and "Stock Symbols"; teachers provide the student bodies and a modem or two.

WEB http://www.santacruz.k12.ca.us/~jpost/projects/TS/TS.html

OLOGIES & OSOPHIES

WE HUMANS ARE ETERNALLY fascinated with ourselves, our brains, our cultures both past and present, and what it all means in the grand scheme of things. Our self-knowledge grows every day, and the Internet is there to help foster that growth. Visit the American Psychological Association for the best overview of those wacky synapses and why they do the things they do. Have your head shrunk on the couch at FreudNet, and if that doesn't clear things up, join the mixed-up crew of Sartre et al in The Realm of Existentialism or go where there are No Dogs or Philosophers Allowed. Find out if you're a social misfit at The Gallup Organization. Then map out the ties that bind at Kinship and Social Organization: An Interactive Tutorial.

▶ ANTHROPOLOGY

ANTHAP—The Applied Anthropology Computer Network According to this site, anthropologists are actually everywhere, applying what they know about human social interaction to advertising, corporate management, forensic science, and more. Could it be that one of the social sciences has—gasp!—a practical application? Find out all about it here.
WEB http://www.acs.oakland.edu/~dow /anthap.html

Anthropology and Culture Rice University's merged gopher collection of anthropology and archeology sites on just about any subtopic.
URL gopher://riceinfo.rice.edu/11/Subject /Anth

Classics of Out(land)ish Anthropology This unusual site applies anthropological principles to modern advertising and journalism by nitpicking at inaccurate borrowings from the field of anthropology and pointing visitors to where they can find resources on the real thing. Nothing is safe, from Indiana Jones to

the Nissan Pathfinder ads.
WEB http://www.lawrence.edu/dept /anthropology/classics.html

Kinship and Social Organization: An Interactive Tutorial The difference between endogamy and exogamy is a consuming interest of all young anthropology students. This tutorial can set them straight in no time, with its clear, easy-to-follow diagrams and text. A gem for those wondering if they accidentally invited their cousin to the prom.
WEB http://www.umanitoba.ca/anthro pology/kintitle.html

sci.anthropology Nobody seems too passionate in this newsgroup. Students ask questions about research or fieldwork, and the few old anthropologists hanging around answer politely. Obsequiousness is recommended.
USENET sci.anthropology

Summer Institute of Linguistics "To study language is to study humanity," say the people at the Summer Institute of Linguistics in Texas. The study of living and dead cultures implies living and dead languages, too, and that's what the SIL site is all about. Download the Ethnologue of Languages of the World, or check out the multitude of links to sites on linguistics, anthropology, literacy and more.
WEB http://gopher.sil.org

▶ PHILOSOPHY

No Dogs or Philosophers Allowed How can anyone resist the title of this British TV show, which was borrowed from a famous London pub's sign, whose frustrated owner erected it to deter poor philosophers who would sit for hours talking but not ordering. The sign's namesake has put up an excellent Web page with lots of facts about the show, its host, and most importantly, contextual background for each of the show's topics, which range from Time to God. If

you're lucky, the show may be airing in your area, so check the listings here.
WEB http://www.access.digex.net/~kknisely/philosophy.tv.html

Philosophy Archive For those who need to hear it from the horse's mouth, this is a great place to find the actual texts of philosophical works. They're well-sorted, so a click on Enlightenment brings up Foucault and Kant, while a click on Descartes yields the thinking man himself. A few links to critiques are included for good measure.
WEB http://english-www.hss.cmu.edu/philosophy.html

Philosophy In Cyberspace All the way from Monash University in Australia comes this exhaustive index of all things philosophical. Beginning with a very basic introduction to Net navigation, the site then lists links, including mailing lists, newsgroups, online texts, journals, and organizations.
WEB http://www.monash.edu.au/cc/staff/phi/dey/WWW/phil.html

The Realm of Existentialism Do you ever feel like you're not really here? Do you constantly contemplate the quality of simply being? If so, you may be an existentialist (just like Sartre and Kierkegaard). Go to this page and read more about the most angst-ridden of philosophies. Its basic guide to the philosophy and its proponents might make you feel more substantial.
WEB http://www.cris.com/~Huntress/philo.shtml

The Sovereign Grace Theology Resource Page Go directly to Hell. Do not collect $200. Okay, so the guys who put up this Web site have a definite agenda and they aren't shy about it. But this page can't be beat for an exposition on the Calvinist and Reformation philosophy that played such an influential role in the early history of the United States.
WEB http://www.conline.com/sovgrace/

ThinkNet Philosopher's Guide Probably the best source for philosophy in a nutshell on the Web, this easy-to-use guide has photos, a biography, major works, and a list of links for each of the great philosophers, from Aquinas to Wittgenstein.
WEB http://server.snni.com/~palmer/philosophy_guide/philos.htm

▶ PSYCHOLOGY

American Psychological Association Of all the special interest groups standing on soapboxes in Washington these days, this is one of the most vocal, which seems appropriate, and not just because of the current debates over the proper treatment of the mentally ill. The APA's Web site is a treasure trove of reader-friendly articles about the profession, with info on psychological disorders and their treatment. The site strikes a balance between catering to professionals, educating students, and supporting those desperate for mental comforting. Visitors can come away with plenty of insight.
WEB http://www.apa.org

Blake's Internet Guide to Philosophy Blake is the classics librarian at the University of Florida, and he has a no-frills list of places to start looking for philosophy on the Net. Don't expect bells and whistles, just a comprehensive page to jumpstart your research.
WEB http://www.clas.ufl.edu/CLAS/Departments/Philosophy/BIG.html

Depression FAQ Depression may well be America's most common illness. About one in five people will suffer a major depression in their lifetime, and many will go undiagnosed until it's too late. Learn the symptoms and find out about the success rate of treatment—it's extremely high. Despite all the rumination about dream interpretation and the virtues of hypnosis, this is where the soul of psychology truly resides.
WEB http://www.cis.ohio-state.edu/hypertext/faq/usenet/alt-support-depression/faq/top.html

The Exploratorium—On-line Exhibits

Oliver Sacks wrote a whole book about *The Man Who Mistook His Wife for a Hat.* At this Web site, those who claim themselves mentally sound can misinterpret memory and the Mona Lisa, and discover just how much psychology depends on a twisted web of synapses, eager to misfire at a moment's notice. **web** http://www.exploratorium.edu /learning_studio/lsxhibit.html

Facts For Families Do you want to kill your little brother because he wets the bed? Has your older sister locked herself in her room for a week, listening to heavy metal and crying? Are you intrigued by the psychological dynamics of everyone in your crazy family? This wonderful collection of 51 fact sheets from the American Academy of Child and Adolescent Psychiatry will spell out the facts on family dysfuntion, from the problems of an autistic child to the horrors of sexual abuse. **web** http://www.psych.med.umich.edu /web/aacap/factsFam

FreudNet His theories have been widely rejected lately (no doubt due to his detractors' sexual repression in early childhood), but somone had to get the psychoanalysis ball rolling and no one could have done the job better than the charismatic Sigmund Freud. Unfortunately this Web site fails to include a picture of the famous velvet-draped sofa (on display at Siggy's London home-turned-museum), but there is plenty to send a Freudian investigator spinning away in all kinds of (id-iotic) patterns. Now, how does that make you feel? **web** http://plaza.interport.net/nypsan

General Psychology—an Introductory Course Here's a chance for advanced high school students to telecommute to Indiana University East, which offers its introductory psych course online. A high school diploma is usually required, but AP credit can be discussed. Topics start with "Introduction to Psychology" and end with "Social Behavior and Group Influences." Those with a fear of commitment can peruse assignments and a

class outline before making a decision. **web** http://www.indiana.edu/~iuepsyc /P103Psyc.html

JungWeb He's got personality, dreams, and he's in touch with his feelings. He's not Prince Charming, but fans of Jung, the so-called father of modern psychotherapy, think he's the greatest thing since the invention of the superego. At this cybertribute to Jung, visitors can take the Meyers-Brigg personality typing test (which does not involve a gauge of words per minute), participate in discussion of dream analysis, and subscribe to a newsletter. **web** http://www.onlinepsych.com /jungweb

PsychWeb A hubsite for students (mostly undergraduate) and teachers of psychology, featuring texts, articles, lists of links, and even commercial sites—but what is that weird little animal at the top of the page? A figment of the author's imagination? **web** http://www.gasou.edu/psychweb /psychweb.htm

Quiz Yourself Designed with a particular college course in mind, these brief tests provides a great way for anyone to find out what they know, if anything, about psychology. Each quiz contains ten questions, and answers are explained, so the clueless can learn something. For those who hate multiple choice tests (which is everybody, right?), there's a long explanation of the psychology behind them, plus tips for taking them successfully. **web** http://www.gasou.edu/psychweb /selfquiz/selfquiz.htm

sci.psychology.misc Talk here is all over the mental map. Much of the conversation is quite civil and perfectly relevant, with topics typically ranging from a discussion of the societal impact of schizophrenia to an argument over whether a woman who killed her baby after refusing psychiatric medicine should have been compelled to take it. The few flame wars can be easily avoided: lurk and lis-

ten for a while to get the tone right.
USENET sci.psychology.misc

SOCIOLOGY

A Sociological Tour Through Cyberspace The tour begins at Texas' Trinity University, where a professor has set up this fantastic page of links and commentary to every imaginable social topic in cyberspace. If all tours were this complete, they'd be worth the price of admission and the cramped buses.
WEB http://www.trinity.edu/~mkearl/index.html

alt.sci.sociology It's never too clear what's going on here, and the posters don't seem to know either. One Net-abuser cross-posted a message about the Soviet Union rising again, but this newsgroup was the only one that cared enough about helping plainly loony members of society to respond. Most of the group's participant are serious students and professionals with important stuff to say on topics such as "the terriorial instinct in humans" and "hip sociology Ph.D. programs."
USENET alt.sci.sociology

American Sociological Association While this site is largely about the ASA, rather than sociology itself, it contains some valuable articles on such topics as the social causes of violence. Plus, a little note at the bottom hints that more information for the general public is forthcoming, making this a site to watch.
WEB http://www.asanet.org

The Gallup Organization It's the undisputed watchdog of social trends, with polls on topics ranging from elections to religion. Gallup wants to know what makes you tick, so fill out a Gallup Poll here, then search for all kinds of vital stats and articles from the Gallup newsletter.
WEB http://www.gallup.com/index.html

Society for Applied Sociology If you're interested in sociology as a career, start with 35 Things to Think About and work your way down the list. Somewhere in that jumble of information might be valuable advice.
WEB http://www.indiana.edu/~appsoc

The SocioWeb Follow the black-and-yellow spider to a prime source of basic sociology information, from Hot Resources such as "Sociology for Very Short Attention Spans," to Sociological Discourse, which includes links to mailing lists and newsgroups. Mostly aimed at college level students, but anybody can benefit from this attractive site.
WEB http://www.socioweb.com/~markbl/socioweb

TEACHERS' LOUNGE

Archeology/Anthropology A long and useful index, which is part of the fantastic history/social studies Web site for k-12 teachers. Searching for newsgroups and university pages? Want dig sites? How about teaching resources? Check out Archeology/Anthropology and be pleasantly rewarded.
WEB http://www.execpc.com/~dboals/arch.html

MetaSelf Most of our perceptions dealing with time and self are spatial. Think about it: We look forward to vacation, look down on an action, and think back on our past. MetaSelf is an interactive metaphorical model of the self and its placement in the world that uses these spatial perceptions as its basis. It's designed for high school teachers and students and has relevant applications for any of the human studies.
WEB http://www.dnai.com/model

Teaching of Psychology in Secondary Schools TOPSS is an organization dedicated to the support of teachers of psychology at the secondary level. Its home page links to lesson plans, an index of Internet resources for psychology teachers, a list of appropriate textbooks, and even information about awards psychology teachers can receive.
WEB http://cscc.clarion.edu/mitchell/topss.htm

ETHNIC STUDIES

CULTURAL IDENTITY IS NEVER black and white. Keeping up with the politically correct ways of referring to different ethnic groups can be hard work. Everyone knows that "Oriental" should only be applied to rugs and vases; people are "Asian" or "Asian American." But is it "Latino" or "Hispanic," "African American" or "black"? Even the term "ethnic studies" is debatable—why should it include only those groups in the ethnic minority? Why not include Irish Americans, Italian Americans, and Greek Americans? No matter which descriptions we use, we're all Americans (hyphenated only in adjective form), and that means that Ethnic Studies is critical in our multicultural nation. In the world-next-door environment of cyberspace, everyone has a chance to mix and mingle. So join the party at the Black Information Network, clue in at soc.culture .asian.american, say hola at CiberCentro and pick up a few Ojibwe phrases at the Fond du Lac Tribal Gopher.

▶ AFRICAN AMERICANS

Afro Americ@ If it's the most extensive collection of 20th-century African-American history you're after, you have come to the right place. While the colorful graphics catch your eye, the almost subliminal bottom-screen scroll suggests the benefits of registering for the Afro American Newspaper Company of Baltimore's bi-weekly updates. The What's New section will give you the numbers behind Farrakhan's seemingly infinite popularity, as well as encourage your online vote for the most influential living musician in black culture today. If you're young and on the scene, or at least trying to find one, Freaknik will tell you where the best parties are happening nationwide.
WEB http://www.afroam.org

Afro-American Culture & Arts Forum
The Salon, a general chitchat board, is the most active section in the forum. It's

where parents discuss how to deal with a teen "indefinitely homebound" (a euphemism for grounded) and where everyone picks apart the media image of the single black mother. Recent immigrants go to Caribbean Meeting to talk about the old countries. The forum also includes serious political talk, occasional accusations of "blacker than thou" posturing, and a group that periodically shares its favorite items from *Weekly World News*—like the one about the 50-foot Jesus terrorizing a small town. The big draws here are the culture topics—art, history, film, theater, and music.
COMPUSERVE *go* afro

AFRONET This online newspaper serves numerous interests and skips the fluff: You don't just have to read and digest, you can talk back, too. If you want to talk about racism in Hollywood (with or without Spike Lee), current African-American flicks, politics, or local news, AFRONET's the place. The "junior posse" gives you all the relevant fashion news, R&B grooves, Def Jam singles, fraternity, sorority, and college scholarship info. Also available is an African-American product catalog.
WEB http://www.afronet.com

Black Information Network Not to be easily categorized, this site has everything from listings of ministries on the Gospel World Wide Network and members of the Association of Black Accountants to sections on adoption, missing children, employment opportunities, real estate, and "friends" (with romantic potential). There is a wide variety of compelling articles, covering issues of transgenderism, politics, and other African-American issues. If it's talk you want, there's no lack of opinions here.
WEB http://www.bin.com/homepage.htm

The Book Stunning graphics are only a hint of the wealth of African-American culture and history offered at this dynamic site. Through text, images and sounds, The Book takes you through a vast library of popular music, photos, video clips, famous speeches and 20th-century icons. The vast educational and entertainment opportunities are regularly updated and easily navigated. Perhaps the most impressive aspect of this site is its thoroughly researched and highly useful compilation of "the best" Web sites, from comics/cartoons to art to science to "wild stuff." For those new to the Web or tired of fruitless searches, The Book could prove beneficial.

WEB http://www.blackhistory.com

Café Los Negros Not your average café, this moody black and Latino Web joint offers a potent cup of art, performance, poetry, fashion, and music. Although this cafe has a cover charge, there are some juicy conversations worth hearing. Complete with a black-and-white photo guide, you can see the hottest threads, or "play" the latest grooves (depending on what's currently available): If you missed a local multimedia performance, or a poetry reading, you just might be able to download it from this funky site.

WEB http://www.losnegroes.com

ClubNubia Online Magazine This self-described "unifying and uplifting" netpaper is geared toward people of color worldwide. You'll find features, reviews and commentary, letters from the editor, and reader responses. Eager readers can also speak directly to the site's editorial staff. A typical feature may discuss your rights as an artist, while other less traditional sections offer poetry and a stream of consciousness-like page entitled Bruhhman's Perspective. Special events, bulletin boards, and classifieds are standard fare.

WEB http://www.directhit.com/clubnubia

NAACP Before you go anywhere else on this site, you'll want to get a first-hand account of the NAACP origins from its first and foremost member, Mary White Ovington. The history, as it was recounted in 1914 by this fascinating woman, is essential for anyone wanting to under-stand in greater depth what the organization is about. From there you might want to become familiar with the NAACP's current functions and concerns, including legislative work and contact with federal agencies, the power of the black vote, civil rights laws, its continued attack on restrictive zoning ordinances, prison reform, modern "lynching" practices, desegregation, military justice, and its recent efforts to introduce low- and moderate-income housing into the suburbs.

WEB http://www.bin.com/assocorg /naacp/naacp.htm

One ON-Line In a letter at the One Nation section of this forum, a black teacher in Japan is on a mission to challenge stereotypes: In another letter, a black Brit living in America questions the relationship between black Americans and black foreigners. Other headings include One Music, Film, Marketplace, and Links—this site offers a targeted, but not very distinctive version of the basic Web service.

WEB http://www.clark.net/pub/conquest /one/contents.html

soc.culture.african.american The African Americans here can be more insightful critics of black politics than any talk-show right-winger, but politics takes a backseat to the mother of all topics—the relationship between men and women. In a recent discussion about love and marriage—"What is it about marriage that women want so desperately?"—more than 100 people weighed in on the subject. Stay around the group long enough and you'll grow accustomed to the monthly "What is racism?" or its sibling discussion "Is that really racism?" After one participant (not an African-American) asked, "Could it be that the funny looks you get in the elevator are more about being male?" An exasperated regular wrote back: "I really think you need a vacation from this group." Perhaps as many as half the regulars on this newsgroup are not African-American.

USENET soc.culture.african.american

ASIAN AMERICANS

A. Magazine *A. Magazine* takes you inside the Asian-American community, through highlighted features and special supplements of its last three (hard copy) editions. Though you won't be able to get the meat of the zine, you will get a hearty gist of what's inside. If it's Japanese animation you want, or hard-to-find classics in Asian-American literature, the @Mall is the place for one-stop Net shopping for must-have pop-culture Asian items. There's also the @Mall video box where you can get a glimpse of the latest Asian animation complete with thematic descriptions, and @Mall music has... what else? Take a virtual tour of Asian-American resources, or explore the ruling topics of the discussion area if you're so inspired.
WEB http://www.amazine.com

ACON: Asian Community Online Network What can the Asian Community Online Network offer you? Essential political, social, civil rights, education, employment, arts, and health service references. They have created a network that allows members of the APA community to exchange ideas on current events, publicize campaigns, coordinate political strategies, and generally provide relevant info to other APA groups regionally and nationally. This site is definitely geared towards the progressive-minded, whether you're actively involved in any of the member organizations, or you're interested in learning about the "who" of PeaceNet, or the "why" of the Anti-Asian Violence Network.
WEB http://www.igc.apc.org/acon

Chinese Community Information Center This is a cybercenter for information on Chinese community publications and their affiliate organizations. Up to 20 papers in Chinese and English can be downloaded for a leisurely read. The CCIC also serves substantial reference lists of Chinese associations, societies and alumni directories, as well as ample resources for literature, music, language, religion, and Internet directories. And kudos for creating a link where you can seek out a former classmate, acquaintance, or even an old, undisclosed crush, from here to China... literally.
WEB http://www.ifcss.org

Filipinas Online The most compelling thing about the Internet edition of *Filipinas Magazine*, is the Your Community section, which has created a venue for Filipino community interaction in the United States and abroad, through "facts, figure and hyperlinks." There is a community calendar of local events, links to newsgroups and mail lists, community news and issues, a study of Filipino American consumer behavior, and where to send your literary and art submissions around the world. Buy a FoneCard, win a subscription to *Filipinas Magazine* with your trivia acumen, comment, suggest, or chat. Whatever your pleasure, your options are many.
WEB http://www.filipinas.com

Philippine News Online So you were seeking the largest Filipino newspaper in North America? You found it. Since 1961, *Philippine News* Online has been providing the Filipino community with headline news, worldwide reporting, community and business news, and entertainment info. Now, thanks to the Web, they now offer commlink, where you can learn, on a more personal level, about who's doing what—and where. You can write letters to the Web master, get a calendar of events, or hometown datelines that give updated news flashes from Antipolo to Zamboanga.
WEB http://www.philnews.com

soc.culture.asian.american Believed to be the granddaddy of identity newsgroups, soc.culture.asian.american has survived years of flesh-searing flame wars to become one of the most exciting newsgroups on the Net. Topics include English-only legislation, immigration questions, the media portrayal of Asian-Americans (any recent movie, TV series, or, for that matter, comic book with Asian-American characters is likely to get a thorough going-over), issues of

violence and cooperation among races and interracial dating. Sometimes these discussions function as mere triggers for flame wars between the two camps that dominate the group. The primary factional breakdown is simple: Non-Asians who consider the group to be a place for all who admire or concern themselves with Asian-American issues versus Asian-Americans who consider the group to be a haven for intra-Asian discussion and bonding. Most people are truly concerned with the issues here, and they post what they feel and think with passion. They're also pretty regular about it: a few hundred new posts a night is not uncommon. Regional RL get-togethers by soc.culture.asia.american members in the Bay Area, Boston, and New York are common.
USENET soc.culture.asian.american

soc.culture.japan Of all of the major soc.culture Asian newsgroups, soc.culture.japan is the only one that seems largely dominated by non-Asians. Quirky discussions of cultural differences prompted by questions from returned tourists or exchange students are common. The handful of regulars posting from Japan are vested with a sort of guru status; they're asked to deliver Solomonic decisions on who's right or wrong about various aspects of Japanese culture. A fair amount of spillover from the newsgroup rec.arts.anime also visits the site.
USENET soc.culture.japan

HISPANIC AMERICANS

The Azteca Web Page Among the many questions you can have thoroughly answered are "What is a Chicano?", "Where is Aztlan?", and "How many people speak indigenous languages in Mexico?" Would you like to view Mexican images, download a game for the PC based on an an Aztec Game (Patolli) learn more about immigration policy, or just hear some interesting stories? It's all possible at The Azteca Web Page.
WEB http://www.directnet.com/~mario/aztec

CiberCentro Recognizing the incredible diversity of Latin countries that often get lumped together by unwitting non-Latino Americans, CiberCentro hosts a customized newspaper/index for each one. If you want newsgroups for Argentinians or a map of Peru, you can get exactly that. You can also find people who are online (and might be able to answer your questions) at the Ciber Citizens page for each country. Although the main menu of the site is in English, knowledge of elementary Spanish is advised.
WEB http://www.cibercentro.com

CLNET (Chicano-Latino Net) Head to this site for information, networking, cultural edification, and a good time. Start at the community center, which provides general assistance on housing, education, labor, and social services information. Stop off at the museum section for a breathtaking view of the murals of Los Angeles and the works of Frida Kahlo, or listen to some mariachi, dance the tango, and get a Spanish-language film review. Then, finish at the library for a quiet read.
WEB http://latino.sscnet.ucla.edu

Latin-American IPR Net This is an information service on Puerto Rican issues, where you'll find a journal of Puerto Rican policy and politics and a socioeconomic profile of Puerto Ricans in the U.S. (including a new feature that allows you to find out statistics on the city's 21 Latino neighborhoods, including population projections to the year 2000). There is a directory of 500 Puerto Rican community organizations in the United States and Puerto Rico, a calendar of events, festivals, and historical dates, essays, poems, and stories on the Puerto Rican experience. If all this isn't enough, you can get on the IPR mailing list with a convenient email subscription form.
WEB http://www.iprnet.org/IPR

LatinoLink Open the pages of this weekly ezine to find timely hypertext news articles and political commentary in Eng-

lish and Spanish. Links to lifestyle, travel, and entertainment pages provide excellent diversions with stories about the struggle over Eva Peron's remains, the Tejano music boom, and the documentary *Carmen Miranda: Bananas is My Business*. In addition, a business section provides online commerce and a growing job bank.
WEB http://www.latinolink.com

LatinoWeb If you were looking for a loan to build a bridge in Buenos Aires, you'd go straight to the business section here and find the home page of Banco Interamericano de Desarrollo. Some of the diverse links take cultural explorers to the Andean Music page or the Ballet Folklorico. No fewer than six sites hold recipes for chimichangas and psole—but if taste dictates, *The Wall Street Journal* and *Las Journada* are just a jump away.
WEB http://www.catalog.com/favision /latnoweb.htm

Mundo Latino This page is one substantial link list. CubaWeb tells you all you want to know about doing business in Cuba, or you can link to Costa Rican coffee, Honduras' participation in the global marketplace, a MexAssist financial newsletter, a Brazilian business directory, Latin American/Spanish language resources, or the Lambda Theta Phi Latin fraternity's national home page.
WEB http://www.mundolatino.org/latingle .htm

soc.culture.latin-america A cacophony of voices and topics, this newsgroup dedicated to the cultures and languages of Latin America lacks focus but it's always interesting. Threads are often carried in both English and Spanish (posters even switch in the middle of sentences, which can be frustrating), and rarely bear any resemblance to their specified topic. But hey, it's fun. One woman is seeking ways to say "I love you" in all languages, and one thread begins, "USA=The Absolute Worst Country."
USENET soc.culture.latin-america

▶ NATIVE AMERICANS

A Guide to the Great Sioux Nation It's not enough to have seen *Dances with Wolves*. In this cyberguide, the Sioux speak for themselves—relating the history of the buffalo hunt, the battle with Custer, the Ghost Dance movement, and the massacre at Wounded Knee. Lavish illustrations of artifacts and landmarks bring the Plains alive. Members of the nation will appreciate links to government and other Native American Net sites.
WEB http://www.state.sd.us/state /executive/tourism/sioux/sioux.htm

American Communication Association The past and present of Native Americans are brought to life in this large collection of links. Ponder the mysterious demise of an ancient civilization at the Anasazi site, or connect with other Shoshone through the InterTribal Network. Links are also provided to the powers that be—the Bureau of Indian Affairs and the U.S. Senate Committee on Native American Issues.
WEB http://www.uark.edu/depts /comminfo/www/native.html

Chattanooga InterTribal Association History is ongoing for this intertribal congress. Re-read the *Last Resolution of the Cherokee Nation*, written in the face of Indian Removal in the last century, or a current article detailing a battle with a Coca-Cola heir over his proposed development atop Native-American graves. Links lead to other sights dedicated to preserving Native-American rights.
WEB http://www.chattanooga.net/City Beat/politics_f/cita_f/index.html

Fond du Lac Tribal Gopher Look here for information on the current Senate Indian Affairs Committee and the reservation education program. If the need arises, this is also the place to translate English into Ojibwe and vice versa: money is *zhooniyaa*, and god is *manidoo*. (Money, as usual, does not equal god).

URL gopher://asab.fdl.cc.mn.us

Index of Native American Resources on the Internet Deceptively simple, this site holds hundreds of pointers to cultural, educational, and political resources. Well worth a visit is the collection of electronic Native-American texts, which holds everything from turn-of-the-century *Atlantic Monthly* stories to the current issue of the ezine *Red Ink Online*. Other pointers lead to language lessons, archeological dig sites, and museums. The selection of U.S. and tribal government sites collected is among the best on the Web.
WEB http://hanksville.phast.umass.edu /misc/NAresources.html

Lakota Information Home Page This collection of documents and bibliography represents efforts to right some wrongs—removing Crazy Horse's image from malt liquor packaging and creating a park honoring the martyrs of Wounded Knee. Debates over teaching religion outside a spiritual setting and a "Declaration of War Against Exploiters of Lakota Spirituality" attempt to protect Native religion and culture in the face of a New Age onslaught.
WEB http://maple.lemoyne.edu/~bucko /lakota.html

The Native American Culture Home Page This is an outsider's guide to the world of the Pueblos of Northern New Mexico. A historical essay brings the reader through the 800 years of history held in the adobe compounds. The calendar of events highlights feast days like the Corn Dances of Santa Clara and the feast of San Geronimo at Taos, where Catholic and native religions combine. Read the online etiquette guide before attending.
WEB http://LAHS.LosAlamos.K12.nm.us /sunrise/work/piaseckj/homepage.html

Native American Languages From a population of 1,800 only 20 Abnaki-Penobscot speakers remain. This database chronicles the demise of native languages. The distinguishing features of

each are described, and linked to others in its language family.
WEB http://www-ala.doc.ic.ac.uk/~rap /Ethnologue/eth.cgi/USA

Native American Tribes: Information Virtually Everywhere Lists are the form of choice here—useful lists of contact information for Native American Organizations like ARROW, Incorporated Americans for Restitution and Rightings of Old Wrongs, or lists of federally recognized tribes like the Barona Capitan Grande Band of Diegueno Mission Indians in California. There are lists of radio stations with Native-American programs, and films and videos where Indians are more than flat, painted villains. The lists of electronic mailing lists and Net links are of great assistance in making further cyberconnections.
WEB http://www.afn.org/~native

Office of Indian Education No longer do Indian boarding schools try to make little white boys and girls out of Sioux, Navajo, or Seminole children. At this home page, read the revised mission statement and find out about ongoing programs like the Native American Arts high school in Santa Fe, N. Mex.
WEB http://oiep.unm.edu/oiep/home.html

Ojibwe Language and Culture This primer teaches a few words, and provides essays on culture and an extensive bibliography. A "values conflict" chart points out the many differences between Anglos and American Indians—guess which is cooperative and which is competitive.
WEB http://hanksville.phast.umass.edu /misc/ojibwe/index.html

Oneida Indian Nation of New York This site reflects more than 200 years of a tense relationship between the Oneida Nation and the United States. The Fort Stanwix Treaty of 1784 (and all those that followed) and a letter dated April, 29, 1994, from President Clinton restating once again the sovereign status of Indian nations are featured. Students of American history will be pleased to learn

about Polly Cooper, who rescued General Washington's starving troops at Valley Forge. But this is also the home page connection for the Oneida Nation, presenting press releases, a calendar of upcoming events, and a tour of the attractions of the reservation, including the Turning Stone Casino and the seat of government, the Council House. Cultural center exhibits are enhanced by audio samples of the Oneida language.
WEB http://one-web.org/oneida

Sisseton Wahpeton Sioux Tribe The virtual reservation of the Sisseton Wahpeton branch of the Sioux tribe from northeastern South Dakota. Outsiders should take the tour, stopping at historical sites and the Tekakwitha Fine Arts Center. Educational and government links keep tribe members up-to-date on local news and national programs, including virtual college courses from the Wahpeton Community College.
WEB http://swcc.cc.sd.us/homepage.htm

ANGLO AMERICANS

Center for the Study of White American Culture This is not a group for people who like to wear bedsheets and dunce caps. Instead, it is a multiracial organization operating on the premise that knowledge of one's racial heritage (even if it is the so-called mainstream) is essential to establishing understanding among races. The CSWAC also believes that people of all races are required in a group to foster a balanced knowledge of a particular race. Follow links to other resources on white culture, and be surprised at how politically correct a group like this can be.
WEB http://www.euroamerican.org/index.htm

TEACHERS' LOUNGE

Diversity Sources Part of a huge collection of links for Social Studies teachers, the Diversity Sources Web site is, well, diverse. You'll be able to find your way to lesson plans or very technical information from here, and there is no eth-

nicity, cause, or organization too specific to be listed.
WEB http://www.execpc.com/~dboals/diversit.html

Ethnic and Cultural Web Quality, if not quantity, is in this AOL directory. Choose one of four ethnicities to search by and the service spits out a set of links to places like LatinoWeb. These are excellent jumping-off places, and many, of course, lead you elsewhere.
AMERICA ONLINE *keyword* clubs→People and Communities→Ethnic and Cultural Groups

Software Bank Download software based on the Interculture Sensitizer technique, which prepares students for encountering other cultures by quizzing them on alternative explanations for problematic incidents. Be advised that one of the programs, which is based on Jane Elliot's anti-prejudice techniques, stars Beavis (of *Beavis and Butthead* fame), which could be a bit annoying.
WEB http://www.soc.umn.edu/~spitzer/softwarebankprw.html

WOMEN'S STUDIES

SIX WORDS FOR THOSE WHO STILL believe that women are the weaker, fairer sex: Gabrielle Reece and Leonardo di Caprio. No one really knows why the male half of society seems to have the upper hand—it certainly isn't due to its superiority. But for generations, women have been trying to rectify the situation in the home, in the workplace, in schools, and now, on the Internet, which has become the newest arena for the sometimes caustic, sometimes elegant feminist debate. Begin your women's studies by solving The Female Equation, then log in an opinion (they're not scarce) at alt.feminism. Need more background? Try On the Issues, then stop for a snack at Woman's Day—it's okay, feminists are still allowed to cook. When you feel refreshed, political action starts NOW. After that cyber-workout, nobody's going to be called the weaker sex.

> **STARTING POINTS**

Feminism and Feminist Related The site's author laments not keeping up with the rapidly growing Web, but the wealth of resources she has collected is awe-inspiring: The Yahoo Women's Studies link, the EINET Women's Resources List, the Women's Web, STOP Violence Against Women, etc.. There's also an online copy of *Heather Has Two Mommies* and links to alt.lesbian.feminist poetry.
web http://www.ibd.nrc.ca/~mansfield/feminism.html

GetNet International, Inc.—The Female Equation Links to interesting sites covering all aspects of the modern gal's life. Celebrate 75 years of women's suffrage with a trip to the NOW site. Check out your stock options at the FIN-Web financial server. Find out what that extra cup of coffee means to your health at the Women's Health gopher. And that's only the beginning.
web http://www.getnet.com/women.html

InforM's Women's Studies Database If for some obscure reason you can only visit one woman-related Web site, make it this one. It links to almost all the womanly sites in cyberspace, and is a terrific compendium of women's studies resources in its own right. You can find a job, a conference on gender and law, the text of *A Vindication of the Rights of Women*, a feminist film review of *Aladdin*, and the email address of your congressperson.
web http://inform.umd.edu:86/Educational_Resources/AcademicResourcesByTopic/WomensStudies

Women Homepage Women here, women there, women absolutely everywhere. Jesse Stickgold-Sarah presents links to a phenomenal number of women-oriented sites. Start by experiencing the intellectual joys of the Women's Resource Project. Broaden your horizons with a trip to the Sexuality and Gender home page. If it's out there, it's probably listed here.
web http://www.mit.edu:8001/people/sorokin/women/index.html

Women's Resources on the Net This attractive site is a great place to start exploring women's resources online. Links to NOW, *Ms.*, women's health sites, bisexual and lesbian resources, bibliographies, biographies, legal resources, support groups, and women's colleges are just the beginning. Stay onsite for an online collection of paintings by women artists, or sound clips of famous women writers like Maya Angelou, and a calendar of links to women's events ranging from a martial arts training camp for women to WisCon 20: The World's Foremost Feminist Science Fiction Convention.
web http://sunsite.unc.edu/cheryb/women/wresources.html

> **DISCUSSION**

alt.feminism "My perception of pregnancy as being stressful, traumatic and unpleasant stems from my observations of friends and relatives of mine who have been pregnant. Are you saying that they are lying?" posts one man in response to an anti-abortionist's challenge, and a typical debate in an alt.feminism day is off and running. Many topics start here, but they all end up somehow or other on the abortion issue, thanks to the pro-life brigade which seems to be regularly prowling and shouting in this unmoderated group. Get in when the threads are young and still original, and you'll find plenty of relevant and interesting debate.

USENET alt.feminism
FAQ: **WEB** http://www.math.uio.no/faq/feminism/alt-faq.html

FEMISA The lively discussions on the Feminist Theory and Gender Studies mailing list range from the philosophical (materialist feminism) to the practical (female genital mutilation). The mailing list, topical bibliographies, book reviews, and papers are archived at the gopher site.
EMAIL listproc@csf.colorado.edu ✍ *Type in message body:* subscribe femisa <your full name>
Archives: **URL** gopher://csf.Colorado.EDU:70/11/feminist

INTERNATIONAL

Global Fund for Women The GFW's focus is international female human rights, and its home page is a smorgasbord of information about the organization and similar efforts worldwide. Find out how to apply for a grant to aid women in developing countries or contribute to the fund.
WEB http://www.igc.apc.org/gfw

Women's International Center Information about numerous scholarships for women of all ages and occupations. Among the women's history tidbits and female words of wisdom are excerpts from a unique cookbook that collects recipes from WIC award winners such as Dame Judith Anderson, the late Bar-

bara Jordan, and Peggy Lee. Make the egg pie, chocolate whoppers, and curry mousse your just desserts.
WEB http://www.wic.org

LAW

The Equal Rights Amendment For three-quarters of a century, feminists have waited for just 57 words. "Equality of Rights under the law shall not be denied or abridged by the United States or any state on account of sex." Read the other thirty-four words at this site.
WEB http://now.org/now/issues/economic/eratext.html

Internet Resources for Women's Legal and Public Policy Information Head to this fabulous site to research rights and redress wrongs. There are annotated connections to gophers dedicated to many women's issues (health care, violence, work) and special interests (lesbians, women of color, disabled women, and mothers). The site also links to women's organizations, publications, and electronic discussion groups.
WEB http://asa.ugl.lib.umich.edu/chdocs/womenpolicy/womenlawpolicy.html

NEWS

Catt's Claws, a Frequently-Appearing Feminist Newsletter Whose claws? Why, the descendants of suffragist Carrie Chapman Catt, one would imagine. In a past issue, the newsletter squarely refuted attacks on affirmative action with statistical illustrations of white male privilege. Other articles described a film project on the early Christian ordination of women, gave pointers on avoiding clinic violence, and printed quotes from allies (Ruth Bader Ginsburg) and enemies (Pat Robertson). Send in your own quotes and comments.
WEB http://worcester.lm.com/women/is/cattsclaws.html

Electric Anima Home Page This new ezine proclaims itself technological fun with a feminine twist. The current issue has an article about girlhood "heroines"

like Wonder Woman, an over-18 only link to Bianca's Smut Shack, and poetry by the likes of "Ed" and "Yan."
WEB http://www.io.com/~ixora

On the Issues A selection of articles from "the progressive women's quarterly," *On the Issues.* The journal covers women and their issues through such topics as female radio talk show hosts, raising male children with a feminist influence, and a regular section of film and book reviews.
WEB http://mosaic.echonyc.com/~onissues

VOW World: Voices of Women "Power tools for visionary women." An online magazine covering the latest in alternative medicines, the state of the feminist movement, and even the gender of God. Check the calendar for workshops to help you realize your sacred inner space or to protect your outer space with self-defense demos.
WEB http://www.voiceofwomen.com

Woman's Day Donna Reed would have felt right at home in the virtual edition of *Woman's Day.* There's a Recipe of the Day (corn niblet casserole), a Tip of the Day (how to get grape juice stains out of the rug), the current table of contents, and an archive of previous articles on shopping, parenting, health, and crafts.
AMERICA ONLINE *keyword* woman's day

▶ ORGANIZATIONS

Feminists Against Censorship (UK) Information and an email link to a British group fighting against the anti-pornography movement. This site also contains info about a U.S. group called Feminists for Free Expression.
WEB http://worcester.lm.com/women /resources/cenfacfe.html

NOW—The National Organization for Women If there was ever a time for women's political action it is NOW. Peruse the hypertext women's issues forums for the latest on court decisions and NOW projects from abortion rights to economic equality. An electronic ver-

sion of the *NOW Times* newsletter is also available. Find out how to join NOW online or whom to contact in your area.
WEB http://www.now.org/now/home.html

▶ ACADEMIC FEMINISM

Feminism and Women's Studies *The English Server* offers a hodgepodge of gender related material, including wry articles such as "Dead Doll Humility" or "The Girls' Guide to Condoms." Philosophical and political tracts such as "Equal Pay" and "Feminists and Cyberspace" are also available.
WEB http://english-server.hss.cmu.edu /Feminism.html

Gender, Sex and Sexuality A collection of documents covering a broad range of topics such as musings on nymphomania, marketing angry women in popular culture, sex and the cybergirl, sexual harassment, and body image.
WEB http://english-server.hss.cmu.edu /Gender.html

Women's Studies Issues on the Net Academic resources for the study of women's issues. Gather bibliographies from the Library of Congress or York University in England, or link to women's studies programs worldwide.
URL gopher://marvel.loc.gov/11/global /socsci/area/womens

▶ TEACHERS' LOUNGE

Women Studies This site is power-packed with jumping-off points designed for teachers who want to bring women's studies into the classroom. The site offers women's studies resources about literature and arts, biographies, history, and even essay contests.
WEB http://www.execpc.com/~dboals /nativam.html

Women's History Month Not every month is women's history month, but who's counting? Visit this page any time of the year.
WEB http://socialstudies.com/mar/women .html

COMPARATIVE RELIGION

MADALYN MURRAY O'HAIR, WHO opposed "The Lord's Prayer" all the way to the Supreme Court, might be shocked to learn that religion is still taught in schools. But nobody's telling you what you should believe anymore. Instead, comparative religion is catching on, with its emphasis on what we can learn from religions worldwide, and how we can better tolerate those who seem very different from us. Religion is everywhere on the Internet. For a crash course in world religions, start at the Ontario Centre for Religious Tolerance. If the spirit of the gospel moves you, worship at the First Church of Cyberspace. For a little Zen, meditate at BuddhaNet. Brush up on the Torah with the Judaism Reading List or find your Mecca at the CyberMuslim Information Collective. No matter what you believe, there's always room to learn something new.

STARTING POINTS

Finding God in Cyberspace Sometimes the title is the best part of a site. In the case of this British page, though, the content lives up to the name. Need Web pages? Journals? Gophers? Electronic conferences hosted by notable theologists and scholars? They're all just a click away; before you know it, you'll be off to the Islamic Resources Gopher, the library catalog of the Jewish Theological Seminary of America, or the Guide to Early Church Documents, and on your way to being a true believer.
WEB http://users.ox.ac.uk/~mikef/durham/gresham.html

Ontario Centre for Religious Tolerance An excellent place to begin your spiritual journey on the Net. The site focuses not only on religious tolerance and freedom, but also on religious abuse, intolerance, and issues relating to religious. Documents written by the center provide extensive analyses of religions and their views on various controversial issues.

Don't miss the indispensable glossary of religious terms.
WEB http://www.kosone.com/people/ocrt/ocrt_hp.htm

Religious Issues Forum Argue about the origin of Satan, consider the theory of evolution, and pose or respond to hypothetical situations to test the philosophy of Natural Law. Religion is on trial in this forum, and both the prosecution and the defense seem inexhaustible. Abortion, the acceptance of gays in the church, and euthanasia are frequently discussed and debated in the Messages section of this forum. On the lighter side, members exchange jokes in the Religious Humor section. Religious symbols, mysticism, and science and religion are also popular topics. In the libraries, the latest theories on the Shroud of Turin turn up as do images of the Sistine Chapel ceiling, texts of the Dead Seas Scrolls, quotes from St. Augustine, a bibliography of African theology, and much more.
COMPUSERVE *go* relissues

Spirituality and Consciousness An annotated list of religion sites on the World Wide Web, with plenty of essays and quotes to inspire you.
WEB http://zeta.cs.adfa.oz.au/Spirituality.html

talk.religion.misc Except for the occasional random posts and flames (no newsgroup is immune), this newsgroup is dominated by genuine religious debate. It's a heavily trafficked newsgroup that attracts people who really like to sink their teeth into an argument. Both religious philosophy (What is the nature of faith?) and religion-related current events (the constitutionality of prayer in school) are faithfully discussed and debunked.
USENET talk.religion.misc

CHRISTIANITY

alt.religion.christian Does God exist?

What exactly is atheism? And how does evolution fit into the discussion? In fact, are you even sure that you exist? All these questions are up for grabs at the highly trafficked alt.religion.christian newsgroup. The only thing guaranteed to be in existence are hundreds of others who are willing and ready to debate them.
USENET alt.religion.christian

bit.listserv.christia Let a satisfied customer tell you about this popular Christian newsgroup: "Boy, when you ask for help on this list you get it… When people help each other things get done. I have seen more love on this list than I have seen for a long time. I've seen some pretty hot topics being discussed and still see communication going on. I think that speaks for itself."
USENET bit.listserv.christia
FAQ: WEB http://rtfm.mit.edu/pub/usenet -by-hierarchy/bit/listserv

First Church of Cyberspace Although the First Church of Cyberspace has an affiliation with the Central Presbyterian Church of Montclair, N.J., this site does not function as the home page for a church. It *is* the church. The sanctuary contains text versions of sermons written for this cyberaudience; the gallery links churchgoers to religious artwork across the Web (including the Sistine Chapel). The library also links to other Christian sites on the Web. Surfers are encouraged to join the congregation and email their opinions.
WEB http://execpc.com/~chender

soc.religion.christian If your parents asked you to kill someone, which commandment (No. 4 or No. 5) would take precedence? A Jew explains the rule of *pikkuach nefesh*, whereby one is not only permitted, but required, to break a commandment to save a life. A Muslim quotes Muhammed: "There shall be no obedience to a creature, in what is a disobedience to the Creator." A Christian prioritizes Jesus' new commandment to "love thy neighbor." When soc.religion.christian is debating doc-

trine, it's an informed, speculative community. Unfortunately, undergraduate atheists bait readers with old chestnuts like premarital sex, the rock too big for God to lift, and bad things that happen to good people. Instead of turning the other cheek, however, Christians flame back.
USENET soc.religion.christian
FAQ: WEB http://rtfm.mit.edu/pub/usenet -by-hierarchy/soc/religion/christian

▶ EASTERN RELIGIONS

alt.hindu Anshuman has a question about the Hindu power ladder: "It seems that most of the quotes given by those pushing Vaisnava philosophy always put the word Vishnu or Krishna in parentheses after the word brahman or prajapati or some other supreme being appears." And Vijay has an answer: "Note that the name 'prajapati' more accurately describes Lord Vishnu than anyone else—although in a lesser sense, it describes Daksa and other progenitors, in another sense, it indicates Lord Brahma (the father of Daksa, etc.), but it more appropriately refers to Lord Vishnu, who is the source of Lord Brahma. We see Lord Krishna referred to as 'prapitamaha' (great-grandfather; Lord Brahma is often called 'pitamaha' or grandfather), 'sarva-loka-mahesvara' (the controller of all worlds; Lord Siva is sometimes called 'mahesvara'), etc. in Bhagavad Gita, 'prajapati' [in addition to many other 'pati' titles] in Bhagavatam, etc. Similarly, 'svayambhu' ('self-born' which often refers to Lord Brahma, but more appropriately to Lord Vishnu) appears in Vishnu Sahasranama, etc." The other participants in this moderately active newsgroup aren't always as onomastically skilled, but they have plenty to talk about from the world of Hinduism—a project to bring water to Thai villages, announcements of the public appearances of Hindu luminaries, and discussions about the nature of sin and dishonesty in the Bhagavad-Gita.
USENET alt.hindu

BuddhaNet Check out the answers to

commonly asked questions about Buddhism and its teachings, learn about meditation, or link to other Buddhist sites. Since BuddhaNet is "Australia's Buddhist Communications Link," Buddhist organizations and meditation practice groups across Australia are just a hop away. The site also contains information about BuddhaNet BBS, a network of bulletin board systems.
WEB http://www2.hawkesbury.uws.edu.au /BuddhaNet/budnetp.htm

Buddhist Studies World-Wide Web Virtual Library Provides links to Buddhist sites—from pictures of Buddha to something called DharmaNet, it's here.
WEB http://coombs.anu.edu.au/WWWVL -Buddhism.html

Introduction to Hinduism In a novel approach to the standard index format of many sites, the author of this site narrates an easy-to-understand basic guide to the Hindu religion. But contained within the text is an extensive index of links to related sites including FAQs, guides to learning Sanskrit, and hypertext versions of important Hindu documents.
WEB http://www.geocities.com/Rodeo Drive/1415/indexd.html

▶ ISLAM

CyberMuslim Information Collective
Welcome CyberMuslims, devotees of Islam on the Internet. Your guide is Selim the CyberMuslim (a graphical character). Join the Digital Jihad to rally against anti-Muslim prejudices; read a newspaper clipping about Bosnia; experience a photo-narrative essay on Muslims in nineteenth-century Russia; and listen to recitations of Al-Fatiha, the beginning of the Quran. Some of the sounds on the site are more random than others, but all in all, this site is a feast for the senses.
WEB http://www.uoknor.edu/cybermuslim

Defenders of Aal-Ulbait and the Companions, Islamic Homepage A comprehensive index (with links) to Islam-related material on the Web, including various Quran translations, Arabic software, information on Muslim countries, pictures, and even 800 numbers for Islamic information. The majority of items listed here are articles about Islam, such as descriptions of Heaven and Hell, and a discussion of the differences between Islam and the Nation of Islam. There's even a category of articles at this site called "Mankind's corruption of the Bible."
WEB http://web.syr.edu/~maalkadh

Islam's Homepage It's tempting to say that if you can't find info on Islam here, it doesn't exist. In addition to an extensive collection of original articles about elements of Islam, this site also includes information about and selected text from Islam-related books and magazines, programming info for Muslim Television Ahmadiyya, an English translation of the Quran, selected prayers, and pictures.
WEB http://www.utexas.edu/students /amso/indext.html

Islamic Texts and Resources MetaPage
Part cyber-encyclopedia, part cyber-reader, the MetaPage carries material on just about everything, like Islamic art, thought, language, scriptures, and prophetic traditions.
WEB http://wings.buffalo.edu/student-life /sa/muslim/isl/isl.html

soc.religion.islam Well-trafficked newsgroup discussing a broad range of Islamic issues, from the role of women to intermarriage to the fate of non-Muslims on the Day of Judgment. The FAQ, with its 15 parts, is equally far-reaching; besides an extensive discussion of Islamic beliefs, there are sections on Islamic Internet resources, human rights, and Farrakhism.
USENET soc.religion.islam
FAQ: **WEB** http://www.cis.ohio-state.edu /hypertext/faq/usenet-faqs/bygroup/soc /religion/islam/top.html

▶ JUDAISM

Judaism Reading List An extensive

reading list of Jewish-related works, divided into the following categories: for non-Jewish readers, general Judaism, general Jewish thought, general Jewish history, Noachide laws, Torah and Talmud, Mishnah and Talmud, Torah and Talmudic commentary, Midrash, halakah codes, becoming an observant Jew, women and Judaism, and science and Judaism. Many of the entries are annotated with explanations. There are also good prefatory discussions of where to find the books.
web http://www.cis.ohio-state.edu/hyper text/faq/usenet/judaism/reading-lists /general/faq.html

The Project Genesis Home Page
Shalom! The most amazing thing about this Web page is that it offers a free (via email) subscription to online classes on a wide range of Jewish topics. Learn about the weekly Torah passage, Jewish law, prayer, Jewish holidays, and even about Jewish attitude toward gossip—all just through an email subscription. Project Genesis is also involved in Jewish activities on college campuses, and the home page provides information about that aspect of the organization.
web http://www.torah.org

Shamash Home Page Its goal is to "help bring the Jewish community into the center lanes of the 'Information Superhighway.'" Links are provided to Reform, Conservative, and Orthodox sites covering everything from Israeli politics to Jewish book lists. Information is also available about the Shamash project itself.
web http://shamash.nysernet.org

soc.culture.jewish "While Jews have argued forever about whether Judaism is more of a 'culture' or a 'religion' or something else, the choice of name for this newsgroup is not proof of anything," declares the FAQ to this newsgroup. In other words, this is the place to discuss just about everything Jewish.
usenet soc.culture.jewish
FAQ: **web** http://www.cis.ohio-state.edu /hypertext/faq/usenet-faqs/bygroup/soc /culture/jewish/top.html

► TEACHERS' LOUNGE

Comparative Religion A splendid guide to the academic study of comparative religion in cyberspace, this popular University of Washington site is frequently updated. Listings range from Baha'i to Sikhism and every faith in between.
web http://weber.u.washington.edu /~madin

Wiretap Library It's just like a library, only the texts are electronic. Religious texts like the Book of Mormon, the Quran, and the Bible are organized by faith.
url gopher://wiretap.spies.com/11 /Library/Religion

PART 6

History

THROUGH THE AGES

IF THOSE WHO DON'T REMEMBER the past are condemned to repeat it, then most of us are probably wandering around living other peoples' lives. It takes a truly original act to go down in history, but most mortals will be satisfied just learning about it. The Internet offers resources that can make the past come alive. The Ancient City of Athens will show you the remains of Greece's golden era. NetSERF will take you to Medieval times. If colonial American history is your thing, Ask Thomas Jefferson. The World History Archives covers the rest of the planet. And the National Women's History Project can explain things from the female point of view. Once you've learned about the way things used to be, act out your wildest fantasies at the Living History Forum.

▶ STARTING POINTS

Archives and Archivists Need to find the records of the Third Municipality Guard in New Orleans from 1836-1846? They're online at the New Orleans Archives, and you can link there from here. Want to trace the South African Constitutional Court's recent decision? They're easily reached, too. How did Gerald R. Ford spend his day as president? Head to the Ford exhibit to find out.
WEB http://miavx1.acs.muohio.edu /~ArchivesList/index.html

Groningen Historical Electronic Text Archive (GHETA) An ever-growing collection of articles and documents from numerous points on the historical map. Documents include late eighteenth-century shipping records from Amsterdam. The bulk of historical data, however, appears to originate in America, dating from the Revolution to the Civil War. Telnet links take you to the History Network at the University of Kansas and the Institute for Historical Research in London.
WEB http://grid.let.rug.nl/ahc/gheta.html

H-Ideas Intellectual history has been called the cocktail-party field—and reading the list will certainly give you some juicy, erudite-sounding tidbits to drop over the canapes. You won't, however, get simple answers. Ask about modern life in Athens and follow a trail of ideas in the ensuing discussion that includes Byron, Hitler, Catherine the Great, and architecture. Don't be frightened away: List members decry pretentiousness.
EMAIL listserv@uicvm.uic.edu ✍ *Type in message body:* subscribe h-ideas <your full name>

H-Net Archive An archive of historical debate, verbiage, and insight from popular history mailing lists. Some lists provide complete collections of dialog, others select popular threads. The H-Women discussion of Lizzie Borden's guilt is a must-read.
URL gopher://gopher.uic.edu/11/research /history/hnetxx

H-State One of the busiest history lists around. Participants are eager to discuss anything that touches on the history of "the state"—social welfare policy, crime and punishment, and public education. The list has a strong international base, which makes for good cross-cultural comparisons of social programs and social needs. H-State is friendly to newcomers.
EMAIL listserv@uicvm.uic.edu ✍ *Type in message body:* subscribe h-state <your full name>

Hargarett Library, Rare Map Collection A collection of maps spanning almost 500 years, from the sixteenth to the early twentieth century. Most of the maps are of the American South during the Civil War era.
WEB http://scarlett.libs.uga.edu/1h/www /darchive/hargrett/maps.html

The Historical Text Archive From the Arctic Circle to Zimbabwe, the Historical

Text Archive covers history and culture in modern process. Understand imperialism, women's history, and ethnic issues in ways you never thought you could. From tracing the roots of African genealogies to a cross-cultural women's history page, this site offers sophisticated information. More conventional resources like George Washington's speeches are also included as a bonus.
web http://www.msstate.edu/Archives/History/index.html

History Sate your appetite for information on history topics from Attila the Hun to the Bay of Pigs. A collection of academic articles has been placed online, and is complemented by primary documents and personal musings. Even Disney makes a showing, with Walt's testimony before the House Un-American Activities Committee.
web http://english-www.hss.cmu.edu/history

History at U Kansas This is it—the repository of all things past, a massive site which takes the mandate "history is everything" seriously. Luckily, it also features a search engine to help historians navigate the wealth of Web pages on art, culture, war, and politics. netsurfers can explore what it was like to be Buzz Aldrin at the U.S. National Space Agency Historical Archives, visit a Roman fort in Scotland, or discuss the Warsaw Ghetto uprising. There are literally hundreds of links to other fascinating sites.
web http://ukanaix.cc.ukans.edu/history

History Departments Around the World Want to know the best place to study the grooming habits of the Emperor Vespasian, the sexual practices of Woodrow Wilson, the subtext of *The Federalist Papers*, or the tactics of Napoleon in Russia? Use this hubsite to link to universities from Dusseldorf to Hong Kong to learn more about history.
web http://gopher.gmu.edu/other/history/research/depts.html

History Forum If you want to pick a fight on the merits or lack thereof of history,

the messages section of CompuServe's History Forum may be the good place to start. The libraries section is a bit less even, however. For example, the Napolean in Love folder supplies some juicy historical tidbits, but other folders, such as History and Science Fiction or Latin American History, remain empty.
compuserve *go* past

Institute of Historical Research This venerable institution, famous for its research into British social history, has become one of the forerunners in the use of the Net for historical research. A good collection of links leads scholars to online resources worldwide, and a primer on Net navigation instructs newbies on how to get to them. An ongoing electronic seminar touches on the hot spots of historical debate, and information is available about the institute's own projects.
web http://www.sas.ac.uk/School/Historical.htm

Library of Congress American Special Collections Brief descriptions of the resources available in the Library of Congress archives, which range from twentieth-century comic books to photos of cowboys to the maps of explorer William Clark.
web http://lcweb.loc.gov/spcoll/spclhome.html

A Selection of History Pages A Net-savvy history buff has put together a list of pages of interest to historians. The author's interests are catholic: you'll find links to the National Library of Medicine, the Armenian Research Center, a Sardinian museum, and the Magna Carta. Feel free to suggest additions.
web http://www.cm.cf.ac.uk/User/Gwyn.Price/history.html

▶ **ALTERNATE HISTORY**

alt.history.what-if What if the South had won the Civil War? Or if the Nazis had won World War II? What if Jesus had never lived? There are serious, well-reasoned questions about Ceasar's effect

on the Roman Empire, as well as fantasy speculations about Atlantis and other "lost" civilizations. The group is always polite, mostly interesting, and sometimes frightening when it plays fast and loose with certain truths.
USENET alt.history.what-if

The Usenet Alternate History List This Web site contains an annotated bibliography of "alternate history" which is a polite way of saying imaginary history. What if the Nazis had won, the submachine gun had been invented before the Civil War, Trotsky had won out over Stalin, or John Lennon hadn't founded the Beatles? While the answer to this last question is obvious—Paul, advertising; George, mechanic; Ringo, circus clown—other questions generate endless, and endlessly fascinating, discussions.
WEB http://www.panix.com/~rbs/AH

▶ LIVING HISTORY

alt.history.living If you've always wanted to wear thigh-high black leather SS boots or imagine yourself as Rhett Butler—but in that pink hooped number Scarlett wore to the picnic—there are other places on the Net for you. If you are serious about recreating the past, uncomfortable shoes and all, alt.history.living is a good place to meet like-minded. Most participants are men who like to play soldier, but who are also concerned about authenticity—which leads to earnest debates. The place of women in battle, the value of "amateur" history, and the "correct" way to act out the past, are discussed with fervor and intelligence.
USENET alt.history.living

Living History Forum If you've ever thought that you may have been born in the wrong century, you might want to start hanging out in CompuServe's Living History Forum which is dedicated to "the re-enactment of selected periods of history." Topics of discussion include how laundry was done in 1198 A.D.? These people are serious about living as

history—even to the point of doing without the spin cycle. The Society for Creative Anachronisms gathers here to play lords, ladies, and lance victims.
COMPUSERVE go living

The Shadow of the Past Home Page Do you envision yourself as Sheriff Matt Dillon riding hell-bent after bank robbers, or perhaps as Calamity Jane downing a drink at the saloon, pistols at her sides? A group of Americans who like to put on cowboy clothes and recreate the wild West have put together a page of instructions for reliving history "properly." A calendar of events is included.
WEB http://www.sptddog.com/sotp.html

▶ MATERIAL HISTORY

Artifact Bob believes that the invention of the vacuum cleaner changed the gender basis of rug cleaning. Alana thinks it was always a woman's place to get thedirt out. Artifact is the home of online discussion of material culture—the real stuff (or junk) of history. Museum curators, historians, preservationists, and the insatiably curious come together on this active list to discuss the evolution of vacuum cleaners, manhole covers, tombstone design, and techniques for preserving faux-marble facades. If, like a recent poster, you want to chat about the origins of gift wrapping, this is the place for you.
EMAIL listserv@umdd.umd.edu ✍ *Type in message body:* subscribe artifact <your full name>

Material Culture Material culture—what is it? The stuff of everyday life—clothes, stoves,dishpans, plows, and guns. Concerned with the "relationship between artifacts and social relations irrespective of time and place" this anthropligical approach to history tries to "explore the linkage between the construction of social identities and the production and use of material culture." This page has a good set of links for anyone interested in perusing history through objects.
WEB http://www.interlog.com/%7 Ejabram/elise/material.htm

▶ THE HISTORY OF...

Association for Gravestone Studies
Cemetaries can reflect the community:
Burial inside the churchyard meant one
was a Christian soul, outside the grave-
yard, the soul was up for grabs. The
Association for Gravestone Studies site
provides some good bibliographic information, but has little content.
WEB http://www.history.rochester.edu
/ags/ags.htm

The History of Medicine The National
Library of Medicine has created several
interesting onlineexhibits. Discover
Paracelsus, a Renaissance physician
known as the "Luther of medicine" for
his radical views on chemistry. Read
about the history of the Caesarean section, which earned its name from Caesar's mandate that all women in danger
of not surviving labor should be cut
open (The common myth that Caesar
was born of C-section seems unlikely
since his mother lived into old age—
almost impossible that she would have
had she had a Caesarean section delivery). Other presentations tell the history
of the Public Health Service and the
National Medical Library. Finally, for
researchers, the library has placed
60,000 images online in a searchable
database covering medicine, showing
pictures such as a 4th century B.C.
Greek vase, Civil War field hospitals, and
modern VD campaigns.
WEB http://www.nlm.nih.gov

The Pickle in History Cleopatra, George
Washington, Thomas Jefferson, Amerigo
Vespucci—they are all appreciated the
pickle. Hey, it's high in vitamin C.
WEB http://www.moonlake.com/pickle
/phistory.htm

rec.food.historic Nutritionists, historians, geographers, and the curious with
good appetites engage in interesting and
unusual discourses about what people
eat and why. Long threads speculate on
how certain spices became popular, why
the tomato was thought poisonous, and
what Scandinavians ate before the pota-
to came from the New World (herring).
Friendly and funny, rec.food.historic is a
place to find new-old recipes—the eighteenth century way to make catsup or
the Bayou variant of fry sauce—and
other food for thought. Perhaps because
of its homey subject matter, this news-
goup has the feeling of a close bunch of
friends chatting over a good meal.
USENET rec.food.historic

ANCIENT HISTORY

IN CYBERSPACE, THE LATEST IN COMputer technology brings you the earliest in human civilization. Why pick up a dusty, old manuscript when ancient documents, from papyrus literature to the Dead Sea Scrolls, are at your fingertips? Start unraveling the cybermummy of knowledge at the Ancient World Web or Worlds of Late Antiquity. If you want to dig deeper, check out ArchNet or the Archaeological Museum of Bologna.

▶ STARTING POINTS

Ancient History Resources Not just old stuff, but really, really, really old stuff—articles about ancient history in Africa, the Americas, Asia, Australia, and Europe.
WEB http://history.cc.ukans.edu/history /subtree/ancient.html

The Ancient World Web Providing links to hundreds of terrific ancient history sites, as well as descriptions of related newsgroups and mailing lists, this Web page author stays on top of what's new in the ancient world, offering netsurfers the very latest from antiquity. If anthropology is more to your taste, the Aboriginal Database and North American Native Culture sites are just a link away. Learn about the Coptic Church, read some of Virgil's works, or stroll through a virtual rendition of the Emperor Diocletian's ornate palace at Spalato with equal ease. This is a great place to start for both teachers and students.
WEB http://atlantic.evsc.virginia.edu /julia/AncientWorld.html

Arachnion: A Journal of Ancient Literature and History on the Web This fledgling publication endeavors to combine the world of the ancients—classical literature and history—with the very modern by creating an electronic scholarly journal. Peruse the table of contents, (Looking for articles on Les rois de Rome? Speech-making and Persuasion in Homer and Apollonius?) then download the current issue.
WEB http://www.cisi.unito.it/arachne /arachne.html

Earthlore: Mysteries? or Lost Histories? Unsolved mysteries for the intelligentsia and lovers of ancient myths and legends, seeking the latest scholarly insights on everything from the lost city of Atlantis to the Holy Grail. The first legend to be examined, which recent data suggests is contrary to widely held Western thinking: Could Moses have been the Pharoah Akhnaton? Read the latest theories from the fields of physiology, archeology, linguistics, and history. It's fun to tug at the pillars of Western thought as a cure for millennial fever.
WEB http://www.globalnet.net/elore /elore10.html

Worlds of Late Antiquity You don't have to be a member of Professor O'Donnell's class to learn from his superb Web course. Lavishly illustrated hypertext essays explore the worlds of St. Augustine, Boethius, and Cassiodorus. The critical works of literary and artistic lights are at your fingertips—take a peek at Priscus's account of a visit to Attila the Hun.
WEB http://ccat.sas.upenn.edu/jod/wola .html

▶ ARCHAEOLOGY

Archeological Fieldwork Server Anyone with an overwhelming urge to spend a summer digging in the dirt with a toothbrush should check out this directory to fieldwork opportunities around the world. Who knows? An archaeological dig may be taking place right in your own backyard.
WEB http://durendal.cit.cornell.edu

Archaeological Museum of Bologna "The Archaeological Museum of Bologna is located in the ancient 'Ospedale della Morte' (Death Hospital). It dates back to the XV century and was inaugurated in

1881." Though the museum occupies the "Death Hospital," this site is very much alive—the only stiffs are mummies. Evoking Italian charm, the museum houses collections of prehistoric, Etruscan, Roman, Greek, and Egyptian archaeological information.
WEB http://www.comune.bologna.it /bologna/Cultura/Museicomun/Archeo logico/ArcheoMuseumHomePage.html

Archaeological Reports Online Dig through this collection of illustrated archeological reports from the near east. Choose from the Tall-E Bakun dig in Iran, the Titris Hoyuk in Turkey, or the Valley of the Kings in Egypt, among others.
WEB http://www.oi.uchicago.edu/OI /DEPT/RA/ABZU/ABZU_SUBINDX _ARCH_SITES.HTML

Archeology of Northeastern North America Get a sense of what life was like for Priscilla Mullins or Squanto by taking a Walking Tour of Plimoth Plantation and Hobbamock's Homesite. Connect to one of the other sites dedicated to pre-expressway New England, such as the dig at Grove Street Cemetery in New Haven, Conn.
WEB http://spirit.lib.uconn.edu/ArchNet /Regions/Northeast.html

Architecture & Architectural Sculpture of the Mediterranean Basin The site houses 2,000 exquisite images of classical and Hellenistic architecture in Italy, Greece, and Turkey, and Medieval and Renaissance architecture in Italy and France. Each image is fully annotated.
WEB http://www.ncsa.uiuc.edu/SDG /Experimental/anu-art-history /architecture.html

ArchNet Obsessed with bones, bricks, and bygone days? Click on the shovel to get to the museum, or the globe to search by region. Link from this Web page to archeological investigations, academic departments, museum, and research facilities, as well as information on the newest techniques in historic archeology, geo-archeology, archeome-

try, and ethnohistory. There's even a page of archeological software.
WEB http://spirit.lib.uconn.edu/archnet /archnet.html

ArchNet-Europe Before Versailles, before Big Ben, and before the Sistine Chapel—find out about the Roman aqueduct system, the rowdy world of the Vikings, and the Neolithic cave paintings of Southern France by linking to some of the excellent sites listed. There are also numerous links to online journals such as Theoretical Anthropology, professional groups, and museum collections from Hungary to Glasgow. Archeological site reports are organized by country.
WEB http://www.bham.ac.uk/BUFAU /Projects/EAW/index.html

Arctic Archaeology After a visit to this informative, illustrated sight, netters will probably know more about how people like the Thule lived—hanging onto the tundra, subsisting on melted ice and qiviut.
WEB http://watarts.uwaterloo.ca/ANTHRO /rwpark/ArcticArchStuff/ArcticIntro.html

Classics and Mediterranean Archaeology Home Page A large searchable collection of links, journals, articles, archeologicalreports, image catalogs, and databases, the Classics and Mediterranean Archaeology Home Page will thrill students with the research short cuts provided.
WEB http://rome.classics.lsa.umich.edu /welcome.html

Society for American Archeology The best part about this pretty site is the very clear introductory information about the science of archeology, which is a whole lot more than just digging. Also check out the section on Participating in Archeology for tips on how to get your hands dirty.
WEB http://www.saa.org

Stone Pages Millions of otherwise normal people are fascinated by stone circles, standing stones, and other ancient manifestations of the human need to

organize (Tetris is a modern one). This site, which is not just for wide-eyed moon worshippers, contains links to archeological sites in England, Ireland, and Scotland.
WEB http://joshua.micronet.it/utenti /dmeozzi/homeng.html

DOCUMENTS

Papyrology Home Page Papyrology has nothing to do with papayas. It is the study of manuscripts written on paper made from the Egyptian papyrus plant. This site offers a chance to scrutinize writing and images from thousands of years ago. Many of the world's largest papyri collections can be accessed from this site, which also houses scholarly literature.
WEB http://www-personal.umich.edu /~jmucci/papyrology

Scrolls From the Dead Sea After remaining hidden in jars in a desert for thousands of years, and enduring 50 years of seclusion in the hands of scholars, the Dead Sea Scrolls have surfaced to be scanned by the entire Net world. Read the fascinating story of the discovery of the Scrolls, and the speculation on the society that created them. View images of selected scroll fragments dating from the third century B.C. to 68 C.E.—1,000 years before the earliest known Biblical manuscripts.
WEB http://sunsite.unc.edu/expo/deadsea .scrolls.exhibit/intro.html

NEAR EAST

Abu Simbel All the majesty and all the mystery comes alive though this virtual rendering of the great pyramid. Abu Simbel can be explored in detail, and the authors of this site have done a good job of explaining its particular symbols.
WEB http://www.ccer.ggl.ruu.nl/abu _simbel/abu_simbel1.html

ABZU: Guide to Resources for the Study of the Ancient Near East ABZU makes writing a paper on ancient Mesopotamia easy. In addition to links to ancient his-

tory and archaeological sites, this collection holds an impressive collection of text documents indexed by author and subject. The University of Chicago's Oriental Institute, ABZU's sponsor, has uploaded incredible artifacts and illustrations to enrich the Near Eastern experience.
WEB http://www-oi.uchicago.edu/OI/DEPT /RA/ABZU/ABZU.HTML

Annual Egyptological Bibliography Home Page If Cleopatra and mummies pique your interest, this site is a good place to begin. The page offers reviews of the new Egyptological studies, and links to other resources.
WEB http://www.leidenuniv.nl/nino/aeb .html

The Institute of Egyptian Art and Archeology Take a look at a 4,000 year old loaf of bread placed in a tomb to nourish a king in the afterlife. This attractive sight offers a full-color tour of Egypt and many insights into the ancient culture. The details are the highlights— an image of a small statue of Nedjemu (c. 2544-2407 B.C.), or stone fragments from the grinding of flour that left ancient Egyptians toothless at a young age. *The Book of the Dead* is available for those wishing to mummify their nearest and dearest.
WEB http://www.memst.edu/egypt/main .html

GREEK & ROMAN

Alexander the Great's Home Page He slept with the *Iliad* under his pillow. His tutor was Aristotle. He was just 4'3". He was Alexander the Great, one of the most charismatic characters of ancient history. This site outlines the life and accomplishments of the famous Greek.
WEB http://www.rmplc.co.uk/eduweb /sites/hampscit/alexander/alex.html

The Ancient City of Athens Maps and slides of the remains of Greece's golden era.
WEB http://www.indiana.edu/~kglowack /Athens/Athens.html

Barbarians on the Greek Periphery An illustrated essay on the relationship between Celtic and Greek art in the fifth century B.C.E. Maps and photos bring you closer to these early forms of art.
WEB http://faraday.clas.virginia.edu /~umw8f/Cze/HomePage.html

Greek and Roman Cities of Western Turkey There is a lot of text here, but this site paints a sweeping portrait of the interaction of the eastern and classical worlds from antiquity to the middle ages—detailing everything from aqueducts to hippodromes. A searchable database, which will hold information of classical architecture throughout the Near East, is under development.
WEB http://rubens.anu.edu.au/turkeybook /toc1.html

Greek Mythology Why do we have seasons? Have you forgotten the story of Persephone, Hades, and Demeter? If so, this essay will explain everything you need to know about ancient gods, heroes, and mythological creatures.
WEB http://www.intergate.net/uhtml /.jhunt/greek_myth/greek_myth.html

Pompeii This is the closest anyone has come in the last 1,000 years to recreating the feeling of walking the streets of Pompeii. In this wonderful, full-color plan of the ancient city, visitors move a little figure through doorways, around corners to temples, villas, and squares—each lavishly illustrated and minutely described. You'll learn about Paganism at the altar of Diana and roofing practice through an architectural animation. It's worth several hours of exploration.
WEB http://jefferson.village.virginia.edu /pompeii/page-1.html

Romarch Want to know how to do as the Romans did? This Web site has general texts on Roman life, law, and aesthetics, as well as detailed archeological reports from all corners of the empire. Use the clickable map to choose an area like Britannia and you'll be thrown into an army encampment in the cold north near Hadrian's Wall. Or head to Gallia and explore a shipwreck off the coast of France. This is a perfect site for Roman researchers of all ages.
WEB http://www.umich.edu/~pfoss /ROMARCH.html

Spalato Exhibit Lifestyles of the rich and famous, circa 293 A.D. A virtual exhibit lets you wander the halls of this gem of late Roman architecture—through the great walls and gate, ornate entrance hall, bed chambers, and even the vaults below, where the Emperor Diocletian tortured his enemies.
WEB http://sunsite.unc.edu/expo/palace .exhibit/intro.html

WebAcropol Suffering from an unfulfilled desire to be a vestal virgin? Take a virtual tour of the Acropolis.
WEB http://www.softlab.ntua.gr/projects /webacropol

AMERICAN HISTORY

WE'VE COME A LONG WAY, BABY. From the collision of Christopher Columbus with native cultures in 1492 to our creation of the World Wide Web, American history has been a short trip to global dominance. But it wasn't easy. NativeWeb: Historical Material will tell you that the "New World" already belonged to somebody else when we "found" it, and the Columbus Menu has enough guilt-inducing tales to make you want to give it back. The Witchcraft Hysteria of 1692 wasn't exactly a roll in the hay, and Slave Narratives will relate an even darker period of American history. Though Abolition Exhibit shows you how America's future was made a bit brighter, the Ellis Island Immigration Exhibit proves that Americans are no strangers to alienation.

▶ STARTING POINTS

African-American History Explore the controversial Black Panthers group via a coloring book. Learn about some of the personalities of the Abolitionists. The National Civil Rights Museum and the *Seattle Times* Martin Luther King Jr. Web site are just two of the stellar links at this compilation.
WEB http://www.auc.edu/~tpearson /hist.html

American History Get the 411 on everything from the Civil War to presidential addresses at this section of AOL's Academic Assistance Center. Post questions on the bulletin board or sign up for tutoring. The truly desperate can access a history teacher by email using the forum's Teacher Pager.
AMERICA ONLINE *keyword* aac→American History

American Memory Pulled from the vast and valuable collections of the Library of Congress, American Memory carries a series of excellent searchable online exhibits. Experience the Civil War through photos of historical battles.

Relive WWII with posters of Rosie the Riveter on a fuselage. Meet ex-slave Mandy Long Roberson in one of the thousands of Depression-era interviews transcribed online. All collections are fully cross-indexed for an easy search.
WEB http://rs6.loc.gov/amhome.html

From Revolution to Reconstruction A great resource of articles by historians, with hypertext links to primary sources, this Web site covers American history from the settlement of the colonies through the Reagan presidency. Choose the link labeled "The search for religious and political freedom" for an illustrated outline of early colonization, the Mayflower Compact, the Charter of Massachusetts Bay, colonial maps, and a law code from the Virginia Colony.
WEB http://grid.let.rug.nl/~welling/usa /revolution.html

Selections from The African-American Mosaic: A Library of Congress Resource Guide for the Study of Black History and Culture More than 500 years of history is covered in this engaging exhibit that traces the African-American experience from slavery through abolition,migration, and the struggle for civil rights. Each section uses a variety of sources to make the history come alive, including the journals of a Quaker shipowner, an anti-slavery broadside, demographic statistics of a black Kansas settlement, newspaper coverage of the Scottsboro trial, and transcripts of the famous WPA slave narratives.
WEB http://lcweb.loc.gov/exhibits/African .American/intro.html

▶ PRE-COLONIAL

Cherokee National Historical Society Follow the Cherokees to the time before thousands were killed by colonizing westerners. Take a cybertour of the ancient village of Tsa-La-Gi or visit present day Oklahoma to see the Adams Corner Rural Village. Find out why the

Cherokees called their trek across the country the "Trail of Tears." Then sign up for membership to the Cherokee National Historical Society and help preserve the history of this nation.
web http://www.Powersource.com /powersource/heritage

Columbus and the Age of Discovery It's 1492 and time to set sail for India. This site lets users find out about the intrepid explorer who stumbled upon the American continent and the myths surrounding him. Check out research papers written by students and take a course on Colonial Latin America. Also learn about the Mediterranean and how its people were affected by the New World.
web http://www.millersv.edu/~columbus

Columbus Menu Essays from a Christian group that opposes the celebration of Columbus Day, as well as protests by Native Americans: "In school I was taught the names Columbus, Cortez, and Pizzaro and a dozen other filthy murderers. A bloodline all the way to General Miles, Daniel Boone and General Eisenhower. No one mentioned the names of even a few of the victims. But don't you remember Chaske, whose spine was crushed so quickly by Mr. Pizzaro's boot? What words did he cry into the dust?" We have all learned that the history of the founding of America was also the unfounding of a long-standing Native American culture. Not only does this site remember those forgotten in favor of Columbus's glory, but it also explains how colonialism worked and how the U.S. still engages in it today.
web http://web.maxwell.syr.edu/nativeweb /subject/quincent/columbus.html

NativeWeb: Historical Material "All that exists, lives. The lamp walks around. The walls of the houses have voices of their own. Even the chamber-pot has a separate land and house. The skins sleeping in the bags talk at night. The antlers lying on the tombs arise at night and walk in procession around the mounds, while the deceased rise and greet the living." These words from a Chukchi

shaman are part of the Native American culture that seemed so different from that of English settlers. Learn about the Battle of Wounded Knee or discover if the names of your towns have Native American origins.
web http://web.maxwell.syr.edu/native web/history/histindex.html

An Ongoing Voyage It may not be so important to know that Columbus lost his shoe in 1492—but Americans should know that he brought tobacco, potatoes, and the hammock back from the New World, in exchange for horses, disease, and destruction. This Web site features a section on pre-Columbian society, and illustrated histories that tell the story of conquest and exploration.
web http://sunsite.unc.edu/expo/1492 .exhibit/Intro.html

▶ COLONIAL

Archiving Early America Why is the word "vessel" printed as "veffel"? "Same" as "fame"? The short answer is that printers used "f"s when a long "s" was used. What is a long "s"? That requires the long answer, and it's available at this site, which archives original eighteenth-century documents.
web http://earlyamerica.com

Ask Thomas Jefferson Even though he's been dead for more than 150 years, Thomas Jefferson is happy to answer queries about rebellion, the price of freedom, divine right, slavery, and scores of other topics. The quotes are all authentic. The selection shows the political leaning of the page's author: libertarian.
web http://www.mit.edu:8001/activities /libertarians/ask-thomas-jefferson /jefferson.html

George Washington: The Making of an Icon This site examines our first president, exploring the ways in which he has come to represent our ideas and hopes for America. Excellent, well-written essays are accompanied by lovely paintings of Martha and George.
web http://darwin.clas.virginia.edu

/~lgg2q/washington.html

H-South Although it was designed as a scholarly list, H-South also provides a great deal of "Southern hospitality" to newcomers and regulars (even offering travel tips). Because H-South is not limited to "history," but also embraces culture, a variety of topics are discussed and relived by the large contingent of Southerners on the list. Recent threads include the sexual abuse of slaves, whether Maryland was a "Northern" state, voodoo, and barbecue.
EMAIL listserv@uicvm.uic.edu ✍ *Type in message body:* subscribe h-south <your full name>

Slave Narratives Enslavement, the horrific middle passage (the Atlantic crossing in overpacked ships), religious practices, family life, punishment, and emancipation are chronicled at Slave Narratives. This site helps to remember some of those who suffered through one of the darkest periods of American history.
WEB http://vi.uh.edu/pages/mintz/primary.htm

Thomas Paine This page's header reads: "Reproducible electronic publishing can defeat censorship." Old Tom Paine would have been proud. You can freely read all the texts that inspired revolutions (The Rights of Man, Common Sense, and The Existence of God) and got Tom in trouble with the English, French, and American governments.
WEB http://freethought.tamu.edu/library/historical/thomas_paine/index.html

The Witchcraft Hysteria of 1692 Eye of newt, tongue of step-sister, toenail of classmate… Budding witches can check out what all the hubbub was about in Massachusetts circa 1692. See pictures of the witch trials and those who were condemned to death. Look at the photo of a witch house in present-day Salem. Find out about the Witches Tricentenary Memorial and how these women protested their guilt. The Witches' League for Public Awareness link will demystify public misconceptions about witches.
WEB http://www.star.net/salem/witches.htm

The World of Benjamin Franklin Come here to appreciate the genius of Ben Franklin, scientist, inventor, statesman, printer, philosopher, musician, and economist. You can download a movie about this master of kite-flying, or explore his life and works through a series of hypertext essays.
WEB http://sln.fi.edu/franklin/rotten.html

19TH CENTURY

Abolition Exhibit Details the end of slavery and how it happened with the help of key figures and parties. Learn about Jonathan Edwards Jr.'s involvement in the early anti-slavery movement and how the issue of black mothers being separated from their children was used to gain sympathy from women abolitionists. Documents, petitions and anti-abolitionist sentiment—it's all presented in black and white.
WEB http://lcweb.loc.gov/exhibits/African.American/abol.html

Abraham Lincoln Was it the beard? The hat? or maybe it was the suit that made Lincoln's brief speech at the Gettysburg Battlefield so memorable. This site has links to pictures, history, and a quiz for those who need to test their trivial knowledge. You'll spit out wooden teeth after checking out the link to a Madlib Gettysburg Address. Find out about Lincoln's family tree, famous quotes, and other things that made Lincoln a great leader. Celebrate Lincoln for the next four score and seven years by checking out the links on Birthday Events.
WEB http://deil.lang.uiuc.edu/web.pages/holidays/Lincoln.html

Abraham Lincoln's First Inaugural Address Text of the famous equivocation on slavery that still didn't stop the war.
URL gopher://gopher.vt.edu:10010/02/115/2

Abraham Lincoln's Second Inaugural

Address "Slavery has become an offense against God." In case you missed it: the full text of Lincoln's second inaugural address.
WEB ftp://ftp.msstate.edu/pub/docs /history/USA/19th_C./lincoln-inaugural-2

The American Antiquarian Society
Three nights prior to the Battle of Lexington and Concord, Isaiah Thomas, friend of the common man and active Whig, smuggled his printing press out of Boston and set it up in Worcester, Mass., and the AAS was born. Since its auspicious beginings, the AAS has become one of the greatest research libraries and societies in the United States. Specializing in the American history to 1877, the AAS is also thought to have the finest collection of American newspapers anywhere. An important resource for American historians, this site houses online searchable catalogs, email addresses of its accomodating staff, seminar information, and the latest Massachusetts weather.
URL gopher://mark.mwa.org:70/1

Amwest-H Could there have been a real Dr. Quinn, Medicine Woman? What kind of music did Indians really play? And what about gays and lesbians in the old West? No query is refused at Amwest-H. Members chat amicably with well-known scholars about the evolution of country music and how mean Billy the Kid really was ("pretty doggone nasty").
EMAIL listserv@umrvmb.umr.edu ✍ *Type in message body:* subscribe amwest-h <your full name>

The Emancipation Proclamation Better late than never—the text of the document that freed the slaves in rebel-controlled territory by invoking "the considerate judgment of mankind and the gracious favor of Almighty God."
URL ftp://ftp.msstate.edu/pub/docs /history/USA/19th_C./emancipation

Frederick Douglass Museum and Cultural Center Take a cybertrip to Rochester (a mecca for information about African-American and womens

rights) and learn about Frederick Douglass, leader and statesman. The site contains a timeline of his life and a calendar of important events in African-American history. Links to other Douglass sites include one to sound clip of an actor reading the speech, "An Appeal to the British People."
WEB http://www.vivanet.com/freenet/f /fdm/index.html

Gettysburg Address If you didn't memorize it in fifth grade, now's your opportunity—the complete text is here.
WEB http://jefferson.village.virginia.edu /readings/gettysburg.txt

Gettysburg Archive The full text of books on the battle of Gettysburg resides here, along with biographies of the major players in this famous historical drama. Choose sides and sing after retrieving the lyrics of "Dixie" or the "Battle Hymn of the Republic." You can even download a .GIF entitled "amputations" from the picture archive.
URL gopher://cee.educ.indiana.edu:70 /11/Turner_Adventure_Learning /Gettysburg_Archive

Sketch of a Three Years' Travel in South American, California, and Mexico In November of 1848, Eugene Ring sailed out of New York City on the Robert Bruce, bound for California and the promise of riches. This is a diary of his adventures in South America, California, and Mexico.
WEB http://uts.cc.utexas.edu/~scring /index.html

20TH CENTURY

A Timeline of the Counter-Culture "A work-in-progress which is a timeline of significant events for baby boomers, bohemians, beatnicks, and hippies, focusing especially on the sixties. 'Significant' so far means it was significant to me, a sixties hippie, and my hippie friends. I started putting together this timeline because I was trying to write about the sixties, and I had to remind myself of what happened when." Too much '60s indulgence may have temporarily affected the memory loss of this aging hippie, but the author has nonetheless put together a useful timeline including the Age of Aquarius, Woodstock, the Weathermen, and Spiro Agnew. Celebrate the advent of the sexual revolution—the pill came on the market in December of 1960. Relive the drug culture—the late Timothy Leary took his first tab of acid on August 9, 1960. And in 1966, John Lennon met Yoko Ono. **URL** gopher://gopher.well.sf.ca.us/11 /Community/60sTimeline

Apollo 11: One Giant Leap Houston didn't have a problem when it launched the Apollo 11 mission. Reach for the moon by visiting this site which includes images from the actual mission (takeoff, picking up samples, coming off ladder onto moon, and that sort of thing). Take off to the Air and Space Museum to learn about what Armstrong, Aldrin, and Collins discovered on the moon's surface and what they brought back with them. Remember that plaque the astronauts left on the moon? You can find out what it said. If you're planning a trip to the moon anytime soon, a mandatory reading of the mission schedule is in order.
WEB http://www.osf.hq.nasa.gov/apollo /apo11.html

The Cuban Missile Crisis: Walden's Paths Go to the brink of war with this progression of the events leading to the Cuban Missle Crisis. Learn about Kennedy, Krushchev, and Castro and their involvement in this potential prelude to full-scale atomic war. Read actual letters between Kennedy ("Let us not negotiate out of fear") and Krushchev and interpret the subtext and conditions of the disagreement. Read first- and second-hand accounts of this two-week event. Includes facts about the geography that made it possible, and a brief tour of Cuba.
WEB http://csdl.cs.tamu.edu/cgi-bin /walden/path_server?cmc-path+

Ellis Island Immigration Exhibit The University of California at Riverside obtained tons of great black and white photos of pre-Statue of Liberty Ellis Island for this online exhibit. You'll feel like an immigrant entering the country at the turn of the century when you see the detailed pictures of baggage inspection and even Christmas celebrations at the port of entry. Observe racist U.S. inspectors examining the eyes of immigrants to enforce the Chinese Exclusionary Act. Boat, port, and aerial views of Ellis Island from 1900 to 1920 are plentiful, along with some shots of Brooklyn and the immigrants who were allowed into the country.
WEB http://cmp1.ucr.edu/exhibitions /immigration_id.html

I Have a Dream Martin Luther King Jr.'s famous speech, delivered from the steps of the Lincoln Memorial in August, 1963. **WEB** http://www.ai.mit.edu/~isbell/HFh /black/events_and_people/005.dream _speech • http://web66.coled.umn.edu /new/MLK/MLK.html

Martin Luther King Jr. "I refuse to accept the view… that the bright day of peace and brotherhood can never be a reality." At its Web site, the *Seattle Times* documents the important political figure who said this in his famous speech. The sound clips of King available here include "I Have a Dream," "Let Freedom Ring" and "The Promised Land." Travel down the King timeline and learn about the January 20th holiday, then converse online with others about the Civil Rights Movement and the life of King. Also check out the electronic classroom with quizzes, and study guides.
WEB http://www.seattletimes.com/mlk

Network Television News Archive Whether interested in media coverage or the actual event, you can find out what America knew and when it knew it at this archive for abstracts of television news stories. To use the archive, choose a year from 1968 to the present, or search by keyword.
URL gopher://tvnews.Vanderbilt.Edu:70

San Francisco Digger Archives Looking for a term paper topic? Write about the San Francisco Diggers, a group of artsy anarchists who took their name from a sect of seventeenth-century English anarchists. Annals of the anarcho-theater group that documented the days of free love and daisies in the Haight in the '60s are available. Time-travel to the era of day-glo and day-trippers with reminiscences of the Merry Pranksters' acid tests. Then, do a quick reread of the Digger Manifesto.
WEB http://www.webcom.com/enoble/diggers/diggers.html

Senator Joe McCarthy: A Multimedia Celebration Listen to the 10-minute soundbites of Senate hearings to snuff out the enemy. Plenty of movie clips and pictures including a mystery guest who was a Nazi sympathizer. Hang out with Joe's friends, Ike (Eisenhower) and Dick (Nixon). Cheer for McCarthy as he gives speeches at the 1952 Republican Convention and brags about the work of his Senate commitee. Then watch the end of McCarthyism when he is bashed by the Counsel for the Army in front of a television audience. Links to satirical sites and audio archives of more famous speeches are provided.
WEB http://webcorp.com/mccarthy

Voices of the Civil Rights Era A brief essay on the hopeful sixties, along with links to audio clips of speeches by Kennedy, King, and Malcolm X.
WEB http://www.webcorp.com/civilrights/index.htm

> **DOCUMENTS**

American Originals "We find the defendant, Alphonso Capone, guilty …" The original verdict paper (with signatures) with which Capone was found guilty for tax evasion is available at this site, alongside many more original American documents. See the determination in Washington's handwriting of his first inaugural address, which talks about how he will make democracy a success. History buffs' wallets will fly out of their pockets when they get to see the Lousiana Purchase deed. Bring back Dick with Nixon's resignation letter or read the police blotter for Lincoln's assassination. Then, sink into the report made by a U.S. Navy officer upon discovering the Titanic's collision.
WEB http://www.nara.gov/exhall/originals/original.html

Presidential Addresses Did you know that when Andrew Jackson was thirteen, he was captured by the British during the Revolutionary War? Or that Woodrow Wilson called the government a "debauched instrument of evil" in his first inaugural address? This site is a great resource for presidental info. Look for biographies of all the presidents, inaugural addresses, and selected State of the Union addresses.
WEB http://grid.let.rug.nl/~welling/usa/presidents/addresses.html

U.S Historical Documents The biggies are all here—the Declaration of Independence, the Mayflower Compact, the Monroe Doctrine, and the Declaration of War on Japan.
URL gopher://wiretap.spies.com/11/Gov/US-History

EUROPEAN HISTORY

WELCOME TO EUROPEAN HISTORY, where kings were kings, and everyone else didn't have it so good. History may not immediately evoke an association with the rules of drama, but the European version had it all: mystery, violence, betrayal, and sexual scandal. For tales of conquest, check out The World of the Vikings. Engage in the Renaissance at the Leonardo da Vinci Museum. Enlighten yourself with Eighteenth-Century Resources. Then find out about more than just furniture at the Victorian Web.

▶ STARTING POINTS

Electronic Sources for West European History and Culture An annotated index of mailing lists, text archives, and Web pages related to history and culture, organized by time period, nation, and resource type. No links provided.
URL gopher://infolib.lib.berkeley.edu /0/resdbs/hist/westeur

Guide to German History Resources on the Net A guide to electronic resources about Germany. The document includes addresses for a German encyclopedia, a dictionary, a directory of German nobility, and mailing lists dedicated to discussion of Attila the Hun, the Hapsburgs, and the Holocaust. (Sorry, no Oktoberfest info.)
URL gopher://una.hh.lib.umich.edu/0 /inetdirsstacks/germanhist:mcbride

The Monarchs of England and Great Britain Sure everyone knows that the Norman Conquest took place in 1066, but can you name each of the Normans individually? Gail Dedrick has provided loads of paintings of English monarchs, from the House of Lancaster to the House of York, as well as brief encapsulations of their lives. Dedrick's "Ye Olde Links" covers the early history of England from castles to the Magna Carta. Take off your spiked hat to explore Anglo Saxon England before the Vikings.

Appreciate modern utilities by visiting the plumbing page in Merry Olde England.
WEB http://www.ingress.com/~gail/index .html

Windows on Italy Windows on Italy is excellent, with terrific articles covering Italian history, on both a national and urban scale. Focus on Milano in general, or the Renaissance in particular. This site is text only, but the quality of the information will keep your interest piqued.
WEB http://www.mi.cnr.it/WOI/deagosti /history/0welcome.html

▶ MEDIEVAL

Feudal Terms of England (and other places) A dictionary of feudal terms from *Abbey* to *Yoke*, with a particularly extensive list of castle terms. You've probably heard of a dungeon, but how about a *barbican* (the gateway defending a drawbridge)?
URL gopher://wiretap.spies.com/00 /Library/Article/Socio/feudal.dic

The Gregorian Chant Home Page A Web site for serious research in medieval music and Christianity, with hypertext essays on ethnomusicology, medieval religious practices, art, and archeology. Sound files will be available soon.
WEB http://www.music.princeton.edu /chant_html

Labyrinth: World Wide Web Server for Medieval Studies You might very well get lost among the offerings of this home page dedicated to the Dark Ages which features links to entire libraries of medieval classics in Latin, French, Italian, and Middle English. Spend a little time with *Sir Gawain and the Green Knight*, or pore over the intricacies of Duc Du Barry's *Book of Hours*. Pages are indexed by culture, country, and topic—everything from medicine to music. You'll be rewarded with Gregori-

an chants and Florentine tax data from 1427-1429.
web http://www.georgetown.edu /labyrinth/labyrinth-home.html

Mediev-L Jay asks, "Could people in the Middle Ages swim?" Did the erudite scholars of the medieval list jump on him and beat him soundly for asking such a silly question? No—they spent a week debating and discussing the query. Charlemagne could swim; most sailors could not (they preferred to drown quickly). One reader suggested that it must have been uncommon or else the dunking test for witches would have been senseless—and another week was spent on the topic of witches and how to spot them. Someone else wondered when people began swimming for pleasure rather than to save their lives. Sure, a lot of those on Mediev-L can quote in Latin, but they'll speak in English too. Newcomers are welcome.
email listserv@ukanvm.bitnet ✍ *Type in message body:* subscribe mediev-l <your full name>

NetSERF This site manages to merge the '90s with the medieval era with a compendium of sites. The section on medieval social history is particularly good.
web http://www.cua.edu/www/hist/netserf

Project Aldus: Early Modern Virtual Library and Resource Center The Johns Hopkins University library has compiled a brief overview of the culture of early modern Europe. There are numerous online texts from the literary lights of the era to downloadable images of important genre paintings.
web http://www.jhu.edu/~english/aldus /aldus.main.html

Richard III Society Richard III was the twelfth of thirteen children, and the youngest of seven siblings to survive childhood. When his family, the Yorks, came into power, it didn't seem likely that young Richard would end up on the throne. Yet he did, and his reign and death became the subject of Shake-speare's famous play. This page is an excellent resource for those interested in Richard III, or fifteenth-century England.
web http://www.webcom.com/~blanchrd /gateway.html

The Vikings An excellent essay on the history of the legendary invaders from the North. Raids in England, Ireland, France, Russia, Iceland, Greenland, and North America hardly made the Vikings the most popular kingdom in the world, but, hey, it's lonely at the top. This essay explains why the Scandinavian warriors were so powerful and successful.
web http://odin.dep.no/ud/nornytt/uda -302.html

The World of the Vikings They may have been the world's first "wind surfers," as one contributor to this site calls them, but Vikings weren't catching waves. This site compiles some very interesting Viking-related sites. The Electronic Beowulf Project of the British Library uses modern technology to retell the tale of Grendel and the She-monster with a new vigor. At other sites, net-surfers can learn medieval ship-building and Runic writing. There's even a Bryggen Runic font available for down-loading and a Runecaster to tell the future. If the sea is in your blood, you might try to join the Viking Network.
web http://www.demon.co.uk/history /index.html

► RENAISSANCE

Aldus The early modern period in Eng-land, otherwise known as the English Renaissance, is brought to life with paintings and writings. The well-bal-anced menu of texts, which include poems written by Elizabeth I, is comple-mented by a beautiful selection of images.
web http://www.jhu.edu/~english/aldus

Electric Renaissance Designed for a college course, this site recreates the Renaissance with an electronic flair. Essays introduce Renaissance social relations, economics, politics, and reli-

gion, to inform readings of the *Canterbury Tales*, Decameron, or Montaigne's Essays. Connect to related sites on the luminaries of the Renaissance—Boticelli, Michelangelo, and Machiavelli. Maps, pictures, and sounds make this a comprehensive multimedia experience.
WEB http://viper.idbsu.edu/courses/hy309

Leonardo da Vinci Museum Exchange punches with the undefeated champion of the Renaissance, Leonardo DaVinci. Sure everyone knows about his "Mona Lisa" or "The Last Supper" but what about his designs for the multi-barrel gun or the giant crossbow? Soloflex has nothing on this da Vinci site, illustrated with plenty of anatomical sketches. Trace the history which includes his meetings with Michaelangelo and Raphael. Forge to the past to find this futurist's helicopter designs and engineering feats that included channeling the course of the Adda River.
WEB http://cellini.leonardo.net/museum /main.html

Louis XIV, King of France Also called the Sun King, Louis XIV was the longest reigning monarch in European history, and ruled in style from his famous palace, Versailles. Besides his commitment to the arts, Louis XIV was an active politician: He took power from the nobility and parliament, rendering himself his own government. Read the details of his life at this site, including the notorious 1685 Edict of Nantes, which reneged the rights of Protestants to worship.
WEB http://129.109.57.188/louisvix.html

Seventeenth Century Resources What brings Miguel de Cervantes and the Mayflower Compact together? The number 16, of course. Peruse this eclectic collection of seventeenth century texts of novels, poetry, political texts, and philosophy tracts.
URL gopher://rsl.ox.ac.uk/11/lib-corn /hunter/Browse%20Alex/Browse%20by %20Date/Browse%20by%20Date%3a %201600s

Vatican Exhibit Chances are good that most of us won't ever get a library card for the Vatican's collection, so visit it through this Library of Congress electronic exhibit. More than just a catalog of this famous repository that held 3,500 books by 1481 B.C., the exhibit is a walk through the history of the city itself, from the ravages of the fourteenth century through archeology, music, and medicine of the last five centuries. The text is accompanied by illustrations from the collection, including the love letters of the many-wived Henry VIII and botanical illustrations by Renaissance masters.
WEB http://sunsite.unc.edu/expo/vatican .exhibit/Vatican.exhibit.html

The Vatican: The City Reborn Just can't get enough of Homer's *Iliad* or maybe you're having Galilean thoughts just looking at the night sky? Visit this site to learn about these topics and more in the Library of Congress's Vatican section. The religious can learn about the Urbino Bible or visit some of the cathedrals. Find out how this city built itself from a mere village of 20,000 people to the flourishing society it is today.
WEB http://www.ncsa.uiuc.edu/SDG /Experimental/vatican.exhibit/Vatican .exhibit.html

ENLIGHTENMENT

The Age of Enlightenment The French seem able to make almost anything beautiful and chic (who else could make frogs' legs a delicacy?). The French Cultural Ministry has put together this stunning guide to the Age of Enlightenment, illustrated and enlivened by carefully selected paintings. With the emergence of secular philosophy, and the rise of the bourgeoisie, French culture shifted from decadence to classical virtue. Explore this evolution at this site fantastique (it's in English).
WEB http://mistral.culture.fr/lumiere /documents/files/cadre_historique.html

C18-L Eighteenth-century discussion for students and teachers alike.
EMAIL listserv@psuvm.psu.edu ✍ *Type in*

message body: subscribe c18-l <your full name>

Class in the Eighteenth Century When, in 1789, Marie Antoinette said "Let them eat cake," she was mocking the hunger of French peasants. In the eighteenth century, class relations erupted into revolution and war—this annotated bibliography is excellent for those trying to get a grip on class warfare.
URL gopher://eng.hss.cmu.edu/11ftp%3AEnglish.Server%3A18th-Century%3A

Eighteenth-Century Resources The perfect source for studying the era of Voltaire, Mozart, and Hogarth, this site gathers sites dedicated to literature, history, philosophy, art, music, architecture, and even landscape gardening. You can ask Thomas Jefferson for his opinions on slavery or read *Paradise Lost.* A collection of home pages of scholars working on eighteenth-century issues provides a unique resource for historians.
WEB http://www.english.upenn.edu/~jlynch/18th.html

French Revolutionary Pamphlets Images of the actual pamphlets that spurred the French populace to storm the Bastille, demanding liberty—and bread.
WEB http://tuna.uchicago.edu/homes/mark/fr_rev.html

▶ 19TH CENTURY

The Napolean Series Napolean fanatics will find their Waterloo at this site. Find out the details of that historic day in 1815. Download paintings of Napoleon or visit the Napoleon Museum. Links lead to more sites about this charismatic military figure. Diehard war buffs can check out the battle sequences of Waterloo and the attack on Russia, then prepare to go to war at The Historical Miniature Wargame Home Page.
WEB http://www.ping.be/~ping5895/links.html

Nineteenth Century British Timeline Actually, this site has several timelines of events in British history. The Humanitas Romantic Chronology covers all the major British literary figures, from Wordsworth to Huxley, and the publications that made them famous. The Victorian Web Timeline covers 1700 to 1983, including such notable events as the abolition of slavery and the Battle of Waterloo. Links to relevant Web sites and a syllabus about British Empire lead to even more historical info.
WEB http://athena.english.vt.edu/Brinlee/TIMELINE.HTML

Nineteenth Century Philosophy Get out the *2001: A Space Odyssey* soundtrack when you read the online text of *Thus Spake Zarathustra.* This site includes black and white illustrations of the notable nineteenth-century philosophers as well as some of their writings. From Kierkegaard to Marx, there are plenty of ways to sit at the computer screen and think about thinking. Cross the boundaries between mind and brain by checking out the online philosophy lectures.
WEB http://www-philosophy.ucdavis.edu/phi151/phi151.htm

The Peninsular War and the Constitution of 1812 In 1808, Napoleon forced the abdication of the Bourbon monarchy in order to install his own relatives in its place. The Spanish people mobilized, and the Spanish War of Independence began. Lasting for six years, the brutal war was memorialized in the paintings of Goya. The essay at this site provides an excellent introduction and overview of this period of Spanish history.
WEB http://www.DocuWeb.ca/SiSpain/history/peninsul.html

Victoria A list dedicated to the Victorian era—repressed sexuality, rooms full of frilly knick-knacks, demure young maids, and Dickens, right? Wrong. Victoria is the most active history list on the Net and it's terrific. There have been long threads about whether or not the movie *The Piano* accurately portrayed Victorian life, and whether young people with pasty skin and black clothing are the conscious inheritors of the Victorian gothic past. What does it mean to be well-bred? What did it mean before Darwin? Victoria is never just an exchange of information. Sit down, have some tea and gossip. Queen Charlotte's divorce (A.D. 1820) or Prince Charles's affairs—it's all allowed here.

EMAIL listserv@ubvm.usc.indiana.edu ✍
Type in message body: subscribe victoria <your full name>

The Victorian Web Furniture is one commonly recognized Victorian contribution but that is only part of the story as this site explains. Such philosophies as feminism, Marxism, and socialism are attributed to this nineteenth-century movement. Agnostics can read about Tennyson's doubt in God. Carpenters might want to look at the section on architecture. Regress with the moderns who write in Victorian literary style (e.g. Thackeray) or compare present-day attitudes with what used to be considered sexual crimes.

WEB http://www.stg.brown.edu/projects /hypertext/landow/victorian/victov.html

Views of the Famine Hungry for more information on this tragedy that occurred from 1845 to 1851? Read the *Illustrated London Daily News* accounts of the Galway Starvation Riots and other horrible events. Check out the Battle of Limerick in Punch, another periodical of the time. This site features bushels of paintings of food riots and armed Irish peasants defending their food supplies.

WEB http://www.emory.edu/FAMINE

▶ 20TH CENTURY

The Berlin Wall Falls The crumbling of the Berlin Wall has become the symbol for the end of the Cold War. This site gives you German, American, and European perspectives on the event. Download QuickTime movies and pictures of the wall, as well as newsreels and personal accounts, including some from those who were kidnapped by East German Police. Information about present-day Berlin is also covered.

WEB http://sti.mit.edu/brc/bigdig/Berlin _contents.html

Bosnia Homepage Get involved in the Bosnian crisis. Download newsgroup threads or listen to some of the NEXUS radio broadcasts or CNN reports. You can virtually feel the pain in some of the Bosnian survivors' accounts. Take a look at artwork inspired by the Bosnia/Sarajevo war and learn about U.S. involvement. This site also provides a form to send messages to people surviving the conflict.

WEB http://www.cco.caltech.edu/~bosnia /bosnia.html

The Dreyfus Affair This isn't about Richard Dreyfuss although there is some resemblance. It's about Alfred Dreyfus, the falsely imprisoned French officer who eventually became recognized as a martyr of anti-semitism. Check out his scholastic activities at the Ecole Polytechnique. Find out about the way he attempted suicide in prison by bashing his head into a wall. This site also accounts for other participants in the Dreyfus Affair, including Zola, Colonel Piquart, and Colonel Henry.

WEB http://www.well.com/user/vision /proust/DREYFUS.HTML

Eastern German Studies Group The EGSG is an "association of scholars interested in that part of Germany once known as the German Democratic Republic." Its newsletter is available, along with other EGSG publications such as Randall Bytwerk's writings on East Germany propaganda. Peruse through some of the links to periodicals such as *Spiegel* (not the clothes catalog) and *Stern* (not Howard). If you've ever wondered what classses might be like at the Humboldt and Leipzig Universities, you can connect to their Web sites. Some links are in German only.

WEB http://www.calvin.edu/cas/egsg

Frontline: Shtethl Before World War II, a significant portion of Eastern European Jews lived in communities called shtethls. Most shtethls existed in

Poland, and consisted of Polish peasants and farming gentry, and Jewish merchants and craftsmen. Small village life had its charms—shared religious bonds and community responsibility—but also its hazards. In the 1940s, these Jewish enclaves, became targets of Nazism. This site, produced by PBS, is a terrific reservoir for those interested in Eastern European Jewish culture. Historical background of the shtethl is given, but the site concentrates on the Holocaust.
WEB http://www2.pbs.org/wgbh/pages /frontline/shtetl

Irish Republican Socialist Movement
This site documents the 20-year struggle of the Irish Republican Socialist Movement. While reading about some of the obstacles the party faced, such as repression from the Official Irish Republican Army and the British Army, you'll learn the meanings of even acronyms such as INLA, IRSP, and SDLP. Find out exactly what Sinn Fein, Nicky Kelly and Devlin McAlisky had to do with anything, and then push forward to the future of Ireland as the Provisionals find allies in the SDLP, call a cease fire, and try to figure out the voice of the working class.
WEB http://www.serve.com/IRSCNA /irsm20yr.htm

The Prague Spring, 1968 Details the events which led to the disappearance of Czechoslovakia and then its remergence after WWII. This site highlights the creation of the KSC, the Czechoslovac National Socialist Party and the Czechoslovac Social democratic Party. Visitors can virtually feel the usurping of power from the Communist dissidents and independent activists. Stalinization and other political currents are traced through the Third Republic. Read about Brezhnev, Dubcek, The Warsaw Pact and of course, The Prague Spring.
WEB http://lcweb2.loc.gov:8080/country -studies/cz_01_06.html#cz_01_06A55

Tito's Home Page Marshall Tito was Yugoslavia's most famous pol, and this site traces his illustrious career. Check out "A Song for Tito," "Flag of the Party" and other songs that can be downloaded. Plenty of speech files let you hear about how Tito felt about the Cold War, fraternity, equality, and unity.
WEB http://www.fri.uni-lj.si/~tito/tito-eng .html

WORLD HISTORY

WHILE THE BANDWIDTH FOR personal time travel doesn't exist—yet—the Internet can offer a pretty reasonable substitute. See the planet from year zero onwards. Marvel at World Cultures from Antiquity to 1500. Roam around worlds past from H-Africa to Latin America to the MESA to Mongolia. Should an occasion demand of you the omnipresence afforded by "synchronopsy," turn your attention to HyperHistory Online.

▶ STARTING POINTS

Gateway to World History This large resource brings together most of the history archives, university history departments, and historical reference works available on the World Wide Web.
web http://neal.ctstateu.edu/history/world _history/world_history.html

HyperHistory Online This ambitious project promises "a synchronoptic display of human history over the last 3,000 years." The word "synchronoptic" means "seeing at the same time," which means that this multimedia site will let you learn about what was going on everywhere in the world at any given time. Is there a connection between Gutenberg and the Reformation? Is the flowering of India somehow linked to the decline of Rome? Draw your own conclusions. The project is based on Andreas Nothiger's wall-sized synchronoptic World History Chart (ordering info provided).
web http://www.hyperhistory.com

Non-Western History HTML Links This constantly growing compendium of links to non-Western culture sites is designed to complement the new national multicultural history standards. Resources range from a text on the Hakka Culture of China to a document entitled "World Cultures form Antiquity to 1500."
web http://execpc.com/~dboals/hist.html

World Cultures from Antiquity to 1500 A professor at Washington State University wants his students to use the Web to discover the whole wide world, and invites all to come along. You can do the class reading, participate in online discussions oneverything from Mesopotamia to The Analects of Confucius, and even take the quizzes—you just won't get a grade. There are resources available for those interested in the history of Greece, Rome, ancient China, the Near East, and Native American culture as well as information on the Middle Ages and the Renaissance. Some of the resources are fabulous, including a hypertext essay on da Vinci that leads to the master's own words, images of his work, and links to other Web sites on the Renaissance.
web http://www.wsu.edu:8080/~dee

World History Find out everything you need to know on the Middle Ages, the history of France, or any other world history topic at this section of the AOL Academic Assistance Center. Post questions on the bulletin board or sign up for basic tutoring. If you need to know something and you need to know it right now, try emailing a question to the Teacher Pager.
AMERICA ONLINE *keyword* aac→World History

World History Archives The author of this Web page uses "history" in the Marxist sense—as aprocess, not an academic discipline. The site has electronically archived hundreds of historical papers and abstracts, and divides its resources alonggeographic lines. Links to international human rights sites and news will help you keep left on a planet tilting swiftly to the right. However, some of the sources are useful to those of all political bents—providing the history of native peoples worldwide.
web http://neal.ctstateu.edu/history/world _history/archives/archives.html

▶ AFRICAN

A Brief History of Tanzania Learn about Nyerere and his creation of the Tanganyika African National Unity (TANU) party, which eventually led Tanzania to independence. Read the Arusha Declaration and understand why Ujamaa ("familyhood") was the slogan for Nyerere's program from 1967. Students brushing up on African history can refer to a chronology that starts in the 18th century and leads to Nyerere's presidency. This page also supplies current information about Tanzania, including its literacy rate, climate, major conflicts, and more.
WEB http://dana.ucc.nau.edu/~mss /history.html

African Reparations Movement Based on the painful history of colonization and exploitation, this group lobbies for reparations from countries that participated in the slave trade. The home page features several articles on how current politics ("Tottenham Refugee Crisis") and historical evidence ("Hijacked African Treasures") inform on the state of Africa today.
WEB http://the.arc.co.uk/arm/home.html

The Battle of Adwa A small site commemmorating the triumph of the Ethiopians over the Italians in 1896. A victory over colonialism as well as Italy, the battle is succinctly explained.
WEB http://www.cs.com/sheba/html /adowa/adwa.htm

Encyclopeadia Africana This site promises greatness. Its editors are Professor Kwame Anthony Appiah and Professor Henry Louis Gates, Jr., two prominent Harvard educators. They assure that in its final form, the site will be "a comprehensive electronic collection of information about black history and culture in Africa, the Americas, Europe, and the Caribbean."
WEB http://web-dubois.fas.harvard.edu /DuBois/Research/EA/EA.HTML

H-Africa Scholars, students, librarians, and teachers participate in this moderated discussion group for the study of African history and humanities. Sponsored by the University of Illinois at Chicago and Michigan State, the H-Africa Home Page contains instructions and tips for subscribing to the list, as well as its discussion logs. Other academics resources are linked there, too.
EMAIL listserv@msu.edu ✍ *Type in message body:* subscribe h-africa <your full name>
Info: **WEB** http://h-net.msu.edu/~africa

The University of Pennsylvania African Studies A terrific resource from one of the best African Studies Departments in America. With links to academic and nonacademic sites, a gallery of photographs, direct links out of Africa, and the Web pages of each African country, this site is indispensable for those getting into the study of Africa.
WEB http://www.sas.upenn.edu/African _Studies/AS.html

World History Archives: Africa A great resource for more recent research on Africa. One can search for information by region. A page of links is also available.
WEB http://neal.ctstateu.edu/history/world _history/archives/archive3.html

LATIN AMERICAN

Cuba A variety of info on Cuba is available at this site. The featured article is "The Cuban Nation, 1898-1959," but there are also links leading to the Cuban History Archives and info on Cuba discussion groups, current events, and Fidel Castro.
WEB http://www.msstate.edu/Archives /History/Latin_America/cuba.html

The Early History of Haiti Learn about the first republic in the world to have been led by a person of African descent. Illustrations of early Haiti depicted include a visit by Christopher Columbus (this guy turns up everywhere in this hemisphere), the transfer of 500,000 slaves from West Africa, and Jean-Jaques Dessalines' revolution over

French rule. Parallel the interesting similarities of Haiti to America and also learn about some of the key figures in Haitian history such as Toussaint L'Overture, Napoleon, Bookman (a voodoo priest), and Sonthonax.
WEB http://pasture.ecn.purdue.edu /~agenhtml/agenmc/haiti/history.html

Eva Perón Eva Perón is not just important because Madonna is playing her in a movie. One of the most important women in Latin American history, she rose from a poor Argentine family to become a famous performer, and then a first lady. This site is a very brief biography of the highly celebrated Argentine.
WEB http://www.middlebury.edu/~leparc /htm/evita.htm

Latin America Mississippi State University has compiled this excellent set of sources on Latin American history. Read about the region's discovery and conquest and national histories on individual countries in the region from Argentina to Venezuela. There are also links to numerous articles on contemporary subjects like Manuel Noreiega and drug trafficking.
WEB http://www.msstate.edu/Archives /History/Latin_America/latam.html

St. Martin: History and Culture Columbus didn't even set foot on St. Martin, but claimed it for Spain as he passed by. This site reveals the island's culture, history, and artifacts.
WEB http://www.interknowledge.com /st-martin/smhis01.htm

The Vanished Gallery From 1977 to 1983, Argentina was under military rule. During this time, thousands of people, a mixture of dissidents, liberals, and innocents, dissappeared, which is of course, a euphemism for murdered. A memorial to the dissappeared, this site also has cogent information on the old regime, and the Falklands War.
WEB http://www.yendor.com/vanished

▶ **MIDDLE EASTERN**

A Basic Help for Middle Eastern Histor- **ical Research** For those researching history papers, this page links to starter bibliographies. The basic research paper method is provided, including desciptions of primary, secondary and tertiary sources and of course, the five Ws (who, what, when, where, and why). Also find out additional information by checking the Library of Congress, people's names and periodicals on the subject. Includes links to all sorts of Middle East sites (none of which are in the Middle East) such as the Middle East Studies Association Bulletin and the University of Texas.
WEB http://alexia.lis.uiuc.edu/~lsmith /history.html

A Brief History of Mecca "Fulfill the inner spiritual void by learning about the place where God's will was revealed to Muhammad (peace be upon him)." Find out why Muslims pray East when in America and West when in India. Get down with your holy, bad self by calling out the list of 11 alternative (but still holy) names for Mecca. This site has a history of Mecca and a brief desciption of the surrounding mountains and entrances to the site of the holy mosque and the Ka'ba. In case you're planning a visit, conversion to Muslim is suggested. Also links to Saudi Arabia and Islam pages.
WEB http://darkwing.uoregon.edu /~kbatarfi/makkah.html

Algeria Allah has stated: "Do not incline toward those who do evil, for hell fire will seize you." These most serious words opened up a communique by Abdelrezak Rejjam in 1993 to the Muslim people of Algeria, the ruling Junta and the rest of the globe. Venture to the past to examine another historic milestone such as the Proposal for the Establishment of a Native Army in Algeria, written in 1830. Then zoom to 1954 to browse the first passionate proposal for the Algerian Front. Mississippi University has archived these three documents and translated them into English. Try to determine why Islamic Salvation Front is abbreviated FIS and why Alger-

ian National Liberation Front is abbreviated FLN. Includes a full color map and links to the Africa page.
WEB http://www.msstate.edu/Archives/History/Africa/algeria/algeria.html

Anatolia Through the Ages Just think, 4,000 years of civilization can be summarized in the space of one Web page. Plenty of sample photos of artifacts from such periods as the Neolithic, Bronze, and Hurri adorn this site, where you can discover diffferent civilizations including the Frygians and Lydians at central Anatolia, and the Karians and Lykians. This history goes back to 9000 B.C.—and through the Byzantine Empire, Roman civilization, and the Ottomans.
WEB http://www.focusmm.com.au/civi_mn1.htm

Jewish Culture and History Through the Ages Shalom! Hear this greeting by downloading the sound file. Then break out the Yiddish dictionaries: It's time to learn about the Jewish culture. Travel to Tour of Israel or the Jerusalem One WWW Network to see pictures of the Western Wall and link to sites with loads of historical and cultural information. Construct an online family tree using the Jewish Geneology Home Page. Visit the Nozyc and Rema synagogues in Poland (pictures included).
WEB http://www.igc.apc.org/ddickerson/judaica.html

Middle East Studies Association of North America MESA, a non-profit organization with international membership, allows all sorts to flip through its newsletter online. Students can read such optimistic papers such as "Is there a future for Middle East Studies?" and the ever-popular, "The End of Civilization is Not So Bad." But there are good sources of more info, both practical and historical: Britannica has got nothing on the Encyclopedia Iranica. The devoted Muslim can reach the highest level of ecstasy possible by looking through the index of Qur'an recitations. The latest Arabic word processor (Arabic system 6.1) is featured and information on the

Project for the Translation of Arabic is available by contacting the University of Pennsylania. MESA membership info is also available.
WEB http://www.cua.edu/www/mesabul/backcov.htm

▶ RUSSIAN

Alexander Palace Time Machine A: For the Jeopardy Daily Double, it's known as the home of the last Tzar of Russia, Nicholas II. Q: What is Alexander Palace? Would-be robbers might want to examine the priceless loot such as the 300-year anniversary commemorative Faberge egg or cigarette cases worth more than an entire tobacco company. The pictures here are so detailed that an average computer would have to magnify the image nine times before seeing any degradation. People running out of closet space will be envious after touring the children's rooms. Think it would be nice to have a maid? Learn how this palace had a cleaning staff equivalent to that of a major hotel. Also, find out about the race to preserve and save what has now become an important European museum.
WEB http://www.travelogix.com/emp/batchison

Black Hole Peripherals, Inc. This visual festival is a homage to pre-Soviet Russia. Step back in time with a photo of a rubber shoe emporium in Riga or a menu from a Russian tea room, circa 1883. This odd collection also holds GIFs of rubles, advertising posters, and WWI propaganda.
WEB http://www-physics.mps.ohio-state.edu/~viznyuk

H-Russia A good place to make contact with scholars, writers, and retired spies in the former Soviet-bloc countries, H-Russia also provides a translated-newsservice from Moscow, with daily updates from the republics. Join members in their efforts to analyze the updates and make sense of the process of history in the making.
EMAIL listserv@uicvm.uic.edu ✍ Type in

message body: subscribe h-russia <your full name>

Russian and Soviet Archive Data This Web site holds an agrarian typology of the provinces of European Russia at the turn of the 20th century, a database of Russian corporations (1700-1914), a history of Sino-Soviet interaction (1950-1957), and some interesting post-Cold War interview projects.
web http://www.eskimo.com/~bwest /icpsr.html

Russian History If Russia conjures images of men drinking vodka and eating at McDonalds in Red Square, this site will open your eyes to its very rich history. From an early history of ethnic diversity to periods of royal tyrany, to the Communist revolution of this century, Russian history gives new meaning to "war and peace." This wonderful site has compiled essays on some of the most fascinating moments of the Russian timeline. Extremely helpful for almost all time periods.
web http://www.bucknell.edu /departments/russian/history.html

Soviet Archives Exhibit The Cold War's on exhibit in cyberspace. For the first time in more than 70 years, the inner workings of the Soviet system are open to view in an exhibit of official documents of the former U.S.S.R. Take a guided tour through the Communist state with exhibits focused on the KGB, the Gulag, propaganda, Chernobyl, and collectivization. Each exhibit is illustrated with documents, letters, and photos. The section on U.S. and Russia relations features the rebuking letter sent by Krushchev to Kennedy during the Cuban Missile Crisis. Each document in this extensive exhibit is accompanied by an English translation.
web http://sunsite.unc.edu/expo/soviet .exhibit/soviet.archive.html

▶ ASIAN

A Brief History of China Can there be such as thing as a "brief history" for one of the oldest cultures in the world? The site's author admits that his intention is less a full-fledged history and more like the Cliffs Notes version. Nevertheless, the site covers the origins of Chinese civilization from 221 B.C., the early empires, the later empires through the birth of modern China.
web http://www.hk.super.net/~paulf /china.html

Chinese History A collection of Chinese historical documents, articles about Chinese history, and sound clips (Mao speaks). The best resources are those related to the democracy movement. Remember Tiananmen Square?
web http://darkwing.uoregon.edu /~felsing/cstuff/history.html

The Great Game: Afghanistan and the Asian Sub-Continent The story is of one of those conflicts that just won't end. The site documents the relationship between Afghanistan and its invaders, from the Crimean War of the 1850s to the Afghan "conflict" of the 1970s. Official studies of her majesty's troops, VD, and Kipling's imperialist stories sit alongside modern news coverage and CIA reports.
web http://www.deltanet.com/users /llambert/great_game.html

Japanese History A series of articles on Japanese history covering ancient times, the feudal age, isolationism, restoration, and the modern period.
url gopher://gan.ncc.go.jp/11/JAPAN /History

Major Events in Japanese History The name says it all. This is a simple document narrating Japanese history from the Asuka Era (592-710 A.D.) to the Showa Era (1925-1989) And while it's not always very complete, sometimes just showing up is good enough.
web http://www.io.com/~nishio/japan /history.html

Mohandas Gandhi Perhaps one of this century's greatest advocates of non-violence and religious toleration, Gandhi

managed to lead India out of colonial rule and addressed conflicts between Hindu and Moslem. This very basic page introduces the great man who has been an inspiration to politicians, peaceniks, and vegetarians alike.
WEB http://www.maui.com/~lesslie/gandhi.html

Mongolia "It would be no exaggeration to say that Mongolia is the only one of the ancient nomad states to retain the tenets of its original nomadic civilization, including the classic migration of livestock and closeness to nature." Though much of the country still lives a traditional nomadic lifestyle, the 20th century has brought several Communist invasions and the insurgence of democracy. Made famous by the Huns, Mongolia's history is well described at this site.
WEB http://www.bluemarble.net/~mitch/mong/cult.html

Nanjing Massacre Some things are neither easy to forget, nor to deny. This site memorializes the 300,000 victims of the 1937-38 massacre of the Chinese of Nanjing by Japanese soldiers. Graphic photos of the carnage are included, along with eyewitness accounts, monographs, and examples of Japanese "historical revisionism."
WEB http://www.arts.cuhk.hk/Nanjing Massacre/NM.html

Romani History In the fifteenth century, Romani people were renamed "Gypsies." The word derived from "Egypt", since it was believed that Gypsies had denied the Holy Family refuge in Egypt. "Gypsy" remains become the standard name for this historically persecuted people of Indian descent. Romani people have spread to most corners of the world, and, for the most part, they have been ill-treated. Research their long history at this site, which also has pages describing how gypsies are represented in popular culture, and how they are being persecuted today.
WEB http://hamp.hampshire.edu/~ratS88/romani/rrwhist.html

Thai History: Ayutthaya Period Sure, you know of a quaint little Thai place around the corner, but did you know that after King Narai's reign in the 1600s, European relations with the country virtually ceased? The Ayutthaya Period is the main focus of this report on Thailand's history, from the fourteenth to eighteenth centuries. Read about Cambodia's influence during the reign of Ramathibodi I, the royal founder of the Thai Kingdom, and the destruction of the capital of Ayutthaya by invaders from Burma in 1767.
WEB http://sunsite.au.ac.th/thailand/history_of_thai5.html

The Turks in History This essay, with sparse hypertext, chronicles the Turkish cilvilization through its initial rise and on to fall of the Ottoman empire. Starting in 1300 B.C., it flies through the ages reaching the present day or, more accurately, 1920. Storytellers will enjoy the Turkish epic *Dede Korkut*, with its positive female view and documentation of the Islamic religion. The devoutly religious might be intrigued by the Church of Aya Sofya and why it was significant to the Turks at the peak of their reign in the 1400s. Even a top military strategist would have to reread some of the passages related to warfare because of all the different factions and groups involved.
WEB http://www.cs.utk.edu/~basoglu/history/tihist.html

Turks & Tatars: 19th Century Muslim Life in the Russian Empire Part of the Interactive History Project, this small site provides a vivid multimedia account of life in Azerbaijan, before the development of the oil fields and the imperialist advances of the Russian empire. The site links to Central Asia resources as well.
WEB http://www.uoknor.edu/cybermuslim/russia/rus_home.html

WOMEN'S HISTORY

"**E**VERY TIME A GIRL READS A womanless history she learns she is worth less," say Myra and David Sadker, in *Failing at Fairness: How America's Schools Cheat Girls*. Written by men, about men, and chiefly for men, history has allowed few women to be recognized for their achievements. Recent history has recorded the advances of women like never before, so find out what you've been missing at the National Women's History Project. Read about women's contributions to suffrage at The Susan B. Anthony University Center. African-American women tell it like it is in Isis: Our Story. If you've got the time, A Calendar of Women of Achievement and Herstory will give you something to celebrate every day.

▶ STARTING POINTS

A Calendar of Women of Achievement and Herstory This unique resource describes something to celebrate every day. For instance, the entry for the month of May, named for Maia the Roman goddess of spring, begins with a brief biography of Mother Jones, a labor organizer who was born on May Day. On May third, there's a note about Belva Lockwood, the first woman to plead before the Supreme Court. By the fifth of the month, you're following Amy Johnson on the first solo flight (by man or woman) from England to Australia.
WEB http://worcester.lm.com/women /history/woacal.html

Multimedia Women's History A compilation of exhibits covering women's history. Most are about Americans, from the history of women working at the famous Wood's Hole Laboratory to the Maryland State Archives featuring portraits of all of the First Ladies.
WEB http://frank.mtsu.edu/~kmiddlet /history/women/wom-mm.html

National Women's History Project Quiz yourself on your knowledge of women's

history, pick up catchy quotations like "History looks different when the contributions of women are included," or get involved with the women's movement in your area. This well-organized site is a must-visit for those interested in why women's history matters today.
WEB http://www.nwhp.org

Notable Women Searchable Database Search for thumbnail sketches in this database of biographies of famous women from all walks of life—like Victoria Woodhull, free love advocate, newspaper editor, stockbroker, and candidate for president on the Equal Rights Party ticket in 1872.
URL gopher://gopher.emc.maricopa.edu :70/11/library/notablewomen

The Susan B. Anthony University Center The Susan B. Anthony University Center provides a comprehensive view of women's history in America. The story of the suffrage movement is available from a link to the National Women's Hall of Fame in Seneca Falls, N.Y., where Elizabeth Cady Stanton and Lucretia Mott held the first Women's Rights Convention in 1848. The Susan B. Anthony Center contains the full text of the Nineteenth Amendment and biographies of famous suffragettes.
WEB http://www.rochester.edu/SBA/index .html

Women of Achievement and Herstory, a Frequently-Appearing Newsletter Irene Stuber, the author of this newsletter, admonishes readers not to "let anyone tell you there weren't notable and effective women throughout history." To prove it, she tells weekly stories of little-known women of power, such as Edith Clara Summerskill, founder of the Socialist Medical Association in England. The newsletter also notes anniversaries to celebrate and offers inspirational quotes.
WEB http://www.lm.com/~lmann/feminist /achievement.html

PRE-MODERN

Diotima: Women and Gender in the Ancient World "For I spoke to her in much the same terms as Agathon addressed just now to me, saying Love was a great god, and was of beautiful things; and she refuted me with the very arguments I have brought against our young friend, showing that by my account that god was neither beautiful nor good." Predictably, Plato went to a woman to get the lowdown on the nature of love. This site is named for Diotima, Plato's ancient Dr. Ruth, and it's full of wisdom and links for those exploring the classical world of women.
WEB http://www.uky.edu/ArtsSciences /Classics/gender.html

The Kassandra Project The Kassandra Project aims to introduce German women writers, artists, and thinkers of the eighteenth and nineteenth centuries. These women have historically been overshadowed, and it is only with the reunification of Germany, and the emergence of writers like Christa Wolf, that their contributions are being re-examined. Explore the fascinating life and writing of Karoline Frederike Louise Maximiliane von Günderrode, whose suicide continues to inspire academic debates about German cultural history.
WEB http://www.reed.edu/~ccampbel/tkp

AFRICAN AMERICAN

Isis: Our Story Two years before Amelia Earhart took flight, Bessie Coleman had earned her wings. Forced to learn aviation in Europe, this young American woman was setting up avaiation schools in America when she died at the tender are of thirty three. Isis: Our Story chronicles some of the greatest African-American women and their accomplishments. There are also links to sites of potential interest, covering topics such as Akan proverbs, Zulu beads, and African studies in the United States.
WEB http://www.netdiva.com/ourstory .html

BIOGRAPHIES

Biographies of Historical Women A terrific compilation of biographies of women from Sappho to Sally Ride. The reading room page hosts links to a searchable database as well as links to important documents in Women's History.
WEB http://www.inform.umd.edu:8080 /Educational_Resources/Academic ResourcesByTopic/WomensStudies /ReadingRoom/History/Biographies

Distinguished Women of Past and Present Meet Jeanne Marie Bouvier de la Motte (1648-1717), known as Madame Guyon. She introduced quietism, a Catholic emphasis on deep contemplation, to France. Like many other mystics, she faced persecution and imprisonment—and has garnered more recognition now than in her lifetime. Come here to discover new women worthy of admiration. Indexes are searchable by name or field.
WEB http://www.netsrq.com/~dbois

WARS

THE HISTORY OF CIVILIZATION IS the history of wars: from Troy to Kuwait, push has come to shove each time the political climate has shifted. Chat, read, even write about war, but don't engage in it. Discuss the history of bellicosity at soc.history.war.misc. Battle your misconceptions at The French and Indian War. Take sides at the Civil War Forum. Relive the horror at the Holocaust Archives. Then, round up the Persian Gulf War with The Operation Desert Storm Debriefing Book.

▶ STARTING POINTS

alt.war "Is the Yugoslav Civil War War petering out?" "Is 'Debt of Honor' evidence?" "Does Proof Exist Of the Rosenberg's GUILT!?!" This newsgroup switches from one war to another more quickly than you can say "ceasefire," but if you're looking for an argument or a kindred spirit, you'll find what you need.
USENET alt.war

MILHST-L Diverse souls meet here—an ex-colonel and a teenager discuss WWII battle plans; a military librarian posts a tidbit about a Civil War general's groundbreaking use of the insanity defense. The list entertains discussion about things nobody could possibly remember, like the dietary requirements of medieval crossbowmen. There are many ex-servicemen on this list, which makes for a friendly rivalry and fosters a tendency toward nostalgia. Newcomers and noncombatants are welcome.
EMAIL listserv@ukanvm.cc.ukans.edu ✍
Type in message body: subscribe milhst-l <your full name>

MIL-HIST Provides a searchable, chronologically organized infoserver for academic research in military history, from ancient and medieval times to the 20th century. An invaluable resource for the battle buff or academic war historian wannabe.
WEB http://www.olcommerce.com/cadre

/milhist/index.html

soc.history.war.misc Battle strategy, favorite generals, and lethal weapons are the subjects of the group. There are many ex-military men here, and in their eyes your credibility rises with trench experience. This is especially evident when the arcane discussion of castle sieges is replaced by modern issues—women in the military is a particular favorite.
USENET soc.history.war.misc

soc.history Soc.history is actually two conferences—a forum for amateur historians and a political battleground. Topics are varied, from Nazis and the economy to the post-Columbian pandemic and the necessity of using the A-bomb in World War II. Marshalling their facts and citing "the experts,"most posters stay generally friendly. But then there's the rabid political character of the group. Ancient Greek history is fodder for a bitter debate over Macedonia and Armenian; Muslims and Turks commit verbal atrocities daily in a constant, ugly reliving of the past.
USENET soc.history

▶ FRENCH & INDIAN WAR

1755: The French and Indian War Nope, it wasn't the French fighting the Indians—it was the British fighting the French in North America. A scholar has excerpted his upcoming history book about the French and Indian War here, and he places an original document a week online to add flavor to the description of battles and political maneuvering. A list of reenactments and related historic sites is included.
WEB http://web.syr.edu/~laroux

▶ CIVIL WAR

Civil War Forum Meet at specific times in the Mason Dixon room to chat about Robert E. Lee. Download photos of old

battlefields. Link up to terrific Web sites. America Online's Civil War forum is a great place to learn about this favorite subject of American history buffs.
AMERICA ONLINE *keyword* civil war forum

Civil War Forum Encompasses a wide range of Civil War topics. From Antietam to Gettysburg, the relevent documents are available, but what makes this site useful are the chat rooms and message boards. Questions are asked, debates rage, and information exchanged. Civil war buffs share their passions, and can be found giving directions to a particularly well-preserved gravestone, or recommending an authority on battle fields.
COMPUSERVE *go* civil war forum

alt.war.civil.usa For some, Gettysburg is more familiar than the Gulf War. All the old controversies are here, but much of the debate slides over into the present, to the persistence of guilt "imposed" on the South and its effect upon the late 20th century. The effects of 130 years of brooding are quite clear. "States rights" are referred to in the present tense and the Confederate flag remains a rallying point.
USENET alt.war.civil.usa

The American Civil War Homepage A page dedicated to making sure no one forgets the War Between the States. There's an immense collection of Civil War-related links that include a minute-by-minute chronology of the five-year conflict, a multimedia exhibit, maps, photos, letters, and diaries—breathing life into the Great Conflagration. Search for great-great-grandpa's unit at the several sites devoted to troop rosters. Battle buffs can arm themselves with info before re-enacting the Battle of Antietam with online soldier's slang dictionaries, artillery and small arms glossaries, and sartorial advice for Rebs and Yanks.
WEB http://funnelweb.utcc.utk.edu /~hoemann/warweb.html

Chronology of the Civil War Single-line descriptions of major events in the Civil War.

URL gopher://cee.educ.indiana.edu/00 /Turner_Adventure_Learning/Gettysburg _Archive/Other_Resources/Chronology _of_the_CW.txt

Civil War Battles Get your uniform pressed for the reenactment or the annual Shiloh party. This site lists the battlefields in the Great Conflagration, from the famous (Antietam) to the not-so-famous (Boonsborough). Each conflict is described, its casualties listed, and results noted.
WEB http://www.cr.nps.gov/abpp/battles /Contents.html

Civil War Diaries The whole bloody story of the Civil War is told here through excerpts of the diary of George Molineaux, a 26-year-old volunteer. The site features a hypertext timeline linked to maps, troop orders, and casualty figures for his unit (the 8th Illinois Volunteer Infantry Regiment).
WEB http://www.augustana.edu/library /civil.html

Civil War Images A small collection of Civil War images.
URL gopher://wiscinfo.wisc.edu:2070/11 /.image/.shs/.war

Civil War Information, Documents, and Archive This Web site provides contact info and schedules for reenactments areaccompanied by a scrapbook of photos from the events. Links here will also take you to the regimental history like that of the 30th Virginia Infantry, the war photo collection of the Library of Congress, or Stephen Crane's classic of war literature, *The Red Badge of Courage.* The site also holds a large collection of diaries and letters.
WEB http://www.access.digex.net /~bdboyle/cw.html

Civil War Letters from the 76th Ohio Volunteer Infantry The illustrated letters of Captain R. W. Burt, a would-be poet, including the classic tale of Phil's encounter with a wild pig while on duty and a homage to Mary Roy, the girl he left behind.

WEB http://www.infinet.com/~lstevens/burt

Civil War Soldiers and Sailors System
Peons at the National Archives are busy entering 5.4 million names into a database of Civil War soldiers. You'll be able to discover whether great-great-great-grandpa caught a musket ball at Gettysburg or came down with dysentery in the Virginia tidewater.
WEB http://www.cr.nps.gov/itd/welcome.html

The United States Civil War Center
Saddle up the horse, put out the flag (yes even the confederate one) and break out the bayonnet, it's time for the Civil War. Inquiring minds might take a sneak peek inside some of the soldier's diaries from both sides of the battle. Cool images of battles, weapons and even Stonewall Jackson's bible bring the war to life. Not sure when the Battle of Shiloh took place? Try the Calendar of Events section which chronicles even some of the most minor conflicts. Collectors can find that miniature soldier attacking with a rifle at the games and entertainment department. Includes all sorts of links to books, films, museums, maps, organizations, etc.
WEB http://www.cwc.lsu.edu/civlink.htm

Letters Home from a Soldier in the U.S. Civil War
Private Newton Scott, a 21-year old farm boy from Iowa, wrote to his sweetheart Hannah Cone from Little Rock in July of 1864 that, because of the illness among the troops, "I have no idea of getting home until the expiration of my time of service. And if permitted to live then I expect to return home and see the people and eat peaches." Newton did live to marry Hannah. Experience the hardships of war in a unique manner through their intelligent and tender correspondence.
WEB http://www.ucsc.edu/civil-war-letters/home.html

Mil-Hist American Civil War
Yet another compendium of Civil War miscellany. Explore the "Vast Sea of Misery"

through the eyes of a field doctor. Link to the Turner Broadcasting Archive or the Byrd collections on army and navy history. Articles, book reviews, and bibliographies provide additional scholarly information.
WEB http://kuhttp.cc.ukans.edu/history/milhst/civwar.html

The National Museum of Civil War Medicine
This new Maryland museum is building a page to tell the grim story of medicine in a war where disease and battle took 800,000 lives. Currently, visitors can read the report made to Congress in the wake of the carnage.
WEB http://www.crcmedia.com/~mcwm

U.S.S. Monitor
Selected .GIFs and sound files from a CD-ROM celebrating this famous ironclad ship.
WEB http://www.evansville.net/~mmd/entert.html

The Valley of the Shadow: Living the Civil War in Pennsylvania and Virginia
What was it like to live in 1863 in Pennsylvania, or in Virginia? Experience the war from both sides through this multimedia exhibit, which boasts online narration and a searchable archive of primary sources from the Civil War era. Search tips help you piece together the story of the past from newspapers, maps, diaries, and government sources.
WEB http://jefferson.village.virginia.edu/vshadow/vshadow.html

► WORLD WAR I

WWI-L
An international discussion list devoted to the history of the First World War in its broadest aspects. The period under discussion is generally restricted to the years 1900-1920, particularly the military conflicts of the period.
EMAIL listserv@ukanaix.cc.ukans.edu ✍
Type in message body: subscribe wwi-l <your full name>

Hell Upon Earth: Personal Accounts of Prince Edward Island Soldiers
"What gruesome sights, pieces of bodies scattered around just like leaves. Oh what a

pity good Canadian blood…" This site describes the book, *Hell Upon Earth* by J. Clinton Morrison, Jr., a teacher, genealogist, and local historian born at Conway, Prince Edward Island in 1948. The book is a personal account of Prince Edward Island soldiers in the Great War.
WEB http://www.peinet.pe.ca/PEIhome page/morrison/author.htm

Lost Poets of the Great War "The rest is silence." What happens to the people who are wholly against something and yet are compelled to participate? The Great War bred these lost poets (who died in action) and this site explains their inner conflict. Discuss the Christian imagery in John McCrae's "Flander's Fields." Search for the hidden meaning in Edward Thomas's "The Cherry Trees," "The Owl or Rain" and find out about his bizarre death, two years after joining the war. A relatively thorough chronology is provided.
WEB http://www.emory.edu/ENGLISH /LostPoets

Gallipoli Seeing the movie would be easier but a more accurate portrayal of the events can be obtained by visiting this site. The beginnings of a world atwar are explained, including the Ottoman Empire's shift from the possibility of joining the Triple Entente (Britain, France and Russia) to joining the Triple Alliance (Germany, Austria-Hungary, and Italy). Read about the naval, land, Ariburnu, Anafartalar and Seddulbahir battles and thank the heavens that war is not on the horizon after reviewing the details of the death toll.
WEB http://www.focusmm.com.au/%7 Efocus/anzac_01.htm

The Zeppelin Library In this case the Zeppelin is the blimp-thing and *not* the rock group. Design majors might want to examine the blueprints (so this is where the *Star Wars* artists came up with the idea for the transport) and get some ideas of their own. Go back to the early days of Count Ferdinand Von Zeppelin and see a picture of kids marveling at his creation. Learn about pre-WWI passenger Zeppelins, Zeppelins at war, and other dirigibles (including some that didn't crash in New Jersey).
WEB http://top.monad.net/~wonko/Zep _HP.html

Fourteen Points Speech Text and commentary on Woodrow Wilson's "Fourteen Points" speech of 1918, which outlined the basic premise of a just and lasting peace.
WEB http://www.edshow.com/civnet /Teaching/Basic/part8/51.html

▶ WORLD WAR II

50 Years Ago Want to know what was Hitler doing on this day 50 years ago? (Hint: he was dead.) This site features a daily column detailing what was happening on specific days during WWII, both on the battlefronts and on the American homefront. Links to photograph collections, and personal reminiscences of battles from soldiers and civilians, enliven the war chronology.
WEB http://www.webcom.com/~jbd/ww2 .html

Anne Frank in the World A Tucson museum is sponsoring a bilingual exhibit on the 12-year-old who functioned as the conscience of a generation. Learn about the upcoming event at this home page. Hopefully, some of the 600 photos and documents will find their way online.
WEB http://www.tucson.com/waller/Anne _Frank.html

Cybrary of the Holocaust This educational site is dedicated to making sure that no one ever forgets the six million. Historical essays on anti-semitism, Nazism, and the Holocaust are rendered terrifyingly real by the personal recollections of survivors and the mute testimony of photographs.
WEB http://remember.org

Holocaust Archives The files here allow documents and perpetrators to speak for themselves. Netsurfers can read through the cold-blooded testimony of captured S.S. Officers, the Wansee protocols,

prison diaries, and trial testimony from Nuremberg to Demjanjuk. Or they can view Holocaust .GIFs, death camp tallies, and blueprints for ovens. Perhaps most poignant are the photos and stories from European Jewish communities annihilated by the war. Historians and Holocaust deniers (ahistorians) both have their say in essays and published articles.
URL gopher://israel-info.nysernet.org:70 /11/hol

Holocaust FAQs The index here includes "Auschwitz-Birkenau: Layman's Guide (parts 1 and 2)," the "Leuchter Reprot," and "Willis Carto & the Institute for Historical Review" (a counterpoint to the revisionists).
WEB http://www.cis.ohio-state.edu/hyper text/faq/usenet/holocaust/top.html

Holocaust Memorial Museum A brief virtual tour of the new Holocaust Memorial Museum's exhibits and research facilities. Information on obtaining tickets and reservations is included.
WEB http://www.ushmm.org

Memories Kids can converse with WWII survivors via this mailing list.
EMAIL listserv@sjuvm.stjohns.edu ✍
Type in message body: subscribe memories <your full name>

Mississippi State University World War II An archive of World War II documents, including an assessment of Japanese fleet strength from 1941, reports on the U.S.S. Arizona and California, and FDR's radio addresses on the Cairo and Casablanca conferences.
WEB http://www.msstate.edu/Archives /History/USA/WWII/ww2.html

The Nizkor Project Dedicated to refuting the plethora of Holocaust denial on the Net, this site houses evidence substantiating the horror of the Holocaust, and a chronicle of the battle against revisionism taking place in cyberspace.
WEB http://nizkor.almanac.bc.ca

Paris-Expos-Liberation Rejoice with the crowds at the Arc d'Triomphe through this bilingual photo essay on the liberation of Paris in 1944. A map of the attack, profiles of the major players, and documents of surrender are all linked to a chronology and glossary.
WEB http://meteora.ucsd.edu/~norman /paris/Expos/Liberation

Revisionist Files "Evidence" that the Holocaust never happened, collected by the denizens ofalt.revisionism and the Institute for Historical Review.
WEB http://www.kaiwan.com/~greg.ihr /misc/misc.html

Salzburg 1945-1955 "Liberation Force/Occupation Power" is the title of this interesting, commemorative site that brings together the history and reminiscences of both victors and vanquished in a hypertext essay. A mixture of oral history, newspaper coverage, children's drawings, and photography brings stories of fear, privation, horror, homesickness, and triumph alive.
WEB http://www.image.co.at/image /salzburg

soc.history.war.world-war-ii Doing a paper on the Battle of Stalingrad and need some help? Post a question here, and prepare to be flooded with helpful responses. A heavily-trafficked list with readers from all over the world.
USENET soc.history.war.world-war-ii

The White Rose The heroic story of the White Rose, an anti-Nazi resistance group led by young students Hans and Sophie Scholl, is told through their affecting pamphlets, letters, photos, and eyewitness testimony.
WEB http://neuromancer.ucr.edu/beauty /rose.html

World War II FTP Archive A collection of World War II resources that include numerous primary documents—the "Green Book" from the Battle of the Bulge, a list of active aircraft carriers, peace treaties, and even an article on the fates of Japanese battleships.
URL ftp://byrd.mu.wvnet.edu/pub/history /military/wwii/Battle.of.Bulge

World War II: The World Remembers A collection of essays, memoirs, and primary sources from both sides of the fatal D-Day invasion. Government documents, photos, *Stars and Stripes* articles, speeches and newsreels make the fateful days of fifty years ago come alive.
WEB http://192.253.114.31/D-Day/Table_of_Contents.html

Yad Vashem: The Holocaust Martyrs' and Heroes' Remembrance Authority Description of the Israeli museum's exhibits, including its ongoing project to record the names of as many Holocaust victims as possible.
WEB http://yvs.shani.net

The Warsaw Uprising To call the Warsaw Uprising a failure is an understatement. This site shows why war truly is hell. The Polish were so underequipped and undertrained that even boy scouts were included in the fighting against tanks and tremendous artillery. The site covers "W hour" set at 17:00 on Aug. 1, 1944, when the slaughter began, to its end on Sept. 2, 1944. To better understand the conflict, maps and brief desciptions of the main participants are provided.
WEB http://www.princeton.edu/~mkporwit/uprising/top.html

History of the Bomb "Now we're all sons of bitches." That's what Ken Bainbridge, the Test Director, said at the experiment for the A-bomb. This site covers the scientific and historical aspects of the Manhattan Project, the development of the weapon that would redefine global warfare. Begin with pre-WWII letters from Einstein to Roosevelt about the purification of Uranium and end (with a bang) at 5:30 a.m. in Jornada de Muerto, N. Mex. The site explains many of the mixed feelings about the "gadget," including Oppenheimer's delight at its success to the protest of many people who signed a petition against it. Strangely enough, the only hypertext is the word Uranium (don't worry—it won't explode if you click on it).
WEB http://www.cs.herts.ac.uk/~csed3ba

/nuke/history.html

▶ **VIETNAM**

alt.war.vietnam "Napalm bomb" could accurately describe the flame wars that ignite in alt.war.vietnam. It is not just the class of '68 butting heads with the ROTCs—several generations of ill will meet up here. These people definitely do not see the war in Indochina (or the Cold War) as over. (When is the last time you called someone "commie pinko scum"?) Simple questions like "What if the U.S. hadn't entered Vietnam?" invite discussions that quickly devolve into name-calling and dogma-slinging. There is also a sharp divide between the "been there" and the "others." Many participants have complained that discussions often deteriorate into attacks on a single individual—and are attempting to correct this. For now, let it be said that President Clinton probably should choose to discuss the 1960s and the Vietnam War in another forum.
USENET alt.war.vietnam

Images of My War An infantry officer's retrospective on his strange odyssey from a jungle training camp in Panama to the real thing in Vietnam. His struggles to maintain morale among his men during this much-hated police action are especially interesting.
WEB http://www.ionet.net/~uheller/vnbktoc.shtml

soc.history.war.vietnam This Web site chronicles cultural debates surrounding the "American experience" in Vietnam. Essentially the same as alt.war.vietnam except that soc.history.war.vietnam is frequented by more civilians, academics, and other people who would be called "commies" on alt.war.vietnam.
USENET soc.history.war.vietnam

Vietnam Archives Includes the Nam Vet newsletter, info about how to obtain casualty files and service records, and lyrics to many songs of the Vietnam war era.
URL ftp://ftp.msstate.edu/docs/history

/USA/Vietnam

Vietnam on Film and Television This massive file lists every film and TV documentary having to do with Vietnam catalogued by the Library of Congress through 1989.
URL gopher://marvel.loc.gov/00/research /reading.rooms/motion.picture/mopic.tv/mp

Vietnam Related Government Documents The words that started it all, and kept it going for ten long years—they're all here. Start with the ever-popular Gulf of Tonkin "all necessary measures" Resolution, then move to the State Department White Paper from 1965, entitled "Aggression from the North." The most recent Senate POW/MIA report is available in its entirety.
URL gopher://wiretap.spies.com/11/Gov /US-History/Vietnam

VWAR-L A mailing list formed to facilitate communication among scholars, teachers, veterans, and anyone else interested in the Vietnam War.
EMAIL listserv@ubvm.cc.buffalo.edu ✍
Type in message body: subscribe vwar-l <your full name>

> **GULF WAR**

The Incredible PBS Gulf War Home Page The online version of the television broadcast that aired in January, 1996. Listen to or read about the war according to key players, pilots and soldiers in the battlefield. The site links to tapes, transcripts, maps, weapons lists, and the BBC Radio Series, Voices in the Storm.
WEB http://www2.pbs.org/wgbh/pages /frontline/gulf/index.html

The Operation Desert Storm Debriefing Book Where did we leave that SCUD? It has to be lying around here somewhere. Powell and Schwartzkopf fans, get ready to be debriefed (your underwear stays on), and military buffs be on guard— this site has plenty of artillery and machinery statistics, including a list of the helicopters and major missiles used. Chuck Norris has nothing on some of

the actual accounts of POWs in the conflict. Find out about all the major players (and some of the minor ones like the media and the anti-war movement) and the countries they came from, as well as a week-to-week breakdown of the important events.
WEB http://www.nd.edu/~aleyden /contents.html

Ronals A. Hoskinson's Gulf War Photo Gallery A collection of snapshots of the Desert Shield and Desert Storm missions (3rd and 13th battalions) and Ronald A. Hoskinson's Gulf War Diary. Enjoy the relaxing bath at the Desert Hilton (actually, it's just a tent). Visit some of the scenic sites such as the "antenna farm" and the many destroyed Iraqi tanks. After shaking sand out of hair, shoes and clothing, relax with a game of cards or better yet, mail call. This photo album is more personal than most online galleries, with candid shots of soldiers and the situations they faced. Includes a neat little map of the "March Through Hell" and other campaigns.
WEB http://users.aol.com/andyhosk /gulf-war.html

Saddam Hussein Biography "He has a large ego...and defeating this may be more difficult than defeating his military forces," says this brief one-page report. Go to the early days of Hussein's military carreer with his attempts to assassinate General Kaseem and overthrow President Aref (ah, those were the good old days). Then, see Hussein hysteria when he murders entire sections of his military out of paranoia, leaving only "yes-men" incapable of assessing the strength of opposing forces (this turns out to be a plus for the rest of the world.) Minor details about his family and education are also brought to light.
WEB http://www.military-sim.com /hussein.htm

PART 7

Foreign Languages

SPEAKING IN TONGUES

A FUTURISTIC WRITER ONCE PRO-posed that in a thousand years lan-guages will merge, and we will all speak a language called Pan-Mandarin. But that's no excuse to skip French class, even if you do have a quiz tomor-row. The study of languages is useful, and not just because you might need it while traveling someday. Leap over lan-guage barriers and cross cultural lines with helpful cues from the Internet. Then set off for a world tour from the Human Languages Page or the Yamada Lan-guage Guides. Got a sentence you can't decipher? Translate it with Multi-Lan-guage Dictionaries. Prepare for your stay at Concordia Language Villages with AOL's On-Line Language Courses. Find a five-letter word that means "Hey, this is in German!" at TransWord Foreign Lan-guage Crossword Puzzles. Brush up your Ferengi at Constructed Human Lan-guages, and then let Say… teach your computer to intone "This is the world's most useless, yet most entertaining Web site." But most of all, study for that French quiz, 'cause Pan-Mandarin ain't quite here yet.

> STARTING POINTS

Foreign Language Forum Feel like the only person in the world studying the Slavic languages? CompuServe says you're not alone—by a long shot. A recent count showed 16 topics and 71 messages in this category. In other words, Foreign Language Forum is full of resources and discussion groups for every language topic you could think of and some you couldn't. *Musis se ucit cestiny!!* (You've simply got to learn Czech.)
COMPUSERVE *go* flefo

Foreign Language Learning Center Southern Methodist University has a super language lab as part of its online presence. Follow the well-marked road to French, German, Russian, Italian, Japanese, Chinese, and Latin, Mexican,

or Spain-ish Spanish sites. It's a nifty collection.
WEB http://fllc.smu.edu/fllc.html

Human Languages Page It's one-stop shopping for all the best Web sites about languages. Cyberguru Tyler Jones has compiled an awesome index, on top-ics like Languages and Literature and Multilingual Resources. A Random Site feature is for the curious explorer—just click and be transported to Hebrew: A Living Language, the *English-Slovene Dictionary*, or any of the other hundreds of sites listed.
WEB http://www.willamette.edu/~tjones /Language-Page.html

International Forum "We are one world with many languages!" intones the intro-duction to this forum, which is a con-glomeration of those many languages and the folks who speak them. Select from French, German, Italian, Japanese, and Spanish resources, visit Foreign Languages for Travelers, or chat in real time at the International Café.
AMERICA ONLINE *keyword* language

Languages Now you can go around the world in minutes with this super index to language sites from Afrikaans to Welsh. This site, as with all of the Willamette language sites, is a must, especially for those lesser-known languages like Gaelic and English.
WEB http://www.willamette.edu/~tjones /languages/WWW_Virtual_Library _Language.html

The Select Ware Complete News Index EXTRA, EXTRA!! Read all about it, and we do mean all. Here's the latest from any country, perfect for that pesky cur-rent events paper or just to practice your Urdu or Czech. The list of more than 100 countries and regions begins with Argentina and ends with Vatican City, and each country links to all the relevant (and free) news sources online. For example, to get the dirt on Portugal,

check out the *Jornal de Madeira* or three other links. Now that's comprehensive.
WEB http://www.select-ware.com/news

University of Richmond Modern Foreign Languages Home Page If you seek Spanish, French, Russian, Japanese, Chinese, Italian, or German sites (and that's most of you right?) here's a complete and useful index to all of the above. What's more, lucky folks with Real Audio should check out the selection of international broadcasts (Cantonese? Korean? Italian?) under Radio. You don't know a language until you can comprehend its native speakers.
WEB http://www.urich.edu/~lang/welcome .html

Yamada Language Guides Tagalog? Hmong? Afrikaans? Even Inuit and Iroquois? For those who would never believe that all these languages and dozens more could exist on the Net, here's proof that the Web is really worldwide. Yamada presents a fantastic collection of mini indexes for any language in cyberspace.
WEB http://babel.uoregon.edu/yamada /guides.html

▶ DATABASES

All the Scripts in the World The title almost tells the story; it's certainly an intriguing collection of scripts from everywhere, taken from the Book of a Thousand Tongues. If a visitor wanted to see Semitic Scripts, he or she would have five from which to pick. But the visitor would miss the best part if he or she failed to see the Language Tidbits page, or Languages (number of speakers). There the visitor might find out that seven million people speak Luba-Lulua. It boggles the mind, doesn't it?
WEB http://idris.com/scripts/Scripts.html

Constructed Human Languages Many languages have never been spoken by even one native speaker. If that sounds strange, then you've obviously never heard of AllNoun, Esperanto, or even Klingon (yes, the *Star Trek* Klingon.) So,

they probably won't be offering classes in the Black Speech (as in *The Hobbit*) at your school, but learning it would make passing notes in class a lot easier.
WEB http://www.quetzal.com/conlang .html

Ethnologue: Languages of the World The Ethnologue, which is also available in print, attempts the impossible: a taxonomy of all the world's languages. From the apparent—Mandarin and English—to the not-so-obvious—Abnaki-Penobscot, anyone?—they're all here, along with detailed information about the country of origin, the number of speakers and who they are, and any dialects. The data base is also searchable by country, so anyone planning a visit to Kyrghyztan can remember to bring along those Dungan and Kirghiz dictionaries.
WEB http://www.sil.org/ethnologue /ethnologue.html

▶ DICTIONARIES

LingWhat? Yesterday in the mail you received a mysterious package. Inside were a few pieces of paper and a computer disk that looked oddly familiar, covered in writing unlike any you have ever seen. Being a Net-savvy soul, you immediately dialed up LingWhat? and answered a simple series of questions. "Does the language use the Latin alphabet?" began the quiz. Finally, your persistence was rewarded, and LingWhat? told you that the package was in Greek. You took it to a friend from Corfu for translation, and finally, the mystery was solved: It was another one of those AOL disks. Thanks, LingWhat?!
WEB http://idris.com/lingwhat/lingwhat .html

List of Dictionaries Whichever language you've got, you can translate it into something else using the links at this site. It's very helpful, or, as they say in Swedish, *enkel*.
WEB http://math-www.uni-paderborn.de /HTML/Dictionaries.html

Multi-Language Dictionary This amaz-

ing search engine will provide you with plenty of *ayuda* or, if you'd rather, *secours* or *aiuto*. In fact, any word you type in may be returned to you translated in up to 30 languages, from the typical romance languages to some rarer gems like Norwegian. It all depends on how many translations of that word have been entered into this database. Do you know a word that isn't here? Add it with the easy e-form provided. But don't worry, there are more than a million words (in all languages combined) already, to be of *hjelp*.
WEB http://dictionary.logos.it/query.html

▶ JUST FOR FUN

Say... Enter a word, phrase, sentence, or dissertation, and listen to a robo-voice try to say what you've typed using phonemic translation. It works pretty well for phonetic words like the French bibliographie (bib-lee-oh-gra-fee) but watch out—*Sprechen sie Deutsch?* became spreck-un-sigh-dooch. There's no inflection whatsoever, either, so the robo-voice sounds permanently blasé. You'll have hours of linguistic enjoyment.
WEB http://wwwtios.cs.utwente.nl/say

▶ SKILL BUILDERS

Concordia Language Villages Need fodder for those "What I Did Last Summer" essays? Impress your teachers by taking a summer language immersion program. Concordia College in Minnesota sponsors summer camps in any one of 10 languages including Danish, Finnish, Swedish, and Norwegian. (This is Minnesota, after all.) The sessions range from two to four weeks, and include overseas programs and wilderness adventures. No prior language knowledge is necessary, but the program will contain "villagers" with all levels of proficiency.
WEB http://home.cord.edu/dept/clv/index.html

International Language Development Master six languages without ever get-

ting up from your computer chair with I.L.D.'s Interactive lessons in French, German, Korean, Japanese, Russian, and Spanish. Sound files in either of two formats (.AU and Real Audio) tell you how to say it, while vocabulary lists and grammar lessons clue you in on what you're saying. To get beyond Lesson One, you need a password, but it's free.
WEB http://www.ild.com

On-line Language Courses At any given time, there are a half-dozen languages classes going on at AOL's Online Campus. What's more, the prices are really nominal—on average about $25 for an eight-week class. For that price, you can't go wrong. Topics include Rank Beginner's Spanish, Travelling in Germany, and Japanese. Join the online revolution and you'll never have to ride the big yellow bus to school again.
AMERICA ONLINE *keyword* ies→Registration and Course Catalog→Languages

SimTel Foreign Language Software If you've mastered URLs, Netspeak, and computer commands, you can learn a little French. This site carries dozens of language tutorials, including some on Chinese calligraphy, Japanese grammar, basic German, Italian, and Turkish for the DOS user.
URL ftp://ftp.coast.net/SimTel/msdos/langtutr

Student Forum Libraries: Teen Global Village This is the source for a multitude of shareware, .GIFs, and study guides for many languages. From Easy Arabic to Lingua Latina, you can probably find it here. It's a grab bag, but you'll want to grab.
COMPUSERVE *go* stufoa→Browse Libraries →Teen Global Village

TransWord Foreign Language Crossword Puzzles If you can already solve the *New York Times* Sunday crossword in less time than it takes to finish off a bagel and coffee, why not try one in a foreign language? They're available in German, Spanish, French, and Italian at this site. This great way to learn vocabu-

lary comes in your choice of three sizes: small, medium, and large (or petite, moyen, et grande).
URL ftp://ftp.dartmouth.edu/pub/LLTI-IALL/365german-news/tw/index.htm

The Virtual CALL Library From French to Farsi, this is the ultimate source of skill building shareware for language learning. Most of the files are in Windows or DOS format, and many are crippled unless you pay (which you always do, right?) but the variety is incredible, from "Tibetan Tools for Windows" to "Kanji for Fun!" as well as the usual stuff like "French Plus! and Learn Spanish." Not interested in shareware? Follow the links to other kinds of Net resources.
WEB http://www.sussex.ac.uk/langc/CALL

▶ TEACHERS' LOUNGE

The American Council on the Teaching of Foreign Languages Its home page is dry as the desert, but this little organization has some staying power. It was founded in 1967 by the Modern Language Association to promote language pedagogy, and as such has insisted on national standards for foreign language study, which are available here. Also, find out about the council's meetings, workshops, and publications.
WEB http://www.infi.net/~actfl

Foreign Language Teaching Forum No foreign language teacher should miss this Web site, its accompanying gopher, or its mailing list, FLTEACH. It's a network of secondary and higher education professionals sharing ideas, information, and occasional laughs (e.g., composition bloopers by students). Archives of the mailing lists and other goodies are linked from the Web site, or you can find them at the gopher address below.
WEB http://www.cortland.edu/www_root/flteach/flteach.html
Info: URL gopher://gopher.cortland.edu:71
EMAIL listserv@ubvm.cc.buffalo.edu. ✍
Type in message body: subscribe flteach
<your full name>

Intercultural E-Mail Classroom Con-

nections IECC lists allow students and teachers to network worldwide with partner classrooms, ask for help with questions, or discuss the ramifications of a global network. At this Web site, browse the archives or find out who's registered on the many lists and where they're from.
WEB http://www.stolaf.edu/network/iecc

The International Channel Does your school have an extra $3,000 for a satellite dish? Beam over to this site to find out why you should be holding fundraisers to get that money. "We speak your language!" exclaims this station, and they do, from Arabic to Thai. In fact, the International Channel broadcasts shows in 20 languages, on all topics, all the time. At its home page, peruse the program schedule, get curriculum ideas, or head to Tech Support to find out the dirty details about cost. If you definitely haven't got the cash, your consolation prize is I-Links, an index of foreign language sites.
WEB http://www.i-channel.com/welcome.html

National K-12 Foreign Language Resource Center Professional development for foreign language educators is the aim of Iowa State's NFLRC. Find out who's participating in its collaborative projects or workshops in your state, or investigate the small but trustworthy collection of foreign language and Internet-related sites. If you happen to be in Iowa, there's a specific directory for you.
WEB http://www.educ.iastate.edu/currinst/nflrc/nflrc.html

FRENCH

"**B**ONJOUR, CLASSE! BIEN-venue a francais!" And so that frightening first day of French class begins. How strange it is when your wild-eyed French teacher begins speaking to you in—eek!—a foreign language. These days you may be past the chapter on introducing yourself and ordering sandwiches au saucisson, or perhaps you're not, and conjugating verbs still makes you feel imparfait. Any way you slice the fromage, you can find dozens of French resources on the Internet. Start with Hapax or travel south for Tennessee Bob's Famous French Links. Build your vocabulary with the French-to-English Dictionary, and find the quick guide to homework cheats at the amazing Verb Conjugation page. If you don't know the difference between l'amour and la mort, try Online French Lessons for Beginners. Travel to the City of Lights at The Paris Pages, and for inflight reading, check the shelves of the University of Virginia's Online French Texts. Bon voyage!

Le coin des francophones et autres grenouilles It's all in French, but that merely lends authenticity to this, the grand-pére of French indexes. It's also one of the few sites to acknowledge that French is spoken in places other than France, so visitors must make sure to follow the signs to "Des informations à l'intention des pays africains francopho-nes" and "Tout Haiti." And for those who are still hungry for pictures of the Eiffel Tower, there's plenty of France here too. **WEB** http://web.cnam.fr/fr/Welcome .html

Tennessee Bob's Famous French Links Tennessee Bob is a professor at the University of Tennessee and he's got a nice set of French links (don't know about the famous part), including subway maps, academic sites, and even the Musée des Beaux Arts. What he doesn't have, you can find with his helpful section on Finding Things. **WEB** http://www.utm.edu/departments /french/french.html

▶ STARTING POINTS

Hapax: French Resources on the Web Cinema, culture, gastronomy, and humor are just a few of the topics of interest indexed at Hapax. A click yields a comprehensive and up-to-date set of links to toutes les choses françaises on the Net. Of special note are the Especially for Students sections and the FAQs about French culture. **WEB** http://hapax.be.sbc.edu

French Language Resources on the Web A long, long list of perfectly described and organized links to just about everything—that sums up this site from the University of Virginia. It runs the gamut from academic (paleolithic paintings at Vallon-Pont-D'Arc) to childish (the Asterix home page). If it's Frenchier than French fries, try looking here. **WEB** http://etext.lib.virginia.edu/french .html

▶ DICTIONARIES

French-to-English Dictionary "Computer"="ordinateur." "Easy"="facile." That pretty much sums up this dictionary. Type in a word in French or English (make sure to follow the instructions for typing accents) and receive the translated word plus its gender—ordinateur is masculine, not surprisingly. Very helpful stuff when you're struggling for that weird vocab word—and it saves trees, too. **WEB** http://humanities.uchicago.edu /forms_unrest/FR-ENG.html

Verb Conjugation Oh, baby, this is going to be great! Click on the verb form (e.g., simple future, subjunctive) enter the infinitive (aller, for example) and "Press to Conjugate" (no comment). A truly climactic experience. **WEB** http://tuna.uchicago.edu/forms _unrest/inflect.query.html

▶ SKILL BUILDERS

EF Bridge from Hypercube. This excellent site carries a searchable English-French dictionary and grammar and vocabulary tests for students of French. **WEB** http://mlab-power3.uiah.fi/English French/avenues.html

Francais a la carte Formation This site's trolling for paid students, but the services they dangle are free. Post an essay on a suggested topic, and receive in return a completely corrected, hypertext copy. Clicking on a mistake leads the essayist to a full explanation of the mistake. *Incroyable!* Also, the section called Learning Tools is a great set of links to learning sites on the Net. **WEB** http://www.accent.net/falcarte

k12.lang.francais A hit-or-miss newsgroup, but any incorrect French posted is sure to be corrected—which can come in handy for students writing essays. The participants come from all age groups and nationalities, and despite the intention of the group to be French-English, several other languages insist on making themselves heard. Posters are always looking for penpals with whom to practice their French, though, so a Japanese speaker may very well correspond with a German—in French. **USENET** k12.lang.francais

La Page de la Plaisanterie An offbeat site in French encompassing all sorts of pithy quotes and tongue twisters. (Les PDTPs) Try saying *"Si six scies scient six cigares, six cent six scies scient six cent six cigares,"* three times fast and you can skip ahead to Conversational French. Well, maybe not, but it's a great way to practice that sexy French accent. **WEB** http://www.idsonline.com/business /quass/french.html

Online French Lessons for Beginners The conversations are very basic, but, thanks to the sound files, you won't come across as a complete fool when asking for *vin rouge* to accompany your *steak frites.* Complete sound files of simple conversations are here, as well as grammatical instruction and common French phrases—giving you something useful to do when you are just *se tournant les pouces* (twiddling your thumbs). **WEB** http://teleglobe.ca/~leo/french.html

Softwares Relatifs a la Francophonie Anyone for French Scrabble? How about a French version of Netscape? This page compiles French-related (mostly shareware) software links. **WEB** http://web.cnam.fr/fr/frsofts.html

Test de grammaire Francaise Students who can get past the instructions en Francais may wish to try this little test of grammar skills. Each test consists of 10 questions, and wrong answers are corrected when the test is graded. *"Annick ecoute. Annick et Guy _____ aussi?"* **WEB** http://www-resus.univ-mrs.fr/Us /France/grammaire.html

▶ LITERATURE

Association des Bibliophiles Universels Forced to slog through *"Chanson de Roland"*? Poor thing. But even if the book's still sitting in your locker you can read it at home with ABU's on-line texts. Contains just about anything that evil French teachers regularly assign. **WEB** http://web.cnam.fr/ABU

Online French Texts Another super source for those reading assignments from hell. *Gargantua* and the pendant *Pantagruel, Le Roman de la Rose,* and even *Candide.* Somewhere, do you hear diabolical laughter and a faint voice (yours) begging, "Can't we just watch the movie?" **WEB** http://etext.lib.virginia.edu/french .browse.html

▶ CULTURE

France and Francophonie Noteworthy sites are marked with a *chouette* (a type of owl, but French slang for "cool"). Topics are plentiful and most deal with French art, music, literature, and culture.

Oh, and of course, Paris.
WEB http://fllc.smu.edu/languages
/French.html

France Forum Most of the conversation is in French, but never fear, every English-language question or comment currently on the board receives a response. The section called La Langue Français is a great place to start for chat about French study, or to post your first attempt at French poetry, but the real meat of this forum is in the cultural sections. Particularly popular are the topics Politique/Société and Tourisme/Voyages.
COMPUSERVE go frforum

The Paris Pages Ah, Paris. The City of Lights, Love, and the Louvre—where everyone lives on bread, jam, and *café* because the rest of the food is too expensive. Travel to your dream city with the Paris Pages. This site claims to be a "collection of everything." That implies jumble, but it is actually attractive, well-organized, and full of pictures. Check the Paris kiosque for the best jazz in the city. Cybertravelers may need no other guide.
WEB http://www.paris.org

soc.culture.france A great place to discuss all things French—from France's nuclear policy in New Zealand to the best discos in Paris.
USENET soc.culture.france
FAQ: **WEB** http://www.cis.ohio-state.edu
/hypertext/faq/usenet/culture-french-faq
/top.html

The Webfoot's Guide to France Another terrific effort on the part of the Webfoot group—this one linking cybertravelers to the French embassy, English-French dictionaries, information on exchange rates, events calendars, and the virtual Town Hall of cities from Paris to Nancy. The Paris Pages are well worth a visit, and Paris Inside Out will keep night owls happy with its What's On listings. The literati will appreciate the site's list of Parisian bookstores. Then there's the cuisine and the cafe guides—they deserve a glance for sheer fantasy value.

Hotel links, transportation maps, and a culture FAQ help ugly Americans (or Brits or Germans) avoid annoying the natives. All that, and we haven't even mentioned the links to French literature collections, such as the Proust Page and the Siege of Paris Page.
WEB http://www.webfoot.com/travel
/guides/france/france.html

▶ TEACHERS' LOUNGE

Apprentissage du français langue etrangere A mysterious Miss ClicNet wrote this site, and among her suggestions for apprentissage is *"Ne surfez pas sans dictionnaires!"* So she provides them, and dozens of other links and suggestions for teaching and learning French on the Internet. But just remember, your students are begging, "Please don't use the *devoirs de vacances.*"
WEB http://www.swarthmore.edu
/Humanities/clicnet/fle.html

Creative French Teaching Methods "Do your students enjoy French? Are you still eagerly teaching the same lessons year after year?" asks Heather Zaitlin, this site's compiler. (Hint: She already knows the answer to both questions.) From networking opportunities to Class Projects, the topics in Creative French Teaching Methods are custom-made for the stressed-out, burned-out French teacher who needs to find ways to use the Internet in the classroom.
WEB http://www.oise.on.ca/~hzaitlin
/teacher.html

Making the Study of French Real with the WWW Every French teacher's dream, this site is part of the Global Village, but it contains everything necessary to teach a year's worth of classes. *C'est vrai*, this site is a gem for high school French teachers. Along with a brief list of suggested lessons is a multitude of links to WWW Foreign Language Instructional Applications.
WEB http://www.urich.edu/~jpaulsen
/pedagog.html#intro

SPANISH

IF YOUR FIRST LANGUAGE IS ENGlish, you're in good company. Nearly half a billion other people speak English, too, which means you can be understood all over the world. But when it comes to choosing a second language, you can't go wrong with Spanish. In fact, after Mandarin Chinese, Hindustani, and English, Español is the most widely-spoken language in the world, and is spoken first in more countries than any of those other three languages. It's pretty easy to learn, too, despite those irregular verbs. If conjugating confounds you, get online and head straight to Comp-jugador. After a quick stop there, Coleman's Websites for Hispanists or the Latin American Network Information Center are the gateways to a round-the-Web tour of Spanish goodies. Join Juan Carlos and Claudia for reading comprehension at the Spanish Practice Page and dream the impossible dream with Don Quixote at Information Relating to Cervantes. Discover Spain and the Spanish-Speaking Countries, but beware teachers bearing Tecla. Then relax with a (nonalcoholic) margarita on the sunny beaches of Mexico. Olé!

STARTING POINTS

Coleman's Websites for Hispanists Despite the Rainbow Brite look of the page, it's a serious and comprehensive index to Spanish sites on the Internet. Topics include learning and teaching, news, Hispanic culture, email lists and penpal sources. There's even a Just for Fun list at the bottom which encourages a click on CyberSpanglish and Sounds of the World's Animals.
WEB http://gpu.srv.ualberta.ca/~scoleman /index.html

Latin American Network Information Center A self-described "Latin American Yahoo!" LANIC lives up to its billing. Although there is a focus only on Latin America and the Caribbean, there are still 27 countries to explore, from Argentina to Venezuela. Each country's page contains a long list of related links, and the index is sortable by any one of 25 topics, from Agriculture to Travel. It doesn't get any more complete than this.
WEB http://lanic.utexas.edu

DICTIONARIES

Comp-jugador Somebody on another Spanish-language Web site calls this "the best replacement I've found for *1001 Verbs.*" We all own a copy of that skinny little cheat book for every language student's nemesis: verb conjugation. With Comp-jugador, you just type in the verb and the proper conjugations pop up. It claims to have over 10,000 verbs in its vocabulary.
WEB http://csgrs6k1.uwaterloo.ca /~dmg/lando/verbos/forma.html

Spanish to English/ English to Spanish Dictionary "This is a very small Spanish dictionary, with a very simple interface," declares this site. True on both counts: it contains only 1,300 words, but the easy search method makes this a valuable quickie tool. Links on either page take the user to the opposite dictionary, but both addresses are provided just in case. Spanish to English is the first one.
WEB http://www.willamette.edu/~tjones /forms/span2eng.html • http://www .willamette.edu/~tjones/forms/spanish .html

SKILL BUILDERS

Basic Spanish for the Virtual Student Even students who don't know *noches* from nachos can benefit from the learning modules at this site. More than 50 lessons are available, from Pronunciation of Vowels to Irregular Verbs—all outlined in an easy-to-follow, step-by-step format. Links to additional resources (such as vocabulary building) are listed throughout.
WEB http://www.umr.edu/~amigos /Virtual

k12.lang.esp-eng Post a request for a Spanish translation and you're quite likely to get a dozen personal and helpful responses to your own mailbox. The overall plan for k12.lang.esp-eng is to enable students and teachers to communicate with others around the world in Spanish or English. It's also a great place to find an e-pal.
USENET k12.lang.esp-eng

Spanish Lessons Homepage His name is Tyler Jones, and he has prepared these Spanish lessons to teach basic knowledge, grammar, and vocabulary of Mexican Spanish. Lesson 1 begins with simple vocabulary like *adiós* and *ustedes*, along with a guide to basic pronunciation. Sound files for each word are available in .AU format. By Lesson 3, the words are organized around a theme like School, with typical entries like *la tiza* (chalk). Verb conjugation and simple sentences, telling time, counting, and self-tests complete the lessons.
WEB http://www.willamette.edu/~tjones /Spanish/Spanish-main.html

Spanish Practice Page Help has arrived for the dreaded reading comprehension part of every Spanish test. Juan Carlos and Claudia are doing something and carrying on a moronic conversation about it. Juan Carlos says: *"Bueno, perdimos el autobús a Madrid y no hay más trenes. ¿Qué vamos a hacer?"* Claudia says: *"Pues, buscar o un hotel o un hostal, ¿no?"* Take the test that follows, continue the dialogue, and submit it for posting. You will receive your score by email.
WEB http://www.ithaca.edu/hs/lang/lang2 /spaform.htm

LITERATURE

Information Related to Cervantes Sooner or later, every Spanish student has to read about Don Quixote and his famous quest against the windmills. Why not find out something about the author while you're at it?
WEB http://csdl.tamu.edu/cervantes/abc _other.html

Latino Literature Home Page When a person loves a topic as much as the author of these Web pages loves Latino literature, it's bound to show. This is a splendid source for information about any Latin American writer of note, with a slight and admitted leaning toward Mexicans. From Gabriel Garcia Marquez to Esteban Echeverria, each author is given affectionate and admiring biographies, often with pictures and a list of works. The site is heavily under construction, but the author assures in an introduction that all will be fixed soon.
WEB http://www.ollusa.edu/admin/alumni /latino/latinoh1.html

CULTURE

Discover Spain Sponsored by the Tourist Office of Spain, the site features an incredible amount of data for travelers and other interested types, including detailed profiles of Spanish towns— from the metropolis of Barcelona to the seaside town of Costa Del Sol. Transportation, trade show, and hotel info is available, as are explanations of social customs and a wealth of images of Spain. Check out the essay on social customs, which explains siesta hours, or pick up some recipes for gazpacho and paella.
WEB http://www.spaintour.com

Hispanos Famosos That's Famous Hispanics, to you non-Español speakers. This site lists them alphabetically or by category of fame—musicians, antiquity, women, and many other headings. Oscar Arias, who was president of Costa Rica, won the Nobel Peace Prize in 1987. Find his biography under Nobel Prizes. Feeling surreal? Summon Salvador Dalí from the Painters category.
WEB http://www.clark.net/pub/jgbustam /famosos/famosos.html

Mexico In Spanish or English, you won't find a more attractive or complete guide to Mexican history, cuisine, art, economy, geography, tradition, science, sports, and tourism than this. (Did you know that Mexico is 1,972,550 square

kilometers, or that November 20 is the anniversary of the Mexican Revolution?) If you read the site's English version, here's a helpful hint: click on the text version of the specific topics rather than the photographic images. For some reason, clicking on the images themselves still spits out Spanish.
WEB http://mexico.udg.mx

Mundo 21: Latin Countries Page While this page is designed for folks using the Spanish textbook *Mundo 21*, that's no reason to stay away for even a minute if you're looking for info about and links to the Latin countries. Click on the image map for the country you want, and be amazed at what you'll find: basic stats, pictures of the currency, maps, and dozens of links to other related places including newsgroups and mailing lists.
WEB http://humanities.byu.edu/spanish/mundo/mundo.html

Sí, Spain Or "*Sí, España*," if one prefers. This site is sponsored by the Embassy of Spain in, of all random places, Ottawa. It's packed with all kinds of details and assorted goodies about the history, population, infrastructure, and everything else about the land of Spanish olives and bullfighting. Even better, it's updated almost daily and contains loads of links to other places. Who could say *¡No!* to Spain?
WEB http://www.DocuWeb.ca/SiSpain

soc.culture.spain Just what exactly are *tapas* anyway? Post a query at this newsgroup and find out. Pose any of your Spanish-culture questions, and receive answers in Spanish and English.
USENET soc.culture.spain

The Spanish-speaking Countries The same señors and señoras who manage Hispanos Famosos bring offer this excellent set of links on every Spanish-speaking country including España herself— "the country originator of the language." A flag of each country is followed by a short but relevant list of cultural links. This just may be the quickest way to the Brazilian Carnaval without booking a

flight to Rio.
WEB http://www.clark.net/pub/jgbustam/paises/paises.html

The Webfoot's Guide to Spain Quick, what numbers do you dial to phone Ada in Madrid? This resource has the answer to that and many other questions about Spain. Links lead to exchange-rate pages, the Spanish embassy, the home page of the city Bilbao, a map of the Barcelona subway, and introductory Spanish lessons. Check here before packing a suitcase for Catalonia or writing that paper on Valencia.
WEB http://www.webfoot.com/travel/guides/spain/spain.html?City

▶ TEACHERS' LOUNGE

ESPAN-L This is a list for those who teach Spanish literature and language. All postings are in Spanish and they come in droves.
EMAIL listserv@vm.tau.ac.il ✍ *Type in message body:* subscribe espan-l

Mailing Lists for Spanish Teachers There's plenty to fill a lonely email box at this site, which is a straightforward list of mailing lists for Spanish teachers. Network. Discuss. Inspire. Be inspired. Never have to plan a lesson again. Hey, now we're talking. Email away for discussion about everything from the country of Spain and its people to the daily news in Chile.
WEB http://math.unr.edu/linguistics/spanlist.html

The Tecla Spanish Educator's/Student's magazine Here is an excellent source for teaching ideas, which can be printed out and given to students "as is" or used as a jumping-off place. Each weekly edition consists of four texts in Spanish, with vocab lists at the end. Also included are four or five ordinary drill exercises. *Tecla* comes *graciàs* to Birkbeck College at the University of London.
WEB http://langlab.uta.edu/langpages/TECLA.html

RUSSIAN

PERHAPS IT'S AN OVERWHELMING urge to read *Pravda* and understand it. Maybe your grandmother was Russian, or you just want to make a killing in Russia's new market economy. Whatever the reason you chose to study the language, learning a whole new alphabet can be intimidating. But don't despair: the SovInformBureau can put you on the right track to all things Cyrillic. Motor over to the Russian-English Dictionary while you're at it and pick up a few new words and a Cyrillic font or two. Then gab about culture and travel in the native tongue of the many Mikhails and Sashas at soc.culture.soviet.

▶ STARTING POINTS

SovInformBureau Vadim Maslok is your host for the ultimate Russian tour. The site provides a friendly and welcoming index to the formerly-Red side of the Web. Check out the link called "Russify Everything" for translation software. Especially noteworthy are the Russian and Soviet Humor links, along with Art, Culture, and Politics.
WEB http://www.siber.com/sib/index.html

Russian and Eastern European Studies Home Page It's not too pretty but it's a superior starting place for Russian resources. Word lists, travel sites, and links to Russian literature repositories are just some of the items available.
WEB http://www.pitt.edu/~cjp/rslang.html

▶ DICTIONARIES

Russian-English and English-Russian Dictionary A simple, searchable dictionary that translates Russian to English and English to Russian. Download Cyrillic fonts which enable you to use the dictionary.
WEB http://www.elvis.ru/cgi-bin/mtrans

▶ SKILL BUILDERS

Russian for Travelers To get the most out of your trip to Russia (even if it's only in your dreams) or to impress your Russian instructor, come to this site to pick up a few phrases in the native tongue. The home page asks you to enter the language you speak and the language you want to learn, and you're set. Learn how to say, "I'd like another vodka, please," and "Which way to the chess tournament?"
WEB http://www.travlang.com/languages /index.html

RusVocab Shareware Type in this week's vocabulary words, and RusVocab will drill you until you are reciting them in your sleep. Choose from a selection of either direct translation or multiple-choice drills. The software even comes with sample vocabulary files. The shareware version of the software is available, and the complete version is still pretty cheap.
WEB http://www.imagi.net/~whitbear /wbrvshar.html

▶ CULTURE

Friends and Partners The iron curtain is down, and communications are up. Friends and Partners opens the lines of communication between Russia and the rest of the world by promoting cultural exchange and introducing Americans and Russians to each other on the Net. People from the heart of Russia can discuss politics with people in the heart of Iowa. Make sure you check out the pronunciation guides (with sound files) to the alphabet, greetings, and farewells in Russian.
WEB http://solar.rtd.utk.edu:81/bc/home .html

soc.culture.soviet Talk about politics, recent news events, and other topics regarding the nation they like to call "sweet mother Russia." A trip to this newsgroup will reward you with a sample of the national culture served à la cyberspace.
USENET soc.culture.soviet

GERMAN

WHEN JFK SO ELOQUENTLY declared, "*Ich bin ein Berliner,*" the Germans heard, "I am a sweet roll," which, quite literally, is what he said. (The proper idiomatic expression is "Ich bin Berliner.") The German people were charmed by JFK's attempt to speak their native tongue, but no student of the language of Bach and Goethe would want to appear so without kultur, and that's where the Internet steps in. The Net is as popular in Deutschland as beer and sauerbraten, so there's no shortage of places to go soak up the atmosphere. With your lederhosen firmly fastened, amaze your friends with your knowledge of some of the stranger idioms at Travlang's German-English Dictionary—"He breaks a fly on the wheel" is Er schiesst mit Kanonen nach Spatzen; and "That's not my pigeon" becomes Das ist nicht mein Bier. Make a lifelong friend at k12.lang.deutsch-eng or curl up with a Grimm fairy tale at 19th Century German Stories. For culture, try soc.culture.german, or for news try The Week in Germany. Then relax with a good schinkenwurst and a bier.

STARTING POINTS

Links for AATG Members From the Potzdamer Platz construction site to Baseball Rules auf Deutsch, the American Association of Teachers of German has got it linked. Investigate the Goethe links or find an e-pal at Deutches Schulnetz—you can do everything but hold a piece of the Berlin Wall.
WEB http://www.stolaf.edu/stolaf/depts/german/aatg/link.html

World Wide Web Virtual Library: German Resources A nicely arranged list of sites not only dealing with Germany, but presented in the German language. Since the Net is so popular among Germans it's a teeming list roaming all across the board from Philology to Plastic Arts. *Ich liebe* WWW Virtual Library, and you will too.
WEB http://www.rz.uni-karlsruhe.de/Outerspace/VirtualLibrary/

DICTIONARIES

Bertelsmann Lexikon A German-language dictionary/encyclopedia produced by Bertelsmann Electronic Publishing. Topics available include Wissenschaft, Kultur and Kunst (Science, Culture and Art.) Instructions are entirely in German.
COMPUSERVE *go* beplexikon

Travlang's German-English Dictionary This dictionary is a powerful search engine for over 120,000 words. Just type in a word—"baby," for example—and the dictionary churns out up to 200 sentences, phrases, and words in German ("baby" is *das Kleinkind*, but "baby face" is *das Kindergesicht*, and "baby grand" is translated *der Stutzfluegel*). Lots of fun when you're just sitting around, procrastinating on homework.
WEB http://www.travlang.com/German English

SKILL BUILDERS

German for Beginners This little set of lessons is complemented greatly by the author's inclusion of reading lists, exercises, and a link to a German-English dictionary. The lessons are in English and well-written, but they are almost impossible to read with a frames-capable browser since they are smashed into one-word columns. So, even if you're tempted to "take advantage" of technology, skip the big button and go for the old-fashioned straight-text version. This means *du*.
WEB http://castle.UVic.CA/german/149

German Practice Page Introduce yourself to Dagmar at the Reading Comprehension and Writing portion of the practice page. Then scroll down for the Fill-in-the-Blank verb form quiz. If you have Java Script, the page let's you know instantly how you did. Otherwise, your

score will be emailed to you.
WEB http://www.ithaca.edu/hs/lang/lang2/tedform.html

k12.lang.deutsch-eng Much more active than some of the other k12.lang newsgroups, this is a highly recommended place to practice your German with other students and native speakers from around the world. Also, there are plenty of Germans (who happen to be major netheads) who want to speak English with you. Bad communication in both directions—can it get any more fun than that?
USENET k12.lang.deutsch-eng

▶ LITERATURE

19th Century German Stories Are you still waiting for *Der Froschkönig* to come along? Every little kid learns this story, about the princess who kisses a frog and—POOF!—gets a prince instead. Now that you're older, read the original German version by the Brothers Grimm, as well as *Rumpelstilzchen* and several other beloved children's tales of yore. Original illustrations and English translations are included.
WEB http://128.172.170.24/menu.html

Internet-Accessible Texts in German A quality list of everything available online that's relevant to German literature. Hypertexts available will include authors ranging widely from Martin Luther to Kafka. Gotta get to Goethe? No problem—*hersehen*…
WEB http://www.lib.virginia.edu/wess/etexts.html#german

▶ CULTURE

Der SPIEGEL Online *Der Spiegel* is Germany's most popular news magazine, as well as Europe's largest. Topics are similar to those found in *Newsweek* or *Time*: politics, the economy, arts, science, and social issues. The online version of *Der Spiegel* comes in either German or English (this link is to the English version, although the text of most articles is German) and is a great chance to practice

side-by-side translation while learning about all the most important German news. Recent article topics include the collective guilt of Germans over the WWII genocide and an interview with the chairman of Daimler-Benz.
WEB http://eunet.bda.de/bda/int/spon/english/e_gruss_inside.html

Deutschland Online Forum *Guten tag* from the gang at the Deutschland Online Forum, where people meet to discuss politics, sports, culture, and music, often in German, but sometimes in English.
COMPUSERVE *go* gerline

Germany Whether you need "Long information" or "Short information," this is an encyclopedic source for maps and interesting facts about the land of biergartens and Wagner. For example, 99 percent of all Germans over the age of 15 can read—and in German, too!
WEB http://www.chemie.fu-berlin.de/adressen/brd.html

soc.culture.german Visit the newsgroup to discuss everything to do with Germany—from the hottest German TV shows to the recent rise in German nationalism. The newsgroup's FAQ is an excellent resource for travelers: It lists the addresses of German embassies worldwide, explains the difference between an S-bahn and a regular Bundesbahn train (the Bundesbahn charges more for the same service), and details the many intercity bike routes found between major cities (they are an excellent way to see the countryside).
soc.culture.german
USENET soc.culture.german
FAQ: **WEB** http://grafton.dartmouth.edu:8001/lrc/culture/europe/scg.faq

The Week in Germany A great site for students searching for current news about Germany, these downloadable newsletters contain articles on cultural and political events; stories and speeches from previous weeks are archived at this Web site as well.
WEB http://langlab.uta.edu/langpages/GIC.html

ITALIAN

"**O**PEN MY HEART, AND YOU will see / Graved inside of it 'Italy,'" wrote an enraptured Robert Browning in his poem "De Gustibus." Millions of people before and since have echoed his sentiment. Italy is a beautiful place, rich both in spirit and in culture, and its language is a lovely reflection of its home. Opera fans know that Italian was meant to be sung, but it also does just fine to summon welcome guests to a perfect dinner of good vino, warm pasta al dente, and pleasant conversation. Grab a cappucino with extra foam, pull up a chair, and prepare to be dazzled by the land that inspired Michelangelo and da Vinci. First, consult the Net and find an Italian/English Dictionary. Learn to speak the language of love at Italian Lessons. You'll find plenty of Divine Comedy at Italian Literature, but for a really wild time, peek through the Windows on Italy. Then, when you have plenty to confess, meet the Holy Father in The Vatican City.

STARTING POINTS

Italy on the Web Here's the master guide to official Italian language, culture, and current events sites around the Net. Its chief goal is to support a section providing links to Italian cultural institutes in cities worldwide, but it also has extensive indexes to cultural information, Italian news, as well as Italian regions and cities. The lists are annotated and hyperlinked to more specific indexes, which is helpful—not to mention the fact that the site's in English.
WEB http://www.geocities.com/Athens /1809/index.html

La Pagina Italiana di Paolo Marcello Araccanci Italiano Paolo has set up a quality index to the best Italian sites for those who may need only a brief tour. There is very little English spoken here, but even non-Italian-speakers can easily comprehend what it's all about: Giornali, for example, lists journals and maga-

zines, while Letteratura links to such written works as the Consitution of Italy. Other categories are Chat, Musica, Il Bel Paese and Per'i Ragazzi. At the bottom are search forms for all the major search engines. All this is perched cheerfully over the Italian flag and a map of the country. Bellissimo!
WEB http://www.panix.com/~moose44 /italiano.html

DICTIONARIES

Italian/English Dictionary It's simple. Type in a word or part of a word and the dictionary returns the translation. The vocabulary is small—only 6,200 words—but that suffices for most beginners to intermediates. There are two URLs: one is Italian to English and one is English to Italian, but don't worry about getting the right one because they're hyperlinked to each other.
WEB http://www.willamette.edu/~tjones /forms/ital2eng.html • http://www .willamette.edu/~tjones/forms/italian.html

SKILL BUILDERS

Italian Lessons Get the most out of your study of Italian by picking up some key phrases at this site. Each lesson consists of subject-related vocabulary instructions: Learn important words to use in restaurants, train stations and at Italian customs checks. And most importantly, learn how to ask for the restrooms. There's an interactive quiz at the end of each lesson to test your newfound knowledge.
WEB http://www.willamette.edu/~tjones /languages/Italian/Italian-lesson.html

Italian Wordlist Have some spare time on your hands? Memorize these complete lists of Italian words, listed alphabetically by letter. There are no definitions or translations, but this is an opportunity to expand your horizons and stay home on a Saturday night to look them all up. You will probably want to

rely on the unzipped versions of the files, because the complexity of downloading the compressed versions may cut into your social time.
WEB http://www.dcs.ed.ac.uk/home/clc/wordlist

Learn to Speak Italian Just for fun, this Ragu-sponsored site is guaranteed to make you smile. Or, if you are desperately trying to figure out how to say, "Carlo, give that Pinocchio doll back to your baby sister right now!" this is your lucky day. Other vital phrases includes "Be a brave man and change little Mario's diaper, OK?" There are sound files in multiple formats for every sentence.
WEB http://www.eat.com/learn-italian/index.html

▶ LITERATURE

Italian Literature Italy's not just the land of spaghetti and the Pope. It's also home to one of the richest literary heritages in Europe. Here's a one-stop source for hypertext versions of all the big stuff, including Dante's *La Divina Commedia* and Boccaccio's *Decameron*. Interested in contemporary Italian poetry? There's a link at the bottom to Caffé Poetel, a searchable index of modern artistes. For basic background in Italian literature, take the topmost link to Letteratura Italiana, part of Windows on Italy.
WEB http://www.crs4.it/HTML/Literature.html

Planet Italy: Culture—Literature Click on Prose or Poetry, and away you'll go to the world of Galileo Galilei and St. Francis of Assisi. This site is lovely to look at and helpful, too, with its narrative English texts briefly explaining the works and lives of several notables. It's not all-inclusive by any means, just very well done. When you're done, the rest of Planet Italy is a worthwhile place to hang around, as much for the pretty pictures as for the culture.
WEB http://www.PlanetItaly.com/Culture/Lit/index.html

▶ CULTURE

L'Unione Sarda Italy's popular daily newspaper is now online. It's a super source for current events and keeping up with trends in your adopted mother country. The main menu is in both English and Italian, but keep a dictionary handy.
WEB http://www.vol.it/UNIONE/unione.html

soc.culture.italian You'll need to know a few words in the language of love in order to enjoy the conversation at the newsgroup, which is almost exclusively in Italian (the only English-language posts are from Americans asking for help with their Italian.) Perhaps more useful is the newsgroup's FAQ—entire sections of it are devoted to tourism, the arts, and Italian customs.
USENET soc.culture.italian
FAQ: **WEB** http://www.lib.ox.ac.uk/internet/news/faq/soc.culture.italian.html

Vatican City An amazingly rich site that opens with the full text of the latest speeches made by the most famous resident of the world's smallest nation. The site also provides a full history of the city, .GIFs of its flag, and maps of its streets. But the best part of the site is the online gallery of images from the famous museums and churches located in Vatican City—at this site you can preview more than 300 images from the Sistine Chapel and close to 600 images from other selected Vatican museums.
WEB http://www.christusrex.org/www1/citta/0-Citta.html

Windows On Italy This site is a large collection of bilingual links for travelers and for Italians, both in the homeland and on Mott Street. Many daily Italian newspapers—right, center, and left—are just a jump away, as are virtual tours of numerous cities from Milan to Naples. You can also read essays on the wine festival in Florence and on taking a tour of the Vatican.
WEB http://www.mi.cnr.it/WOI

JAPANESE

SOME TIME IN THE 1970S, AMERIca discovered Japan. Sure, we knew it was there all along—an island halfway around the world—but until the critical gas shortages made us notice its excellent manufacturing skills and supreme social order, we had thought of the Japanese as they were after World War II—tragically beaten. We were wrong. We were impressed. We still are. Japanese cities are virtually crime-free. The people are healthy and educated. What's more, they've taken the trouble to learn our language. Some of us, the lucky ones with a good school curriculum, have been able to return the favor. Now anyone with access to the Internet can learn Japanese and appreciate the language of the Land of the Rising Sun. So hop on a crowded Tokyo subway and cruise over to TN's Japan-Related Web Links, armed with Jeffrey's Japanese-English Dictionary Server. Climb Mount Fuji with your copy of 100 Poems by 100 Poets. Don't forget the wasabi at Wade's Virtual Sushi Parlor and when your snack is done, make a friend in the blue sea of the Japan Forum.

▶ STARTING POINTS

Japanese Information Listen to the national anthem, read some Japanese proverbs, download the constitution of Japan, get a list of mailing lists in Japan, take a tour of Kyoto, explore Japan with maps, check in for travel updates or learn the essential phrases to get around Japan. You can do all of these with the links available on this site. Sound clips are included.
WEB http://www.ntt.jp/japan/index.html

sci.lang.japan FAQ This is a good introduction to some basic facts about the Japanese language.
URL gopher://gan.ncc.go.jp/11/JAPAN/SLJ

TN's Japan-Related Web Links Hang on to your boushi, because if it's Japanese, TN has found it and posted it. More than 2,000 links—that's more links than there are common kanji—make this the mother of all Japan Web guides. Whether it's kabuki or Honda you seek, you'll be so intrigued by the other links that you may never get there. But they're featured, along with haiku, Fuji Film, Buddhism, origami, Sony, sushi… and bless TN's soul, it's all in English.
WEB http://www.panix.com/~tn/japan.html

▶ DICTIONARIES

Jeffrey's Japanese-English Dictionary Server A sophisticated dictionary for English-to-Japanese translations. Words can be translated into *romaji* (romanized) and then to *kana* and *kanji*. Although browsers supporting Japanese text are encouraged, Netscape users can view illustrated representations of Japanese characters. The site also has a searchable database of 6,000 *kanji* characters.
WEB http://www.itc.omron.com/cgi-bin/j-e

The Quick & Dirty Guide to Japanese Grammar "An educational institution obviously has a financial stake in dragging out your language learning as long as possible (and confusing you along the way)," says Tad Perry, the author of this brief work of linguistic education. Using the K.I.S.S. method ("keep it simple, stupid"), Perry offers a funny, readable, and most of all informative guide to the sometimes bewildering rules of Japanese. Topics include particles, subjects and deletions.
URL gopher://wiretap.spies.com/00/Library/Article/Language/grammar.jap

▶ SKILL BUILDERS

The Japanese Tutor This is an in-depth program which contains units on language, people and culture. There are several levels of study, from beginner to advanced. For proper pronunciation,

download the sound files of native Japanese speakers, and watch the video clips to master your kanji strokes.
WEB http://www.missouri.edu/~c563382

Travelers' Japanese with Voice "With Voice" means that there are download-able sound files in .AU format of helpful sentences like "I'm looking for someone who speaks English" and "Please tell me where to go to buy it"—both incredibly critical phrases to know. There's also a simple pronunciation guide.
WEB http://www.ntt.jp/japan/japanese

▶ LITERATURE

100 Poems by 100 Poets (Ogura Hyakunin Isshu) Not only is *Hyakunin Isshu* one of the most influential books in Japanese literature, but it inspired an extremely popular card game based on the poems. Not only does this Web site have both an English and a Japanese version of the *Hyakunin Isshu*, but it also has an on-line version of the card game, *Uta Karuta*. Oh, life is sweet sometimes, you think, until you realize that playing the game involves memorizing all 100 five-line poems, called *waka* and *tanka*.
WEB http://etext.lib.virginia.edu/japanese /hyakunin/index.html

Classical Japanese Texts on the World Wide Web Even if you can't view *kanji* on your computer, which means you can't read most of the literature these links point to, you'll want to check out this amusing and informative page. Plus, there's a really cool Japanese mask at the top.
WEB http://www-leland.stanford.edu /~patkins/texts.html

▶ CULTURE

Japan National Tourist Organization Coins are 1 yen, 5 yen, 10 yen, 50 yen, 100 yen, and 500 yen. Bank notes are 1,000 yen, 5,000 yen, and 10,000 yen. There. That's your first lesson in Japanese currency. This official online outpost of Japanese tourist information is packed with mini-lessons to help the

traveler navigate his or her trip to Japan. The site describes everything from the climate of the country to the drinking etiquette, from the costs of a Japan Rail Pass to the best places to shop in Tokyo. The National Tourist Organization includes a list of recommended restaurants, suggestions of tour itineraries for budget travelers, maps, and listings for museums and galleries across the country.
WEB http://www.jnto.go.jp

Japan Window The window is a cooperative site, with information on technology, business, government, and living in Japan. Kids visiting the site are invited to learn hiragana and origami. Adults can read about the Japanese diet, review tax law, find out what's on at the theater, or meet in an online live chat room to talk about the Kobe earthquake or last night's baseball game.
WEB http://jw.nttam.com/HOME/index .html

▶ TEACHERS' LOUNGE

Center for Educational Media The CEM is dedicated to providing teachers with educational materials about Japan and Asia, and as part of their quest have a large online database available for searching. It also publishes a free newsletter and offers other educational packets.
WEB http://www.cs.earlham.edu/~cem

Teaching and Learning About Japan "Welcome to this hypertexted narrative introduction to selected aspects of Japanese civilization and culture," begins this site. You may want to dial this site right in front of easily bored students and send them on the Japanese cybertour of their lives. Explore places like Joseph Wu's Origami Page, Kabuki for Everyone, and the Godzilla home page, while enjoying Lee Makela's tour guide spiel.
WEB http://www.csuohio.edu/history /japan.html

CHINESE

CHINA IS HOME TO A BILLION PEOPLE, or one-fifth of the world's population. Mandarin is spoken by more people than any other language in the world. So shouldn't we all learn it in school? There's a real case to be made for studying China and its once and future territories like Hong Kong and Taiwan, but it can mostly be stated in one word: culture. Chinese culture has been one of the purest and most protected, as well as one of the richest in the world, for thousands of years. To most Americans, it remains a completely undiscovered treasure. But learning the basic language and its many dialects could give you nightmares, so cuddle up to your computer and sleep a little easier. Your very own Chinese dynasty begins at Chinascape or Hu Wenze's Home Page. Study for Mark Bosley's Chinese Radical Exam and then check out the wacky St. Olaf's gang and their Practical Chinese Reader. Find the "way" to Lao Tzu at Classic Chinese Literature, or book your flight for a Tour In China. We promise that these pages will give Chinese take-out a whole new cultural relevance.

▶ STARTING POINTS

Chinascape This Web index is a jumping-off place for so many points of Chinese interest, in topics such as News, Culture, Entertainment, Sports and Martial Arts, that it can get overwhelming. To help, the creators of Chinascape provide news headlines and other noteworthy material in an unmistakable Hot section. The coverage extends to Mainland China, Hong Kong, Taiwan, and Macau.
WEB http://harmony.wit.com/chinascape

Chinese-Language-Related Information Page A well-organized and reliable set of links to Web sites pertaining to Chinese language study. Sections include links to Chinese courses and tutorial software, as well as academic connections and cultural sites. This one is a must-visit for any Web tour of China.

WEB http://www.webcom.com/~bamboo/chinese/chinese.html

Hu Wenze's Home Page One of the most comprehensive indexes to things Chinese on the Web, Hu Wenze's Home Page begins with a brief introduction and a primer containing links to sites about reading Chinese online (hint: It's not automatic). After that, click to such index categories as arts, business, magazines, and literature. Anything worth visiting is probably listed here.
WEB http://pears.lib.ohio-state.edu/China/homepage1.html

▶ SKILL BUILDERS

Audio Tutorial of Survival Chinese Greeting, shopping, dining, travelling: this is linguistic survival, kids. There are sound files in .AU format for each topic, and pinyin romanization for each phrase. "How are you, Mr. Wang?" is *Ni hao, wang xiang shen?*
WEB http://pasture.ecn.purdue.edu/~agenhtml/agenmc/china/ctutor.html

Chinese Character Pronunciations You have no idea how to read Chinese script, but you speak Chinese and you are lucky enough to have JavaScript and this page. Cut and paste your Chinese text (in certain specified formats) onto this page, and it will return a romanized pronunciation guide for your selection. Then, you can read it—helping you bridge a cultural gap that may alter the course of history.
WEB http://www.webcom.com/ocrat/reaf

Mark Bosley's Chinese Radical Exam No, this is not a test to see if you should have held a megaphone at Tiananmen Square. Chinese radicals are the building blocks of Chinese calligraphy—a stroke or a swash of the brush. This site is host to a Windows program designed to tutor students of Chinese until they master the radicals. No Chinese font is necessary, and a demo version is available for free

here—the full version costs $29. Features of the program include flash cards, pop quizzes, and other goodies. Not interested? There's more to see, under Related Information.
WEB http://execpc.com/~mbosley

Practical Chinese Reader While there are a lot of people in cyberspace doing their best to help you learn languages from Spanish to Ojibwe, not many of them have worked as hard as these people. At this site, you'll find 17 Quick Time videos of elementary Chinese conversations at the "Hello, how are you?" level. They're designed to accompany the textbook for which the site is named, but so what? It's fun to watch people look a little silly for the sake of education.
WEB http://www.stolaf.edu/people/hess/pcr.html

► LITERATURE

Chinese Classics You'll need to brush off those Chinese fonts for this site, but at least it's in English, too. Chinese Classics "aims at collecting as many Chinese classic literature as possible for the benefit of the Internet community." They're doing well, with nine topics including Pre-Qin philosophers, poetry, prose, and even a chronology of Chinese history. Make sure you check out the aptly-named "Poetry about Moon."
WEB http://www.cnd.org/Classics/index.html

Classic Chinese Literature Here's the spot for English translations of Confucius and Lao Tzu. Need more information about these famous Chinese guys? This site goes beyond fortune cookies and contains links to both philosophy sites and bibliographies.
WEB http://pasture.ecn.purdue.edu/~agenhtml/agenmc/china/classlit.html

► CULTURE

China Home Page China's big. It's very big. This home page is as well. Buried among links to Chinese universities and personal home pages for Chinese citizens, the site offers an extensive tour of China (Web pages for each of the Chinese provinces with recommendations for sites to see and things to do), general information about the mammoth country, and pages on Chinese music, art, and language.
WEB http://solar.rtd.utk.edu/~china/china.html

Finding News About China If you want to keep abreast of happenings in China, Hong Kong, Taiwan, or Tibet, check out this list of resources for Chinese news on the Internet. There are links to weekly journals of Chinese current affairs, daily Hong Kong and Taiwan Stock Exchange reports, human rights bulletins, and newswires from Beijing from Hong Kong.
WEB http://www.hk.super.net/~milesj

soc.culture.china China, Hong Kong, and Taiwan aren't part of the same country. In fact, one of the most frequent topics in these three newsgroups is the distinctions and political hostilities among the "three Chinas." Soc.culture.china is dominated by PRC students doing study-abroad programs in the States, and most are taking the time to freely post anti-government messages, since they are safely out of reach of rolling tanks: Tiananmen and its aftereffects remain high-volume topics. Much conversation is conducted with embedded Pinyin phrases, so don't be surprised if you suddenly find the discussion entirely incomprehensible. Be sure to read the FAQ for detailed instructions on reading and writing in Chinese on-line.
USENET soc.culture.china
FAQ: WEB http://www.cis.ohio-state.edu/hypertext/faq/usenet-faqs/bygroup/soc/culture/china/top.htm

Tour in China Click through Web pages for each of the provinces of China. Resources include photos of popular attractions, essays on the history of regions, and descriptions of famous tourist sites.
WEB http://www.ihep.ac.cn/tour/china_tour.html

LATIN & GREEK

ONE IS ALIVE (AT LEAST IN SOME form) and the other is dead (cold on the floor). But other than that, Latin and Greek have a lot in common. Two hundred years ago, a proper education consisted almost entirely of digesting Greek and Latin texts on such subjects as politics and religion, written by a bunch of guys with only one (weird) name, like Plato or Aristophanes. The general consensus was that all the knowledge of the world resided in these classics. Today, the only Greek learned by the modern student is the name of his fraternity or her sorority, and the only type of Latin learned is pig. But plenty of people at all levels of education are making it their business to keep these languages going. Join them at Pagina Latina, then glean some ancient wisdom from The Tech Classics Archive. Practice your Sanctus and Missa with the naughty nuns from the Council of Remiremont. Then read Cicero and Caesar the way they wrote at Project Libellus. If it's all Greek to you, head straight for Hellenic Greek Linguistics. But remember: a language is only dead when it's entirely forgotten.

▶ STARTING POINTS

Communications Connections: Latin
For the budding classicist, this page hosts a bright collection of links to both the ancient world and the modern challenges of learning Latin. Many of the sites are both Greco and Roman, so the "Latin" is a bit of a misnomer. Try The Classical Collection of the Otago Museum, or pay a visit to the Palace of Diocletian.
WEB http://www.widomaker.com/~ldprice /#Sofia

MAC Education: Latin and Greek Modern technology to help you bone up on some ancient languages. The two games available teach either Latin or Greek. Both are identical except for the vocabulary lists they use. Both have something

to do with hungry frogs (the frogs of Aristophanes, perhaps?) Each game's vocabulary list stores about 2,000 words, and can be augmented by the student. Don't forget to pay for your shareware if you like it.
WEB http://www.sciedsoft.com/#Latin

Pagina Latina Rome by way of Springfield, Mo. is kind of an indirect route—unless one happens to be visiting this page put up by Springfield's Kickapoo High School. It's got a great collection of links to Cultura Romanorum and Medieval Latin, as well as Other Stuff. We also discover that Latin isn't a dead language after all, since the folks at Kickapoo have invented a new word: hyperlinkos.
WEB http://www.orion.org/ed/sgfschls /kickfl/latlinks.htm

The Tech Classics Archive Desperate students can find more than 400 Greek and Roman texts online, along with the three most beautiful words one can hear: in English translation. Plus, if you've been assigned to read the *Iliad*, but the only Homer you can understand is Simpson, this site may help—all the texts have commentary available. You'll never have to dread the words "read and discuss" again.
WEB http://the-tech.mit.edu/Classics /index.html

▶ LATIN

Allen and Greenough's New Latin Grammar Sometimes there's no need for frills. Allen and Greenough's New Latin Grammar is a concise and understandable grammar guide for those who already have some background in Latin, but probably not complete enough for those who don't know veni from vidi or vici. This is pretty much of a bargain-basement site, but it makes an excellent reference.
WEB http://ccat.sas.upenn.edu:80/jod /AG/allgre.contents.html

The Council of Remiremont "This is a story about nuns who are just a little bit naughty and settle down with each other to talk about what sort of men they like," begins the introduction to *The Council of Remiremont*. Does this sound like something a teacher would let kids read? Don't ask any questions, just enjoy the poem in hypertext Latin. If you see a word you don't know, that's OK—the difficult ones are clickable, and lead to a helpful glossary. Extensive interpretation and historical annotation are provided at the level needed by students who are still learning the language.
WEB http://ccat.sas.upenn.edu/jod /remiremont.html

Latin Practice Figure out how to download PERL, the software that reads the Latin practice exercises available here, and you'll be wiser than Athena. There are complete instructions, but the process is complicated. It's worth it, though, for these huge files of exercises on topics like nouns, verbs, and patterns. Included are large databases of nouns, verbs, and phrases, which may be used as a dictionary.
URL ftp://ftp.u.washington.edu/pub/user -supported/libellus/aides/lquiz/unpacked

Project Libellus Caesar? Cicero? Livy? Nepos? Here they are in their mother tongue. Go to it, get through it and you won't have to tell your teacher "*mea culpa.*"
URL gopher://wiretap.spies.com/11 /Library/Classic/Latin/Libellus

Study Guide to Wheelock's Latin by Dale A. Grote Make sure your computer has plenty of memory if you download this book-length guide to using the most popular Latin college textbook. Whether or not you've ever seen Wheelock's, this study guide is an immensely useful tool for learning the language. Its discussions of grammar presume almost no knowledge of the parts of speech, which is helpful for those of us who slept through that scintillating lecture on gerunds.
URL gopher://wiretap.spies.com/00

/Library/Classic/latin.stu

► GREEK

Brief Tours in Greece These brief illustrated tours—City of Drama, Around the City and Prefecture of Ioannina, and Aristotle University of Thessaloniki—leave you wanting to know more about the beauty of Greece. You'll be thankful for the link to the Hellas discussion group, where the subject of conversation runs from stuffed grape leaves to politics.
WEB http://www.lance.colostate.edu /optical/Leo/Greece

The Greek Connection The Greek Connection is not a new thriller starring Gene Hackman. It's a collection of links to Net sites maintained in Greece. Link to such gems as a guided tour of the International Festival of Patras and the complete texts of epic poetry at the Perseus Project, or chat in Greek at soc.culture.greece. Just click and take a chance—you're sure to be rewarded.
WEB http://www.algonet.se/~nikos /greek.html

Hellas OnLine Greece—the home of feta cheese and Aristotle. Learn about Greek culture while you drink in the sites at this excellent hypertext guide. Links lead to overviews of classical art and literature, a photo album of magical locales (Thessaloniki, Corfu, and Naxos), pages on sailing the Aegean and Ionian Seas, and even an homage to Greek Nobel Laureate Odysseas Elytis.
WEB http://www.gsc.net

Journey to the Greek Islands If you're in a hurry, skip the texts and go straight to the luscious pictures of the Aegean Islands. You'll see why the gods stuck around. But if you have time, flip through the history and travelogues with such names as "The Voyage to Light and Smiles." They're not half-bad.
WEB http://paros.ariadne-t.gr/islands /islands.html

PART 8

The Arts

ART CLASS

MANY OF THE GREATEST artists didn't live to see the beginning of the Internet. Picasso, for example, died just after the defense department began work on ARPAnet. Frida Kahlo didn't survive that long. And while Leonardo da Vinci probably had a schematic for the entire online world buried in a notebook somewhere (he even sketched a plan for the helicopter), Michelangelo—whose Creation of Adam is a perfect symbol for connectivity—couldn't have imagined a world where millions were joined by a network of machines. But their memories are being preserved and protected by the Net. Start out with World Wide Arts Resources—that should keep you busy for a few days—then move on to Art History: A Preliminary Handbook, before venturing on a tour of the hundreds of pages dedicated to specific artists and online museums. Find the contemporary art scene at Hot Lava Magazine, then follow your muse to The Joy of Painting, Focus on Photography, The Charcoal Page, rec.crafts.pottery, A World of Crafts, or all of the above. Those who seek art simply cannot miss.

►STARTING POINTS

The Art Line With one of the best online illustrated guides to periods and styles from Neoclassical to Dada, this hubsite has enough art history resources to fill a textbook. But don't forget to scroll down on that black, purple, and green home page to the encyclopedic index of museums, university departments, and artists—both the masters and contemporary. If you know nothing about art, you'll be ready for that Advanced Placement test by the time you're done reading. **WEB** http://grimmy.santarosa.edu /~sfaught/art.html

Fine Art Forum This is an active place, host to images, tools and techniques, and discussion on the creative process. As a forum, it is a mixing bowl for art criticism, chat rooms, interactive galleries, and much more. Check out the libraries for a large number of .GIFs and .JPEGs in all styles and genres from Florida Wildlife to Portraiture. **COMPUSERVE** go fineart

The Incredible Art Department Some of this site is geared to elementary and middle school-aged students, but it's a must-see for anyone who fancies art. This is the spot for anything creative, from art games to public domain pictures, plus plenty of annotated links to museums, artists, art journals, architecture… do we need to continue or are you already typing in the URL? **WEB** http://www.geocities.com/The Tropics/1009/index.html

The World of Art The World of Art is home to a Masterpiece of the Week, with a review. Also featured are Q&As about current arts events and a nice set of links to museums. The Masters contains an exhibition of Michelangelo, Rodin, David, Raphael, and Bernini. All told, it's a site that's as pretty as its subject. **WEB** http://ezinfo.ucs.indiana.edu /~mworkman

World Wide Arts Resources Need links to galleries, artist home pages, festivals, agencies, museums, and crafts? Don't miss this incredible source for everything on the Net. "You will notice that WWAR offers the most comprehensive information available," assures the home page. They're not just tooting their own horn—it's the truth. Plus, if you know exactly what you want, you can save time with the handy search engine. **WEB** http://wwar.com

►ART HISTORY

Art History: A Preliminary Handbook Dr. R.J. Belton, a professor at Okanagan University College in British Columbia, has written this helpful little guide to

studying art history. While there is no information about periods or artists, reading this handbook is ideal for getting into the artistic mindset and learning how to write about art. "Why Study Visual Culture?" and "What is Art?" along with "Some Basic Reference Materials" are just a few of the topics. This is what you should read before you even look at a painting.
WEB http://oksw01.okanagan.bc.ca/fiar/hndbkhom.html

The PartheNet It's got Impressionism. It's got Ancient Egypt. It's got Man Ray, the Vatican, and the Taj Mahal. In short, it's got a helpful index to all of art history on the Net. All you have to do is take a look.
WEB http://home.mtholyoke.edu/~klconner/parthenet.html

The WWW Virtual Library-Art History University of London's Birkbeck College comes through again, with a dazzling array of constantly updated Art History links. It's not very well-organized, but is definitely worth wading through since some of the links—The Unicorn Horn for Liverpool Museum, for example—probably won't be found elsewhere.
WEB http://www.hart.bbk.ac.uk/Virtual Library.html

▶ ART TALK

alt.artcom Art aficionados exchange information about Internet art resources, art college versus university education, and employment opportunities; discuss creative blocks and the pending dismantlement of the NEA; and digress, digress, digress.
USENET alt.artcom

The Art Bin A Swedish magazine featuring articles and essays on the local arts scene. Be among the first to see oil paintings, lithos, and photography by up-and-coming Swedish artists. The texts, as well as a guide to events and exhibitions, are in English and Swedish.
WEB http://www4.torget.se/artbin/aaehome.html

Artcrit An art criticism discussion forum.
EMAIL listserv@yorku.ca ✍ *Type in message body:* subscribe artcrit <your full name>

Fine Art Forum This electronic news service reports on art and technology. It is available in three formats: A monthly email digest, an online gopher database, and a fully interactive color version on the Web. In addition to current and back issues, the site has an online gallery and links to individual artists, museums, mailing lists, newsgroups, and international associations and events.
WEB http://www.msstate.edu/Fineart_Online/home.html

Hot Lava Magazine This graphically intense (many thumbnails and JPEGs) monthly displays the works of independent artists and photographers, poets, and musicians. There are links to artists' home pages and there's information on designing one of your own.
WEB http://www.interverse.com/interverse/lava/index.html

Oversight Magazine The alternative arts community of Los Angeles is the primary focus of this online magazine, featuring profiles of individual artists and information on local shows. Visit the Studios section (featuring such artists as Bertha Big Butt), or links to *Oversight*'s critical zines, which include *Coagula*, *Frame-Work*, and *Caffeine*. If time permits, visit the multi-roomed Galleries, especially the ever-popular Empty Gallery.
WEB http://home.earthlink.net/~oversight

▶ ONLINE COURSES

The Alphabet of Art Learn a new alphabet here, one that will help you describe and work with art to your fullest. "Alphabet" is a misnomer, since the site is more of a course in art criticism and creation, but read it anyway, starting with Line and working all the way through The Picture Plane. You'll never look at, create, or talk about art in the

same way again.
WEB http://www.atl.mindspring.com
/~massa/alphabet.html

Art 101: Art Appreciation Southern
Utah University offers this course on an
ongoing basis. It's entirely online and
even includes virtual field trips. The
course is self-paced and fully interactive,
including discussion via email.
WEB http://www.suu.edu/WebPages
/MuseumGaller/artapp.html

PAINTING

The Joy of Painting Join the millions of
amateur painters who just want the late
and lamented Bob Ross for a dad—or
those who've rediscovered PBS's *The
Joy of Painting*. Of course there are
plenty of liner brushes and tubes of
Phthalo Blue for sale, but scroll down
and check out Tips and Techniques or
the Painting Project for hands-on fun.
Naturally, you can also find out where
Joy of Painting classes are being held
or find TV listings. Now make a "happy
little tree," and we guarantee life will
seem "sun-shiny" again.
WEB http://bobross.com

**Painting: Color Theory, Materials, and
Techniques** Have you been hypnotized
by the Color Wheel? Pulled a hamstring
while stretching a canvas? Think egg
tempera is what you ate at a Japanese
restaurant? In short, do you need information about painting? Then run, don't
drip, to this Web page for the most lucid
guide around.
WEB http://www.herron.iupui.edu/faculty
_html/larmann/chlkpt.html

DRAWING

The Charcoal Page This Web site is all
about the wonderful, messy drawing
medium called charcoal. Suitably, the
site is done up in black and white. Click
on the charcoal frog—the doorman—
and enter the actual page. Links is a
pretty thorough set of pointers to charcoal exhibits and fine arts resources on
the Web, as well as a list of recommended books. Tips and Tricks is a disap-
pointing collection of one so far, by the
author of the page, but he invites submissions. The gallery is much more useful, and unlike other sites' Picks of the
Week, this one is actually updated every
week.
WEB http://www.clearlight.com/~donschjr

**Drawing: Perspective, Shading and
Composition** It seems that no matter
how many perspective drawings we
make in school, the vanishing point is
always our grade. If that sounds familiar,
then take a trip to this site, a how-to
guide for drawing something other than
stick figures and doodles. Find out about
the horizon, the bird's and worm's eye
views, how to judge and create the illusion of depth, and how to shade. Even if
you know these things already, don't
miss the hints and links to exemplary
works.
WEB http://www.herron.iupui.edu/faculty
_html/larmann/chlkdrw.html

PHOTOGRAPHY & DESIGN

@tlas magazine This online magazine
for photography, multimedia, design and
illustration features a new and radically
different design for each seasonal issue.
A recent edition was all lower-case
Courier and featured plenty of ASCII art,
taking you back to the bad old days of
the Net. But a click on the Photo section
revealed a whole new side of *@tlas*, and
a great exhibit of photography by contemporary artists. Design, multimedia,
and illustration get the same treatment.
WEB http://atlas.organic.com

Communication Arts Magazine It's "The
Essential Creative Resource," or at least
it's close. This magazine is glossy on the
newsstand and has a Web site to match.
But it provides form a substance with
well-written articles on everything from
Design Technology to Book Reviews.
The *CA* folks online do not attempt to
simply mimic their print format: Instead,
they've created a hubsite with links to
graphics-related sites, plenty of chances
to give feedback or to network, and pro-

vide an inspiring exhibit section.
WEB http://www.commarts.com

Focus on Photography Here's an essential how-to guide to photography, which will help even those who are challenged by the words "point-and-shoot." This site asks questions like, "What kinds of photography are there?", reviews Camera Basics, and provides additional references on the Web in an easy-to-understand style. This is where to start if you don't know a shutter from a lens.
WEB http://www.goldcanyon.com/photo /index.html

A History of Photography Sir John Herschel, a well-known British astronomer, is credited with inventing the word "photography," when the process was first developed in 1839. From its cumbersome beginnings, when capturing an image would take several minutes of absolute stillness—which explains why no one smiled in those old family photos—to the modern days of one-hour processing and digital photography (never mind movies), photography has had a fascinating history. Read about it, then visit the photography museums indexed at the top of the home page.
WEB http://www.kbnet.co.uk/rleggat /photo

Mac Graphic Arts & CAD Forum
Although most of the information is presented on the Macintosh platform, a link to the PC Graphics Forum is provided. Conferences, a software bonanza, and a chance to interact and learn from all types of graphic artists are featured at this site.
AMERICA ONLINE *keyword* art

The Photojournalist Coffee House Photographers can't have poetry slams, they don't want to sip espresso and talk about Joyce or Thackeray—maybe some of them can't even string a paragraph together—but that doesn't mean they have nothing to say, as the Photojournalist Coffee House shows eloquently. For the inspired visitor, the coffee house has also helpfully provided an excellent set

of links to related sites.
WEB http://www.intac.com/~jdeck/index2 .html

Sight Magazine *Sight* bills itself as "the online magazine from some of the world's finest photography." As such, it's not crowded by ads for a print version of the magazine. It's focus on the Web is a visual treat. The Departments section contains reviews, pictorials, and a chance to talk back. Editorial contains the meat: from photojournalism to documentary photography. This is a class act.
WEB http://www.sightphoto.com/photo .html

▶ CERAMICS & SCULPTURE

Clayart An active ceramic arts discussion list. Many of the members are academics, but any topic from kiln firing to getting a grant is fair game.
EMAIL listserv@lsv.uky.edu ✍ *Type in message body:* subscribe clayart <your full name>

The Potter's Page All the way from South Africa comes this index for online ceramics fanatics. It covers everything from software that calculates glaze, to wood-fired stoneware artists in Japan.
WEB http://www.aztec.co.za/users /theo

rec.crafts.pottery No one's more serious about pottery than a recreational potter, and no one has more questions. Amy laments, "I am a novice in pottery/ceramics, and recently made what I think is a fairly common mistake in the craft: the top for a hand-built container was glazed to the container (accidentally)." Several experienced potters leap to her rescue, with techniques ranging from using a diamond-tipped saw to rhythmic tapping. People ask questions about wheels or kilns, and someone posted a Glaze FAQ. Newbies are welcomed warmly. This is a cozy and active place for people who share a common interest. Those who like slabs and coils will like it, too.
USENET rec.crafts.pottery

Years of Italian Sculpture View images by period or by sculptor—there are dozens of options and hundreds of images. Whether you need to find a good fig leaf to model or prefer your sculpture like Michelangelo's "David" (*au naturel*) there is guaranteed to be something inspiring in 1,200 years.
WEB http://www.thais.it/Scultura

CRAFTS

The Creativity Connection The Association of Crafts and Creative Industries would very much like visitors to become hooked on this site, which it sponsors. But it's okay to be a lifelong crafter—at least it's safe, legal, and fun—more than can be said for most addictions. The site is organized from Ideas—creative, fun, and occasionally attractive projects—to Exchange—newsgroups and a bulletin board. In between are Events, Sources, and Craft Business, not to mention the always-fun-at-parties Links. Plus, visitors who register may win craft supplies.
WEB http://noi.noli.com/cc

rec.crafts.misc Overburdened with leftover dryer lint? The posters in rec.crafts.misc have ideas for crafts using this and other valuable commodities. No matter what someone has, a dozen people have used it in a craft that wowed the family on Christmas morning. Besides the sometimes wacky suggestions, there are extremely serious artisans here, too, discussing paints, embroidery, leather carving, and other topics.
USENET rec.crafts.misc

A World of Crafts Be a cybershopper of craft supplies, find on-line publications, peruse a Crafter's Guide Encyclopedia, get free Projects and Patterns, join Associations, and as if that wasn't enough, follow some Links. Yes, Virginia, there is A World of Crafts.
WEB http://www.craft.com//menu.html

GALLERIES

Art on the Net This site, created by and for artists, is a studio for 100 artists throughout the world. It displays the work of visual artists, sculptors, and animators, as well as poets, musicians and bands. Stroll through the virtual gallery to view works-in-progress, or listen to sound clips and new music from alternative bands. Art is blossoming in the sculpture garden (a recent addition to the site), and the presence of video art will be expanding in the near future. There are links to other artists online, as well as a list of events planned worldwide. It's also possible to submit your work for review, and to open a studio of your own.
WEB http://www.art.net

ArtCity Recent exhibits at ArtCity have included "Pierced Hearts and True Love: A Century of Drawings for Tattoos" as well as others both mainstream and offbeat. The galleries and artists listed are paying for the privilege, but the work is quality and the presentation sumptuous. There are articles from *Art & Auction Magazine*, a Newsstand, and a small but intriguing index. Visit, though, for the pictures.
WEB http://www.artcity.com

Artplace Browse ArtPlace with student and professional artists, dealers and the like. Drop in on Clark Kelley Price's studio at 24 Artplace to have a look at some of his western oil paintings, cruise the student art area, where middle and high school students exhibit their best work, or post a classified net-ad. Visit the Virtual Gallery where you can show up to five of your paintings or drawings for free. If you're ready for the big time, you can "rent" a Web studio, (designed, built and maintained by Artplace, Inc.), where prospective buyers can see your work, read your bio and descriptions—and maybe—make a purchase.
WEB http://www.artplace.com

ONLINE MUSEUMS

The Akron Art Museum Works from the permanent collection (Frank Stella's "Diepholz" and Chuck Close's "Linda")

are displayed. The color and detail quality of the images is outstanding. Upcoming museum events are also available.
WEB http://www.winc.com/~aam

Allen Memorial Art Museum Want to see some lesser-name, quality works? Try Allen, home to 14,000 pieces. The images, which include some big names like Monet and Klimt, too, are large and detailed.
WEB http://www.oberlin.edu/wwwmap /allen_art.html

The Brooklyn Museum From the second-largest art museum in New York comes a rewarding set of images from their permanent collection, organized by period and artist. Explore painting, sculpture, prints, drawings, and photography, or perhaps the Arts of Africa. Want to visit? Location and hours are provided.
WEB http://wwar.com/brooklyn_museum

The Butler Institute of American Art It's "America's Museum," situated in Youngstown, Ohio. A good portion of Butler's collection is online, and some of America's best artists are represented. See Edward Hopper, Winslow Homer, Mary Cassatt, and many others of varying degrees of fame. Of course, there's plenty of background on the museum and its programs, too.
WEB http://www.butlerart.com

The Chrysler Museum This museum isn't dedicated to the auto. It holds a collection of 30,000 objects, spanning almost 4,000 years, including a world-renowned glass collection, art nouveau furniture, and works from African, Egyptian, pre-Columbian, Islamic and Asian cultures. There is also an extensive collection of European and American painting, sculpture, and decorative art.
WEB http://www.whro.org/cl/cmhh

Cleveland Museum of Arts This classy site hosts a selective exhibit from the museum's 30,000 works, and provides a detailed "Curator's Choice" article

(changed periodically) describing a particular artwork. Collection highlights include Picasso, Caravaggio, Rubens, several works of antiquity, and works by Impressionists like Degas and Renoir. It's a beautiful and comprehensive grouping.
WEB http://www.clemusart.com

Dallas Museum of Art Online Reproductions of works from a number of periods and cultures; major pre-Columbian and contemporary works are featured. More than 200 digital images are currently available, and the site's still expanding. Every gallery, the sculpture garden, and even the Dallas skyline and local tourist attractions are displayed. The GIFs are all quite large (visiting online could take more time than walking through in person). There is also information about the museum's comprehensive programs and resources.
WEB http://www.unt.edu/dfw/dma/www /dma.htm

Detroit Institute of Arts There's more to the Motor City than cars and Motown, as the DIA artfully demonstrates. Almost every period of Western art is. Click on images to reveal the artist, period, and medium of any painting in the exhibit. Information on museum-sponsored events is also available.
WEB http://www.dia.org

Dixon Gallery and Gardens A specialized art museum with a dual focus—19th-century French and 18th-century German porcelain.
WEB http://gray.music.rhodes.edu/Dixon .html

Glenbow Museum This collection of Western Canadian artifacts and art draws from native cultures and contemporary artists.
WEB http://www.lexicom.ab.ca/~glenbow /museum.htm

The Guggenheim Museum Home to one of the world's finest collection of modern and contemporary art, the museum (the one that looks like a big, white spiral) is

almost as famous for its architect (Frank Llyod Wright) as for its exhibits. It's also the world's first international museum, comprised of the Solomon R. Guggenheim Museum, the Guggenheim Museum SoHo and the Peggy Guggenheim Collection in Venice.
web http://math240.lehman.cuny.edu /gugg

Heard Museum Contemporary and historical Native American and Southwestern art is featured at the Heard Museum.
web http://hanksville.phast.umass.edu /defs/independent/Heard/Heard.html

High Museum of Art Nestled on one of Atlanta's 23 Peachtree Streets is the High Museum, famous for its diverse collection of traditional and contemporary European and American art. The Information page teases with an image of the museum's acclaimed façade; unfortunately, the graceful interior is currently not displayed. The online gallery samples the permanent collection—from the work of the Italian Renaissance masters (Bellini's "Madonna and Child") to modern artists (a Warhol silkscreen of Marilyn Monroe). Pieces from the furniture galleries are also represented. Special exhibitions have featured Jacob Lawrence's *Migration* series and *The Treasures of Venice*.
web http://isotropic.com/highmuse /highhome.html

Huntsville Museum of Art This small museum in Alabama displays works by several local artists.
web http://www.hsv.tis.net/hma

Indianapolis Museum of Art This site features thumbnail images from the museum's special exhibitions, including *Art By Four African-Americans* (contemporary artists John Wesley Hardrick, William Majors, William Edouard Scott, and Hale Aspacio Woodruff), *Juxtapositions*, and *Dutch and Flemish Painting from the Royal Library, Windsor Castle*. You can't download images, but color and sharpness are excellent.
web http://ws2.starnews.com/ima

Internet Arts Museum For Free (IAMFREE) A multimedia (paintings, music, photography, video art, and literature) art site. Read A TriAngle of Stories, a collection of short stories by Kevin McCaughey. Listen to albums created for the site by composers like Mike Frengel. Past "exhibited" albums have included The Dance of Antoine, reportedly the first album created specifically for the Internet. GIFs and short video clips are also available.
web http://www.artnet.org/iamfree /index.html

Lin Hsin Hsin Art Museum This artist from Singapore incorporates images, sculptures, poetry, and music in her work. This cyberspace-only museum presents several dozen images of Hsin's work, with emphasis on her prints and other works on paper. A small selection of her 800 digital-art images are featured. Learn about the printmaking and wash processes, as well as the history of paper.
web http://www.ncb.gov.sg/lhh/lhh.html

Los Angeles County Museum of Art This site is filled with artistic masterpieces from L.A.'s premier art museum, including selections from decorative and Eastern art, costumes and textiles.
web http://www.lacma.org

Luxembourg National Museum of History and Art Visiting Le Musée National d'Histoire et d'Art will expand your knowledge of the tiny Grand Duchy, a nation roughly the size of Jacksonville, Florida. The site's elegant entry hall leads to exhibits on the art and lifestyles of Luxemburgers. Special exhibitions include the collection of the Prince of Liechtenstein (Liechtenstein is an even tinier European nation than Luxembourg). There are also links to several other online museums worldwide. Some information at this site is available only in French.
web http://www.men.lu/Musee/LUXMUSE .HTML

MOMA: The Museum of Modern Art

Click on that stark red logo, and head to the menu of the online guide to the mother of all modern art museums. MOMA began with eight prints and one drawing, and has mushroomed into a museum housing approximately 100,000 pieces, not to mention the thousands of films and books in the library. Visit Mondrian, Matisse, and van Gogh, just to name a few, and find out all about exhibits like the huge Picasso and Portraiture.
WEB http://www.moma.org

Montreal Museum of Fine Arts Masterpieces in Motion: A Century of Automobile Design and The Symbolists (works by Rodin, Munch, Maurice Denis, and Alfons Mucha) is a collection of works that has been exhibited at this site. The permanent online collection, which emphasizes modern Canadian and European art, is growing; images are being cross-referenced with an index of artists.
WEB http://www.interax.net/tcenter/tour/mba.html

The Palmer Museum of Art ONLINE A wonderful collection of American landscapes, sculpture, and portraits. The online catalog represents only a portion of this Centre Hall, Pa. museum's holdings, displaying art by Milton Avery, Edward Hopper, John Sloan, and others. The Online Catalog Preview contains more than 40 thumbnail images (some with links to larger versions).
WEB http://cac.psu.edu/~mtd120/palmer

Philadelphia Museum of Art A few of the museum's more prominent works are shown, such as Vincent Van Gogh's "Sunflowers" and Marcel Duchamp's "The Large Glass (The Bride Stripped Bare by Her Bachelors, Even)." Image sizes (39K, for example) are small, making it difficult to appreciate the detail of pieces such as The Large Glass.
WEB http://www.libertynet.org/~pma

Smithsonian Institute Navigating the Web pages and floor plans at this site requires patience and skill. But if you are persistent, you can view paintings and sculpture as if you were actually inside the immense complex. The site is expanding as the museum adds new collections (e.g., the Royal Benin Gallery in the National Museum of African Art). There are links to all the galleries in the Smithsonian complex (the National Portrait Gallery and the Museum of American Art are particularly rich), as well as to off-site museums (such as the Cooper-Hewitt in New York City). Netters access the libraries, Marine Station, and astrophysical observatories from here. The resources at this site are extensive. America Online's Smithsonian site also offers links to Smithsonian publications and an excellent photo archive.
WEB http://www.si.edu
AMERICA ONLINE → *keyword* smithsonian

Teyler's Museum A Dutch art and science museum.
WEB http://www.nedpunt.nl/teylers museum/engels/hal.html

WebMuseum One of the most comprehensive art resources available on the Net. New exhibits, curated by Nicolas Pioch, are presented several times a week. In one recent week, significant paintings by Giorgio De Chirico, Edward Hopper, Wassily Kandinsky, Paul Klee, Amedeo Modigliani, Pablo Picasso, and Jean Renoir were shown. Special exhibitions have celebrated Gothic and medieval art and the works of Vincent van Gogh. The site also offers a Famous Paintings collection, which heavily emphasizes Impressionism. There is an index of more than 100 artists (from Josef Albers to Joseph Wright of Derby) with biographies and several images of the artists' prominent paintings. Works are also cataloged by style (Early Gothic, Fauvist, Cubist, and Abstract Art); pieces that best exemplify the various styles illustrate the catalog. The site's glossary links to artists who represent the styles defined. Some information is also available in French and Japanese. Fast data access is achieved through a network of sites in the U.S. and worldwide.
WEB http://sunsite.unc.edu/wm • http://www.cnam.fr/louvre

▶ TEACHERS' LOUNGE

Art Education/ Advocacy Here's one of the best places for art teachers to start looking for resources to use in the interactive classroom. Literally everything is gathered, including a wonderful selection of relevant mailing lists and newsgroups. Pop over to to the artist-run artnetweb; Belly Button, the favorite works of an art history teacher; Clay Works; or even Crayola Art Education from this page.
WEB http://www.geocities.com/TheTropics/1009/artedu.html

Arts Education As encyclopedic as the rest of the World Wide Arts Resources site, this index sorts links to all levels of art education, from primary to postgraduate. Also points to the main index on arts councils and associations.
WEB http://wwar.com/institutschools.html

▶ ARTISTS

Adams, Ansel
WEB http://www.book.uci.edu/AdamsHome.html

Bernini, Gian Lorenzo
WEB http://www.thais.it/scultura/bernini.htm

Bougereau, Adolphe-William
WEB http://www.primenet.com/~byoder/artofwb.htm

Cassatt, Mary
WEB http://sunsite.unc.edu/louvre/paint/auth/cassatt

Cezanne, Paul
WEB http://www.oir.ucf.edu/wm/paint/auth/cezanne

da Vinci, Leonardo
WEB http://www.leonardo.net/museum/main.html • http://sunsite.unc.edu/wm/paint/auth/vinci • http://banzai.msi.umn.edu/~reudi/leonardo.html • http://www.glasscity.net/~omoral/leonardo.html

Dali, Salvador

WEB http://www.mercon.com/mercon/carl/dalilink.html • http://www.mercon.com/mercon/carl/dalitour.html • http://www.ionet.net/~jellenc/dali.html • http://www.highwayone.com/dali/daliweb.html

David, Jacques-Louis
WEB http://silver.ucs.indiana.edu/~mworkman/jldframes.html

Degas, Edgar
WEB http://sunsite.unc.edu/wm/paint/auth/degas

Donatello
WEB http://www.thais.it/scultura/donatell.htm

Duchamp, Marcel
WEB http://www.val.net/~tim/duchamp.html

El Greco
WEB http://sunsite.unc.edu/wm/paint/auth/greco

Escher, M.C.
WEB http://www.texas.net/esche • http://kite.preferred.com/~joey/escher.htm

Gauguin, Paul
WEB http://sunsite.unc.edu/wm/paint/auth/gauguin

Goya, Francisco
WEB http://www.primenet.com/~image1/goya/goya.html

Homer, Winslow
WEB http://web.syr.edu/~ribond/homer.html

Hopper, Edward
WEB http://sunsite.unc.edu/wm/paint/auth/hopper

Kahlo, Frida
WEB http://www.cascade.net/kahlo.html

Kandinsky, Wassily
WEB http://www.oir.ucf.edu/wm/paint/auth/kandinsky

Klee, Paul

WEB http://www.oir.ucf.edu/wm/paint
/auth/klee

Lichtenstein, Roy
WEB http://helios.augustana.edu/~lag/rl
.html • http://www.fi.muni.cz/~toms
/PopArt/Biographies/lichtenstein.html

Magritte, Rene
WEB http://pharmdec.wustl.edu/juju/surr
/images/magritte/magritte.html

Matisse, Henri
WEB http://www.oberlin.edu/~dfortune
/groupHome.html

Miro, Joan
WEB http://pharmdec.wustl.edu/juju/surr
/images/miro/miro.html

Mondrian, Pieter
WEB http://titan.glo.be/~gd30144
/mondrian.html • http://www.desires
.com/2.1/Toys/Mondrian/mond-fr.html

Monet, Claude
WEB http://hops.cs.jhu.edu/~baker/monet
.html • http://vinny.csd.mu.edu/~howard
/monet.html • http://www.columbia.edu
/~jns16/monet_html/monet.html

Munch, Edvard
WEB http://sunsite.unc.edu/wm/paint
/auth/munch

O'Keefe, Georgia
WEB http://helios.augustana.edu/~lag
/gok.html • http://info.umd.edu
/Pictures/WomensStudies/Picture
Gallery/okeefe.html

Palladio, Andrea
WEB http://www.gpnet.it/ashmm/monu
_pal.htm

Picasso, Pablo
WEB http://watt.emf.net/wm//paint/auth
/picasso • http://www.clubinternet.com
/picasso

Pollock, Jackson
WEB http://www.calvin.edu/~efernh85
/jackson.html

Renoir, Pierre Auguste
WEB http://www.ukshops.co.uk:8000
/gallery/renoir.html

Rodin, Auguste
WEB http://www.paris.org/Musees/Rodin
• http://silver.ucs.indiana.edu/~mwork
man/rodframes.html

Rossetti, D.G.
WEB http://jefferson.village.virginia.edu
/rossetti/rossetti.html

Rousseau, Henri
WEB http://hades.sckcen.be/wm/paint
/auth/rousseau

Sanzio, Raffaello ("Raphael")
WEB http://silver.ucs.indiana.edu
/~mworkman/rapframes.html

Sargent, John Singer
WEB http://sunsite.nus.sg/wm/paint
/auth/sargent

Seurat, Georges
WEB http://www.pride.net/~dbirnbau
/seurat.html

de Toulouse-Lautrec, Henri
WEB http://www.mcs.csuhayward.edu
/~malek/Toulouse.html

van Gogh, Vincent
WEB http://hops.cs.jhu.edu/~baker
/van_gogh.html

Vermeer, Jan
WEB http://www.ccsf.caltech.edu
/~roy/vermeer

Warhol, Andy
WEB http://www.warhol.org/warhol

Whistler, James McNeill
WEB http://www.glyphs.com/art/whistler

Wright, Frank Lloyd
WEB http://flw.badgernet.com:2080/flw
.htm • http://www.mcs.com/~tgiesler
/flw_home.htm

MUSIC APPRECIATION

HAVE YOU EVER FALLEN ASLEEP TO Beethoven's Moonlight Sonata, swooned to Glenn Miller's In the Mood, waltzed to Strauss' The Blue Danube, daydreamed to Edith Piaf, or sung along with South Pacific? Well, your parents probably have. Musicals probably aren't your thing and Mozart may seem like a relic—even though he was the Jim Morrison of the eighteenth century. While the contemporary sounds of rock, pop, and rap are easier for us to relate to, their musical predecessors often require a lesson in listening to be fully appreciated and enjoyed. When you're ready to get down with Debussy, head to the Classical Net Homepage, or open your mind and ears at JazzNet.

► STARTING POINTS

All-Music Guide In addition to a list of this week's most popular albums and singles, this site offers access to one of the largest music databases in the world. With hundreds of thousands of albums listed, and thousands of artists cataloged in genres such as rock, pop, punk, funk, hip-hop, reggae, classical, jazz, soundtracks, vocals, and experimental music, this is a stellar resource—one that no music fan should ignore. The Web site is a discussion forum and information site for the guide; entries are linked to band descriptions in the CDNow! data base.
COMPUSERVE *go* allmusic
WEB http://cdnow.com

The All-Music Guide Music Glossary
The exploration of musical terminology at this site is broad and thorough, covering technical explanations (de capo to dynamics), general knowledge (Nashville to note), instrument definition (zheng to zither), and more. The links are organized alphabetically, so obviously you can't work backwards by trying to find a word that fits a definition. In addition, broad terms such as "punk rock" get the same quip definition as simple terms like "guitar," and genre-specific terms like "loft jazz." Use this list to define particular terms, not for an overview of genre terminology.
WEB http://205.186.189.2/amg /mus_Glossary.html

Mammoth List of Music
Festivals Mama mia! Mama mia! It's a Cyberian Rhapsody, here at this site, with links to more than 100 music festivals, hoedowns, and shindigs. Links to music festivals worldwide.
WEB http://www.pathfinder.com/vibe /mmm/music_festivals.html

Musi-Cal A listing of live musical performances that are searchable by performer, city, venue, or event. Want to know where Neil Young is playing in upcoming months? Enter his name, designate "performer," and search. Looking for something to do this Saturday night in your area? Search by city name (not just the big cities), and listings for performances at local night clubs, bars, colleges, and arenas are retrieved. Listings include dates, performer names, and contact numbers. Anyone can submit listings, and while the site is certainly not comprehensive, it's pretty amazing.
WEB http://www.calendar.com/concerts

Wilma Tour Directory This index of concert and venue information links to city guides, tour schedules, and even concert reviews. Visitors can preview hundreds of cities for information about arenas, clubs, theaters, colleges, and coffeehouses. (New York City has more than 100 listings, while L.A. has approximately 200.) In many cases, venues have their own home pages and the Wilma Tour Directory links directly to these pages. Record labels have also deluged the Net. Wilma links to many of these labels, most of which feature extensive concert tour information for their artists. Wilma also has a directory of artists who are currently on tour, and features links to tour schedules and concert reviews.

WEB http://wilma.com/tour.html

WWW Music Database More than 5,700 albums by more than 2,000 artists; each listing includes catalog numbers, tracks, total playing time, comments, and pertinent Web links. While coverage is spotty, this is one of the best organized data bases, one that allows fans to move quickly from discographies to fan pages. If your favorite album isn't listed, you can submit a listing with an easy-to-use form. **WEB** http://www.gcms.com/~burnett /MDB

▶ BLUES/JAZZ

Artists of Jazz Index Northwestern University's WNUR has created dozens of profiles for jazz artists, from the major (Louis Armstrong, Miles Davis) to the minor (Shaun Baxter, Tatsu Aoki), and they're all here, along with discographies, biographies, and supplementary links. **WEB** http://www.acns.nwu.edu/jazz /artists

Albert Ayler An innovative biography of sax player Albert Ayler in which notes on Ayler's life are interspersed with quotes from the subject himself. Of his move from Cleveland to Stockholm, for example, Ayler says, " I remember one night in Stockholm, I tried to play what was in my soul. The promoter pulled me off the stage. So I went to play for little Swedish kids in the subway. They heard my cry." The page also includes images, sound clips, and a discography. **WEB** http://ernie.bgsu.edu/~jeffs/ayler .html

Da Capo Press One of the great pleasures available to a jazz fan is listening to the music; another is reading about it. When it comes to reading about jazz, there's no better place to go than Da Capo. With more than 100 jazz and blues titles on artists ranging from Benny Goodman to Eric Dolphy to Miles Davis—each of whom is afforded a dedicated Web page with a full table of contents, back cover blurbs, price information, and supplementary multimedia— this catalog takes on the feel of a museum. **WEB** http://www.dnai.com/~lmcohen /dacapo.html

Eric Dolphy Eric Dolphy played clarinet and saxophone, played them brilliantly, and then died young, the echo of his music still suspended in the air. This page pays tribute to his music. **WEB** http://farcry.neurobio.pitt.edu/Eric .html

Don Ellis A fan page devoted to the innovative bandleader, composer, and trumpet player who died in 1978 at the tragically young age of 44. This page contains a discography and links to other Ellis sites. **WEB** http://www.mbnet.mb.ca/~mcgonig /donellis.html

Hogan Jazz Archives This archive is dedicated to the preservation of New Orleans jazz, and includes oral history interviews, music samples, an archive of historical photos and films, sheet music, manuscript materials, and hundreds of articles and books about the form. While the online component of the archive is relatively new, the curatorial staff is in the progress of creating an online catalog of all materials. **WEB** http://www.tulane.edu/~lmiller /JazzHome.html

House of Blues The house specials here are Blues Talk, hosting an open chat daily at 8 p.m.; Guitar Shop open Tuesdays and Thursdays at 8 p.m.; a magazine rack of blues zines, gig schedules from New Orleans to Harvard Square; and a *Blues Brothers* site well-stocked with historical info, Aykroyd and Belushi quotes, bios and filmographies, complete with sound clips. For the lowdown on midnight rider Gregg Allman, you'll want to pull up a seat at the *Blues Revue Magazine*, where you'll hear how his "familiar opening blues guitar chords enveloped in a searing slide solo, and an ominously beautiful soul-laced vocal

cuts through the concert hall like a rising phoenix."
AMERICA ONLINE *keyword* musicspace→ House of Blues

Jazz Clubs around the World A directory of jazz clubs, mostly U.S. listings but also a sprinkling of European clubs and even a few from Israel. The clubs are listed by cities and the info is limited to phone numbers and addresses. There are no reviews and the list doesn't specify whether the clubs are exclusively jazz venues.
WEB http://www.acns.nwu.edu/jazz/lists /clubs.html

JazzNet While it's not really limited to jazz—there's plenty of blues information here, too—this site contains a wealth of resources for jazz fans. Want updates on the Monterey Jazz Festival or the San Francisco Blues Festival? Interested in ordering the U.S. Postal Service's jazz stamps? You can do all those things from this page, and check on labels, artists, newsletters, and academic resources, as well.
WEB http://www.jazznet.com/index.html

Charles Mingus A discography of the brilliant and temperamental bassist's work, (both as sideman and bandleader), as well as anecdotes about the aforementioned brilliant and temperamental bassist and a poll that asks jazz fans to nominate the best Mingus album of all time.
WEB http://www.siba.fi/~eonttone /mingus

rec.music.bluenote What color is jazz? Blue, of course. Blue like the sky. Blue like the Miles Davis record (kind of). Blue like the links on your Web browser. Internet jazz chat is blue, too, mostly because there's so much to talk about and so little time. What are the best CDs of solo drumming? What rock bands have most successfully integrated jazz signatures into their work? What's the best septet ever? When they're not comparing lists, fans are talking about jazz movies (the Oscar-nominated documentary *A Great*

Day in Harlem gets high marks), wishing Louis Armstrong a happy posthumous Fourth of July (and a very happy birthday), and wondering what jazz songs are being used as the soundtracks for network TV shows these days.
USENET rec.music.bluenote

WNUR-FM JazzWeb WNUR is only a college radio station, sure, and Northwestern isn't exactly the first university that springs to mind when you think of jazz. But maybe it should be. Among Internet jazz sites, WNUR's JazzWeb is the rarest of rare birds, a Sonny Rollins among reed hacks. With a large hypertext document ramifying jazz into its styles and substyles, an archive of artist bios, an essay on jazz instruments, a list of jazz venues nationwide, and links to labels, there's precious little in the jazz world that's not covered.
WEB http://www.nwu.edu/jazz

▶ CLASSICAL

All-Music Guide Classical Section This enormous classical music recordings database will help you get your hands on that hard-to-find recording of Chopin's "Aeolian Harp Etude." Search the database by any of the following criteria: performance, performers, composer, instrument, period, or rating. Every release is described by listing its composer, title, genre, period, form, instrument, key, date, number, performance quality, performers, and the record company that released it.
COMPUSERVE *go* amgclassical

Classical Music Download a copy of AOL's classical calendar, have a classic chat at the Sounding Board, where 1,843 postings under 48 headings can be located by topic or date, peruse the music library where you can get a description of Beethoven's "5th Symphony," or scan NPR's guide to Schubert's unfinished works.
AMERICA ONLINE *keyword* musicspace→ Classical Music

Classical Net Homepage The Basic

Repertoire List will give you the option of seeking out classical information by period (Medieval, Baroque, Modern), while Composer Data can take you right to the music's source. If you have a purchase in mind, you will be guided to your choice of classical CDs by the Classical CD Buying Guide or the Recommended section. A read through their reviews and articles can put you in touch with some much admired classical music opinions on individual CDs, records, and the composers themselves. **WEB** http://www.classical.net/music

rec.music.classical Are you a tubist looking for work? Need to sell a cello? Looking for a conductor? In addition to addressing the basic fiscal queries of various starving musicians and composers, this newsgroup serves as the central clearinghouse for classical music chat—from polls inquiring about your favorite sublime musical fragments, to debates on using a pedal when playing Scarlatti. Whether you're looking for a favorite Figaro recording, used record stores in Boston, or a Stravinsky biography, you will get ample attention. If you don't want to sort through the general list of messages, check out the rest of the groups in the hierarchy, which focus specifically on classical guitar, performance techniques and announcements, and recordings.
USENET rec.music.classical

rec.music.classical.performing Searching for a place to confide your deepest performance fears? Need some advice on vocal technique or interpretation? Dying to discuss conducting or performers' medical issues? Well, this is the most likely spot to have all your performance related questions and concerns, answered, addressed, or at least echoed. An FAQ is available for quick reference. **USENET** rec.music.classical.performing

▶ COMPOSERS

The Great Composers All the masters, from Albeniz to Mozart to Wagner, are profiled at this extensive site. In fact,

this is one of the few places on the Net to get even a quick sketch of the lives of major composers like Schubert, Stravinsky, Handel, and Hayden. Locate your favorite by searching the index alphabetically or by period. This site is brought to the Net courtesy of BMG Classics. **WEB** http://classicalmus.com/composer .html

Bach Home Page Learn about the extraordinary life and works of this classical composer through the essays on his life and the lists of his compositions. **WEB** http://www.classical.net/music /composer/works/jsbach/bwvindex.html

Ludwig van Beethoven
Even though Beethoven's father was a heavy drinker, he still realized that his boy had talent and made sure the young lad had some piano lessons. Read about Beethoven's life and scan a list of his compositions. **WEB** http://www.ida.his.se/ida/~a94johal /beet.chtml

Giovanni Bottesini: A Life
The International Bottesini Society sponsors this biographical site dedicated to the famous opera and contrabass composer and conductor. **WEB** http://www.webcom.com/~redwards /gbmain.html

John Cage By reading Cage's autobiographical statement at this site, you'll discover that the world-renowned composer was also a good storyteller. The story of his life and career is accompanied by an annotated discography. **WEB** http://newalbion.com/artists/cagej

Frederic Chopin An annotated list of Chopin's piano compositions is the centerpiece of this site. With descriptions of each piece, as well as playing tips and difficulty ratings, the annotations will be especially helpful for players looking for the right piece to match their skills. **WEB** http://www.cs.cmu.edu/afs/cs/user /pscheng/www/chopin.html

Philip Glass Explore modern minimal-

ism through the work of its most representative composer, Philip Glass. Glass is currently promoting his opera adaptation of Jean Cocteau's *Beauty and the Beast*. A discography on the composer, and sound files of some of his better-known works, including "Knee Play 1," are offered.
web http://www-lsi.upc.es/~jpetit/pg

Gustav Mahler Home Page This site features informative lists relating to the artist, including annotated notes on his works, a timeline, lists of festivals, books, concerts, societies, and organizations. Visit the Mahler picture gallery to see what the visionary looked like.
web http://www.netaxs.com/~jgreshes /mahler

OPERA

Casta Diva, Inc. Home Page For those interested in the costuming side of opera, Casta Diva, a major costume supplier, has assembled a JPEG gallery of its famous costumes (most are designed by Lelia Barton) in action on the stage. And although the images are presented as thumbnails, you can download larger versions for wall display.
web http://www.access.digex.net /~castadiv/gallery.html

Cyberspace Opera An opera is being composed online, and you can contribute by sending in rhymed couplets based on concepts or quotes from the storyline. The couplets will then be set to music and incorporated into a real opera to be performed in Austin, Texas. The opera's working title is *Honoria in Ciberspazio*, and its main characters include Rez, a passionate young writer and philosopher of virtual communities, and Sandy Stone, a cyberspace goddess who "flips her long black hair before saying something wonderfully brilliant." It's opera for the computer age.
web http://www.en.utexas.edu/~slatin /opera

Opera Houses of the Past and Present Opera houses were smaller in the seven-

teeth century—the largest venues seated around 2,000 opera-goers, while today's average house seats between 4,000 and 6,000 people. This interesting study lists the size (in cubic feet) and seating capacity of every opera house worldwide, beginning with the Wiener Staatsoper, built in 1639, up to Washington, D.C.'s Terrace Theater, completed in 1979.
web http://www.cc.columbia.edu/~km34 /theater.html

Opera Schedule Search this worldwide opera schedule by artist, location, or time to find out when and where the next performance of your favorite opera is taking place.
web http://www.fsz.bme.hu/opera/main .html

rec.music.opera Put a bunch of opera buffs in the same room and there's bound to be trouble. If you're having difficulty choosing between a Bartoli or Larmore *Barber of Seville* recording, don't expect any straight answers. You'll most likely be buried in piles of still more recommendations, along with a combination of some on-the-nose and long-winded reviews. And when the fans leave, the performers remain, exchanging performance tips, tipping each other off to potential gigs, and recommending instructors.
usenet rec.music.opera

Weaver's Opera Field Notes If you think opera is something you only listen to when you are at the dentist's office, these self-proclaimed "field notes of a rookie opera lover" might make you take a closer look at the genre. A mysterious opera fan identified only as Weaver has collected loving observations of the many, many, many performances he has taken in over the past seven years.
web http://www.alaska.net/~hweaver /opera-index.html

MUSICAL THEATER

alt.music.lloyd-webber What do you know about the animated film version of

Cats? Are you aware that *Starlight Express* was originally conceived in the '70s as an animated musical? These and other Webber-related issues are addressed by the few Webber fans chatting online.
USENET alt.music.lloyd-webber

Gilbert and Sullivan Archive Sponsored by the Savoy Theatre, this page offer bios of the famous collaborators, synopses of their works, a G&S festivals schedule, a list of G&S clubs, and links to other G&S Web sites.
WEB http://math.idbsu.edu/gas/GaS.html

Hair: The American Tribal Love-Rock Musical The age of Aquarius lives with a synopsis, show history, profiles of former cats members, a photo archive, and descriptions of current productions.
WEB http://www-leland.stanford.edu/~toots/Hair/hair.html

Hallelujah! A plot synopsis of this musical about two teenagers growing up in religious schools.
WEB http://www.unt.edu/~cjk0001/hal.html

Jekyll and Hyde Info on the current Broadway production, its cast, the scheduled tour, show-related merchandise, and how to join the *Jekyll and Hyde* mailing list.
WEB http://reedycreek.stanford.edu/RecArtsJH

Jesus Christ Superstar Ralf Southard just loves *Jesus Christ Superstar*, so he assembled lists of past and present performers, lyrics to the show's songs, the latest tour dates and productions worldwide, and info about the movie.
WEB http://www.webcom.com/~sabata/jcs/welcome.html

Jesus Christ Superstar: A Resurrection A promotional page for the two-disc CD put out by Daemon Records. Read reviews of the recording, scan a track list (with song lyrics), and read bios of the performers, including the Indigo Girls.

WEB http://www.hidwater.com/jcs/jcs.html

Les Miserables Contrast the novel with the musical by reading the essays on both.
WEB http://www.ot.com/lesmis

Miss Saigon Dedicated fans of *Miss Saigon* constructed a site with a synopsis of the show, profiles of the actors, sound bites of the famous songs, and subscription information for the fanzine *Sun and Moon*. A section of this site is devoted to the finale—at various times during the show's run, three different songs have been sung at the end of the show—and this page allows you to download bites of each song and vote for the one you prefer.
WEB http://www.clark.net/pub/rsjdfg

Newcastle Gilbert and Sullivan Society The home page of the Newcastle University club offers info on their performances, their society, lists of theaters in the UK, and links to other G&S societies in the U.K. and U. S.
WEB http://www.ncl.ac.uk/~n314699/Gilbert.html

Playbill Online Playbill Online helps put the Great White Way online, and in spectacular fashion. With the latest news briefs from the busy street; listings for local, regional, national, and international shows; and chat rooms where musical fans can meet and discuss their favorite performers and shows, this is the premier source of information about the musical theater. But it doesn't stop there—Playbill also features online live chat with stars like Rachel York, Gregory Jbara, and even Patrick Stewart. There's also a trivia topic to test your Broadway knowledge: "Name a musical biography of Tchaikovsky that played at the Adelphi Theater in 1947." It's *Music in My Heart*, of course.
AMERICA ONLINE *keyword* playbill

rec.arts.theatre.musicals The newsgroup discusses a variety of topics, including the history of musicals, the lat-

est live chat session at America Online's Playbill topic, and the debate of Andrew Lloyd Webber's status as a modern-day Mozart (on that subject Margaret stated, "I don't think even ALW would put himself in the same category with Mozart!").
USENET rec.arts.theatre.musicals

Steven Sondheim Stage The definitive site on the master. Find an FAQ on his life and work, current and back issues of the *Sondheim Review*, sound clips of his songs, synopses and info on *Assassins!*, *Follies*, and *Into the Woods* (among other shows), and links to other Sondheim sites.
WEB http://www.sondheim.com

▶ LYRICS AND SYNOPSES

Shows & Soundtracks If you spend a lot of time at the movies with your eyes closed and your ears wide open, meet others who share your affliction and chat about favorite composers (Henry Mancini's name surfaces frequently; George S. Clinton's name somewhat less frequently). Entire threads of these messages are archived in the library of this site, so you'll find lengthy repartee about music in motion pictures, on television, and even in animated cartoons (great for Carl Stalling fans.)
COMPUSERVE *go* musicarts→Libraries *or* Messages→Shows & Soundtracks

Synopsis Archive Not just Cliffs Notes for popular musicals—such as *Guys and Dolls*, *Cabaret*, and *West Side Story*—but also pictures and reviews of various performances.
WEB http://www.mit.edu:8001/activities /mtg/archives/mtg-archives.html

▶ CHOIRS

Akateeminen Laulu — The Academic Choral Society Links to concert info, contacts, FAQs, general information, recordings and training opportunities. A good place to start the day, and also a good place to Finnish.
URL gopher://gopher.helsinki.fi/11 /jarjestot/kuorot

Ars Nova This Web site for Michigan's renowned choir contains links to upcoming concert info, reprints of past concerts, audition information, and a list of Ars Nova personnel.
WEB http://gopher.orsps.wayne.edu/nova /arsnova.html

Austin Handel-Haydn Society The society is not exclusively dedicated to choral music of the Classical and Baroque periods, but performs works from a wide range of eras and genres. This site features links to a schedule of events, society history, and bios, as well as contact and ticket information.
WEB http://www.quadralay.com/www /Austin/FineArts/HHS

The Bach Choir of Pittsburgh Pittsburgh's oldest and largest choral organization. You can find a detailed schedule for the group and links to other Bach and classical music sites.
WEB http://www.lm.com/~lmann/bach /bach.html

Cantatille Cantatille is the "first Belgian choir on the Web," but you can bet it won't be the last. One hopes that future choir pages will be more interesting than this one, which offers a short plea for contact with another small choir and a links to Belgian resources.
WEB http://zorro.ruca.ua.ac.be/~windels /cantatille

Gyuto Tantric Choir The perfectly synthesized, subtly disturbing music of Buddhist choirs has somehow worked its way into pop culture. These choirs have been sampled by everyone from Enigma to the Beastie Boys, but to hear them in their pure, transcendental state, come to this site and listen to their sound clips. You can also get a schedule of the Tantric Choir's U.S. tour, learn more about Tibetan Cultural Survival, the Endangered Music Project, and seek enlightenment by linking to other Buddhist resources on the Net.
WEB http://www.well.com/user/gyuto

Melbourne University Choral Society

This Australian choir offers an informative page providing bios of the choir members and the conductor, rehearsal information, and highlights of the season's performances.
web http://www.cs.mu.oz.au/~winikoff/mucs/mucs.html

Sacramento Master Singers This accomplished choir of 40 singers from the greater Sacramento area maintains a lovely Web site, with links to bios, concert and CD info, and the choir's most recent repertoire, and dozens of other similar pages.
web http://www.dcn.davis.ca.us/~jcrowel/sms

Sonoma County Bach Choir An earnest mission statement for earnest Bach supporters and links to the Sonoma State University Academic Foundation.
web http://www.sonoma.edu/scbs

Studentkoret Aks A Norwegian choir offering info on their concerts and history and some pictures. An English-language version is also available.
web http://www.stud.unit.no/studorg/aks/index.html

Trondhjems Studentersangforening This page has information on Dagens Kor, Undergrupper, and Relaterte Linker.
web http://www.stud.unit.no/studorg/tss

TVRC A mammoth home page for those interested in the music of children's choirs.
web http://www.iac.net/~spock

University of Notre Dame Shenanigans Enter the archives to dig up photos, reviews, and schedules for University of Notre Dame's singing and dancing ensemble.
web http://www.nd.edu/~shenana

Whatcom Chorale Discover the history of the society that has brought 25 years of music to Bellingham and Whatcom counties.
web http://www.pacificrim.net/~arvann/pages/whatchor.html

Yale University Choir Just a few of the hosts in the Battell Chapel offering heavenly instruction. Learn the history of the Yale Choir.
web http://www.cis.yale.edu/uchoir/index.html

▶ WORLD MUSIC

alt.music.exotic "Sound is the same for all the world," said Youssou N'dour in "Eyes Open." International music fans who agree with him converge to discuss the music, exchange record reviews, and occasionally ask for playing tips; for example, Mike writes, "Rednecks of Tennessee want to know: Who's new, bad, and blue in African guitar music? All our Sunny Ade tapes are worn out, and the bootlegger who used to go North and cop for us has crashed his '57 Chevy." It is a small world after all.
usenet alt.music.exotic

The Gypsy Kings Often thought of as the Omar Sharifs of the music world, no one is ever really sure where these guys originated. No one, that is, except Sony Records, and they'll tell you where the Kings started out if you visit their site. You'll also get a discography and preview of *Love and Liberty*, the the group's latest release.
web http://www.music.sony.com/Music/ArtistInfo/GipsyKings_LoveAndLiberte.html

World and Ethnic Music Visitors to World and Ethnic Music can go to the message boards of this site and meet other international music fans who are just as impassioned. They can also enjoy the library which features some real gems—like a recording of a live gourd dance song and a list of Brazilian music radio stations. Overall this site is not very busy, but the information and discussion is informed and interesting.
compuserve *go* musicarts→Libraries *or* Messages→World/Ethnic

▶ AFRICA

alt.music.african Who is the hottest

guitar player in Zaire today? Is it Syran Mbenza, Rigo Star, or Diblo Dibala? If you have an opinion on this, or any other topic having to do with African music, express yourself at alt.music.african. Jim recommends Samite who is from Uganda and specializes in all traditional Ugandan instruments, including the madinda. The Kadinda is the Kabaka's (king's) own royal madinda.
USENET alt.music.african

Music from Africa and the African Diaspora Want to read an article on popular trends in Kenyan music? Or a biography of King Sunny Ade (he was born in Nigeria, the son of a Methodist minister)? Then visit this site, which offers resources and info on the music of every African nation. You'll find the site organized alphabetically by country.
WEB http://matisse.net/~jplanet/afmx /ahome.htm

CHINA

Chinese Music Mailing List A mailing list to keep you updated on CD and laser disc releases in Taiwan, Hong Kong, and China. Some announcements are in Chinese.
EMAIL newwave@rahul.net ✍ *Type in message body:* subscribe whatsnews

FRANCE

French Music Mailing List Two lists, one for male singers (chanteur) and one for female singers (chanteuse). What French singers spring to mind? Well, Francis Cabrel, Daniel Belanger, Patrick Bruel, Mitsou, and Edith Piaf. Mailing lists are multilingual.
EMAIL majordomo@wimsey.com ✍ *Type in message body:* subscribe chanteuse-list <your email address> • majordomo@wimsey.com ✍ *Type in message body:* subscribe chanteur-list <your email address>

INDIA

Indian Classical Music Learn about the basis of classical Indian music, the raga, which is "The combination of several notes woven into a composition in a way which is pleasing to the ear." Then scan the list of Karnatic and Hindustani ragas listed to find one to play. Also, find bios of some great masters of Indian classical music and an online CD catalog where you can shop for and order their music.
WEB http://www.vt.edu:10021/org /malhaar/music.html

rec.music.indian.classical The overwhelming majority of posts to this group advertise or ask for listings of Indian classical music concerts and performances ("Are there any events in the St. Louis area?" asks Frank). However, conversations consisting of such subjective commentary as: "Zakir can forge a chemistry with most great artists. The way he accompanies Ravi Shankar is much different from his treatment of Shivkumar Sharma…" are not entirely uncommon. Visitors will also be able to read the occasional CD review, but it's clear that most fans who post here prefer to hear the music live.
USENET rec.music.indian.classical

IRELAND

Celtic Music Calendars Never miss another Celtic music event in your area again. Celtic Calendars is a family of mailing lists, one for every U.S. state and Canadian province, and each list posts a monthly calendar of Celtic musical events.
EMAIL majordomo@celtic.stanford.edu ✍ *Type in message body:* subscribe info lists <your email address>

JAPAN

Bonsai's Pop Page Bonsai's site will keep you up-to-date on the Japanese pop news. In the Idol Database section, you can read over 150 biographies of the hottest Japanese pop stars (43 percent of the bios also contain pics of your fav pig-tailed, Sanrio clad performers). Search the data by artist name, then check out the ranked lists of physiological minutiae, including body mass and height (Mochida Maki is a shade under five feet tall, while Mizuno Miki is a towering 5' 7"—more than three inches taller than the average height for a Japanese female pop star). You can also read the top ten pop list, which is updated weekly. Bonus: There is an extensive collection of links here, too, which take you to the home pages of Japanese TV shows, karaoke sites, and pop star pages.

WEB http://www.net5.co.jp/~bonsai

Key Aspects of Japanese Culture Learn about Japanese culture through its traditional music and theater at this thoroughly comprehensive site.

WEB http://www.ewco.com/home.htm

LATIN AMERICA

Andean Folk Music Latin folk music and culture, including technique, announcements, instruments, sources, discographies, and related gossip.

EMAIL majordomo@lvande.us.net ✍ *Type in message body:* subscribe andino <your email address>

Brazilian Music Antonio Carlos Jobim. Gilberto Gil. Gal Costas. These are the artists who put Brazilian music on the map and are keeping it there. This site explores Brazilian music through sound clips, pictures, and bios of its most popular artists.

WEB http://orathost.cfa.ilstu.edu/public /OratClasses/ORAT389.88Seminar/Exhibi ts/GerryMagallan/Artists.html

La Musica Latina A Spanish-language site that features links to Web sites dedicated to Latin rock, Brazilian, tango, Caribbean, tejano, and flamenco music. The site is in Spanish, but many of the links are written in English.

WEB http://www.bart.nl/~dtheb/musica .html

rec.music.afro-latin Where else would you learn about the Finnish samba school Imperio do Papagaio in Helsinki, Tito Puente's September performance in Dallas, or the Web address of the organization producing the show? This group covers a lot of ground in English and Spanish, from reggae to salsa to Spanish-language rock. And if you happen to know whatever became of the "great drummer" Ray Barreto, you'll satisfy one newsgrouper's curiosity.

USENET rec.music.afro-latin

MIDDLE EAST

Kereshmeh Records Persian music fans need search no further for their classical, folk, and contemporary recordings. Kereshmeh's CD catalog features album covers, sound clips, and ordering info for artists like Alizadeh and Torkaman. There are absolutely no renditions of "Misty" offered here.

WEB http://www.kereshmeh.com

Middle Eastern Music Fans of Middle Eastern music can meet other fans and discuss the genre by joining this Finnish mailing list.

EMAIL middle-eastern-music-request @nic.funet.fi ✍ *write a request*

NATIVE AMERICA

Rainbow Walker Profiles of native artists like the Young Singers of the Puget Sound, two men from the Lummi Nation of Washington State. Also find primers on the flute and whistle tradition in native music as well as pow wow music and dance traditions.

WEB http://www.teleport.com/~rnbowlkr

NEW ZEALAND

Kiwimusic A page of album reviews, band bios, and links to other New Zealand music info sites, most of it culled from the Kiwi music mailing list.

EMAIL kiwimusic-request@mit.edu ✍ *write a request*

WEB http://www.sanger.ac.uk/~sd /kiwimusic/HOME

MAKING MUSIC

EVER SINCE THE FIRST GRADE when you picked up the recorder (that was the only instrument you couldn't break), you've rather enjoyed blowing through hollowed tubes to make noises. A few years later, you discovered a world of other instruments that required blowing, as well as banging, tooting, plucking, and strumming. Whatever instrument you play, the Net can help you play it better, from Accumulated Accordion Annotations to Tuba Tunes. Don't forget that the voice is an instrument, too. If you need advice on keeping it in top shape, refer to "I need advice on maintaing my vocal chords." If you'd like to work on writing the songs that make the whole world sing, try Music Theory Online.

INSTRUMENTS

The Big Used Gear List People selling used drums (including cymbals), bass guitars, guitars, amps, effects, and outboard gear (bass compressors, noise gates, and entire studios) can post classified ads for free.
WEB http://cord.iupui.edu/~badrian/list .html

Tools of the Trade Several companies—including Peavy, Blue Ribbon, and Coda—showcase their new products. Preview the new Peavy guitar by checking out the sound clips, then go to the message boards to discuss the products with owners or other interested shoppers. Many of the manufacturers post their company histories and newsletters.
AMERICA ONLINE *keyword* music Space→ MusicTools

ACCORDION

Accumulated Accordion Annotations This accordion sites has it all—FAQs, a list of accordion music companies nationwide, a bibliography of accordion books, and even pics of the site creator's trip to the Petosa's accordion shop in

Seattle. In addition, there are links to concertina sites, including a calendar of "squeeze-related" events.
WEB http://www.cs.cmu.edu/afs/cs/user /phoebe/mosaic/accordion.htmlFAQ?

BAGPIPE

Bagpipe Music Ned Smith's been piping for 35 years, making him well-qualified to have a page of his own where he can share his instrumental experiences and advice with fellow pipers. In addition to a brief educational bio, Smith gives you a written sampling of some of his original tunes, including "Running in the Rain," a song "vaguely inspired by Duncan Johnston's 'The Streaker,'" and a page where beginners can learn the notes of the bagpipe scale and the correct fingerings.
WEB http://www.agate.net/~smithr /Bagpipe.html

rec.music.makers.bagpipe How did bagpipes come to be associated with fire and police departments? Where can urban pipers practice without being hauled away by their piping friends at the police department? Is there a good bagpipe band for hire in Akron, Ohio? Bagpipe fans gather to discuss these and other piping issues.
USENET rec.music.makers.bagpipe

BANJO

alt.banjo Pick noise is a constant concern for beginner banjo players. They come here for advice from more experienced pluckers, who advise them not to fret—it's just a matter of practice. Find sound advice about buying, playing, and enjoying the banjo.
USENET alt.banjo

BASS

Bass Instruction For consummate instruction, tablature, FAQs, newsgroups, effects, and just about anything else you could want or need to know

about playing the bass.
WEB http://www.harmony-central.com/Bass

BASS GUITAR

alt.guitar.bass A beginning bass guitarist asks of his fellow musicians: "I am going to buy my first bass. For my money, would it be better to buy a Fender standard jazz or a carvin LB20?" A seasoned pro wonders if anyone has "ever seen an 8-string bass bridge with four of the tuners built into the bridge so you don't need an oversized headstock?" Most of the impassioned debates here revolve around determining the best and worst guitarists, guitars, styles, etc. Your questions and bass-related issues of choice should be well served.
USENET alt.guitar.bass

Bass Resources at Harmony Central Within the depths of the massive musical site known as Harmony Central is this amazing section devoted to the bass. Click on Bass Instruction for the basic tenets of playing the instrument. A link to the rec.music.makers.bass FAQ provides more fundamental playing knowledge. In the Effects section, discover how to get maximum distortion from your bass and how to cheaply concoct original bass effects at home. Info on bass and amp manufacturers will help you build your first (or best) bass rig ever. If you're feeling scholarly, link to *The Bass Digest* for bass briefs by the experts.
WEB http://harmony-central.mit.edu/Bass

BRASS INSTRUMENTS

Brass Mailing List A repair technician/clarinet player needs advice on the best way to lubricate a customer's graphite trombone. A trumpet player asks of the brass audience: "If you were able to ask any famous lead trumpet player a question who and what would it be?" Although this list is intended mainly for musicians in small brass ensembles, other interested parties such as wind bands, orchestras, woodwind or percussion players, and composers, are also welcome.
EMAIL brass-request@geomag.gly.fsu.edu ✍ *Write a request*

DRUMS

The Drummer and Percussion Page Don't be scared off by the bad drummer jokes at this site—there is some good information here, too. Like the events calendar that covers drum/percussion festivals worldwide. And the link to The Groove Archive, which features .GIFs of 13 standard drum rudiments recommended for beginners (followed closely by a second 13). There's even a directory of drummers and percussionists on the Net that's long enough to be the drummer's yellow pages.
WEB http://www.cse.ogi.edu/Drum

rec.music.makers.percussion Have an opinion on the Mapex Mars Pro series drum set? How do you feel about the Electronic Roland TD-5K? Want some info on free concerts around the country? To respond, you need look no further than this enthusiastic group of percussionists. Have your questions answered by one or more of it's innumerable members, or sit back and watch the percussive discussions unfold.
USENET rec.music.makers.percussion

FLUTE

Flute Mailing List Discussions of the instrument and the music made with it.
EMAIL flute-m-request@unixg.ubc.ca ✍ *Write a request*

The Flute Player Home Page The most interesting section of this site is the Master classes topic, which features interviews of famous flutists like Herbie Mann. Also featured are player profiles, model reviews, and manufacturer info.
WEB http://www.windplayer.com/wp/flute.html

FRENCH HORN

International Horn Society Mailing List

This list is dominated by discussion of the French horn, its repertoire and pedagogy, workshop and festival announcements, alternate fingerings, horn humor and anecdotes, instrumental repair and technology, and scholarly reports.
EMAIL majordomo@spock.nlu.edu ☜
Type in message body: subscribe horn <your email address>

GUITAR

Acoustic Guitar Home Page From the folks at rec.music.makers.acoustic comes interesting guitar facts, an intimate guitar lesson with Bo Parker, an explanation of equal-temper tuning, and a dissecting look at guitar resonances. Also find an extensive list of guitar mail-order companies, reviews of instructional material, and profiles of legendary acoustic guitar players.
WEB http://www.io.com/~galvis/rmmga.html

Guitar Lesson The indispensable guitar cyberlesson. You'll learn everything from the basic chord formations, major and minor scales, to advanced chord theory, all with the help of a jazz improvisation primer, chord theory charts and other useful tools.
WEB http://www.harmony-central.com/Guitar/instruction.html

HARMONICA

Cyber Harp World Describing itself as the "Home of the Harmonica Heroes of the Future," this site offers a list of events in the harmonica world (festivals, concerts, and seminars), and links to harmonica players' home pages, the Harp-L mailing list archives (including its picture archive), and other harmonica sites, including the *Irish Harmonica News.*
WEB http://www.wku.edu/~pierccm/harp_home.html

PIANO

The Piano Page Three cheers for the Piano Technicians Guild for assembling this great collection of links to piano-related sites on the Net. Links to the technicians' archives will teach you how often and how to service your piano. A directory of piano technicians, teachers, and manufacturers in the Industry Guide puts you in touch with the personnel needed to get your piano up and running. A collection of piano images includes photos of refurbished vintage pianos as well as paintings with pianos as their subject. For piano conversation on the Net, there are also links to newsgroups and mailing lists.
WEB http://www.prairienet.org/arts/ptg/homepage.html

SAXOPHONE

The International Saxophone Home Page Because there are very few saxophone sites on the Net, enthusiasts will appreciate the well-rounded information available. Visitors can find in-depth reviews of current CD releases that highlight every song's construction and career history of the album's artist. A nationwide directory of used instrument dealers and price lists organized by model is also featured. The site's creator has even taken the time to list all the multiphonics fingerings he has discovered. Soon The International Saxophone Home Page will offer an online beginner's playing manual and interviews with famous players.
WEB http://www.teleport.com/~jdumars

TROMBONE

The International Trombone Association Yes, there really is an annual Trombone Festival, and all the info you need to get there is featured at this site. With approximately 4,200 members from more than 50 countries, the ITA certainly has cause to toot their own horn, and if you want to hear them do it, make a pit stop in Austria for their weeklong festival/workshop. Before you go, however, you might want to apply for the Robert Marstellar Memorial Scholarship, the ITA award, take part in other trombone competitions or subscribe to the ITA quarterly journal.

web http://www.niu.edu/acad/music/ita
.html

Trombone An entertaining and informative site about the trombone. Featuring sound files of master trombone player Alain Trudel rendering "Blue Bells," this page also offers a mouthpiece chart for selecting the right piece for different models, a trombone-related bibliography, discography and record reviews, and an archive of the Trombone-L mailing list.

web http://www.missouri.edu/~cceric
/index.html

TRUMPET

The International Trumpet Guild Viewable, readable, and downloadable from this site, are selected articles from the *ITG Journal*, information about ITG programs and services, news from the trumpet world, music/record/book reviews, contest info, and sheet music.

web http://www.itg.dana.edu/~itg

rec.music.makers.trumpet Continuous breathing is a normal function for all humans. But for trumpet players, it has special meaning: By using the continuous breathing technique, blowers can "literally sustain a note until their horn fills up with saliva," according to one post. Besides playing techniques, you can also find horns for sale and bands seeking horn players.

usenet rec.music.makers.trumpet

Trumpet Mailing List There's no trumped-up talk about the instrument at this mailing list. Get the facts on playing techniques, instrument models, music, and concerts.

email listserv@acad1.dana.edu ✍ *Type in message body:* subscribe trumpet <your full name>

TUBA

Tuba Tunes Listen to the tuba section of the University of Wisconsin marching band play "Semper Fidelis," "Beer Barrel Polka," and "On Wisconsin." These songs will make you feel like you're in the stadium at kickoff with a hot dog in one hand and a beer in the other.

web http://www.engr.wisc.edu/~haack
/tuba/index.html

VIOLIN

Violin Makers: A. Stradivari Located in Cremona, Italy, the Stradivari violin making school is the onlyItalian state school of its kind. This page provides information on the school's programs, as well as links to other violin sites.

web http://graffiti.telnetwork.it/stradivari
/welcome.html

VOICE

Barbershop Web Server This page acts as a directory for fans, participants, and professionals of the barbershop community. Looking for a copy of "Play That Fussy Rag"? Hoping to get a good spot for the SIA International in New Orleans? Even if you're just casting about for a limerick to tell while the bass fumbles for his pitch pipe, the FAQs from this site will smooth out all your harmonizing glitches.

web http://timc.pop.upenn.edu

Primarily A Cappella From Anonymous 4 to Toby Twining, from the Bobs to Vocal Nation, from Black Umfolosi to ZapMama, get the scoop on every facet of a cappella—contemporary, vocal jazz, barbershop, R&B, classical, gospel, world, collegiate, doo-wop, folk, and Christmas—at this well produced site. Links to title and group listings, online buyers' clubs, CD reviews and other a cappella directories.

web http://www.accel.com/pac/index
.htm

rec.music.a-cappella A dream was realized for Malaika, an eclectic four-woman a cappella group, at Canada's "Stone Angel," when they recorded their first CD, but the question remains: "Should you use body mikes for vocal percussion?... and oh, did you make it

to the Coffeehouse in Cambridge to see Five O'Clock Shadow, Ball in the House, and Deadline Poet?" If these sound like excerpts from a conversation you'd like to be having, then don't miss another minute of a cappela chat with this enthusiastic group.
USENET rec.music.a-cappella

"I need advice on maintaing my vocal chords" This Schoolhouse Discussion Group topic is as much general vocal assistance as you're likely to find on the Net at this time. Voice experts provide helpful advice on how to maintain the health of your vocal chords.
WEB http://www.webcom.com/~velan /discuss/tl/tl9.html

Vocals/Barbershop Talk about barbershop quartets, quintets, sextets, septets, octets, nontets, and minyans with other members of CompuServe.
COMPUSERVE go musicarts→Libraries or Messages→Vocals/Barbershop

▶ MARCHING BAND

Links to Marching Bands Want to link to marching band pages? Go ahead—in fact, with this list, linking will be so easy that you'll have enough energy left over to march in lockstep with other tuba-toting football fans. The page contains links to Usenet newsgroups and instructions on how a drum major or bandleader can set up a Web page.
WEB http://seclab.cs.ucdavis.edu /~wetmore/camb/other_bands.html

rec.arts.marching.band.high-school What do marching band members talk about? Choreography. Music. Politics. Football. And sometimes even fashion: "We've decided to go with a new kind of hat, and some of us are in favor of the toboggan, that knit cap that grunge rockers wear. We want our theme to be 'Smells Like Team Spirit,' and we want to smash up our instruments when we are done playing them. What do other drum majors think of this idea?"
USENET rec.arts.marching.band .high-school

▶ COMPUTER MUSIC

Apple II Music and Sound Forum Dedicated to music composition and sound on a PC. Download sound players, editors, and converters from the Applications Library, then pay a visit to the sound libraries, where you'll find hundreds of archived sounds. There are also libraries for MIDI and MOD programmers, with original compositions by members of the forum. Questions about sound digitizing, music education, and MIDI? Post them on the message boards and get feedback from others who make music on the Apple II.
AMERICA ONLINE keyword a2→Music and Sound

Audio Virtual Library An index of links to newsgroups, utilities, and support for audiophiles, this is where you'll find links to the sound archive at Oxford, Michigan State's voice library, John Lennon sound files, a place to discuss binary sounds on computer, IBM PC sound cards, and audio equipment, and listen to the online radio programming of AudioNet and Virtual Radio. If you're in the market for audio software, you can pick get them free at BSD Unix, or purchase some from RealAudio.
WEB http://www.comlab.ox.ac.uk /archive/audio.html

Midi Music Forum Let's say you've just developed an interest in MIDI. In this forum, you could head to the message board and ask for a recommendation for a MIDI player, instructions on how to convert a MIDI file to a .WAV file, or advice on how to get started. If you're more of an old hand at MIDI, you might engage in a discussion about Motown's treatment of strings, computer-controlled sound systems, or composing jazz MIDI. Each of the major computer platforms has its own message and library section. In the library, the resources include MIDI players and editors for several computer platforms, samples, song files, sound card files, and programming guides.
COMPUSERVE go midiform

COMPOSITION & THEORY

Music Theory Online This bi-monthly online journal from the Society for Music Theory is the essential companion for students of music theory and composition. A recent table of contents offers you access to such articles as the "Overlapping Hemiolas of Handel" and "Two Interpretations of the First Movement of Beethoven's Piano Sonata in E-flat Major," a review of the John Cage Symposium, job postings from the Irish World Music Centre, article commentary from previous issues, plus reviews, new dissertations, announcements, and correspondence. Music Theory Online will tell you how to retrieve MTO items, including musical examples and graphical figures, give you a basic rundown of FTP, gopher, and the Web, and clue you in on how to post announcements.
WEB http://boethius.music.ucsb.edu/mto /mtohome.html

Online Music Instruction Online Music Instruction offers a friendly, pressure-free classroom where you'll learn the basics of music theory, including notes, the staff, clefs, note names, steady beats, measures, rests, and dynamics. If you're so inclined, challenge your knowledge of music with the various tests provided. Beginning students will get the most out of this site, and move comfortably onto more advanced musical concepts, such as ledger lines, time signatures, beamed notes, and triads. Downloadable instrument sounds are provided as a helpful teaching tool.
WEB http://orathost.cfa.ilstu.edu/public /KenFansler/onlinemusicpage.htm

The (Online) Wholearts Music Conservatory Classes here in music theory and composition require a working knowledge of scales and modes, intervals and basic chords. Lessons are based on a progressive series of readings, each of which is linked with one or more musical examples downloadable (as MIDI files) and playable on computer sound card, electric piano, or synthesizer. Students are guided through the readings

and exercises according to their needs. Wherever you live, you can make your interests and contact information available to other musicians through the Whole Arts Music Mall, the largest Web resource for directories, calendars, services and education, while "Categorical Links" can put you in touch with the archives of the traditional folk song database.
WEB http://www.wholarts.com/music/ed /theory.html

Sheet Music Online Don't be fooled by the name, this is every musician's home base for retailers of musical instruments and supplies, software home pages, free entertainment and online services, MIDI and other music-making resources, and links to music magazines from the folkzine *Dirty Linen* to *Internet Music World*. There's no place like SMO for personalized educational resource materials, not to mention free downloads, transcription services, and sheet music ordering and delivery.
WEB http://sheetmusic.cenornet.com /default2.html

TEACHERS' LOUNGE

k12.ed.music At k12.ed.music you may find a notice from a private school in the Bronx seeking a music teacher, or an Illinois music major offering his opinion on the poor treatment music gets in high school, (string instruments in particular). A soon-to-be preschool music teacher needs some advice on lesson plans. Perhaps you can help.
USENET k12.ed.music

Music Education Online Nearly all essential music links converge at this hubsite. Music Education Online allows you to contact a variety of online resources, and post questions and comments about music to interactive bulletin boards. Includes links to multicultural resources, newsgroups, and magazines.
WEB http://www.geocities.com/Athens /2405

DANCE

THE WORLD OF DANCE IS COMposed of many realms; some ethereal, some earthy. There are those to whom dance is the silent physicality of the human body challenging its environment, exploring and experiencing space, air, light, and gravity. To others, it's a good way to exercise. Still, if you have dreams of pirouetting across a stage or tap dancing in a musical, the Internet can point you in the right direction. Even if becoming a professional dancer is not in your plans, an online dance class might prove to be your ideal form of exercise and self expression.

▶ STARTING POINTS

rec.arts.dance Participants of this newsgroup talk about everything from what you can expect to make in awards money if you win a professional dance contest to the facts of music licensing. Don't be shy; it's a friendly place to discuss dance steps, workshops, music, and social and competitive dancing.
USENET rec.arts.dance

▶ BALLET

alt.arts.ballet This is a well-traveled, friendly, and informative newsgroup for ballet/modern discussion, where you're as likely to run into a 16-year-old, professional-level ballerina from Israel, as you are a Nebraskan father concerned about his potentially embarrassing participation in his daughter's dance recital.
USENET alt.arts.ballet

The American Ballet Theatre The home page of America's premier classical dance company lets visitors witness what goes into the building of a ballet. Behind this 60-year-old company are both creative and administrative forces envisioning the company's future and developing programs to fulfill it. You'll get a good sense of the artistic inclinations of the ABT's current directors via bios and choices for the upcoming sea-

son. Biographies of the dancers, conductors, and other members of the artistic staff are also featured. For more visual stimulation, you can browse the photo gallery, or refer to the ABT's schedule of events, including live performances, premiers, new programs, and classes.
WEB http://www.abt.org

Ballet Archive Japan Ballet is big in Japan. How big? Find out by surfing through this site's impressive array of worldwide links, including extensive information on six of the country's top dance companies. Heading east? Pick up an online schedule for the Asami Maki Ballet or the Tachibana Ballet School. For a sneak peek at Japanese ballet without getting a visa, peruse this site's exquisite photo section.
WEB http://www.bekkoame.or.jp
/~arakawai/index.html

Ballet Web A basic, if not overly impressive page, which changes periodically. Standard features include a photo and quote of the week (e.g., "True strength is delicate"), commentary, and analysis of issues currently affecting the ballet community. Links to other dance Web sites are provided.
WEB http://users.aol.com/balletweb
/balletweb.html

Cyberdance The grace and precision with which a ballet dancer moves is not a gift given at birth, but the result of years of passionate commitment and rigorous training. This expansive Web site opens a door into the world created by the sweat and inspiration of ballet dancers and choreographers. Learn about the people and organizations who create ballet's great works of movement through links to classical ballet and modern dance resources, including dance companies from Singapore to South Africa. The online library section lets you test your dance trivia or cruise the list of dance education programs, with worldwide links from Australia to

Rotterdam. If you're ready to market yourself as a dancer, peruse the list of potential managers and agents and obtain information on funding programs and grants.
WEB http://www.thepoint.net/~raw/dance.html

Dance Pages Get lost backstage at the Paris Opera Ballet, the Royal Ballet, or even the Birmingham Royal Ballet. Meet the dancers and choreographers of famous dance companies and learn about the ballets they've brought to life. Uncover a wealth of biographies, histories, and stunning photographs. Links lead to everything related to ballet, including FAQs, guides to stretching exercises, and even the Degas page of the Web museum.
WEB http://www.ens-lyon.fr/~esouche/danse/dance.html

George Balanchine If you've never heard of this man, than you're overdue for a trip to his biographical page. Outlined in a thorough fashion are the details of his impressive dance career, including his choreography and stories behind the founding of the New York City Ballet.
WEB http://www.ens-lyon.fr/~esouche/danse/Balan.html

▶ JAZZ & TAP

Jazz Tap Center You may not think of Israel as a hot spot for tap dancing, but after a visit to the home page of The Israeli Hoofers, you're likely to change your mind. The tapping duo of Avi Miller and Ofer Ben have created, among other things, Tap Tel-Aviv, a professional tap dance company, and the Tap Jazz Center, a school that trains prospective company members. In addition to providing all the basic info on history, classes (in New York and Israel), upcoming performances, and other tap studios across the country, you can link up with some mighty useful worldwide resources like the Dance Teacher Database, Dance Events Database, and an updated list of dance festivals and contests. You need

not be Israel-bound to benefit from this page.
WEB http://www.isratap.co.il

Tap Dance Homepage This is the place to be for the brush, pull, flap, scuff, and shuffle: If these words sound like what you do when washing your dog, you may want to head to the site's helpful glossary first. The multimedia activities at this site let you take a listen to Gregory Hine's fast-tapping feet, or catch a clip of Ira Bernstein's Appalachian Flatfoot Clogging video. For those of you who read tap, there's a diagram of the shim-sham, or if you're looking for ways to learn some of these smooth steps, tap into a list of videos, books, supplies, and festivals.
WEB http://www.hahnemann.edu/tap

▶ MODERN

Chamecki/Lerner Dance Company Dive into this engaging site to discover the inner world of the daring company that created it. Begin your journey with biographies of the company's Brazilian founders, then take an inspirational walk across the landscape of "The Butterfly Effect," one of their many original and eloquent dances. Glide through the gallery of riveting photos from various performances, study the company's eclectic repertoire, and end on a cinematic note, with a preview of their latest work entitled "Homemade."
WEB http://www.users.interport.net/~tintin

Dancemakers For a jolt of inspiration, head to this illuminating site put together by "Toronto's foremost contemporary troupe." The eclectic members of Dancemakers offer eloquent descriptions of their work in words and pictures. There is much to be learned about the language of dance by examining the ensemble's current repertoire. Indulge in the finer details of the company's history by reading the "who's who" list, with biographies of its members and artistic director. For a lesson in the politics of arts funding, you'll want to have a look at Some Carefully Chosen Words.

WEB http://www.interlog.com/~dncemkrs

Dancing on a Line This artist-run, New York dance zine extends its coverage beyond the physical dance realm. One compelling feature gives voice to choreographer Stephen Petronio's "Struggle With The Body," and how it resulted in his "exalting, exploiting, and exposing" of those bodies interpreting his work. To understand the methods of an "electronically enhanced" dance company, you'll want to read DOAL's interview with Troika Ranch. Regularly updated previews and listings are standard fare at this Web site, while a music archive full of sound clips is proof of the benefits of Net over paper magazines. A highly original ongoing story section, featuring the "Chronicles of Dancer 'X'" is good for a comic breather, and "The Artist Speaks" provides a forum for dancers to write about their own creative processes.
WEB http://www.cipsinc.com/dance/doal.html

Second Hand Dance Not the term for copping moves off the disco diva next to you, but the name of a company whose post-modern interpretation of life on earth includes such pieces as "Waltzing Dogs," "Businessman at Rush Hour," and "Crazy Chefs in a Kitchen." The Second Hand Dancers move to the sounds of jazz, rock, and classical music, and utilize some pretty funky handmade props and costumes, about which they're happy to tell you. You'll get the lowdown on how this company got started, what the founders did before Second Hand, a schedule of upcoming performances, and where to find other modern-minded companies and musicians on the Net. Photos will help give you an idea of what this exciting company is all about.
WEB http://www.clarityconnect.com/webpages/secondhand

Trish "Asha" Hanada-Rogers This dance coordinator/teacher/ performer, offers an excellent dance history resource base through the Brand Library Dance Series, where you can read about such great dancer/choreographers as Ruth St. Denis, Martha Graham, and Charles Weidman. The thrust of this page however, is to get you familiar with "Asha" herself. You can read her resume, dance history, and schedule of upcoming performances.
WEB http://home.earthlink.net/~rogers

▶ TEACHERS' LOUNGE

Dance Events Database This is an excellent way to locate and/or list any style dance event by country, state or city, week, month, or season. You'll find all the necessary information about the event, including brief descriptions, time, and date. Phone numbers are occasionally listed, but all can be accessed by email.
WEB http://www.net-shopper.co.uk/dance/database.htm

Dance Teacher Database This searchable list of dance teachers worldwide is the forum for both those looking for a new dance teachers and instructors wishing to advertise. But that's not all. Links lead to commercial dance resources, the latest news on contests and festivals, a band search-and-listen option, shareware and software, plus an email form for questions.
WEB http://www.net-shopper.co.uk/dance/teacher.htm

Dance Teacher Now Flip through this informative magazine to learn how to computerize your studio, devise techniques for teaching those with special needs, or have a chat with fellow dance educators worldwide. Place an electronic ad in the classified section, read the latest nutritional tips, or start building your Spanish and tango dancing library. Everything is possible at this detailed site—whether you're interested in teaching techniques, dance styles, employment, studio management, business issues, competition, or personal success stories. Four special issues are published yearly.
WEB http://www.dc.enews.com/magazines/dance

PART 9

Electives

HOME ECONOMICS

L ADIES AND GENTLEMEN, STRAP on those aprons tightly, this could get a tad messy. Boy meets girl across a crowded mixing bowl. Girl drops nose ring in cookie batter. Teacher chips tooth on strangely hard oatmeal raisin. Its name may be a nod to the Beaver Cleaver years, but this sure isn't the same home economics class your mom took in high school while dad was down the hall rebuilding Edsel engines. Boys and girls dice and sew side by side, and often with equal incompetence. Offended masculine and feminine sensibilities will have to find a different outlet for political insurgency. The conversation at newsgroups like alt.sewing and rec.food.cooking is all about pragmatic advice, while the domestic diva of the Family and Consumer Education Home Page avoids the political implications of domesticity with admirable grace and obliqueness.

along quite nicely with a national membership of over 273,000 "young men and women." How many young men are actually members, and what invectives are hurled their way in the high school hallways? The male to female ratio is not included at the group's home page, but there is no mistaking its nod to the barefoot-and-pregnant days of yore—images of apron-clad boys are glaringly absent. Even as the mission statement is careful to emphasize the possibility of "wage earning" and the "multiple roles of family members," the focus is on the promotion of "home economics, home economics careers and related occupations." And what colors do these bustling little housewives-to-be wear as they learn the ins and outs of balancing the grocery budget? Red, to represent the rose, "because it gives joy through its beauty and fragrance. It symbolizes a desire for beauty in everyday living." **WEB** http://www.inc.net/~clonge/fhahero .html

▶ STARTING POINTS

Family and Consumer Education Home Page Tipper Gore, rejoice. Family values have arrived in cyberspace, and not a moment too soon; at least not according to Chris Longe. A Family Consumer Education Instructor at a Wisconsin middle school, Longe makes Martha Stewart look like a dangerous radical. Her classes stress the importance of family identity, self-confidence, and resisting peer pressure. While she does not ignore the more tangible home economic issues of nutrition, health, and sewing, she is far more concerned with the "big picture." Is this a case of conservative indoctrination cleverly disguised as unbiased life training? Longe is careful not to come down too strongly on either side of the white picket fence. **WEB** http://www.inc.net/~clonge

Future Homemakers of America Paleontologists, don't go digging for this group's charter quite yet. The Future Homemakers of America are chugging

▶ SEWING

alt.sewing "I tat; what do you need help with?" begins a representative thread at the busy sewing newsgroup, where expert advice is the top order of business. The seamless dialogue between the needle-impaired and the deft inspires faith in the utilitarian power of the Internet. **USENET** alt.sewing

Excerpts from Needlecrafter's Computer Companion Lifting thousands of benighted crafty types out of the dark ages, Needlecrafter's Computer Companion exemplifies the ubiquitous nature of computer technology. You won't see robots doing needlework at this site, but interested parties can learn how to attend virtual reality quilt shows, turn ordinary photos into cross-stitch charts, and even "morph" Sunbonnet Sue. Of course, the book isn't free, but excerpts are included for the curious.

WEB http://www.execpc.com/~judyheim
/needle.html

Margaret Minsky's Sewing Page A visit
to Margaret Minsky's page yields more
than simple information on the art of
sewing. This page is an unintentionally
intimate look at the sewing expert's life,
and that of her family, as detailed by
past sewing projects. Visitors to the
page know, for instance, that in 1994
Minsky's baby was 14 months old, and
that he received a jumpsuit for Christmas. They also know what Minksy wore
in her hair at her wedding and what her
husband received for Christmas in 1995.
Minsky provides detailed images of her
impressive sewing projects, as well as
text descriptions to aid emulators over
some of the difficult hurdles.
WEB http://www.media.mit.edu/people
/marg/sewing.html

Martha's Sewing Room Martha Pullen's
how-to sewing show, which airs on PBS
in 44 states, "shows you how to make
everything from beautiful quilts to heir-
loom sewing. Doll dresses... Antique
clothing..." The list is long and illustrious. The show's home page invites
sewing enthusiasts to order videotapes
of previous shows they may have
missed.
WEB http://www.sa.ua.edu/brent/msr.htm

Phinney Fabrics Sewing Source Now,
you can place your order for fabrics, patterns, and other sewing supplies without
dropping a stitch. At the "Ask Mrs. Phinney Corner," the goddess of the stitch
doles out tips and advice to tangled neophytes.
WEB http://www.halcyon.com/homestyl

Sewing and Quilting Quilting and quilt
swaps are the hottest topics of discussion in the forum, but sewing topics are
also covered in impressive detail. Subdi-
visions include general sewing, machine
embroidery, and dolls and bears.
Although the forum features many regulars, it is a meeting spot for everyone
from the hobbyist to the frustrated Bar-
bie owner.

COMPUSERVE *go* crafts→sewing and
quilting→message sections

Sewing with Bernina The undisputed
queen machine of the cross-stitching
scene, Bernina is the Michael Jordan of
the sewing world, with a following the
size of a small country. If Bernina's min-
ions came together, their combined quilt
would span the globe three times over.
Bernina products are celebrated at various sites across the Net. The Bernina
home page, fan club, and one related
site are listed. The fan club page contains access to the Bernina Mailing list, a
forum for the further discussion of
sewing with Bernina products.
WEB http://www2.ari.net/home/rain/lalu
.html • http://quilt.com/BFC • http://www
.bernina.com

► COOKING

The Cooking Club With scheduled chats
every day of the week, interactive
instructions for food preparation, and a
special area for kids, this may very well
be the tastiest club online. The cookbook
section contains thousands of family
recipes, and has its own message
boards subdivided into topics like hors
d'oeuvres, sauces and salads. The Cooking Club is also the home of Vegetarian's
Online, for herbivores and the people
who love them.
AMERICA ONLINE *go* cooking club

Cooks Online Forum Join the ranks of
the Cooks Online Forum, and taste the
magic of cyberspace. Where else can
one address a question to Betty Crocker
and receive a prompt answer (from a
publicist, but even so...), or sift through
43 messages on chili peppers? The
forum is open to anyone with an interest
in cooking.
COMPUSERVE *go* cooks

Flora's Kitchen Her favorite recipes—
for cheesecakes, chocolate desserts and
other healthful treats—all in the Master-
Cook format.
WEB http://www.deter.com/flora/kitchen
.html

FoodWeb Gourmands and gluttons alike gather at this "site with bytes galore". A stewpot of diverse information, Food-Web offers links to recipes, general food and nutrition information, as well as a selection of resources for the avid or aspiring drinker.
WEB http://www.foodweb.com

Jayne's Food Page Jayne "particularly enjoys baking bread and cooking Italian dishes and soups." She is also an avid cybersurfer, having gathered more than 40 of the richest links to cooking, baking and recipe resources on the Internet.
WEB http://www.webbuild.com/~jmkizer /hob-food.html

Kath's Meal-Master Recipe Swap Kath adores the Meal-Master recipes, and she's culled her favorites to share with her spatula-wielding peers.
WEB http://www.cyberspc.mb.ca/~pickell /recipe.html

Meal-Master FAQ All cooking roads on the Internet lead to Meal-Master. A shareware recipe database program for MS-DOS-compatible computers, Meal-Master allows recipes to be stored, searched and shared with other Meal-Master users. A FAQ provides detailed information for the would-be cyberchef, including the means for Meal-Master procurement.
WEB http://ourworld.compuserve.com /homepages/S_Welliver/mmfaq.htm

Meal-Master Resource Page Download-able recipes in the Meal-Master format, organized by country of origin.
WEB http://members.aol.com/DonW1948 /mealmast.htm

rec.food.cooking Alternative meats any-one? Yes, this newsgroup is a fine place for the discussion of specific recipes and cooking techniques; but it is so much more. A sardonic discussion of the Frugal Gourmet's wig sits alongside a plea by the unofficial spokesman for the unofficial People for the Ethical Treatment of Lobsters. Humor, ethics and chicken fried steak; who could ask for more?
USENET rec.food.cooking
FAQ: WEB http://www.cis.ohio-state.edu /hypertext/faq/usenet/cooking-faq/faq .html

Secrets of Really Good Chocolate Chip Cookies It's just as you've always suspect-ed: Follow the original Tollhouse recipe, but never, ever skimp on the butter.
WEB http://www.well.com/user/vard /cookies.html

> **NUTRITION**

Arizona Health Sciences Library Nutrition Guide This short index is a good starting point, offering approximately two dozen links to nutritional sites across the Web and organized in alpha-betical order by subject and format.
WEB http://128.196.106.42/nutrition.html

Blonz Guide to Nutrition Hands down, the best index for nutritional sites on the Net. Thousands of links to government dietary guidelines, health and medical rescues, publications, food associations and companies, academic resources, food-related links, food and fitness, gar-dening and much, much more. Just in case laughter is the best medicine, visi-tors get a handful of humor links. A great resource for both professionals and health-minded consumers.
WEB http://www.blonz.com/blonz/index .html

Food Pyramid Guide This graphic repre-sentation of the food pyramid, the post–rice cake revamp of the four food groups, offers extremely brief descrip-tions of the food divisions and daily doses.
WEB http://www.ganesa.com/ganesa /~misc/foodpyramid.html

International Food and Information Council (IFIC) The home page for the IFIC holds a tremendous amount of information for parents, educators, health professionals, and consumers. Linked in a circular manner, the same nutritional information for children can be accessed via the parents' page, the educators' page, the Food Safety and Nutrition Information page, and the consumer page.

web http://ificinfo.health.org

Nutrition and Your Health: Dietary Guidelines for Americans The fourth edition of this official government guide to healthy eating contains both general advice (explaining the new food pyramid), and very specific guidelines (1½ ounces of natural cheese counts as a serving of the milk group). Also addressed are the different nutritional needs of children, women, and vegetarians/vegans. A must-read for everyone who cares about their diet.

url gopher://gopher.nal.usda.gov:70 /00/infocntr/fnic/dga

Nutrition Pages This great page gets kudos for both design and well-produced content. There are a series of articles on such topics as Aspartame and Neurotoxicity, The Great Saturated Fat Scam, Militant Vegetarianism, and Amputees and Powerlifting (OK, so it's a little off-topic, but what a great water cooler conversation.) Visitors can comment on articles and send in their own. There are also three excellent FAQs on basic stuff (What do the terms RDA, RDI, and USRDA stand for?), lifestyle (Why shouldn't I just take vitamin pills to balance my diet?) and sports nutrition (Why should I exercise when it's such a pain?). Also featured is a collection of links to about half a dozen nutrition hubsites.

web http://deja-vu.oldiron.cornell.edu /~jabbo/index.html

Virtual Nutrition Center Possibly the best online resource for health students and professionals. There are hundreds of links to pages on metabolic pathways and genetic maps, interactive anatomy browsers, online journals, glossaries, courses, consumer information, and nutrition databases. Access to the similarly comprehensive law, medical and dental centers are also included and adding flavor are a selection of some-

what unlikely links to such things as the current time in Singapore, the position of the planets, a card-sending service, travel warnings and immunization info, and, of course, the weather.

web http://www-sci.lib.uci.edu/HSG /Nutrition.html

INDUSTRIAL ARTS

THE DEVIL MAKES WORK FOR IDLE hands, but one way to stay on the side of good is to keep them occupied with tools. Whatever your ambition—to build your dream furniture, replace a fan belt, or make a nice gift for your mom—you'll probably need some help along the way. So before you pick up that saw or open the hood of your car, consult the Internet's industrial arts resources. The Net's got instructions on everything. Try making jewelry at Art-Metal Project. Then try making your car run smoothly at Autosite. If you're not heavy into metal, carve out some time for learning to deal with lumber at WoodWeb.

▶ AUTO REPAIR

Automotive Guide Does fuel-injection cleaning really help a car? How do I know when I need an alignment? The tips and maintenance advice given are intended for people with some basic mechanical skills. They don't go into too much depth. Links to more detailed instructions are provided.
WEB http://www.eecs.uic.edu/~abuduan/auto.html

Autosite Stop at the garage for some of the best repair and maintenance tips to be found on the Web. This virtual mechanic leads you around the car, with diagrams to illustrate what you need to do to get your motor running reliably. There's also a wealth of information on buying cars, new and used, and finding a good driving school, as well as a library of current consumer advice.
WEB http://www.autosite.com

CarTalk Maybe you've heard them on the radio or read their syndicated columns. Now you can find them on the Web. Those lovable mechanic philosophers Tom and Ray Magliozzi (a.k.a. Click and Clack) bring their inimitable style to the CarTalk pages. Even if you've never looked under the hood of a car,

you'll find yourself reading about brake cylinders and fuel injection, and feeling like it all makes some kind of sense. If you have a question or concern, there are real answers among the amusing one-liners.
WEB http://cartalk.com

Mark's Automotive Web Site If you think you have a "hot car" and you want other people to see it, Mark will post a picture of it at his Web site. He also provides advice on maintenance and repair and lists links to other car-obsessed sites and surfers.
WEB http://www.iceonline.com/home/markp/index.html

On the Road Car fans will enthuse over the impressive array of links to information on pretty much whatever you want to do with cars, including buying, selling, repairing, and driving them. Click on the logo of a car to get to brand-dedicated sites.
WEB http://www.slonet.org/~rschafer/carsites.html

rec.autos.* FAQ "What are understeer and oversteer?" "What is double clutch downshifting?" This FAQ, compiled from rec.autos.misc. and four other newsgroups, has the answers, plus an index of the rec.autos.* archive and links to other automotive documents.
WEB http://www.emi.com/~rwelty/FAQ

Womanmotorist What kind of maintenance should I be doing on a regular basis? How can I tell if my brakes require repair? Questions are answered clearly—no jargon spoken here. Most reassuring is that no question is too "simple." Apart from the pink-and-white color scheme, there's nothing about this site that restricts it to women. Additional features discuss racing, travel, and cars reviews.
WEB http://www.womanmotorist.com

WPRO Drive Thru Radio The Zangari

brothers compiled questions and answers from their radio show about car maintenance and put it on the Web. Queries range from the simple ("I need new tires—what do I need to know?") to the simpler ("What oil should I use in my car?"). All advice is easy to understand and put into practice.

WEB http://www.wpro.com/drive.html

▶ METALWORKING

The ArtMetal Project From blacksmithing to jewelry, The ArtMetal Project covers it all. Go to the Gallery to see the great things that can be achieved with malleable metals, then return to the resources and newsletters to get guidance for doing it yourself. A complete list of the materials and methods used in metalwork is provided. Once you've finished a project, ArtMetal offers the opportunity to show off your work on its pages and to publish your own words of wisdom.

WEB http://wuarchive.wustl.edu/edu/arts/metal/ArtMetal.html

Metal Web News Having trouble making that anvil? Feeling the urge to do some welding? *Metal Web News* will hold your hand through these tricky projects by providing lots of how-to articles and advice. *Metal Web News* is the online newsletter of the Metalworking newsgroup, and its home page features a good collection of links to other metallic sites.

WEB http://tbr.state.tn.us/~wgray/index.html

rec.crafts.metalworking "I've been told that drinking milk is an effective antidote for the effects of breathing the smoke caused by welding galvanized metal. Anyone confirm this?" "I'm looking for suppliers that could sell me 20,000 stainless steel split rings." "I need welding instruction. Where do I go?" Commercial companies, industry professionals, and hobbyist alike converge at this newsgroup for advice and information on making things with metal.

USENET rec.crafts.metalworking

▶ WOODWORKING

W5 Wood Working on the World Wide Web is a comprehensive list of woodworking resources, including those found on the online commercial services. Particularly helpful are the links to woodworking newgroups and FAQs. There's so much data that you really need to have some idea of what you're looking for before you begin. For techniques and how to, refer first to the W5 Helpline.

WEB http://www.iucf.indiana.edu/~brown/hyplan/wood.html

WoodWeb An incredible resource for everything pertaining to wood, from prescriptions for bending it to the best kind of glue. There's an email forum on the subject, a collection of articles such as "Drawing Attention to Drawers," and information about woodworking products. There's not too much for a real beginner, but if you're already into it, you'll get a lot out of it.

WEB http://www.woodweb.com

Woodworker Explains everything you ever wanted to know about wood, but didn't know who to ask. Post queries about how to perform even the simplest woodworking task and receive help from both hobbyists and professionals. Join nightly chats about finishing, turning, designing, and other topics, hosted by the staff of *American Woodworker* magazine. If you're looking for new ideas for woodworking projects, browse through back copies of the magazine.

AMERICA ONLINE *keyword* wood

LIFE SKILLS

SOMETIMES IT DOESN'T SEEM LIKE life requires a lot of skill. You roll out of bed in the morning and stumble through the day, right? Well, yes. But what do you do when you run into a situation that's new to you? Or unexpected? Or threatening? You could just hope this situation will go away, but chances are it won't. Chances are that you won't want it to just go away, either. Fortunately for you, thousands of people have been through the same situations and they want to help via the Internet. Online resources can help you cope with everything from sunburn to sexually transmitted diseases, parallel parking to typing. It's all here: the good, the bad, and the ugly of being out there on your own. Anyone taking Al Bunny's Typing Class this semester?

▶ CPR & FIRST AID

CPR: You CAN do it! CPR, in case you've forgotten or never knew, stands for "cardiopulmonary resuscitation," and it's something that you can learn to do by following the six steps shown here. A great feature of this page is the CPR pocket guide you can print and carry around at all times. There's also a video demonstation and links to CPR training sites.
WEB http://weber.u.washington.edu/~gingy/cpr.html

Family Health This site offers a series of two-and-a-half minute audio files providing practical answers to frequently asked questions about health. Be prepared: each file is about 1.2 megabytes in size. Topics covered run the gamut from such basic subjects as hand washing, removing splinters, and staying cool in summer, to sleep apnea, peptic ulcers, and radial keratotomy.
WEB http://www.tcom.ohiou.edu/family-health.html

First Aid Online This site is no replacement for a doctor, but it has some good tips for treating minor accidents. The real problem is knowing when you can help and when you should get help. Still, if the injury is just a bruise or a sprain, you should be able to follow these brief instructions and keep the situation under control until help arrives.
WEB http://www.wps.com.au/business/firstaid/firstaid.htm

MedAccess MedAccess promotes family health by providing downloadable health workbooks to keep track of children's immunizations and illnesses (user-friendly for the organizationally challenged) and a health and safety alert section direct from the Federal Food and Drug Administration for the latest toxins reports on common household goods. A section called You Are What You Eat investigates just what's in that chicken and rice casserole.
WEB http://www2.medaccess.com/

MedicineNet Are there any side effects to Advil? Is it safe to take antihistamines during pregnancy? Can you take too much vitamin A? Find out at MedicineNet, a cyber medical reference. Look up those tricky doctor terms in the site's dictionary; find out how you can control, say, acne; find your nearest poison control center in Diseases & Treatments; or catch up on the latest medical news. While MedicineNet does not attempt to replace your doctor, it is a useful health resource.
WEB http://www.medicinenet.com/

▶ DRIVER'S ED

Reasonable Drivers Unanimous Do you agree that driver's education and testing in America "in one word—sucks"? You will find sympathy with this Web page. Operating on the belief that driving and traffic laws in the United States need some improvement, Reasonable Drivers Unanimous sets out to examine a few of the areas it thinks are particularly ripe for change. Check out some of its arti-

cles about driver's ed in the USA and elsewhere. The site also features tips on the art of driving, stories of true driving adventures, and articles about DWI, speedtraps, and more.
WEB www.clark.net/pub/kevina/sl/home2.html

Teen New Driver's Homepage Ryan is a teen. Ryan is a new driver. This is Ryan's home page. He gives helpful advice on driving in various conditions as well as general safety tips and info on how to buy your first car. It's brief but thorough, and really zeros in on what's important to teenage road-users.
WEB http://www.ai.net/~ryanb

Traffic Safety Information Village
Behind this Web page lives a town full of tiny people (about the same size as the little men in the ATM machine) working to make sure all the traffic safety information you'll ever need is available online. The village has a bookstore, newsstand, library, and even a highway linking to more traffic safety sites. Don't miss the off-ramp to this hub of resources on your fast track to becoming a good driver.
WEB http://www.scbe.on.ca/pde

▶ DRUG EDUCATION

AL-ANON and ALATEEN If you need help with a drinking problem, either your own or that of someone close to you, you'll find support at this Web page. If you're unsure that there is a problem, a 20-item questionnaire helps you to find out. Toll-free numbers are included for more information.
WEB http://solar.rtd.utk.edu/~al-anon

Alcohol, Drugs, and Smoking At this site, both pictures and text explain the uses (including medical) and effects of alcohol and other drugs (both "hard" and "soft"), plus a list of symptoms of abuse. Some of the illustrations seem more like how-to instructions than anything else, but if you believe that you need to know the enemy, then start your inquiry here.

WEB http://www.uncg.edu/health/drugs.html

Drug Education Page If tobacco and alcohol are legal, why isn't marijuana? Does prohibition work? How do we decide which substances should be controlled and how? This is a collection of writings about all kinds of drugs, with a focus on their effects relative to each other. For example, which is worse for you, beer or pot? The site has a good section on Drugs In The Media. Be prepared to leave with as many, if not more, questions than you had when you arrived.
WEB http://www.magic.mb.ca/%7Elampi/new_drugs.html

Go Ask Alice! Sponsored by Columbia University, Go Ask Alice is an extensive Q&A that covers all kinds of health concerns including issues related to the use of drugs and alcohol. Questions include just how dangerous is light to moderate use of marijuana? What exactly does "blacking out" from alcohol mean? The answers are clear and straightforward, never moralistic. Alice doesn't promise to answer every individual's questions, but the list covers many concerns.
WEB http://www.columbia.edu/cu/healthwise/cat2.html

Life Education Network Despite a somewhat moralistic tone, there's good stuff to be found at this Web site, including a dictionary of slang terms for drugs, and the facts about specific drugs and their effects. The Life Education Network hopes that the info it provides will help prevent drug abuse, as well as other forms of "personal harm related behavior."
WEB http://www.lec.org

The Master Anti-Smoking Page This really is the master anti-smoking page. From here you can get to hundreds of other anti-smoking pages, including the Bureau of Alcohol, Firearms, and Tobacco home page and the No Smoke Cafe. An excellent resource for research about cigarettes and how they affect us.

web http://www.autonomy.com/smoke.htm

Web of Addictions "You won't find glib, hip treatment of this very serious topic here," cautions this site about addictions. Web of Addictions is indeed very serious, and it provides information in such a no-nonsense way that it ends up being kind of boring. But don't be put off; there's some very helpful stuff, especially in Facts About Addictions, which covers addictive substances.

web http://www.well.com/user/woa/facts.htm

▶ SELF-DEFENSE

Assault Prevention Information Network "A woman is a victim of a violent crime every 14 seconds. And that is just the reported ones." And that also doesn't include men who are victims of violence. So it's probably a good idea to check out this site, which links to tons of articles about self-defense. Especially helpful are the Guidelines for Choosing a Self Defense Class and the lists of instructors. You might even find a new vocation when you check out the Bodyguard HomePage.

web http://galaxy.tradewave.com/editors/weiss/APINintro.html

DangerHigh Presented by the Nashville Polics, this game promises to "teach consequences of actions or inactions." A demo of the DangerHigh Game leads you through a variety of threatening school situations, like being insulted or beaten up, or being offered drugs. You get to choose your responses and then see the potential outcomes. The Web site also provides information on risk reduction and self-protection. Its tactics are heavy-handed at times and the solutions are a little simplistic, but it provides good awareness training. The Self Defense Tips have pictures and sound clips to lead you through some of the basics of looking out for yourself on the street.

web http://www.nashville.net/~police/dangerhi

PrePARE Self Defense You read newspaper headlines like "Central Park Stalker!" or "Three Men, Three Guns!" and you're shaking in your boots. PrePARE (that's Protection Awareness Response Empowerment) wants to help you protect yourself. Read the success stories and discover your particular self-defense needs. It's not all about fighting—it's about about using your voice and your brains, too. This site tells you where you can learn these invaluable skills.

web http://www.cybergrrl.com./health/prepare/index.html

SEX EDUCATION

AIDS 101 Everyone's talking about AIDS, HIV, and antibodies—and you don't want to say anything in case they think you're dumb—but what exactly are they talking about? Visit this Web site which reviews the basic information you might have missed in Health class while you were doing your Math homework. There are no pretty pictures to distract you from understanding the facts—which is probably just as well—because this is serious stuff.

url gopher://gopher.hivnet.org/00/hivtext1/aids101

alt.romance.FAQ Is virginity something you lose or something you give? Does sex equal love? Can sex be purely physical? The alt.romance.FAQ addresses these and other complicated questions. The answers here are subjective, but definately worth a look. The FAQ also features Lyrical Interludes, an overview of a Christian perspective on sex and marriage, and some useful suggestions for dealing with uncomfortable sexual situations. Phone numbers for free advice and information are also provided. If the FAQ doesn't have the answer, you can try the newsgroup— alt.romance—but expect a fair number of less-than-serious responses.

web http://www.fredonia.edu/students/watson/virgin.htm

Coalition for Positive Sexuality For straight talk, go straight to the Coalition

for Positive Sexuality. Created to meet the needs of young adults in the Chicago area, this site is dedicated to being totally honest about sex and sexuality. Some people (like your parents) might be offended by just how frank the language at this Web site is, but for giving clear answers to direct questions, CPS can't be beat. There's tons of valuable information and it is supportive of all kinds of sexual choices, encouraging you to "just say yes" to whatever is best for you. Some sections are also in Spanish.
WEB http://www.positive.org/cps

Condomania Online Aside from trying very hard to sell you condoms of many colors, styles, and sizes, this site also does its part to educate visitors about safer sex. Its safe-sex manual first advises you that "you deserve respect," and when you decide to have sex, you need to know "what is safe sex?" Then read "all about condoms" at this colorful site, decorated with condoms to point the way.
WEB http://www.condomania.com

Gay and Lesbian Community Forum One of the highlights of AOL's gay and lesbian forum is the opportunity to make contact with gay, lesbian, and bisexual teenagers nationwide. The concerns of the forum range from the serious to the silly, from those looking for love to those looking for like-minded friends. A resource library with news and information about the gay and lesbian community at large make this a valuable source of support for teens coming out.
AMERICA ONLINE *keyword* glcf

Healthy Devil On-line If you need factual information, practical advice, or support about nearly any sex-related question, you'll probably find it at this Web site sponsored by Duke University. It contains detailed sexual health information on everything from abstinence to contraceptives, plus information on more general health concerns, including acne, sunburn, and itchy feet. Check out the huge Q&A. If your problem isn't covered, submit a question and get an email

answer. Selected Q&As are added to a permanent list.
WEB http://h-devil-www.mc.duke.edu /h-devil

Internet Public Library Teen Division The IPL's teen division offers a social services section covering many issues of concern, including sexuality. It contains a good overview of sexual health sites.
WEB http://aristotle.sils.umich.edu/teen

!OutProud! If you're gay, lesbian, or bisexual, and you want information or affirmation, you have found a friend. !OutProud! can help you discover the non-heterosexual side of the Internet, and provides a forum for getting in touch with other lesbian and gay teens. Heterosexuals can educate themselves, too, about the realities, both problematic and positive, faced by their lesbian and gay peers.
WEB http://www.cyberspaces.com /outproud

Peer Health "Surf-In" Williams College hosts this service dealing with general and sexual health concerns. Although some of the information is aimed directly at Williams College students, most of it is applicable to anyone with a sexual health concern. After all, how different can Williams students be from normal people? This site also offers sound advice on alcohol and drugs, eating and body image issues, and other health concerns.
WEB http://wso.williams.edu/peerh

Rock the System In order to rock the system, you first have to understand the system. These pages are packed with facts about all kinds of health issues that affect young people, especially those concerning sexual activity (pregnancy, STDs, HIV, and AIDS). "Our articles explain where we're at as a country on each of these issues, and how different ideas for healthcare reform might affect [young people]."
WEB http://www.southern.com/RTV

STD Homepage How's your knowledge

of sexually transmitted diseases? Can you name the most common ones? What kind of behavior puts you at risk of getting an STD? Take the quiz to find out how much you really know about AIDS, gonorrhea, syphilis, venereal warts, herpes, and other conditions. If you find that you didn't know much, you can learn more. A warning to the squeamish: the descriptions of STDs are accompanied by some very graphic and slightly disturbing pictures.
WEB http://med-amsa.bu.edu/people /sycamore/std/default.html

Teen Sexuality Going to this site is like visiting a museum with a bunch of really smart friends as your tour guide. In this photo-essay, six teens speak their minds about sexuality in thoughtful and direct language. They are accompanied by short commentaries written by psychologists and suggested questions for discussion. No preaching—or links to support groups—just a lot to look at and think about.
WEB http://www.intac.com/~jdeck /habib/intro/index5.html

WomenSpace The girls at WomenSpace "talk frankly and take no-holds-barred looks at what's important to you—from your love life and sexuality to issues affecting your health and happiness." The site's just like a virtual big sister who will fill you in on the facts, from birth control to the dos and don'ts of shaving. The site dishes the dirt about bad dates, bad roommates, and bad hair. It even takes you shopping at the Grrl Store for everything from tampons to books by and about young women. The site also hosts a regular series of live discussions.
WEB http://www.womenspace.com

▶ TYPING

Al Bunny's Typing Class A downloadable game that teaches and improves typing skills.
WEB http://www.softsite.com/win3/edu /oth/albun12.html

Common Typing Errors So you think you know how to type? Maybe you do, but do you know how to type correctly? Are you perhaps a leaner? Or a clacker? A lounger or a sloucher or a presser? Pictures will help you to determine which, if any, of these risky typing styles is yours. Learn to avoid these errors and you'll never have to find out what RSI stands for.
WEB http://www.esu.edu/LOCAL_WWW /cpsc/rsi/unsafe.html

Mario Teaches Typing That's Mario as in Nintendo. The site amounts to an ad for a fun-sounding way of learning to type. If the thought of Mario teaching you typing excites you, download the demo.
WEB http://www.interplay.com/website /sales/salemari.html

PART 10

Phys. Ed.

GYM CLASS

THE WORLD IS DIVIDED INTO TWO distinct classes: those who don't mind P.E. and those who can't stand it. But however you feel about gym class, at least today's public schools don't force students to wear embarrassing pastel-colored bloomers or absurdly mismatched polyester shirt-and-short sets, as they did a decade ago. Enthusiastic gym classicists are well-plugged in to the Net, with such comprehensive online arenas like the Cyberstadium and America Online's SportsLink. And for those who detest physical activity, the Internet has many resources that can help make gym class seem less of a loathsome chore. A good place to start might be the Newbie's Guide to Sports—gym uniforms aren't required online.

▶ P.E. 101

All Sports.Com "You can't claim to cover all sports without doing just that," exhorts All Sports.Com, and at first glance, it would seem an appropriate boast. If you can't find your sport here, you'll probably find a link that will get you there. This quick-loading, no-frills list links to plenty of team home pages as well as general interest groups. However, a quick buzz through the links reveals a lot of them to be woefully out of date; many either connect to a forwarding page or just don't exist anymore. All the promise and potential fades in a frustrating bout of pointing and clicking.
WEB http://allsports.questtech.com/nfl

America's Sports Headquarters This mammoth-sized site is a well-stocked database of sports on the Web, from fantasy-team pages to sport-employment opportunities to three (count 'em, three) Web pages devoted to Shoeless Joe Jackson. A wide range of sports is available, including such far-flung choices as Broomball and Kinesiology, as well as the standard fare (baseball, football, hockey, and a particularly good collec-

tion of basketball links). There is no original information in this site, only links to other sites. Although it can be a bit difficult to find what you're looking for, as there is no search screen, it's still a great place to start a search for athletic information if a general Web search hasn't turned up what you're looking for.
WEB http://www.csn.net/sport

Awesome Sports Sites Who decides what makes a sports site awesome? You do, at this populist site that compiles visitor's nominations and posts links to the eight most wanted each month. After you visit the nominees (which are none too shabby—recent contenders included America's Sports Headquarters, 1996 Summer Olympics, and Mudball), you can vote for your favorite. Perhaps even more useful are the awards archives, which offers links to other nominated sites, their monthly standings, and full descriptions of each month's winner.
WEB http://www.awesomesports.com

Cyberstadium A comprehensive index to baseball, basketball, football, ice hockey, soccer, golf, tennis, and other sports sites, Cyberstadium covers all the bases. Creator Michael Van Hoek's basketball page carves up the Basketball Server by team and division for the latest information, and offers a handful of related hoop sites. Van Hoek also makes it easy to find Cyberstadium's newest entries (check out his New Sports Sites page), and offers links to such hot sites as ESPNET SportsZone, CNN International Sports, and Sports Spectator.
WEB http://www.interlog.com/~mvanhoek /cyber-stadium/cybrstad.html

The Newbie's Guide to Sports An offshoot of Steve's Page, Steve Franklin's comprehensive (and generally pretty good) guide to the Internet, Newbie's Guide to Sports unfortunately suffers from low maintenance. At first glance, one might consider it to be a no-frills connecting point to a panoply of sports-

related Web sites—including such sports as skydiving and auto racing—but click around and most of what you'll find are a lot of outdated addresses. Perhaps this exercise in futility is precisely the author's ironic intention.
WEB http://www.ug.cs.dal.ca/pub/sports .html

Physical Education Resources A graphics-free list of P.E. links. Includes such handy sources as the Abdominal Training FAQ, the Endurance Training Journal, and a game to develop tennis skills.
WEB http://www.iac.net/~buckrich/phys .html

Sport World Where else can you go to find the North American Orienteering home page, sail with the Goowla Regatta (wasn't that a song from *The Lion King*?) Yacht Club of Australia, or catch the latest Hong Kong soccer results? Featuring a point-and-click map of the world to connect you to the sporting events of various continents, Sport World is an easy-to-use and refreshingly cosmopolitan connection to international sports. Coverage of Olympics sites is also featured, and external submissions are encouraged.
WEB http://susis.ust.hk/~danny/sport /sport.html

Sports Illustrated Online Just what you'd expect from the leading sports magazine, *SI*'s Web site provides news, scores, and statistics for football, baseball, basketball, hockey, tennis, and golf. To illustrate: The Hockey page gives league news, game previews, box scores, game recaps, team-by-team stats, and the latest league standings. You can also do your basic magazine business here, such as subscribing, ordering back issues, reading previous cover stories, and sending letters to the editor—and yes, there are swimsuit shots, including some never-before-seen pix.
WEB http://pathfinder.com/si/greet.html

Sportsline USA SportsLine is best known for its involvement with Joe Namath and Mike Schmidt; both host

forums here. But the site also boasts play-by-play recaps and close-to-real-time updates on all major games, breaking stories, and compiled statistics. The site is Java-enabled and hosts regular columns from scores of major newspaper columnists, so even if you're far from your favorite team, you're in the midst of home-team hysteria. To get all of SportsLine's benefits, though, you have to pay. Many features are open to subscribers only.
WEB http://www.sportsline.com

SportsLink The first stop at America Online for any sports-related information. SportsLink features every connection from ABC Sports to the World Wide Wrestling Federation, plus a generous list of magazines and forums, and a full schedule of chat.
AMERICA ONLINE *keyword* sportslink

Sportsworld: The Stadium Connections to SportsChannel's local team news and to NewSport's national sports network both offer news, stats, and other miscellaneous sports info. Contests, chat rooms, and interviews are also promised, as are pre- and post-game summaries that will utilize new technology to avoid the standard long downloads.
WEB http://sportsworld.line.com

Sportz Internet University offers a refreshingly broad look at sports on its Sportz page. You'll find news on major professional sports as well as good stuff about alternative sports like sky diving, snow boarding, rock climbing, mountain biking, water polo, racquetball, cricket, broomball, hacky sack, and Korfball. Never heard of Korfball? All the more reason to check this page out.
WEB http://www.internetuniv.com /sportsz2/index.htm

Sportzine The fact that this zine is on the @Toyota site is both good and bad: good because they have money to make it look good, bad because you're barraged with Toyota ads. If you can get past that, check it out for regular, family-

oriented features on topics like balancing the life of a parent/ coach, "hell holes" (the toughest miniature golf holes in America), and training advice for the couch-potato-turned-weekend-warrior, as well as fantasy league information and sporting-gear reviews.
WEB http://www.toyota.com/hub/sportzinecover

USA Today Sports *USA Today*'s traditional sports formula works great on the Web. Great graphics (and quick at 28.8 kbps), a lot of color, and all the sports news you could want without the price tag of *SportsZone* and *SportsLine*. This site also boasts a wealth of team-by-team statistics, schedules, and commentary. If you pick up the print version of *USA Today* for the sports section, you'll love this site. It's everything the paper version is—only free.
WEB http://www.usatoday.com/sports/sfront.htm

Wide Web of Sports Eye-catching and in-your-face, this is an excellent destination for hard-core fans. The emphasis here is on baseball, basketball, hockey, and football—big surprise. Its best feature, the Players Personal Page, allows you to view snazzy pics of your fave player, read up on his stats and bio, and even send him email (perhaps to tell him not to screw up in the next game). The Autograph Central Store hawks signatures, collectibles, and the usual sports merchandise. At the Cyber Sports Auction you can bid for a chance to meet top players, such as Braves pitcher John Smoltz. Upon completion of reconstruction, Wide Web promises post-game chat sessions with coaches and players.
WEB http://www.wwwsports.com

Women in Sports A site comprised of the biographies and personal stories of female athletes and their experiences. Although it could be more comprehensive (for instance, Women in Bowling offers a single link), Women in Sports lets you search by name or by sport (including some entries you wouldn't immediately consider, like auto racing,

kayaking, rugby, and rodeo); read heartfelt accounts from female athletes discussing joy, fear, discrimination, role models, and motherhood; and browse a reading list of books, periodicals, and special-interest documents. One of the pages' most prominent links connects you to The Sports Pages by Amy Lewis, the ultimate guide to women's sport pages on the Web.
WEB http://www.mother.com/~asw/skywomen

Women Sports This well-laid-out site covers sports that involve women, mostly on the collegiate level, including volleyball, basketball, skating (figure and speed), soccer, softball, gymnastics, golf, and tennis, as well as a mysterious section called Athletics (which consists of mostly track and field). Each sport is represented by a selection of news items, opinion pieces, schedules, and statistics, although for some of them the information is a bit scant.
WEB http://www.womensports.com

▶ TEACHERS' LOUNGE

k12.ed.health-pe A rather infrequently visited forum for grade-level physical education teachers to discuss topics ranging from the side effects of the job (e.g., shingles) to supplemental income opportunities for those who wish to "stop coaching spoiled high school brats." One rather unimaginative gym teacher asked for help on what to do with old tennis rackets. The obvious reply? "Donate them to the art teacher."
USENET k12.ed.health-pe

National Association for Sport and Physical Education NASPE is an association of more than 18,000 physical education, sport, fitness, and kinesiology professionals whose goal is to promote quality physical activity programs. Its Web site contains outlines of the national standards for physical education and athletic coaches, materials for legislators, and updates on NASPE activities.
WEB http://www.aahperd.org/naspe.html

BALLS

I N THE MOVIE *CLUELESS,* ONE OF the Beverly Hills high schoolers attempts to get out of gym class by whining that her plastic surgeon doesn't want her to play any sports involving balls flying into her face. Of course, the sport she was forbidden to play was tennis, which leads us to the question of why all sports involving balls do not have the suffix "ball." Soccer is another sport which does not contain the suffix "ball" and yet is played with a ball (not to mention the fact that in England the same sport is called football). Sometimes the sports world makes little sense, but what do you expect from a bunch of jocks? For a bit of insight, make a cyberstop at The Dugout, take a scenic drive along The Basketball Highway, have a ball at any age with Slow-pitch Softball, drop in at The Kop, set yourself up at Volleyball Worldwide, or just watch with the computers at Computers Watching Football.

▶ BASEBALL

Baseball Fans passionate about baseball debate great plays, key stats, the direction of baseball, and the likelihood that their favorite players will become tomorrow's baseball legends. Or, perhaps like Dave, they come looking for movie suggestions—baseball movies that aren't just about baseball, but about life. So far, he only has *Field of Dreams.* Eddie suggests *Fear Strikes Out.* Rod tosses in *It Happens Every Spring, Bang the Drum Slowly, The Natural,* and *Bull Durham.* Lance mentions *Angels in the Outfield.* In another topic, dozens of fans are speculating on the best all-time defensive team. And still in another topic, fans are trying to answer a trivia question: What were the three monuments in the old Yankee Stadium? Answer: plaques to Mantle, DiMaggio, and Pope Paul VI. The Pontiff, apparently, had a mean slider.
COMPUSERVE *go* fans→Messages→Baseball

Baseball History Newsletter With scores of avid readers, this newsletter is the definitive place in cyberspace for historically minded fans of academic inclination. Brett is writing his senior thesis on baseball during the Civil War. Sue is writing a paper comparing George Will's theory on the designated hitter rule with conservative and liberal ideals. A baseball history professor in Ausburg, now blind, remembers Blackwell's 16-game winning streak and Williams's career climax (a home run in his final at-bat). *The Baseball History Newsletter* publishes statistical trivia in every issues as well as a sampling of reader contributions.
EMAIL godux@teleport.com ✍ *Write a request*

Baseball Library CompuServe gives you a library filled with trivia quizzes, team logos, stats management shareware programs, Little League scheduling software, historical stats databases, Major League Baseball schedules, rulebooks, proposals for fan strikes, player interviews, and—get this—even baseball poetry.
COMPUSERVE *go* baseball library→Libraries →Baseball

The Dugout Smart, quick use of graphics make this site disarming from the get-go. Baseball fans can find information about (and links to) their favorite major league teams as well as the Little League, the Baseball Hall of Fame in Cooperstown, N.Y., other sports sites, tips on coaching, fantasy leagues, where to find hard-to-get tickets, and how to buy tickets online. If you like baseball, this site belongs on your bookmark list.
WEB http://www.elee.calpoly.edu/~sware /baseball.html

The Dugout Cincinnati Reds fans speculate about the depth of their pitching staff on the Professional Baseball message board while would-be baseball managers build teams for AOL's Fantasy

Baseball League. Clemson and Rice fans argue about the NCAA pennant race on the College Baseball message board and gamers with baseball simulators play in the forum's ongoing simulation league, raiding the library for files of favorite ballparks and memorable games. And while they're in the library, fans collect images of Ty Cobb, Yaz, Roberto Clemente, and the Yankees logo. This elaborate baseball resource and entertainment center also features team schedues, baseball news, and live baseball chat.

AMERICA ONLINE *keyword* gs→Baseball

Internet Baseball Archive Web Page An archive of baseball information, including schedules, statistical analyses (e.g., The Davenport Translations), archives of the hypertext magazine for baseball, *Online Drive*, and the baseball FAQ. The archive also carries a small collection of links to other baseball Web sites.

WEB http://www.baseball.org/baseball

John Skilton's Baseball Links This handsome and extensive catalog of baseball links—almost 1,000, and growing daily—is a must for all boys and girls of summer. Every imaginable aspect of baseball—buying and selling, fantasy/rotisserie leagues, official and unofficial team hangouts, trivia contests—are all represented in this obvious creation of a high priest in the church of baseball.

WEB http://www.pc-professor.com/baseball

rec.sport.baseball Whether analyzing lineups, debating the merits of interleague play, advocating or trashing players up for election to the Baseball Hall of Fame, or discussing last night's game, the newsgroup garners hundreds of messages from baseball fans every couple of days.

USENET rec.sport.baseball

The National High School Baseball Coaches Association Home page for the national organization dedicated to promoting high school baseball. Carries articles from its newsletter, high school baseball rankings, and extensive information about the association.

WEB http://www.highways.com/baseball

Society for American Baseball Research Want to know the email address for your favorite baseball team—or all of them, for that matter? Been wondering how you could get your hands on perhaps the greatest baseball essays ever written? How about a complete guide to the American Baseball Archives and Wax Museum? Among this baseball-scholar site's features: An index of, and musings on, the greatest ballparks (major and minor leagues), trivia, links to the Society for American Baseball Research (SABR), and a baseball-only search engine.

WEB http://www.skypoint.com/sub scribers/ashbury/_hhdir/hhhotlinks.html

▶ BASKETBALL

The Basketball Highway Former college player and coach Alan Lambert has made a site for basketball coaches at any level, whether you're in the pee-wee league or varsity. Lambert has created an effective virtual community for players and coaches, providing job listings, basketball camp information, coaching articles, downloads, links to software providers, and anything else you might need. With pleasing graphics (a nice wood-tone background—the basketball imagery is toned down) and a very user-friendly, simple format, TBH is ideal for those who feel more comfortable with the basketball net than the Internet.

WEB http://bbhighway.com

The Journal of Basketball Studies Every Monday, fans across the country get together to discuss which NBA player should be traded and why. Now, Web master Dean Turcoliver, a former college-level player with a Ph.D., has unleashed his statistical formula for trading players upon an unsuspecting world (get out your slide rules). Most of the results, he says, are surprisingly "counter-intuitive." This professional-

looking site makes a science—the titular Basketball Studies—out of the various statistics and strategies of the game. Analytical articles and an online book, *Hoopla*, make this a complete resource for those who would take the guesswork out of the sport.
WEB http://cmr.sph.unc.edu/~deano /bball/index.html

Off the Glass/Basketball When basketball fans talk, they talk the way that basketball players play—with style. Some people favor the inside game, lots of capital letters and arguments of indisuptable authority ("JORDAN IS ONE OF THE GREATS!"). Others wheel, whirl, and slash, always keeping an eye out for the unseen opening ("Do you think that the Heat could package off another set of trades to get Steve Smith back? It might take some dealing, but it would be worthwhile"). And then there are the perimeter shooters, the message board regulars who deliver their opinions with a certain aloofness, relying on statistics and conventional wisdom rather than passion. As Sly Stone once said, "It takes all kinds."
AMERICA ONLINE *keyword* gs→Basketball

On Hoops Love talking, thinking, and reading basketball? Go here, now! These guys ("Los Chucks") definitely have too much free time on their hands—or too little else on their minds—but their loss (of mental health and social survival) is the gain of every true basketball fanatic. Hear inside information; read and post theorizing and gossip on such topics as Nellie's departure from the Knicks, the Lakers' bump epidemic, and Rachel meeting her basketball hero; or vote for the chump of all times. It all goes both ways—everybody here loves not only the game but the culture of basketball, and they speak personality fluently.
WEB http://www.onhoops.com

▶ **FOOTBALL**

Allsports Football Hotlist When you need football information, you need football information. You don't want to sit around mulling over the issues, reconsidering, wondering to yourself whether or not your obsession with the pigskin is indicative of a deep-seated resentment of vinyl. You want hard data, and lots of it. And you'll find all you need at the Allsports Football Hotlist, which links to dozens of the best football sites on the Web—not only one-stop-shopping sites such as the Nando football server and Satchel Sports but individual team pages.
WEB http://allsports.questtech.com/nfl /football.html

Computers Watching Football It's hard enough to track football players and their moves with human beings behind the video camera. But can a computer be taught to do it better and even label what it films? Maybe, if it is programmed with the rules of the game and a history of common plays. This is the sort of artificial intelligence research conducted at MIT's Media Lab, and this page houses ongoing results.
WEB http://www-white.media.mit.edu /vismod/demos/football/football.html

Football Get your fill of pigskin in AOL's football area, which includes a wide variety of message boards, libraries, and news services devoted to the game that brought new meaning to the phrase "illegal motion." Start out talking NFL at the pro football message board, then relive your days rooting for Notre Dame or Nebraska on the college football message board. And if you've chatted until you just can't chat anymore, check out the scores, news, and especially the file libraries, which are filled with .GIFs of team logos, rosters, and even some wonderful multimedia clips.
AMERICA ONLINE *keyword* gs→Football

Football Mostly NFL in the Pro Football topic, as you might expect, and mostly offseason chat that veers between awe and disgust over the way that free agency has changed the game. "Every year it's like the league gets a total facelift," writes one fan. "And while I was repulsed by it at first—it seemed

like a betrayal of everything that football is supposed to be, hometown heroes and stable teams to root for—now I think it's the most exciting thing to happen in sports in many years."
COMPUSERVE *go* fans→Libraries *or* Messages→Football

Football Central Ode to the Gridiron. Football Central was designed, say its makers, for people who are sick of going back and forth to Yahoo! to get football scores. It boasts links to the NFL, arena football, the CFL, and the World League, as well as to the football pages of many major universities, high schools, and some of the best fantasy sports sites. Best viewed with Netscape 2.0 and Java, Football Central is neat, clean, quick, and worth a look.
WEB http://www.dnai.com/~foley/football central

rec.sport.football.misc "Well, my friend wanted me to post this. He is 5'11" and 220 lbs. He doesn't have that great of hands. He also is not that strong right now. He wants me to ask how he can improve himself to make our school JV team? He also wants to know how he can get stronger." Wannabes and pigskinoholics alike turn up in this newsgroup, which is mainly comprised of a group of men talking about what floats their boats most—football.
USENET rec.sport.football.misc

World Wide Virtual Library: Football Get your tea and crumpets ready, because a great reference site for American football pages is based in the United Kingdom. Since "football" overseas is "soccer" in the States, "American football" is something of a growing cult sport in Europe. The page's designers have picked an excellent array of football sites on this side of the Atlantic to feature, and they also offer an intriguing index to European teams. Ever wondered about the fortunes of the Graz Giants or the Dublin Tornadoes? The team statistics have to be seen to be believed.
WEB http://www.atm.ch.cam.ac.uk/sports /gridiron.html

> **SOCCER**

International Soccer Cybertour True to its name, International Soccer Cybertour will take you around the World Wide Web, Usenet, and beyond in order to find the soccer resource or article you're looking for. ISC is good for the professional soccer enthusiast, amateur, coach, or parent. An abundance of background art can make some pages slow at lower speeds, but at 28.8 bps, the art adds a great deal to the site, making it much more interesting. The proprietary search engine works well.
WEB http://www.cybergoal.com/soccer

The Kop/Soccer Named after an area of Liverpool Stadium, this center for things soccer has an area for discussion, news, and files. You don't have to head down to Merseyside to find home team chat. The message boards are full of patriots from around the world painstakingly dissecting the efforts of favorite players. Blackburn believes the Rovers have the season sewn up: Do you? Muse on the future of football. Will high salaries remove players from their working class roots just like baseball did? Or dispute an offside call: "It was a push against Shearer when he headed square across the box!" Every country has its own message folder or folders. Don't miss the action.
AMERICA ONLINE *keyword* gs→Soccer

Pure Web No soccer-related site in cyberspace has missed being caught in Pure Web. Start out with up-to-the-hour scores provided by Premier League Soccer Results and clarify the name of the goalkeeper for Italy in the '72 World Cup at the International Soccer Server. There are links to club pages from the Tottenham Hotsputs to the Zurich Grasshoppers; and competitions from the mod Coca Cola Cup to the venerable European Cup. Last but not least, there are links to a U.S. TV soccer programming schedule and an FAQ about the World Cup.
WEB http://www.atm.ch.cam.ac.uk/sports /webs.html

rec.sport.soccer This newsgroup is sometimes as much a political science primer as a site for soccer discussion. In the midst of a Croatian supporter's tussle with a Slavonia fan comes a discussion of just what happened to those Yugoslav players when the country split up. If you take note of the vituperative accusations of hooliganism flying among fans, it's obvious that the union of England and Scotland under James I (VI) in 1603 has yet to take root. Someone will always be here willing to rate players, share stories of the most unusual goals and greatest games, and wonder fearfully about the future of Van Basten's ankle. Sven wonders, "does beating Nigeria mean more than beating Estonia?" Enquiring soccer minds want to know.
USENET rec.sport.soccer

rec.sport.soccer—The Web Page A massive soccer site with links to the newsgroup, a multi-page list of mailing lists for soccer fans from Austria to South Africa, a hypertext guide to the British FA Premiership (bookmaker's odds, a list of up-and-coming players, top scorers, "bad boys," and links to the team pages), FIFA rules, soccer terminology, and a list of FTP sites with Football Manager computer games.
WEB http://www.atm.ch.cam.ac.uk/sports

Soccer Flash: Qatar is replacing Nigera in the World Youth Championships. Check here for all the latest news from the world of soccer, courtesy of Reuters. There are news flashes, in-depth match analyses, and even player gossip.
AMERICA ONLINE *keyword* sports→ Choose a Sport→Soccer

Soccer America Online Goooaaalll! Soccer America Online is good-looking, well-organized, and has both domestic and international coverage. This electronic version of the soccer-based news weekly is a lot more interesting than your average magazine, with substantial interactivity—plus a super-cool place where you can ask the editors questions. It shoots, it scores.
WEB http://www.sportsite.com/SA

Soccer Games If you can't join 'em, then pretend to be their manager. Downloadable soccer games place you in the role of a manager trying to get his team as far from the bottom of the league as possible. These PC-only games are addicitve and give you the choice of playing Italian, German, Scottish, or English soccer team managers.
WEB http://www.atm.ch.cam.ac.uk/sports /games.html

United States Soccer Federation Soccer's on an upswing, so why isn't this page? Where's the beefcake pic of Tab Ramos? In spite of some of the most heinous presentation and horrible design on the Web, this is a decent place to get information about American soccer, detailing the activity of the men's and women's teams and offering a play-by-play of many games.
WEB http://users.aol.com/socfed

▶ **SOFTBALL**

Amateur Softball Association Did you know that softball is America's newest Olympic sport? The ASA's 4.5 million members are very proud of that fact. The organization's home page boasts more information about the sport, including its history and team stats, plus links to *USA Softball Magazine* and the ASA Hall of Fame.
WEB http://www.softball.org

Fastpitch Softball Life's a pitch at this Web site devoted to fastpitch softball, complete with links to all modes of the sport, including amateur, college, men's, women's Olympic, and more.
WEB http://www.mcs.net/~sluggers /softball.html

Slow-pitch Softball "People of all ages play softball. Young children play softball. Middle-aged adults play softball. They have 35 and older slow-pitch softball leagues. There are 45 and older slow-pitch softball leagues. There are 55 and older slow-pitch softball leagues. I have even read about a blind softball league." But what's the difference

between fastpitch and slow-pitch softball? Perhaps the answer is obvious, but find out for sure at this Web site, which contains links to tips, tricks, and info on new equipment.
WEB http://ux1.cso.uiuc.edu/~j-danner

▶ VOLLEYBALL

rec.sport.volleyball Did anyone see the Ball State men's volleyball team during their appearance on *The Price is Right*? Does anyone have any experience with torn tendons? Can anyone think of any really wild (but perfectly legal) plays? This newsgroup covers all levels of volleyball, from professsional to high school, from indoor to beach. When not concerned with serve reception tactics, jumping shoes, and tournament announcements, the group's participants sometimes veer into odder areas, such as this agonized, if not exactly lucid, lament by a high-school v-ball coach: "We coaches have to be very careful. Can you believe that you can be successfully sued by a player for not teaching them everything you said you would. If I tell Molly Middle-hitter that I'll teach her how to set and I'm unsuccessful, regardless of the reason, she can sue my tail off for 'breach of verbal contract' or something like that."
USENET rec.sport.volleyball

Volleyball Can Stanford go undefeated this season? Why did Karch Kiraly fall off the grandstand while receiving his trophy at a tournament? While the talk on this maessage board tends toward the crushingly specific—top players at local leagues in Venice Beach and Texas—there's a lot of activity and enthusiasm.
AMERICA ONLINE *keyword* grandstand→ Sports Message Boards→Other Sports →Volleyball

Volleyball News from around the volleyball world—match results, tournament announcements, and even the occasional obituary, such as a report on the death of Russian-born star Andrei Kuznetsov in Chieti, Italy.

AMERICA ONLINE *keyword* sports→Choose a Sport→Volleyball

Volleyball Worldwide According to the home page, Volleyball Worldwide is "an attempt to centralize information on the sport of volleyball." In addition to a wealth of general documents about the sport—everything from team names to volleyball stats to lists of books and magazines—the page has a number of more specific categories on international volleyball associations such as Federation Internationale de Volley-Ball (FIVB), and the United States Volley Ball Association (USVBA).
WEB http://www.volleyball.org

RACKETS & PADDLES

IF ALL THE GUNS IN THE WORLD were replaced with rackets and paddles, the world might be a safer place—although it would be a lot harder to get court time at the public park, and that could lead to some nasty fist fights. In fact, competitive sports were invented as a more civilized form of war. Thus we have ping-pong diplomacy, the Olympics, and the "friendly" game of tennis to assert superiority over conniving little brothers. The Internet can certainly improve your standing, with its many resources devoted to racket sports. The Badminton Home Page is a good place to bat the shuttlecock around, while The Code of Tennis helps you play by the rules. They don't call it the Net for nothing.

▶ BADMINTON

The Badminton Home Page Brought to you "as a service to the world's badminton community," and opening with the New Age/medieval-style logo of the Unicorn Badminton Club, this heavily text-focused site lists links and more links. Learn everything from the laws of badminton to how a shuttle is made. There's a directory of international badminton organizations, practical advice on running a competition, training and coaching advice, and badminton humor. Correct behavior is encouraged: "The Unicorn Badminton Club believes that it is important that the sporting image of the game is maintained and therefore expects members to play in white…" Or else.
WEB http://mid1.external.hp.com/stanb/badminton.html

▶ RACQUETBALL

AARA Racquetball Rules Is your racquetball partner driving you to distraction with delays on his serve? Then visit this site and dazzle him with a recitation of the Official American Amateur Racquetball Association Rules: "Except as noted in Rule 4.5(b), delays exceeding ten seconds shall result in an out if the server is the offender or a point if the receiver is the offender…" Want the lowdown on how to resolve conflicts over hinders? It's here, too.
WEB http://www.cs.washington.edu/homes/rex/rb/aara.html

alt.sport.racquetball Big in the United States, slightly less popular in less enlightened nations (Britain, for example, where they still call gasoline "petrol" and use it to drive their cars on the wrong side of the road), racquetball has a fairly interesting newsgroup that can fairly be called unpopulated. Between questions about floor coverings and top-of-the-line equipment ("How will the Helix compare to my Mirada? Will I be disappointed or will I never notice the difference?"), the group lists racquetball tournaments and tips, and occasionally posts updates to the FAQ.
USENET alt.sport.racquetball

Racquetball FAQ General questions, techniques, and rules for the sport of kings. What racquetball videotapes are available? Are there any good mail order supply houses for racquetball aficionados in the boondocks? And what happens if you bust your racket over an opponent's head and the strings make that "whang, whang, whang" noise as they do in cartoons?
WEB http://www.mcs.com/~toma/www/files/rqb.faq

Tom Arneberg's Racquetball Page As sparse and gray as a racquetball court, Tom's page offers straight text with few visual surprises. That's fine if you're looking for FAQs and figures, upcoming tournament dates, and an interesting "ladder algorithm" for determining racquetball rankings, because all the straight dope on the sport is certainly here. For flashier stuff, use this page for its many links to other, more graphically-enhanced racquetball spots on the Web.

web http://www.mcs.com/~toma/www
/pages/rqb.html

SQUASH

alt.sport.squash How beloved is
squash? How hard is it to become an
expert? Will Michael Jordan leave basketball to join the squash circuit? Rankings,
tournament announcements, tips from
veteran players to beginners, and even
the occasional squash recipe crowd this
newsgroup, which also includes the
occasional odd posting—a writer for a
national deaf newspaper seeking a picture of deaf squash champ Rebecca
Macree.
usenet alt.sport.squash

Internet Squash Players' Association
The home page for the Internet Squash
Foundation aims to promote this racket
activity as "the leisure sport of the
future." ISPA links to sites in Canada,
Southeast Asia, and Britain, and also
archives articles relating to squashy
matters.
web http://www.ncl.ac.uk/~npb

Squash Rules As every fan of the sport
knows, squash rules! Seriously, though,
this document explains the ins and outs
of the world's second-favorite racket
sport. Here's a quick quiz: What's it
called when the ball, after being served
and before it has bounced more than
once on the floor and before it has been
struck at by the receiver, touches the
server or anything he wears or carries
(yes, girdles count)? Answer: "Down."
The excitement never stops.
web http://ptoon.ccit.arizona.edu/NMSRA
/Rules.html

TABLE TENNIS

rec.sport.table-tennis For no apparent
reason someone's compiling a list of
famous Barrys in ping-pong, and Tubby
has another name to add to the list—
Rutledge Barry, former U.S. Junior
Champion from the 1970s, made the
semifinals of the U.S. Nationals in 1978
or 1979, now semiretired, but still

ranked in the top 30. There are listings
of tournaments, tips on play, and even
posts about table-tennis demographics
("At the place where I work, the population of table tennis players are 80% blue
collar and 20% white collar").
usenet rec.sport.table-tennis

Table Tennis FAQ As FAQs go, they don't
get much more businesslike than this
one, which has information on rankings,
players associations, scoring, and the
terminology of the game (ball, racket,
and the ever-popular speedglue). Did
you know that in Spanish this sport is
called *el tenis de la mesa*, which translates literally as "the tennis of the table"?
web http://peacock.tnjc.edu.tw/ADD
/sport/faq.html

**WWW of Sports—Table Tennis (Ping
Pong)** Based in Taiwan, this site links to
the Usenet newsgroup for table tennis,
and also includes results and capsule
summaries of action from important
table tennis events worldwide.
web http://peacock.tnjc.edu.tw/sports
.html

TENNIS

alt.tennis Not nearly as active as
rec.sport.tennis. The crowd's younger
here, or so it seems: You're likely to find
netheads who quote Stone Temple Pilots
and Queen. That's not to say the group's
devoid of tennis discussion. Take Steve,
for instance, who brought his concern
about the purported "decline" of tennis
to the newsgroup: "What should the
powers that be in the world of tennis do
or promote to build enthusiasm for tennis and interest in it among a broader
audience? What can they do to entice
more people to start playing, especially
kids?"
usenet alt.tennis

The Code of Tennis This guide covers
customs and traditions not covered in
the tennis rule book, like what to do
when you're not sure a ball is in or out
("your opponent gets the benefit of the
doubt").

WEB http://www.tennisserver.com/code .html

rec.sport.tennis If you say Agassi's a boring player, don't plan to walk away from this group flame-free. "Get a life, buddy," one fan replied. Another praised Agassi for playing "rock 'n roll tennis." O.K., enough about Agassi. Didn't you know that "Sampras is God." Fan talk aside, there are a lot of serious discussions, like the one about whether you get more power with looser strings, and the thread about the sexiest woman player. Fan talk isn't easy to keep on the sidelines here.
USENET rec.sport.tennis

The Rules of Tennis The official rules of tennis—the code of the International Tennis Federation—are divided into sections on singles, doubles, and wheelchair tennis. Everything's here, from the simple rules everyone knows, even if you've never played—e.g., "the players shall stand on opposite sides of the net"—to the more arcane details, like the size and weight of the ball (between 6.35 and 6.67centimeters and 56.7 and 58.5 grams). The code certainly comes in handy for resolving common disputes, like what to do when the ball hits a permanent fixture or how to score a tiebreaker. Unfortunately, most people don't have courtside Web access.
WEB http://www.tennisserver.com/rules .html

Tennis Country Describing itself as "the total tennis site on the Internet," Tennis Country is packed with information, but is plagued by intro screens at every level: Using it feels like walking through all the doors in the opening-credits sequence of the old *Get Smart* TV show. The info, once you get to it, is good, and the graphics, once they load, are equally impressive. You enter this site, which fancies itself a club, by signing up as a member or by visiting as a guest. Once inside, the areas of interest include a playing-hint library, fitness tips, and a guide to resorts and camps where tennis is celebrated and elevated.

WEB http://www.tenniscountry.com

Tennis Forum An eclectic and interesting spot for online tennis bums, with talk of everything from tennis drills to broken strings. Special areas of the forum focus on events, trivia, equipment, and players' bios. The libraries offer a diverse selection of tennis resources, including results, lists of tennis camps, info on resorts, and a Tip of the Week.
COMPUSERVE *go* tennis

The Tennis Server An atmospheric painting of a tennis racquet and a palm tree greets all the netheads who visit to this attractive site, which is anchored by links to the best tennis info on the Web. Aside from the usual info on equipment and rankings, you'll find .GIFs of Steffi Graf, Michael Chang, Stefan Edberg, and others, along with a Player Tip of the Month, offering detailed advice on such topics as the role of the server's partner in doubles.
WEB http://www.tennisserver.com/Tennis .html

Tennis Web A listing of links to everything tennis on the Web, with a handy look at latest additions, Tennis Web offers brief but helpful insights into what to expect at each site. Categories include tennis camps, fan pages, FAQs, newsgroups, resorts and hotels, and travel and weather. It's a fine starting point for novices and longtime tennis devotees. Learn to play like a pro.
WEB http://www.xmission.com/~gastown /tennis/tweb.htm

STICKS & CLUBS

MANY COMPETITIVE SPORTS evolved from the primitive rituals of our distant ancestors. Archery originated as a mode of hunting. Croquet was first played with dried animal bones. Golf was once a form of networking among Neanderthal tribes. And hockey—well—hockey really hasn't changed much. The Internet, a modern incarnation of smoke signalling, provides many ways to get in touch with your more basic instincts. You can aim at the bull's eye at Traditional Archery, check in at Hockey, or take a stab at rec.sport.fencing.

▶ ARCHERY

alt.archery Traditionalists and non-traditionalists talk bowstrings and feathers on this newsgroup, but beware the political twists in which the group can sometimes become embroiled. Politics in the archery community can be vicious, and the direction of archery in the U.S. and the balance of power among different archery organizations are often the subjects of bitter debates here. But equipment and technique are not overlooked either. Are feathers better than vanes? The group's divided evenly. Which is better: right or left helicol? "Doesn't matter" was the overwhelming response. "I've shot 5-inch feathers and vanes, 4-inch feathers and vanes and 3-inch feathers. The helical provides spin, just like the rifling in a gun barrell, which makes them inherently more accurate," explains Stephen of the Maurice Thompson Archery Association.
USENET alt.archery
FAQ: WEB http://rtfm.mit.edu/pub/usenet/alt.archery/

Archery Bow benders inspired about upcoming 3-D shoots discuss techniques and equipment. But, bowhunters, despite the no-hunting-discussions rule, account for most of the messages here. Writes one excited archer, "I think the 3-D helps your shooting of course but also

helps your mind get on track for the HUNT! Let's talk trigger vs. release."
AMERICA ONLINE *keyword* grandstand→ Sports Message Board→Other Sports→ List topics→Archery

Archery Michael is trying to figure out what he should use as a backstop when shooting broadheads (the arrows are real pain to get out of hay bales). Other archers are chatting about equipment, stories, and technique. And then there's Ted, who believes that there are about 380,000 bowhunters in Michigan and assumes some credit for the impressive number—he's done a lot to publicize the sport in Michigan. Archery has a lot of public advocates in this forum.
COMPUSERVE *go* outdoorforum→ Messages→Archery

Archery on the Internet An aptly-titled comprehensive list of online archery resources, broken down by country, with a special section set aside for Olympic archery pages. A brief summary of each site is given to help you find exactly what you're seeking. The list itself tells an interesting story—whereas the rest of the world (in particular the United Kingdom), is mostly interested in the particular challenges of the sport and in mastering the skills involved through tournaments and the like, America's numerous sites seem mostly concerned with the process of killing big (and not-so-big) game—then boasting about it online.
WEB http://www.ilinkgn.net/commercl/author/links.htm

rec.sport.archery A recent poster to this newsgroup wrote worriedly: "I have heard many horror stories, such as the bow collapsing and causing serious injury to legs, face, etc. Any truth to this???" He came to the right place. This is a devoted group of people, serious in their pursuit of the finest equipment, stance, and score. The members of this well-versed newsgroup can provide illumination into any facet of the sport

imaginable.
USENET rec.sport.archery

Traditional Archery Devoted to archers who hunt, the topic includes both traditionalist and compound bowhunters. Messages are exchanged about stalking versus standing hunting and equipment ("Right now I'm experimenting with arrow woods. I've tried cedar and yellow pine so far. I believe that arrow wood is more of a preference that an accuracy question"), but the division between the two camps is a diverse topic that just won't die.
AMERICA ONLINE *keyword* grandstand→ Sports Message Boards→Outdoor Sports→List Topics→Traditional Archery

▶ CRICKET

CricInfo-The Cricket Database Absolutely everything anyone anywhere ever wanted to know about cricket, stuffed in 7,459 files in 786 directories. Included in this vast collection are the latest news, tour schedules and scorecards, as well as cricket articles from papers and magazines around the world. The depth of cricket trivia contained here is amazing—everything from the results of the first match in 1877 to a play-by-play of today's test match. You can learn who won the toss in the India/Australia match in 1947 (India), view maps of cricket grounds across the world, or consult profiles of the best bowlers and fielders. The whole site can be searched by keyword for fact-finding ease. For a light-hearted break from fact gathering, check out the humor section: "There once was a bowler from Hampshire…" Also featured are cricket rules, information on the IRC channel, FTP and WWW links, and pictures.
URL gopher://cricinfo.cse.ogi.edu:7070/11/link_to_database

RSC Test Cricket Home Page Apparently, it took an American cricket-o-phile to make a truly fun page on this perplexing sport. If you have Windows, download the "pretty darn statistically accurate" cricket simulator. If you're like the guy who created the site—desperate to play his favorite game in the cricketless U.S.—this home page will at least permit you the vicarious satisfaction of making up teams of your favorite players and pitting them against one another. You can even coach your team and see whether your strategies help or hurt. No Windows available? You can still play via email or check the links to other cricket sites.
WEB http://www.epix.net/~brett/cricket.html

Ultra Cricket Born in Sussex, living in Utah, and missing a good game of cricket? Well, don't think about ending it all with a final-exit swim in the Great Salt Lake. Instead, alleviate your homesickness through Ultra Cricket, the world's premier cricket simulation. The site explains how the game is run and provides information on getting started with a team of your own. Be a manager, field a team of players with varying skill profiles, and watch your players either gain skills or lose agility with age. Don't worry about a lack of competition—there are already 72 teams playing.
WEB http://diana.ecs.soton.ac.uk/~ta/uc_home.html

The Wonderful World of Cricket It's always a wonderful day at this site, which is packed with links to cricket sites across the world. Search all the links for your favorite player or team, or add to the fun by using the on-site template for submitting links.
WEB http://wwwmbb.cs.colorado.edu/~mcbryan/bb/22/22/summary.html

▶ CROQUET

American Croquet Rules Have you ever seen the movie *Heathers*? Remember that game those nasty girls would play? That was croquet, and it's not always a way of showing up your friends—in fact, fans know it as a somewhat quaintly old-fashioned diversion and one of the world's most endearing, if not romantic, lawn games. This document contains a complete set of rules for the American version of the game.

web http://clarisse.wustl.edu/~brian/Croquet/rules.html

The Virtual Greensward You're not the type to crave just stats: you live for the philosophy behind the balls and mallets. Well, you're among friends. The Virtual Greensward is a nicely presented collection of croquet philosophy, links, contacts, and organization lists. But it's mostly just a lot of good, opinionated writing on the meaning and origins of the only legal way to knock people out or "bang 'em in the balls."

web http://www.comzone.com/croquet

▶ FENCING

The Art of Fencing If you're into fencing, this is a must-see, with drawings, photographs, lots of links, and info on fencing-related books and articles, such as "The Value of Timing in Tactics" and "A Brief History of Fencing." If you're a fencing newbie, you'll find illustrated definitions of the foil, epee, and sabre. Other highlights include lists of competition results and information on upcoming events. You'll even find a FAQ on Japanese sword arts.

web http://www.ii.uib.no/~arild/fencing.html

Clothing Requirements for USFA Tournaments Get the latest on clothing and equipment regulations for competitions. The document should answer all your questions about masks, plastrons, and whether you can include advertising on your uniform.

web http://csclub.uwaterloo.ca/u/mabuckle/fencing/rules/updates/USFA-clothing-Nov.94.text

Fencing FAQ What's in the fencing FAQ? Well, answers to questions like "Which is the best weapon?" and "What kind of cross-training will help my fencing?" This document, available at multiple Net locations, addresses everything from the basics of getting started at a local club to the details of fencing equipment and

rules. It includes an excellent list of resources, such as fencing organizations, outfitters, books, videos, and even software.

web http://www.cis.ohio-state.edu/text/faq/usenet/fencing-faq/faq.html
url ftp://rtfm.mit.edu/pub/usenet-by-hierarchy/rec/sport/fencing/www

Fencing FTP Site An archive of information and illustrations related to fencing, swords, and swordplay. Line drawings of everything from an epee (a type of fencing sword) to a plastron (a quilted pad worn by fencers). The text ranges from the by-laws of the Durendal Fencing Club in Madison, Wisc., to a list of fencing concepts and terms. The document fensafe.txt outlines the "inherent risks in the activity."

url ftp://bbs.macc.wisc.edu/pub2/fencing

rec.sport.fencing Discussion varies from debate about the merits of the French grip vs. the pistol grip to talk of interesting club names, like the Vampire Fencing Club, Foiled Again!, and Swash and Buckle. A friendly, yet serious group, gathers to talk about rules and strategy. Posts about tournaments are always welcome.

usenet rec.sport.fencing

▶ FIELD HOCKEY

Field Hockey The youth-power movement (mostly high school students) directs the focus from the usual in-depth analyzing of college and professional games and players. If you're interested in getting information on joining local teams, playing in college, going to field hockey camp, or buying equipment, definitely visit this well-traveled area.

america online *keyword* grandstand→ Sports Message Board→Other Sports→ List Topics→Field Hockey

rec.sport.hockey.field Advice and hints, such as "Of course, you should make an attempt to save the ball, but that should not stop you having a go at the players!!" and "the side tackle will probably remove the player for the rest of the game," are not uncommon and are occasionally accompanied by the reminder that "[field] hockey is a non-contact sport!" However, discussions do veer from these dangerous encouragements to something a little more tame, like scores, schedules, and team rosters. **USENET** rec.sport.hockey.field

GOLF

19th Hole Golf information—from golfing headlines to equipment ratings. Diehard golf fans will be gratified by the Almanac section of the service, which provides extensive information for PGA and LPGA tours. This is one of the best golf pages in cyberspace and a reminder that they don't call them links for nothing. **WEB** http://zodiac.tr-riscs.panam.edu/golf/19thhole.html

Golf Golf isn't the most discussed sport on CompuServe—in fact, given that it shares a message board with tennis, it's hard to separate the clubbers from the racketeers. But if you persevere, you may run into interesting threads on golf tips and the longevity of golf balls. ("I read somewhere that the ball manufacturers make all their balls the same way and then sort them according to the way they turn out due to manufacturing variances.") **COMPUSERVE** go fans→Golf/Tennis

The Golf Home Page Everything you've always wanted in a cybercaddy, but were afraid to ask, including links to other important golf sites, tips on club customization, score cards from local golf courses across the country, and a golf FAQ. The site also contains a few golf cartoons. **WEB** http://ausg.dartmouth.edu/~pete/golf

Golf Web Some golf sites offer PGA scores and consider it "extra duty" if they toss in a little LPGA. Golf Web goes the extra mile without patting itself on the back. It even covers golf in Scotland, where the game was invented. If that's not enough, a good proportion of their

text is available in both English and Japanese. Its library even includes movie reviews. (Happy Gilmore vs. Caddyshack—the debate rages on…) If you have questions about buying stock in a golf-related company, you've come to the right place. Even the financial soundness of golf-club makers is in here somewhere. **WEB** http://www.golfweb.com

GolfData Web On-Line Home Page One of the most comprehensive golf sites on the Web, with a database of 15,000 American courses; discount coupons for those courses; online subscription information for a variety of golfing publications (Northeast Golfer, Par Excellance); playing tips from a PGA player (Jeff Maggert); an electronic golf shop; an electronic travel service; and a listing of more than 300 golf schools. While this site is a pay service ($4.95 per month), it also has a selection of materials available for free, including essays on famous courses such as Turnberry and a program guide to The Golf Channel. **WEB** http://www.gdol.com

In the Fairway "Compression is really only a measure of how much a ball deflects when a standard load is applied to it in a lab test. For the record, many Tour Professionals actually use 90s because they prefer a softer feel in their short game." Sounds complicated, huh? But compression, deflection, and standard loads constitute only a small part of the golf talk on AOL's Grandstand Golf message board. There's also plenty of talk about clubs, computer simulations, courses across the country, and even a thread on "the biggest wimp in golf"—Chip Beck, John Daly, and Paul Azinger each net a handful of votes. **AMERICA ONLINE** keyword grandstand→ Sports Message Boards→Golf

On the Green What does AOL's golf area have to offer online fans? News and notes, a chat area, a simulation game, and a library that includes golf digests and a number of fantasy courses for

downloading.
AMERICA ONLINE *keyword* gs Golf

rec.sport.golf This is a huge newsgroup, with thousands of posts on topics ranging from balls to clubs and shoes to blues. While posts occasionally discuss pro golfers, most of the traffic is concerned with golf as a participant rather than spectator sport, and the group has a number of fascinating threads about the the dangers of golf ("golf as a contact sport"), cost-cutting while putting ("budget golf"), and the sport's steep learning curve ("new course = higher score?"). There's even a thread about the legal ins and outs of cloning popular club designs.
USENET rec.sport.golf

Simulation Golf AOL's golf simulation area is home to two versions of electronic golf—the Access League Pro Tour and the Grandstand Golf League. This area has rules for the golf simulations, along with a leaderboard listing current cybergolf luminaries and a library with courses for downloading.
AMERICA ONLINE *keyword* ggl

The Virtual Golfer With interesting uses of Java and tables, The Virtual Golfer is a good destination unless you're Netscape-deprived. It's got golf chat and a Virtual Golfer Message Board, where you can communicate with the similarly fanatical. Your golf-talk options include clubhouse talk, a PGA "pool" where you can pick the winners, a locker room, and a classifieds area for hawkers, hackers, and buyers.
WEB http://www.golfball.com

▶ ICE HOCKEY

The Blue Line Besides bulletin boards for discussing college and professional hockey teams, the forum features a fantasy hockey league, hockey schedules for each month, archives of Internet hockey news, and a hockey library with logos, schedules, game sound clips, player photos, stats databases, newsletters, and other hockey information.
AMERICA ONLINE *keyword* gs hockey

The Goaltender Home Page Dedicated to those daring kamikazes of the hockey rink, the underappreciated goaltenders, this home page is a profusion of links, stats, awards lists, pix, news, and articles of interest to fans of the Jason Voorhees-lookalikes. Presided over by University of Colorado student Doug Norris, the GHP should keep hockey fans busy for quite a while, especially with entertaining features like "How to Talk Like a Goalie," and a listing of the biggest peeves of goalies (drunken fans tossing Hostess Ring Dings toward the net is one).
WEB http://amath-www.colorado.edu /math/student/norrisdt/goalie/goalie.html

Hockey This hockey message board hosts professional as well as amateur hockey discussions. For team logos, hockey pool programs, databases to organize your hockey stats, NHL fan guides, team schedules and rosters, booster club info, lists of referees, information about amateur and international hockey leagues, salary lists, and other topics, browse the hockey library.
COMPUSERVE *go* fans→Libraries *or* Messages→Hockey

Hockey-Goalie Goalies unite! Or, at least share experiences. Maybe you're in the market for knee pads, even though you still love your three-year-old Brown's that fit like a second skin. Or, perhaps you're shopping around for a good goalie school. Then again, maybe, like list member Stormwind, you just need to talk about last night's game with other goalies—her team shut out the competition. Most people on the list are doing the same thing—trying to stop a puck—and they come here to talk about it.
EMAIL majordomo@xmission.com ✍ *Type in message body:* subscribe hockey-goalie

Hockey Links on the Web David Strauss has compiled an extensive listing of hockey sites on the Net. He's linked not only to dozens of NHL team sites, but also to the International Hockey League FAQ, the Canadian Junior A Hockey Standings, the Usenet hockey news-

groups, the German Hockey Home Page, and the Fantasy Hockey League. All told, the site links to more than a hundred hockey Web sites.
WEB http://www.eskimo.com/~dstrauss /hockey.html

Jean Pelland's Hockey Emporium Monsieur Pelland has compiled an incredibly extensive set of links to hockey sites around the globe (AHL, CHL, ECHL, amateur, high school, fantasy, ad infinitum). Doubt us? He's even got the South China Hockey League home page. For fun, check out the page for defunct teams— Pelland is currently featuring the Kenora Thistles, 1907 Stanley Cup Champs.
WEB http://www.feldspar.com/~pelland /hockey.html

WWW Hockey Guide We went to the fights last night, and a hockey game broke out. If you've heard that one before, you've likely seen a slapshot or two in your day. Maybe you're even missing a few front teeth. If you're a hockey enthusiast, you've come to the right place. From here you can link to over 1,100 hockey sites, including professional and college leagues, rotisserie leagues, and roller and field hockey. Navigating from this index is fairly painless. You can also access an intimidating array of hockey-related newsgroups.
WEB http://www.hockeyguide.com

▶ LACROSSE

alt.sport.lacrosse You don't have to be a lacrosse expert from Maryland, the lacrosse center of the world, to join discussions in this newsgroup. Get information on year-round local leagues. Talk about NCAA lacrosse—"the fastest game on land!!"—and compare visits to the Lacrosse Hall of Fame. Although this newsgroup is largely focused on men's lacrosse, it touches occasionally on the expanding world of women's lacrosse. During the offseason, for instance, you can find insights into the history of the "WWF of field sports"and explanations of unclear crease rules and penalties. Predictions of scores and rankings, such

as the "'TOP 25' list of NCAA lacrosse schools," also hold seasonal lacrosse fans until the start of the new season. During the season, the group lists not only the scores of both professional and NCAA games, but also serves as a forum for heated debates about the sport's stars, intense crease rolls, and unbelievable breakaways.
USENET alt.sport.lacrosse

Lacrosse (Indoor&Outdoor) Some of the comments on this message board— "lacrosse looks like field hockey with a lacrosse stick"and "I had a terrible time trying to get the ball into the air. It just dove back to the ground"—suggest that participants aren't so savvy about lacrosse, and newbies are in fact the dominant force. But becareful, because the frustrated vet will occasionally step in to pull rank—when a neophyte asked about the importance of elbow pads, a long-time lax player blasted back: "Yes, of course they're necessary, you fool, it will reeeally hurt without them." Between the witty exchanges, there is useful information about teams, games, and statistics, as well as fundamental advice for the active lacrosse player ("eat more, run a lot, lift weights").
AMERICA ONLINE *keyword* grandstand→ Sports Message Board→Other Sports→ List topics→Lacrosse (Indoor&Outdoor)

SKATES, SKIS, & FLYING DISCS

IF ALIENS FROM OUTER SPACE landed in Central Park in July and witnessed a game of Ultimate, they might think at first that they'd never left home. After observing the scores of inline skaters trolling the Big Loop, however, they would have to conclude that they were definitely on another planet—one inhabited by a slave species whose master goes by the name "Rollerblade." Shortly thereafter, the aliens would infiltrate the Net, where they would find reasonable explanations for these phenomena at The Frisbee Page and alt.skate.

FIGURE SKATING

ABC Figure Skating Need to know the difference between a camel spin and a death spiral? Click here to look up skating terms and lingo in the figure skating glossary, read skaters bios and personal interviews, and skim through USFSA info. A good place for spectators to learn the basics, ABC's site even has a Fun Facts area that lists endless championship trivia.
AMERICA ONLINE *keyword* abc figure skating

Figure Skating Home Page Besides results from current figure skating events, this site offers links to information about upcoming tours and competitions, a comprehensive FAQ list, details on movies of jumps and spins and facts on Nancy Kerrigan. On the humorous side, the page includes links to the campy Scott Hamilton ("pictures of Scott when he still had hair") page to the "Frogs on Ice" illustrations.
WEB http://www.cs.yale.edu/HTML/YALE/CS/HyPlans/loosemore-sandra/skate.html

The Kristi Yamaguchi Home Page Okay, so you follow Kristi Yamaguchi like paparazzi follow Alec Baldwin and Kim Basinger. Let's just hope it doesn't border on obsession. But should you have a mild fascination with Kristi, satiate it

here. "Pictures, pictures, pictures," the page tantalizingly beckons. It delivers with—wait for it—pictures. Print 'em and post 'em on your wall. Just about everything you'd want to know about the woman—from her history to her friends, to the charities she endorses.
WEB http://www.polaris.net/user-www/shanhew

FLYING DISCS

The Frisbee Page With an endearing sad-sack disclaimer ("I know, it's not colorful or fancy, but it'll get you there"), this page serves as a net discography (*disc*-ography, get it?), with links to documents on Frisbee technique and rules.
WEB http://www.sccs.swarthmore.edu/~dalewis/frisbee.html

George Ferguson's Ultimate Page A page devoted entirely to competitive Ultimate, with very little overlap into flying-disc culture.
WEB http://www.cs.rochester.edu/u/ferguson/ultimate

rec.sport.disc A discussion hub for Ultimate players and other Frisbee aficionados, this newsgroup accomodates everything from disc rhapsodies ("Good spirit tip: If you foul someone, call it on yourself ! Everyone thinks you're bitchen") to announcements of tournaments and pickup games to more practical advice about nail care ("I wear a golf glove on my right hand to play ultimate, indoors or out. This is because I am a guitarist as well as a (very bad) Ultimate player, and I need something to protect my fingernails. It's not 100% effective, but I do come away with fewer damaged nails than before I wore the glove").
USENET rec.sport.disc

Ultimate GIFs Pictures of Frisbees in flight, and the brave men and women who lay their lives on the line—and the fresh-cut grass—to catch them.
WEB http://www.sccs.swarthmore.edu

/~dalewis/frisbee/frisbeegifs.html

The Ultimate Players Association What happens when you mix football, soccer, and a Frisbee? You get the team sport, called Ultimate, featuring plastic disks whistling across college campuses from Hampshire to Stanford. The Ultimate Players Association oversees varsity and club competitions in the U.S., so zip over to see how your college team is doing in the polls. If you just can't get enough of the sport that uses an adjective as a noun, you can link to multiple newsgroups, featuring heated discussions on various pressing matters of the ultimate concern.
WEB http://komodo.hacks.arizona.edu/~upa

The Ultimate Timeline A history of Frisbee, from Fred Morrison's historic disc of solid tenite (first carved in 1947 and manufactured in the mid-fifties by Wham-O) to the proliferation of summer Ultimate leagues across the United States. The page also includes famous Frisbee quotes, such as the ultimately pretentious "Ultimate doesn't build character, it reveals it."
WEB http://pipkin.lut.ac.uk/ftp/gumpf /Ultimate/ultimate_timeline

Ultimate Web Pages Are these the ultimate Web pages, or Ultimate Web pages? Huck on over to this site for Frisbee links galore.
WEB http://www.access.digex.net/~erics /ultimate.html

UPA Home Page The official home of the Ultimate Players Association, this page includes membership information, addresses (both email and snail mail) for UPA officials, newsbriefs about the sport, and raw statistics from last year's tournament.
WEB http://www.upa.org/~upa

UPA Rules of Ultimate "Ultimate is a non-contact sport played by two seven-player teams." It's not exactly the Declaration of Independence, but this document is just as important for Ultimate players, with coverage of end zones,

substitutions, observers, field planning, and even tournament etiquette.
WEB http://www.cs.rochester.edu/u /ferguson/ultimate/ultimate-rules.html

▶ INLINE SKATING

alt.skate There's heated discussion between rival skate factions—"Rollerblading sucks unless you can jump the Gonz… Everyone else shoud be shot, and pissed on. SKATEBOARDING RULES"—and chat includes everyone from mild-mannered figure skating fans to radical, separatist skateboarders who think alt.skate-board is too fashion-conscious. Others simply swap shopping tips or dream the great dream of rolling.
USENET alt.skate

Inline Online Best of the inline skating Web zines, Inline Online boasts links to profiles of companies and products, skate park addresses worldwide, archives of an emailing list on inline skating, a movie and picture archive, individual and team profiles, and classifieds for skating equipment. Inline Skating is in the process of building a mini-empire of online skatezines, offering space and links to DailyBread, Box, Roller Hockey, and XSk8 (none up at press time).
WEB http://galaxy.einet.net/galaxy /Leisure-and-Recreation/Sports/daniel -chick/io_org.html

Inline Skate Companies List A comprehensive list of inline skate retailers and equipment manufacturers.
WEB http://www.outdoornet.com/inline /inllist.html

InLine Skating Want to find out the best way to clean your ball bearings? How about advice on a purchase? This board is friendlier than most skating discussions, so newbies need not worry admitting they've never owned a pair of skates before.
COMPUSERVE *go* outact→Libraries *or* Messages→Inline Skating

Inline Skating Get down to the nitty-gritty of buckles and bearings on another inline message board on AOL. What kind of skates should you buy? Well, there's Bauer (experts in the ice hockey arena but newcomers to the roller world), but neophytes may opt for a pair of Rollerblades, the Kleenex of inline skate manufacturers. Equipment advice, technique debates, and anecdotal chat are all part of the discussion.

AMERICA ONLINE *keyword* exchange→ Outdoor Activities→Outdoor Activities Board→List Topics→Inline Skating

Inline Skating FAQ Looking for first-hand tips on how to perform a front-side curb grind? Can't decide whether to buy the Hyper Hop-Up kit or the Lazzy Legs? If you're confused about which features are a priority, this is where you can learn to decipher SSHA ("Silly Sales Hype Acronyms"). Net skaters can look up local skating clubs in their area, and accessory hounds will find a listing of retail outlets around the world.
URL ftp://rtfm.mit.edu/pub/usenet/rec.skate
FAQ: **WEB** http://garnet.acns.fsu.edu/~adchen/rec.skate.html

Inline Skating Picture Index One-stop source for pictures of flips, soul skating, and Team Skydigger.
WEB http://ftp.sunet.se/ftp/pub/pictures/sports/skating/inline

Skating the Infobahn You can get anywhere in the inline skating world from this page, which includes everything from local FAQs, information about organizations, and announcements of events to retail outlets to pictures and newsbriefs from the U.S. Consumer Product Safety Commission press releases.
WEB http://www.panix.com/~rbs/Skate

Tony Chen's Inline Skate Archives If you don't feel like hustling down to the local skate shop to browse over the latest models, check out this archive of skate photos.
WEB http://garnet.acns.fsu.edu/~adchen/picsdex.html

Wheel World Find everything from shopping tips to a new skate partner in AOL's Blading message board. Roller hockey enthusiasts are allotted their own folder. Add the Artistic Roller Skating, Speed Skating, and Roller Derby folders, and AOL makes it to the top of the list for commercial service offerings to inline enthusiasts.
AMERICA ONLINE *keyword* grandstand→ Sports Message Boards→Roller Skating

SKIING

GORP Internet Skiing Resources There certainly are other Web sites with more comprehensive ski coverage, but GORP's numerous links are well organized and annotated. Select World Ski Reports to see where the powder is best, then head to the local resort pages for prices and pictures of Bozeman, Mont. or Sunday River, Maine. If you're looking for ski buddies, try GORP's list of ski clubs. Cross country advocates will find links to several good Nordic pages as well.
WEB http://www.gorp.com/gorp/activity/skiing.htm

Marc's Home Page for Skiing Information Marc spends his free time as a volunteer ski patrol member at Jay Peak in Vermont and Willard Mountain in New York. When he's not rescuing inadvertent tree huggers, he is constructing a great skiing Web site. For skiers in the northeast this is the best place to start. Check the Ski Vermont HomeLodge feature with whatever questions you may have about Vermont skiing and get up-to-the-second weather reports from Vermont Hydrologic Observations. The rest of the northeast is equally well-covered. Marc has also linked his site to several home pages for local ski areas across the country and internationally. His careful annotations of every link are a special bonus. Don't miss them.
WEB http://www.rpi.edu/~guidom/First Tracks.html

Other Ski Info The rather modest title does this page a huge disservice. No other Net ski site has more links to worldwide ski areas, from Slovenia to Santiago, than this one. What can you expect to find? Most local sites provide their slope details, as well as prices, local tourist information, and often trail maps and enticing pictures.This is a great place to dream, and to comparison shop—jump easily from Sugarloaf to Sunday River. If that's not enough, there's an impressive collection of weather links, ski clubs, ski sites, and retail Web pages on board. Ready to go? The collection of travel links can help with air fares and adventure vacations through a dozen online travel services. **WEB** http://gamera.syr.edu:2345/SKIING /other.html

rec.skiing.alpine Why oh, why did anyone ever invent the snowboard? This is a constant refrain in the very busy newsgroup dedicated to what steep snowy slopes were really meant for—skiing. Novice skiers get pointers on turning from experts. Steve and Dan debate the physics of skiing. Is it the friction or the pressure of skis on snow that causes it to melt? They even resort to equations. Skiers exchange tips on favorite slopes and ski boots, but discussion can sometimes take on quite an edge.The group recently divided over the ski patrols right to ticket racers for excessive speed on crowded slopes. Are racers arrogant and dangerous? Do ski resorts make more money off day trippers and thus pick on racers? Or is it that Americans just don't get the culture of skiing? Jump right in if you've got an opinion. **USENET** rec.skiing.alpine

SkiMaps Maps, yes, but so very much more. SkiMaps has everything a Net skier could possibly need, including links to other ski sites from around the world. Try the Snow Page's European ski collection or jump to Ski Colorado. Maps—more than 70 to date—collected by the site's creator and downloaded by other eager Web skiers are also provided. If you want to relive your last trip to Sundance, there's a map for you, too. Have recurrent James Bond super-skier fantasies? Take a look at the map of Murren in Switzerland, the site of the Bond film *On Her Majesty's Secret Service*. Missing Aspen? There always Beau Jo's pizza menu to bring back the whole Colorado experience. **WEB** http://www.skimaps.com

Skiing Why is a boarder like a vacuum cleaner? Both come with a dirtbag attached. So says Mike, generously inviting any boarders to come forward with skier jokes. Boarders and skiers do seem to peacefully coexist on this board, where the snow-happy exchange ice advice and agony-of-defeat stories. Join the never-ceasing discussion of free heels between telemarkers and Alpinists. Listen to those "in the know" boost Mammoth's double blacks or Tahoe's nightlife. You might even find a cyberpal to meet on the slopes of Big Sky. **COMPUSERVE** *go* outact→Libraries *or* Messages→Skiing

Skiing This Breckinridge-based Web site takes skiing seriously, posting the skier's responsibility code, complete with its warning that "skis don't kill people, skiers do." The site provides you with a set of good connections to international ski Web sites and, for those who ski American, forecasts from the University of Michigan's weather server. **WEB** http://gamera.syr.edu:2345/ski.html

The Snow Page This is the best skiing site going—a massive collection of links to resorts, newsgroups, archives, and home pages worldwide. There are also maps, conditions reports, travel services, and online ski shops to assist in every aspect of a cyber ski-bum's life. You can jump to several online cyberzines or find outabout the "snow people" on the Net by linking to their home pages. Email them with comments through the Snow Page's automatic email link. If that isn't enough, there's a picture gallery and the results of a gopher search—900 ski-related documents to while away those sultry summer hours. **WEB** http://rmd-www.mr.ic.ac.uk/snow /snowpage.html

MIND & MUSCLE

BRAIN VERSUS BRAWN. THE OLD conflict has often been repeated—from David vs. Goliath to Dr. Peter Burns vs. Bobby Parezi. Brain always wins. Or is this just wishful thinking on the part of scrappy writers who pen trite story lines? In real life, isn't it always the hunk who has the last laugh, the burly blond who gets the cute worm? Indeed, isn't brawn itself a kind of intelligence? One must admit, it takes a certain kind of mind to develop a certain amount of muscle. But brain and brawn need not be mutually exclusive. On the Internet, one can exercise both. So take a load off at Weightlifting, overcome a fear of flying at Trampolining, or try a hand at the Karate HyperCard Stack.

BODYBUILDING

Weightlifting Weightlifting news from around the globe, including results of international competitions and links to the sports pictures database.
AMERICA ONLINE *keyword* sports→ Choose a Sport→Weightlifting

Weights-L Nutrition, injuries, workouts—it's all fair game on this active list. You don't have to be an experienced bodybuilder to join, although many of the contributors clearly know their stuff—and have strong opinions—when it comes to issues such as diet supplements and steroids. "If the Republicans are serious about 'getting government off our backs,'" wrote one lifter, "then they should be at the forefront of restoring our freedom by repealing the laws that make some drugs legal (alcohol, caffeine) and others not (steroids, marijuana, etc.)."
EMAIL weights-request@fa.disney.com
✍ *Type in message body:* subscribe weights-l <your full name>

The Women's Bodybuilding Forum It's a good thing that female bodybuilders have broad backs, because they have to bear the brunt of numerous sterotypes about physically powerful women. With discussion about sexual orientation, sexual potency, and the rules of attraction interweaved with weights and workout talk, this is a list with a social conscience. Did your brother look at you strangely when your bulging abs started picking up distant radio signals? Did your boyfriend break up with you when you dead-lifted his Volkswagen Rabbit? Toss those wimps to the side and subscribe to this list.
EMAIL femuscle-request@lightning.com
✍ *Write a request*

GYMNASTICS

Gymn: An Electronic Forum for Gymnastics What are the standings for the men's prelims in the Pan American Games? How about the final standings for the women's American Classic Senior All-Around? Brought to you by the same folks that run the Gymn mailing list (an archive of the list is available here), the site reliably tracks results at recent meets, features a calendar of gymnastic events, and monitors the collegiate rankings. And, that's just the beginning. Check out *The Gymn Reporter*, an onsite newsletter, indexed for easy use, that provides professional commentary on meets and training tips. You can also look up the address of the Azerbaijan National Olympic Committee in the list of gymnastics organizations or get details on other gymnastics publications.
WEB http://www.rmii.com/~rachele /gymnhome.html
URL ftp://ftp.cac.psu.edu/pub/gymn

Gymn Forum Subtitled "an electronic forum," this page is lovingly dedicated to all things gymnastic. There's quite a bit of stuff crammed in here—where to get the best videos on the subject; who placed where, when, and why, at which recent competition; who the up-and-comers are, and so on. The forum has its own mailing list too, so if you prefer, the site can basically come to you. Don't forget about the

email addresses to the stars. If your favorite's got one, it's here.
WEB http://rainbow.rmii.com/~rachele /gymnhome.html

Gymnastics Young gymnasts frequent this board for comradeship, advice, and, occasionally, some soul searching. Meet 12-year-old Laurie, who recently quit gymnastics because it wasn't fun any more. She strongly advises others to rethink their Olympic hopes—is it all worth it? And, while gushing about favorite gymnasts is rather common, gymnast activism is also alive: Coaches and athletes recently banned together to fight a program's demise at Temple University—and won.
AMERICA ONLINE *keyword* grandstand→ Sports Message Boards→Other Sports→List Topics→Gymnastics

Lisa's Gymnastics Archive Lisa was frustrated about the lack of gymnastics-related resources on the Net so she created her own site with pictures and links to all the online gymnastic resources she could find.
WEB http://humper.student.princeton.edu /~lcozzens

Trampolining Trampoliners dream the little dream of flying, and this German-English Web site is dedicated to those who like to bounce. Trampolining history, an events calendar, results of meets, trampolining statistics, archives of trampolining, and contact information for the sport are avalable. German required.
WEB http://este.darmstadt.gmd.de:5000 /misc/tramp/trhome_en.html

USA Gymnastics Association Need to discuss something with the USA Gymnastics Association? Send them email.
EMAIL usgf@delphi.com ✍ *Write a request*

USA Gymnastics Online With the Olympics taking place in Atlanta, the excitement surrounding the world of amateur gymnastics in the United States has reached an all-time high. If you've got a passing interest in the sport or are a seasoned veteran (which probably makes you a freshman in high school), check this place out. It's got insider tips and strategy articles from some of the industry publications, as well as news on events like the World Championship, held in April.
WEB http://www.usa-gymnastics.org/usag

▶ MARTIAL ARTS

Aiki Jujitsu Introduction to and information about Stanford's self-defense curriculum, encompassing Karate, Jujitsu, and Zen Budokai. The FAQ is clear, concise, and, best of all, a quick read.
WEB http://jujitsu.stanford.edu/jujitsu .html

Aikido FAQ Is Steven Seagal really an aikidoka? Well, that depends on how much of a purist you are, but this FAQ can fill you in on the debatable issues. Find out precisely how to strike someone without really hurting them. Learn about the unbendable arm and and how "ki" can get you there. And if you feel you've got two left feet on the mat before you've even started, the primer in "Dojo Etiquette" can help you maintain a modicum of face.
WEB http://www.ii.uib.no/~kjartan /aikidofaq/aikido.html

The Dojo If the gruesome UFC-style fighting grosses you out, then hold your typing fingers in the UFC folder. You're likely to be told to go away until you stop complaining. If, on the other hand, you're interested in reality-based training, get some first-hand advice on eye jabs: "grabbing the head by pushing the thumbs into the eyes and grabbing the nerve center under the jawline is a wonderful method of slamming the head into the ground or up against a wall or tree or car, etc." On the spiritual side, you're as likely to be bashed: "*never* ask what is chi force around here! sheesh, the negative responses from shogusha alone will fill up the folder!" Still, you can get through the History folder relatively unscathed. Safe areas also include the non-interactive Tourna-

ments and School Listings A-Z folders. Otherwise, explore at your own risk.
AMERICA ONLINE *keyword* grandstand→The Dojo

Howard A. Landman's Aikido Index

Aikido's non-violent status among the martial arts is reflected in this page's information offerings: e.g., "How to put on a gi" and "The technique of kote-gaeshi" (wrist arm lock). Once you've mastered these basic lessons, use the links to move on to other, more advanced sites.
WEB http://www.hal.com/~landman/Aikido

Japanese Sword Arts FAQ

Kendo, Kumdo, Iaido and other Japanese sword arts revealed and explained.
URL ftp://anon-ftp rudolf.nscl.msu.edu /pub/iaido/swordfaq.txt

JUJUTSU

List for discussing Jujutsu that carries announcements and discussion about technique and philosophy.
EMAIL listserv@psuvm.psu.edu ✍ *Type in message body:* subscribe jujutsu <your full name>

Kendo and Iaido Terminology

Dictionary of Kendo and Iaido terms.
URL ftp://rudolf.nscl.msu.edu/pub/iaido /terms.txt

MARS—Martial Arts Resource Site

One of the most impressive martial arts resource pages in cyberspace. The site links to several essays including "Ki Breathing" and "The Real Meaning of the Black Belt," texts like "The Art of War" and "TaoTe Ching," terminology lists and bibliographies for several forms of martial arts, dozens of FAQs, and many related sites.
WEB http://www.lehigh.edu/~sjb3/martial .html

Martial Arts

There's an international focus on martial arts at this Swedish-based site. Besides local information for Scandinavians, find out where to practice Karate in the U.K., Judo in Norway, or Tae Kwon Do in Virginia. If you're looking for pictures of "kicks 'n' punch-es," check out the Martial Arts Gallery. Confused about how to spell Ju jutsu (Jiu jitsu or Ju jitsu)? Acccording to Rico's Ju Jutso Page, it doesn't make a difference. You can also read up on the early armored grappling origins of Ju Jutsu in 10th-century Japan, and look for more substantial resources in the bibliography.
WEB http://www.docs.uu.se/~rico /martial_arts

Martial Arts Events

Any event even remotely related to the martial arts is chronicled, including happenings that are set for more than a year in advance. Kickboxing matches, pressure-point seminars, women's-safety classes, the Ultimate Challenge—all these events and more are posted. All you have to do to get on the list is ask. You can't knock a free ad, but it would all be a lot more useful if the events were in some semblance of order.
WEB http://www.centuryma.com/tourney .shtml

Martial Arts Forum

Variety of chat topics from Tae Kwon Do basics to promo ideas for your fledgling Kung Fu academy. The library contains extensive workout lists, a primer on Tai Chi, Usenet FAQ files, and Chinese icons for Windows 3.1.
COMPUSERVE *go* goodhealth→Messages *or* Libraries→Martial Arts

Martial Arts Mailing List

Wondering how to throw the Kusari Fundo (weighted chain)? "Avoid throwing it at the head unless you're willing to kill the guy… The kusari can be used like a Bolo on steroids." You don't have to be a killer to join this mailing list, although sometimes you might think it would help. Postings also range from the difference between "tumbling" in gymnastics and "rolling" in Aikido to announcements about non-lethal Kyusho Jitsu seminars.
EMAIL martial-arts-request@martial-arts .eng.sun.com ✍ *Write a request*

Michael Boyce's Universal Martial Arts

The intro page to this virtual dojo

promises quite a bit, but a few short black-and-gray paragraphs on Gung Fu, as they call it here, and a check-back-later request in place of a newsletter are the only things around to complement the online resume of a West Coast black-belt instructor. It's the journey, and not the goal, that are important here—so says this Gung Fu master. Let's just hope he journeys to a few larger and more informative Web sites and picks up a few tips.

web http://members.aol.com/montablo/univer.htm

Pekiti Tirsia: Philippine Kali The wooden sword known as the Kali not only killed Magellan in the 16th century (1521 to be exact), but also became the namesake of the primary Filipino fighting style. You'll find the full history of the sport, details on the underground years after the Spanish succeeded in overtaking the Philippines, plus a description of the hierarchy of sticks, groupings of techniques, and how to use them.

web http://www.cecm.sfu.ca/personal/loki/kali.html

rec.martial-arts Is Tae Kwon Do or Judo more effective on the street? Do Aikido or Jujutsu techniques work better against resistance? Rivalries among the martial arts run rampant. Even video game fighting simulations come into the mix. The newsgroup is a great place for Movie IDs when you just can't remember where that fantastic fighting scene came from.

usenet rec.martial-arts

Shotokan Karate of America This North American non-profit Karate organization provides a basic outline of Karate's history, from its origins in Chinese Shaolin Boxing to Okinawa to its introduction to mainland Japan in 1922. There are addresses of dojos in the U.S., Canada, and the Netherland Antilles.

web http://www.hmt.com/martialArts/ska/ska.html

PERSONAL FITNESS

Personal Fitness Got a soreness in the left hamstring? Tried rest, stretching, heat, and ice? Post your message to these boards, and wait for the onslaught of advice. Everyone's welcome, whether you're a slow-moving tennis player ("I can't get to hard shots"), a beach babe wannabe ("I have a lot of blubber on the bottom of my legs, and I need to get rid of it soon, cause I'm embarrassed to wear a bathing suit"), or a runner from St. Louis looking for a training partner (6:45 pace). These people lead active lives, or so it seems. There's little off-topic discussion. The most active topics? Bodybuilding, lifting, cycling, marathon training, and running.

america online *keyword* sports boards→ Personal Fitness

WRESTLING

Wrestling Information Page If you forget the lack of graphics (Hulk Hogan's body is probably a registered trademark), as well as the typos that grace these pages—the work of a 19-year-old Swede—you're left with very little to remember. This fanboy's love note to the oft-bloodied denizens of the square circle includes a TV guide to European wrestling shows and pages and pages of the basics of nearly every wrestling matchup since 1985.

web http://www.mds.mdh.se/~dat95pkn/wrestle

The Wrestling Page A page that bodyslams the competition. Most impressive here are the 52 audio clips of wrestlers screaming that they're going to "get revenge!!!" Another nice feature is the list of wrestlers' real names, some of which may explain their often anti-social behavior. A definite must-see for any fan—or anyone who just wants a new .WAV file to play when starting Windows—are quotes like, "I'm gonna pulverize you in the ring tonight!"

web http://adscape.com/wrestling

GOING THE DISTANCE

ATTENTION SPAN IS A SINGLE quality that can determine many aspects of a person's life. Those with long ones have the potential to excel at practically any career. Those with short ones, on the other hand, might fare better as toll-takers. The world of distance sports, with its marathoners and sprinters, holds opportunities for both those who are long and short of attention (distance is relative). The Internet clearly favors the latter, but even those with long attention spans might find appropriate online places at which to linger. It may take more than a minute to learn the proper way to put a shot at The Thrower's Page. Become a gearhead by memorizing Bike Terminology, get into the swim of things at rec.sport.swimming, or join the lively Dead Runners Society.

► CYCLING

Bicycle Enthusiasts Mailing List During a typical week on this list, the Virginia Bicycling Federation posted the agenda of its upcoming retreat; Charlotte inquired about urine testing in the Olympics; a member of the New Orleans Regional Bicycle Awareness Committee asked for suggestions on producing a city map specifically for the cyclist; and dozens of people engaged in a rather graphic and quirky discussion about road kill.
EMAIL email listproc@yukon.cren.org ✍
Type in message body: subscribe bicylce <your full name>
Archives: **URL** gopher://list.cren.net:70/11 /archives/bicycle

Bike Chat Room Live discussions about cycling including mountain biking, bicycle advocacy, and long distance touring are scheduled every night of the week on AOL and attended by members of both the BikeNet forum and Bicycling Magazine Online. A schedule is posted in the BikeNet Conference Room Folder.
AMERICA ONLINE *keyword* bikenet→

Conference Room & Schedule→ Conference Room *keyword* bicycling→ Bike Chat Room

Bike Terminology Spend any time in a biking discussion and you'll hear about "campys" (a nickname for the Campagnolo bicycle company), "gear capacity" (a front derailleur mechanism), and a "recumbent bicycle" (a bicycle meant to be ridden in a supine position). Learn the vocabulary.
URL gopher://draco.acs.uci.edu.:1071/00 /glossary

BikeNet—The Bicycle Network This forum is one of the most impressive biking sites in cyberspace, featuring representatives from the biggest biking organizations in the country (the Bicycle Federation of America, the United States Cycling Federation, and the League of American Bicyclists, and others). Its message center has garnered over 25,000 messages in categories such as components, accessories, classifieds, racing, training and fitness, regional trails and tours, and mountain bikes. Live BikeNet chats happen several times a week and there's always a schedule for the chats posted in the conference folder. The Software Exchange area of the forum stores biking images, FAQs, guides, tip sheets, chat logs, and a large collection of biking software.
AMERICA ONLINE *keyword* bikenet

Bill's WWW Sports Page Cycle racing is Bill's obsession, and he's compiled links to several racing news and results resources on the Net as well as links to regional cycling pages, image archives, and training instructions.
WEB http://econ-www.newcastle.edu.au /~bill/billspor.html

Cyber Cyclery Whether you need a new helmet (a wide variety of sponsors have pages accessible through links), the date of the next dirtbiking workshop in

your area, or just want to meet some new bike buddies, this is the place for you. Good categorization allows easy access with minimal trial-and-error searching, and subjects vary from chat, events, and activity resources, to online bike shops and a great bulletin board with posted offers of companionship and cycling adventure ideas.
WEB http://cyclery.com

Cycling on the Internet Still more links to cycling sites online. Pedal over to the Central New Jersey Bicyle Racing site or perhaps the home page for the 1994 Tour de France. Keep going until you're tired. Hey, was that the Colorado Mountain Bike Racing page you just blew by?
WEB http://wwwhost.cc.utexas.edu /students/utcycling/internet.html

The Cycling Page Although this Web site has links to quite a few resources for cyclists in the San Diego, there are also dozens of links to other cycling pages.
WEB http://psy.ucsd.edu/~mtaffe/cycle .html

The Cycling Page A page with a message: "Think globally, cycle locally." The site carries the latest results of Classic, World Cup, and Stage races as well as the International Cycling Union and the World Cup rankings. European team information, racing calendars, explanations of scoring systems, and the historical results of important races long past are also here. Looking for a list of Tour de France winners since 1903? How about the winner of the results of the Amstel Gold race since 1966? Links are made to "technical stuff," including a metric gearing table and speed/pedal revs tables. A small collection of photos from championship races resides on this site as well.
WEB http://sunwww.informatik.uni -tuebingen.de:8080/sport/rad/rad.html

Cycling the Net It's quite probable that you could access all your biking information needs from this one Web site. Race results? College club info? Biking

images? Still not satisfied. How about mountain biking resources, endurance training tips, archives of dozens of mailing lists, and a place to order Spinergy wheels?
WEB http://www.eskimo.com/~cycling /breakaway.html

rec.bicycles FAQ Mike Iglesias, rec .bicycles moderator of sorts, compiled a list of answers to questions that have been repeatedly asked on the seven biking newsgroups, and the result was a huge reference guide to biking and biking resources online. How do the organizers determine the ratings for the climbs in the Tour de France? What exactly is Polarlite? What are the pros and cons of Terrybikes for women? Can you reuse old spokes in new wheels? Why do heavier people roll down hills faster than the scrawny people? These and hundreds of other biking questions are addressed, primarily in the form of answers that have been posted to the newsgroup.
web http://www.cis.ohio-state.edu /hypertext/faq/usenet/bicycles-faq/top .html
URL ftp://draco.acs.uci.edu/pub/rec .bicycles/faq

VeloLinQ Every imaginable link for the cycling enthusiast, accessible through quick and colorful category buttons, is available. Browse through more magazines devoted to two-wheelers than you thought possible. It's attractive, fun, and mind-boggling, although some of the links are not quite up to speed. But with any attempt of this size, its hard to ensure absolute perfection with each link.
WEB http://www.velolinq.com

VeloNet: Global Cycling Network This electronic information desk for cyclists is like a sign-up clipboard on your computer; its great (MajorDomo) system allows you to subscribe or delete yourself from many cycle-related emailing lists at the click of your mouse. See nothing you love? Start your own emailing list instead. Or, if you're looking for a

particular club or organization, check the 365 individual listings in the phone book. As a part of the vaster Cyber Cyclery site, there are now even more links among the various lists, as well as a growing number of member organizations.
WEB http://www.cycling.org

WOMBATS on the Web Female mountain bikers of the world unite! Actually, they already have, and they're here, at the online forum of the Women's Mountain Bike and Tea Society. This fun arena features women helping each other stomach and surmount the mountain biking community's omnipresent macho lingo and techno obsessions. Talk about biking, form a group, learn about events in your area, or just vent through the reader's forum: You're bound to feel better after you visit with these noncompetitive, pro-personal-best women.
WEB http://www.wombats.org

> ▶ RUNNING

Dead Runners Society Despite its ominous name, the Dead Runners Society is actually a lively symposium of similarly lively folks who like to talk about running. Covering everything from meditation to marathons, the society's listserver brings together people interested in pounding their feet on the earth—over and over again. Trot on over to learn how to subscribe, and take advantage of their streamlined link index of track clubs and upcoming events around the country.
WEB http://storm.cadcam.iupui.edu/drs /drs.html

Internet Resources for Runners If you're a hard-core runner, the Internet Resources for Runners page is worth a bookmark. We found the most valuable link on the site the injury resource library. Manned by Dr. Fernando Dimeo, there are common diagnoses, cures, and insights to even the most minor problems runners encounter. And naturally, there are links to studies, industries, standings, and post-mortems on just

about every running event.
WEB http://www.nauticom.net/users /kenecon

Planet Reebok Such a huge planet—it's a wonder you can find any straightforward information about shoes. Start by checking out Reebok's listings for online IRC interviews with Jimmy Connors and Nancy Kerrigan, wade through the company's Sole Difference human rights campaign page, and end up at a press release of the company's latest women's athletic shoe. There's more—preseason workouts and coach interviews, plus a bulletin board featuring hundreds of Reebok and running-related sites, mailing lists, and retail outlets (Planet Reebok, strangely enough, offers no retail service), even a place to criticize the company's advertising campaign.
WEB http://planetreebok.com

rec.running No pain, no gain. If you run a lot, then you probably won't squirm when people start recounting the details of their various knee injuries or the bunions they can't get rid of, and, most of all, how much it hurts. Besides countless postings on where to run, local running clubs, and first-hand feedback from runners about the latest footwear, debates run wild over how to handle those ferocious dogs in the park. When the solution to kick, hit, or spray ammonia in the face of a dog is suggested, users might get a warning: "If you ever kicked / hit / punched my dog in the face or ribs or anywhere I would take this as an act of animal cruelty and as an attack on what is basically 'my child'. In other words, I would do my best to make you regret the hell out of such vicious behavior." Runners of the world may not unite, but they sure like to fight and complain.
USENET rec.running
FAQ: **WEB** http://www.atm.ch.cam.ac.uk /~oliver/H_and_H/runfaq.html

Runner's World Are you worried about your "Popeye legs" (big calves)? Sounds like you need to work out your thighs a little more. Exercise ideas are frequently traded here, both to improve running

and to even out disproportionately exercised muscles. Besides postings with advice for marathon training, 10K races, and what to do if your "toes are beat up," dog talk runs amuck.
COMPUSERVE *go* fitness→Health & Fitness Forum→Runner's World

The Running Page Going to L.A., Portland, and Florida but afraid you won't know how to fit in your workout? This is a great place to get detailed information on running scenes around the world. Dedicated to linking you to information about running organizations on the Web, it is a good starting point for information about upcoming races, local clubs, and becoming a member of USATF (USA Track and Field). You can also post your own running tips or compare personal bests.
WEB http://sunsite.unc.edu/drears /running/running.html

Triathlon FAQ What's a brick? In the triathlon world, it means a bike ride followed by a run: It also describes how your legs feel for the first part of the run. Before you dismiss competing in a triathlon—assuming you're absolutely not cut out for the Hawaii Ironman— think again. This FAQ offers helpful suggestions for all levels of athleticism. A short triathlon only involves a one kilometer run at the end, compared to the Ironman's 42.1 kilometers, while a Decatriathlon is 10 times the Ironman, taking a maximum of 18 days to complete. Most basic questions are answered, from "What are the typical events in a summer triathlon?" to "Why do so many atheletes get upset about wetsuit usage in races?"
WEB http://fas.sfu.ca/0h/cs/people/Grad Students/zaiane/personal/trifaq.html

USATF Addresses and Phone Numbers In order to participate in the major races and marathons, you must be a member of the USA Track & Field, the governing body for track and field, cross country, and road racing events. More than just a list, this page saves you money. "Believe it or not USATF will not give all the

addresses and phone numbers of their associations, but will sell it as part of a $10 book." Luckily, someone had the bright idea to catalog most local branches around the country here. If your local office is missing, you can send in the information.
WEB http://sunsite.unc.edu/drears /running/usatf.html

▶ **SWIMMING**

Aquatic Team of Mecklenburg Home Page Though it may sound obscure, ATOM Swimming in Mecklenburg, N.C., is one of the best swim programs for young people in the U.S., and many of its graduates make it to the Olympics. Here you can find out how to get involved, and you can also access a schedule of North Carolina meets and local swimming committees.
WEB http://web.sunbelt.net/atom

The Long Distance Swimming Calendar Find out what YAABA's up to. But first, find out what YAABA is (Ye Amphibious Ancients Bathing Association) in the acronyms-explained-here page. If you're a future Diana Nyad looking to swim across the English Channel, or if you just want to cross the 20-kilometer Rottnest Channel in West Australia, look no further than this page.
WEB http://fas.sfu.ca/0h/cs/people/Grad Students/zaiane/personal/longswim /swimlist.html

Masters Swimming More than just masters, this message board serves as the only place to chat about swimming on CompuServe. Get feedback on swimming and pregnancy or find out about meets in your area. Don't forget to backstroke over to the file library, which includes meet schedules and dozens of articles on virtually all swimming topics—training, breathing, cramps, nutrition, Autralian crawl, and breaststroke.
COMPUSERVE *go* goodhealth→Libraries *or* Messages→Masters Swimming Library

rec.sport.swimming Looking for the perfect off-season workout? Need advice for a good stretch program to alleviate cramps? Even if you're simply suffering through a swimmer's fashion dilemma, like whether mirrored swimming goggles will go down well at the local Y, this discussion group takes all types. The chat covers diving, as well as broader issues such as Greg Louganis's disclosure that he has AIDS.

USENET rec.sport.swimming

FAQ: **WEB** http://lornet.com/swimming /FAQ/swimfaq.txt

SwimChat The next best thing to actually swimming is, of course, talking about swimming. Swimmers and swim fans who get to feeling a little out of their element on dry land need only dial up SwimChat to get right back into the swim of things. There are three daily discussion groups—at 4, 7, and 10 p.m. (EST)—and options are available for private conversations. There's also a subscription option to notify those interested in scheduled chats.

WEB http://www.4-lane.com/sportschat /newsc/sw_index.html

Swimming Find out the latest on the Chinese performance-enhancing drug scandal, which 17-year-old World Cup sprinter put Egypt on the swimming map, and World Cup results from up-to-date Reuters' swimming news briefs.

AMERICA ONLINE *keyword* sports→Choose a Sport→Swimming

Swimnews Online Swimnews Online opens with a sharp index of its various components, including the magazine, a photo library, meet results, rankings and records, a calendar, and a list of links. The index is easy to use, and the rankings come up quickly and cleanly. There are no excessive graphics to slow things down here, just stats. It took only a few quick clicks to learn, for example, that on day one of the April 21 swimming races in Sydney, Australia, Susan O'Neill placed first in the women's 100-meter freestyle, with a time of 56:24.

WEB http://www.swimnews.com

▶ TRACK & FIELD

Pole Vault Development Page A page with an attitude about altitude. This expansive Web site put up by USA Track and Field hosts its own bulletin board, The Pole Vault, where visitors can post messages typically ranging from the exclamatory "Big sticks for sale!" to the plaintive "Help me invert." Another page announces age-graded competitions from 8 to 80+, proving that "old vaulters never die, they just get softer poles." At the coaching area, vaulters-in-training can learn how to improve their approach, plant, and top from dozens of veteran vaulters.

WEB http://www.stcloud.msus.edu /~khanson

The Thrower's Page For the community of sports enthusiasts who specialize in tossing heavy objects around, this page lists contact information (and sometimes links) for organizations and publications of interest. Need expert advice on how to put that shot (or throw that discus or hammer)? Several specialists are available to email. Visitors can also read thrower's bios and stats or engage in live chat at The Ring.

WEB http://www.geocities.com /Colosseum/3027/throhome.html

USA Track and Field Long Distance Running Pages Wondering how your time on that last 12K holds up against the U.S. record? Race down here to find a full field of long-distance-running record books, measurements for 14,000 courses, national rankings, and other services geared to the long-distance runner in general, and to serious competitors in particular. Extensive Olympic coverage of every qualifying page is also featured, down to the last shoelace.

WEB http://www.usaldr.org

PART 11

School Library

REFERENCE DESK

IN THE DAYS BEFORE *STAR TREK* role-playing games and ordering by email, the Net wastouted as a new kind of reference library, an electronic environment that put a galaxy of knowledge at the fingertips of even the least experienced computer user. While reference sites may not be the most glamorous offerings in the online world, they remain a rich source of useful information. Need to find out about zymurgy, Namibia, or the ibex? Browse Grolier's Academic American Encyclopedia or Britannica Online. Confused about the conversion from ounces to grams, or Celsius to Fahrenheit? Consult the Conversion Table page. Flummoxed by the word flummoxed? Satisfy your etymological hankerings with The American Heritage Dictionary or the Hypertext Webster Interface. If your query requires knowledge of a higher degree, try emailing it to the Ask An Expert Page.

▶ STARTING POINTS

Ask An Expert Page Experts are standing by to answer your email on topics that include science, literature, economics, computers, and the Internet. More esoteric expert pages include Ask the Web masters about Stoves and Fireplaces and Ask Ken! You can even Ask the Amish, but because it's against their religion to use the Internet, responses will be relayed through a spokesperson.
WEB http://njnie.dl.stevens-tech.edu /curriculum/aska.html

Reference Center Modeled after a comfortable library room, the center makes finding valuable references online as easy and intuitive as possible. Click on the science shelf, the humanities book that's lying on a sofa, the computer on the librarian's desk, the entertainment magazine on the coffee table, or one of several room fixtures, and link to an annotated list of Internet resources. The newspaper, for example, links to ABC News, National Public Radio, and the Associated Press newswire. But the site is more than a good collection of hotlists: It also staffs librarians to help cybertravelers find the resources they need. Fill out a form and a librarian student will guide you. Currently, a MOO is being developed at the site to allow librarians to be on call in real time.
WEB http://www.ipl.org/ref

Reference Help Think of it as the reference desk at your local library—complete with a friendly librarian. Post questions on the bulletin boards for the Smithsonian, *National Geographic*, the Academic Assistance Center, and other AOL research-oriented presences that are linked to this area. In addition, a live reference assistance session is held every evening from 8 p.m. to midnight (EST).
AMERICA ONLINE *keyword* reference help

Reference Index A long list of links to large Internet resouces such as library catalogs, dictionaries, newsstands, subject guides to Internet resources, and other reference sites.
WEB http://www.lib.lsu.edu/weblio.html

Reference Works Area code servers, foreign currency exchange rates, libraries, atlases, census statistics, and dictionaries are just a few of the reference guides linked to this site.
WEB http://english-www.hss.cmu.edu /reference.html

The Virtual Reference Desk Purdue University's sleek set of links to Web sites containing government documents, dictionaries, thesauri, phone books, maps, and more.
WEB http://thorplus.lib.purdue.edu /reference/index.html

▶ CALENDARS & TIME

Date and Time Click on a country's time zone for the current date and time.
WEB http://www.bsdi.com/date?

Monthly Calendar Heidi was born May 20, 1973. What day of the week did that fall on? Sunday. What day will it fall on in 1996? Monday. And what day does payday fall on next month? Wouldn't you like to know? Type in a month and a year and the server will return the month's calendar. Type in just the year and the server will return a full year's calendar.
WEB http://www.cmf.nrl.navy.mil/calendar

WWW Calendar Generator Choose a month and year. Give the calendar a heading. And if you're using Netscape, the site will generate a calendar.
WEB http://www.intellinet.com/CoolTools/CalendarMaker

> **CONVERSIONS**

Conversion Table Measurement and temperature conversion tables.
WEB http://www.uwosh.edu/students/wallip27/convert.html

Koblas Currency Converter Select a country (China, for instance) and the currency of any of the countries listed will be converted relative to the currency (in this case, the Chinese Yuan) of the country selected. Updated weekly.
WEB http://bin.gnn.com/cgi-bin/gnn/currency

Unit Conversions Enter a mile and convert to centimeters. Enter days and convert to seconds. Enter Celsius and convert to Kelvin. The site supports conversion programs for time, temperature, volume, density, kinematics viscosity, and several other units.
WEB http://eardc.swt.edu/cgi-bin/ucon/ucon.pl

> **DICTIONARIES**

A Word a Day The mailing list introduces more than 15,000 subscribers to a new word each day. The Web site carries today's and yesterday's word, and you can even download the pronunciation of the word.
EMAIL wsmith@wordsmith.org ✍ Type in

subject line: subscribe <your full name>
FAQ: WEB http://www.wordsmith.org/awad/faq.html
Info: WEB http://www.wordsmith.org/awad/awad.html

American English Dictionary A searchable version of an English dictionary.
URL gopher://odie.niaid.nih.gov/77/deskref/.Dictionary/enquire

The American Heritage Dictionary A searchable version of the third edition of the *American Heritage Dictionary* with over 303,000 words, phrases, people, and geographic locations.
COMPUSERVE *go* dictionary

Casey's Snow Day Reverse Dictionary (and Guru) Submit a definition and the server spits out the word you had in mind. The success rate of this service, unfortunately, is low.
WEB http://www.c3.lanl.gov:8075/cgi/casey/revdict

College Slang Dictionary A list of college slang terms and their definitions. If you "flail" at UC Berkeley, you're not doing very well. If you are a "fleshling" at Swarthmore, you have three more years of college (at least) to go. If you are a "cow" at Carnegie Mellon, you belong to a sorority. And at Wellesley, many women try hard not to be "Wendy," a term for the stereotypical waspy Wellesley woman.
URL gopher://wiretap.Spies.COM/00/Library/Article/Language/slang.col

The Devil's Dictionary According to *The Devil's Dictionary*, an abstainer is "a weak person who yields to the temptation of denying himself a pleasure" and a female is "one of the opposing, or unfair, sex." Written by Ambrose Bierce in 1906, this is not your typical dictionary. It offers a cynical, acerbic twist to the definitions of hundreds of words, often supplying witty quotations along with the definition.
WEB http://nti.uji.es/CPE/ed/0.0/bierce/dd.html • http://www.alcyone.com/max/lit/devils

Hypertext Webster Interface Search *Webster's Dictionary* for hypertext definitions and examples of a term's usage. Click on one of the terms in the definition and link to a definition of that term. It's a great tool for feeling your way around the English language.
WEB http://c.gp.cs.cmu.edu:5103/prog webster

Merriam-Webster's Collegiate Dictionary Search by entry name or the full text of the dictionary. If you're uncertain of a word's spelling, enter the first few letters of the word followed by an asterisk and a list of possibilities will be returned.
AMERICA ONLINE *keyword* dictionary

Merriam-Webster's Thesaurus Search for synonyms and antonyms.
AMERICA ONLINE *keyword* thesaurus

Merriam-Webster's Word Histories Research a word's history—its etymology—with this searchable reference.
AMERICA ONLINE *keyword* histories

The NASA Thesaurus Related terms for several hundred space, astronomy, and NASA-related vocabulary words.
WEB http://www.sti.nasa.gov/nasa-thesaurus.html

Roget's Thesaurus Looking for a perfect word to capture the essence, meaning, or substance of an idea? Search 1,000 entries (by full-text or entry name) in the 1991 edition of *Roget's Thesaurus*.
WEB http://tuna.uchicago.edu/forms _unrest/ROGET.html

Webster's Dictionary A searchable version of *Webster's Dictionary*.
URL gopher://sfsuvax1.sfsu.edu:3015 /7default%20SPEL

WordNet Enter a word and search for synonyms, antonyms, group senses, homonyms, and other word relations.
WEB http://www.cogsci.princeton.edu /~wn/w3wn.html

The WorldWideWEB Acronym and Abbreviation Server When you need an acronym or abbreviation defined ASAP, search this extensive, easy-to-use database.
WEB http://curia.ucc.ie/info/net/acronyms /acro.html

▶ ENCYCLOPEDIAS

Britannica Online For less than the price of buying the real set of books, you can subscribe to the online version of Britannica's encyclopedia, *Britannica's Year in Review* and the tenth editon of the *Merriam-Webster's Collegiate Dictionary*. The editors have hot-linked some of the encyclopedia text to Internet resources.
WEB http://www.eb.com

Compton's Encyclopedia Updated twice annually, Compton's has over 5,000 long articles and 29,000 shorter articles. The encylopedia is searchable and the site offers tips for effective searching.
AMERICA ONLINE *keyword* encyclopedia

Global Encyclopedia With fewer than 200 articles, this encyclopedia has been written by and for the netter.
WEB http://www.halcyon.com/jensen /encyclopedia/welcome.html

Grolier's Academic American Encyclopedia This searchable, online edition of Grolier's Encylopedia has over 33,000 articles (many with bibliographies) and is updated quarterly.
COMPUSERVE *go* encyclopedia

The Hutchinson Encyclopedia A continuously updated British encyclopedia with over 34,000 articles. Users can also search for and download images from the encyclopedia.
COMPUSERVE *go* hutchinson

▶ PERIODICALS

Ecola's Newsstand An index of links to newspapers and magazines worldwide organized by region, nation, and state. A search engine allows a more specific search for news.
WEB http://www.ecola.com/news/press

The Monster Magazine List Despite the sleek, trim interface of this index, you will be struck by a sense of awe at the tremendous amount of resources this index promises. If you're looking for a magazine, search for its title or browse the categories ranging from arts and entertainment to travel. Looking for a magazine about monsters? You might be out of luck, but a power search will yield scores of references to monsters in the news.
WEB http://www.enews.com/monster

My Virtual Newspaper Hundreds of sources of global, national, and local news are available at this section of My Virtual Reference Desk. A search engine also lets you find an instant weather report for any region you choose.
WEB http://www.refdesk.com/paper.html

Newsstand Delivers what its title promises. Dozens of magazines and newspapers are housed at the news section of this commercial service. Biggies like *The New York Times* are available here, but so are more esoteric periodicals, such as *American Woodworker*.
AMERICA ONLINE *keyword* newsstand

▶ QUOTATIONS

Bartlett's Familiar Quotations It's the day before an important speech and you need the perfect quotation. Who are you going to call? Bartlett's, of course. Search by keyword or choose from a list of hundreds of people quoted in the book, including Elizabeth Barrett Browning, Edgar Allan Poe, Charles Dickens, Dante, and Jean Jacques Rousseau. The book was published in 1901, so don't expect to find quotations from the likes of Noam Chomsky, Susan Sontag, Andre Sakharov, or Elie Wiesel.
WEB http://www.cc.columbia.edu/acis /bartleby/bartlett/index.html

▶ TELEPHONE NUMBERS

Airline Toll-Free Numbers A list of airlines and their toll-free telephone numbers.

URL gopher://odie.niaid.nih.gov/77 /deskref/.areacode/index

Area Code Look-Up Enter an area code and the site returns the U.S. region covered. Enter a city and the site returns the area code.
URL gopher://odie.niaid.nih.gov/77 /deskref/.areacode/index • gopher://coral .bucknell.edu:4320/7areacode

AT&T Toll-Free 800 Directory A searchable database of 800 numbers registered with AT&T.
WEB http://www.tollfree.att.net/dir800

World Wide Yellow Pages Search or browse by business name, type of business, or geographic location. Information includes address and telephone number.
WEB http://www.yellow.com/cgi-bin /SearchWWYP

▶ ZIP & COUNTRY CODES

Internet Country Codes Have you received an email with "se" at the end of the address and not been sure what country it came from? Refer to this A-Z list of countries and country codes used in Internet addresses.
WEB http://www.ics.uci.edu/WebSoft /wwwstat/country-codes.txt

National Address Server Type in the full address, minus the ZIP code, and the site will return a nine-digit ZIP code.
WEB http://www.cedar.buffalo.edu/adserv .html

U.S. Postal Service Address Quality & ZIP Code Locator Enter exact address for a nine-digit ZIP code or city and state for a five-digit ZIP code.
WEB http://www.usps.gov/ncsc

LIBRARIES

BOOKS ARE OUR FRIENDS. REALLY. They calm us when we're we're feeling agitated, remind us of happier times—and if we're really sad, we can blow our noses in them. Maybe that's why they hide from us. And maybe that's why people, always thinking a step ahead, invented libraries—so those little leather-bound suckers could be located, checked out, and loved to death. On the Net, libraries are plentiful, and as easy to use as a pocket comb. To discuss everything from research to fines, visit soc .libraries.talk. You don't even have to whisper.

▶ STARTING POINTS

Boston Library Consortium No library card is required to access the catalogs of BC, BU, Brandeis, MIT, Northeastern University, Tufts, Wellesley, UMass/Boston, UMass/Amherst, the Boston Public Library, and the State Library of Massachusetts. Simply visit this site for links to these Massachusetts institutions. Browse the catalogs and be as loud as you want—no librarians!
TELNET telnet://blc.lrc.northeastern.edu

CLIO—The National Archives Information Server The full resources of the National Archives—7.4 million still pictures, 300,000 rolls of microfilm, 1.7 million cubic feet of textual documents, and much more—aren't all online, but information about the archives, a guide to its holdings, articles about how to use the regional resources, microfilm catalogs for geneological research, and elaborate online exhibits using archive resources are all available. Past online exhibits have included poster art from World War II, a day in the life of the president, and a tribute to the Declaration of Independence.
WEB http://www.nara.gov

Hytelnet An index of catalogs for public, college, and specialty libraries worldwide. Hypertext links get you to a library, and the site provides log in instructions. A listing of library-related resources, including access to hundreds of electronic books, is also available here.
WEB http://www.cc.ukans.edu /hytelnet_html/START.TXT.html

Internet Public Library Hundreds of library catalogs in more than 30 countries are available at this site. To find a specific library, browse the menu, which is alphabetized by country. There are also links to over 1,800 online books (including banned books) and other texts.
WEB http://ipl.sils.umich.edu/ref/RR/LIB /opacs-rr.html

Library of Congress The Library of Congress is the largest library in the United States, of course, and one of the largest in the world, with millions of volumes and hundreds of thousands of other documents—government charters, codes and regulations, maps, and transcripts of Congressional hearings, and more. Online, the Library of Congress offers several services, including a telnet-accessible catalog of its holdings (searchable by author and keyword) and an extensive Web site with electronic exhibits on everything from African-American history to Renaissance culture to the Dead Sea Scrolls. Pay a visit to the national library.
WEB http://www.loc.gov
TELNET telnet://locis.loc.gov

Libweb Visit libraries worldwide with this collection of links to the card catalogs of institutions in the United States, Asia, Australia, New Zealand, Canada, Europe, and Mexico. In addition, the site features links to library-related companies (database providers and vendors, ILS vendors, and bibliographic tool providers), library and information science schools, and libraries with their own Web sites.
WEB http://www.lib.washington.edu /~tdowling/libweb.html

New York Public Library The formidable skyline of New York City greets you at this Web site, which comprises the entire 12 million volume collection of the world's largest public library. Learn about the library, its history, its architecture, and its sponsorship of humanities events in Manhattan; and click on the Catalog link to launch a telnet application and access the library's holdings.
WEB http://www.nypl.org
TELNET telnet://nyplgate.nypl.org→<your password>→nypl

Smithsonian Institution A catalog of the 1.2 million works in the Smithsonian Institution's holdings is online. One-stop shopping for researchers, this site offers 40,000 rare books, 15,000 journals, and 1,800 manuscripts, as well as extensive collections on many subjects (like African and African-American Resources at the Smithsonian).
WEB http://www.si.edu/organiza/offices/silib/silguid.htm
TELNET telnet://siris.si.edu

▶ LIBRARY CATALOGS

All library entries listed in this section are displayed in the following form:
Name of Library
telnet address of catalog→login
Info: url of informational page

Air Force Institute of Technology
telnet://sabre.afit.af.mil→library
Info: http://www.cc.ukans.edu/hytelnet_html/US000OTH.html

Arizona State University
telnet://carl.lib.asu.edu→carl
Info: http://www.lib.auburn.edu

Auburn University
telnet://131.204.82.10
Info: http://www.lib.auburn.edu

Berkeley Public Library
telnet://198.31.22.250→library
Info: http://www.ci.berkeley.ca.us/bpl

Boston University
telnet://128.197.130.200→library

Info: http://www.cc.ukans.edu/hytelnet_html/US002.html

Brigham Young University
telnet://library. byu.edu:2000
Info: http://library.byu.edu

Brown University
telnet://library.brown.edu→library
Info: http://www.brown.edu/Facilities/ University_Library/library.html

Bucknell University
telnet://library.bucknell.edu→library
Info: http://www.bucknell.edu/departments/library

California Institute of Technology
telnet://clas.caltech.edu→clas
Info: http://www.caltech.edu/~libraries/homepage/homep.html

Carnegie Mellon University Libraries
telnet://library.cmu.edu
Info: http://www.library.cmu.edu

Case Western Reserve University
telnet://129.22.138.1→library
Info: http://www.cc.ukans.edu/hytelnet_html/US008.html

Chicago Public Library
telnet://database.carl.org
Info: http:// cpl.lib.uic.edu

Citadel, the Military College of South Carolina
telnet://155.225.6.2→info
Info: http://www.cc.ukans.edu/hytelnet_html/US008.html

Claremont College
telnet://library.claremont.edu
Info: http://voxlibris.claremont.edu

Colgate University
telnet://library.colgate.edu→library
Info: http://www.cc.ukans.edu/hy_html/US008.html

Colorado State University
telnet://csn.carl.org
Info: http://www.colostate.edu/Depts/LTS/libhome.html

Columbia University Libraries
telnet://columbianet.columbia.edu
Info: http://www.cc.ukans.edu
/hytelnet_html/US008.html

Cornell University Library
telnet://ez-cornellc.cit.cornell.edu→
library
Info: http://www.cornell.edu:3002/library
/cul.html

Dartmouth College
telnet://lib.dartmouth.edu
Info: http://coos.dartmouth.edu/~library
/LibHomePage.html

Duke University Libraries
telnet://ducatalog.lib.duke.edu→library
Info: http://www.lib.duke.edu

Emory University Libraries
telnet://euclid.cc.emory.edu→euclid
Info: http://www.cc.emory.edu/MENUS
/libraries.html

Five College Consortium (Amherst, Hampshire, Mount Holyoke, Smith, and UMass/Amherst)
telnet://lib.amherst.edu
Info: http://www.amherst.edu/amherst
/admin/library/text/rflib.html

Indiana University
telnet://infogate.ucs.indiana.edu→guest
Info: http://www.indiana.edu/~libweb

Iowa State University
telnet://scholar.iastate.edu
Info: http://www.lib.iastate.edu/welcome
.html

Jewish Theological Seminary of America
telnet://jtsa.edu
Info: http://www.cc.ukans.edu
/hytelnet_html/US008.html

John Marshall Law School
telnet://catalog.jmls.edu
Info: http://www.jmls.edu/jmlshome.html

Johns Hopkins University
telnet://janus-gate.mse.jhu.edu→ janus
Info: http://www.jhu.edu/libraries.html

Kansas State
telnet://ksuvm.ksu.edu→lynx
Info: http://www.lib.ksu.edu

Kent State University
telnet://catalyst.kent.edu→prompt
Info: http://www.cc.ukans.edu/hy_html
/US008.html

Lafayette College
telnet://139.147.42.4→Library
Info: http://lafsun.lafayette.edu/home
.html

Library of Congress
telnet://locis.loc.gov
Info: http://lcweb.loc.gov/homepage/lchp
.html

Los Alamos National Laboratory
telnet://admiral.lanl.gov
Info: http://barnowl.lanl.gov

Lunar and Planetary Institute
telnet://cass.cass2.jsc.nasa.gov→
cass online
Info: http://cass.jsc.nasa.gov/ols.html

Massachusetts Institute of Technology
telnet://library.mit.edu
Info: http://www.cc.ukans.edu
/hytelnet_html/US008.html

Miami University
telnet://watson.lib.muohio.edu:1500
Info: http://www.lib.washington.edu
/~tdowling/libweb.html#usa

Michigan State University
tn3270://dialmagic@magic.lib.msu.edu:23
Info: http://web.msu.edu/library

Middlebury College
telnet://lib.middlebury.edu→LIB
Info: http://www.middlebury.edu/library

Museum of Fine Arts, Boston
telnet://flo.org→guest
Info: http://www.cc.ukans.edu
/hytelnet_html/US008.html

National Archives
telnet://ux1.cso.uiuc.edu
Info: http://www.nara.gov

National Center for Atmospheric Research
telnet://library.ucar.edu
Info: http://www.cc.ukans.edu
/hytelnet_html/US008.html

National Library of Medicine
telnet://medlars.nlm.nih.gov
Info: http://www.nlm.nih.gov

New York State Library
telnet://nysl.nysed.gov→catalog
Info: http://unix2.nysed.gov/library

North Carolina State University
telnet://library.ncsu.edu→library
Info: http://dewey.lib.ncsu.edu

Northwestern University
telnet://library.ucc.nwu.edu
Info: http://www.library.nwu.edu

Oberlin College
telnet://obis.lib.oberlin.edu
Info: http://www.oberlin.edu/Default.html

Oregon State
telnet://oasis.kerr.orst.edu→oasis
Info: http://fubar.kerr.orst.edu:70

Princeton University
telnet://catalog.princeton.edu
Info: http://infoshare1.princeton.edu
:2003/online/Catalog2.html

Purdue University
telnet://lib.cc.purdue.edu
Info: http://thorplus.lib.purdue.edu

Rensselaer Polytechnic Institute
telnet://infotrax.rpi.edu
Info: http://www.rpi.edu/Library/LibInfo
.html

Rice University
telnet://library.rice.edu
Info: http://riceinfo.rice.edu/Fondren

Rochester Institute of Technology
telnet://wally.isc.rit.edu
Info: http://wally.isc.rit.edu

Rutgers University
telnet://info.rutgers.edu

Info: http://info.rutgers.edu/rulib/liac
.shtml

Rutgers University Law Library, Newark
telnet://law-new.rutgers.edu
Info: http://www.rutgers.edu/lawschool
.html

San Diego State University
telnet://library.sdsu.edu
Info: http://www.sdsu.edu

Skidmore College
telnet://lucy.skidmore.edu→pac
Info: http://www.cc.ukans.edu
/hytelnet_html/US008.html

Smithsonian Institution
telnet://siris.si.edu
Info: http://www.si.edu/organiza/offices
/silib/start.htm

Southern Methodist University
telnet://129.119.64.2
Info: http://www.cc.ukans.edu
/hytelnet_html/US008.html

Stanford University
telnet://forsythetn.stanford.edu
Info: http://wwwsul.stanford.edu

Stevens Institute of Technology
telnet://database.carl.org
Info: http://www.lib.stevens-tech.edu

Temple University
telnet://library.paley.temple.edu
Info: http://www.cc.ukans.edu
/hytelnet_html/US008.html

Texas A&M
telnet://128.194.4.1→notis
Info: http://www.cc.ukans.edu
/hytelnet_html/US008.html

Tufts University
telnet://library.tufts.edu→tulips
Info: http://library.tufts.edu

U.S. Military Academy
telnet://library.usma.edu
Info: http://www.cc.ukans.edu
/hytelnet_html/US008.html

University of California at Berkeley
telnet://gladis.berkeley.edu
Info: http://infolib.berkeley.edu

University of California at San Diego
telnet://infopath.ucsd.edu
Info: http://www.ucsd.edu/library/index
.html

University of Chicago
telnet://libcat.uchicago.edu
Info: http://www.lib.uchicago.edu/LibInfo
/Catalogs

University of Colorado
telnet://arlo.uccs.edu→arlo
Info: http://www.uccs.edu/lib/arlo.html

University of Florida
telnet://luis.nerdc.ufl.edu→luis
Info: http://www.uflib.ufi.edu/uflib.html

University of Illinois at Chicago
telnet://uicvm. uic.edu→luis
Info: http://www.uic.edu/depts/lib

University of Iowa
telnet://oasis.uiowa.edu
Info: http://www.arcade.uiowa.edu

University of Maine
telnet://ursus.maine.edu
Info: http://libinfo.ume.maine.edu

University of Maryland
telnet://victor.umd.edu
Info: http://umbc7.umbc.edu/~curnoles
/aokweb.html

University of Michigan
telnet://mirlyn.lib.umich.edu→mirlyn
Info: http://www.lib.umich.edu

University of Missouri at St. Louis
telnet://umslvma.umsl.edu→libcics
Info: http://www.umsl.edu/~libweb

University of Notre Dame
telnet://irishmvs.cc.nd.edu→library
Info: http://www.cc.ukans.edu
/hytelnet_html/US008.html

University of Oregon
telnet://orbis.uoregon.edu

Info: http://www.uoregon.edu/UOlibrary

University of Pennsylvania
telnet://mpg.library.upenn.edu
Info: http://www.library.upenn.edu

University of Southern California
telnet://uscinfo-net.usc.edu
Info: http://cwis.usc.edu/Library

University of Texas at Austin
tn3270://utxdp.dp.utexas.edu→ ucat
Info: http://www.lib.utexas.edu

University of Washington
telnet://uwin.u.washington.edu
Info: http://www.lib.washington.edu

University of Wisconsin at Madison
telnet://nls.adp.wisc.edu
Info: http://www.lib.washington.edu

Vanderbilt University
telnet://ctrvax.vanderbilt.edu→acorn
Info: http://www.cc.ukans.edu
/hytelnet_html/US008.html

Virginia Tech
telnet://vtls.vt.edu
Info: http://vatech.lib.vt.edu

Wake Forest University
telnet://wfunet.wfu.edu
Info: http://www.wfu.edu/Library

Washington University
telnet://library.wustl.edu
Info: http://library.wustl.edu

Wesleyan University
telnet://129.133.21.140
Info: http://www.wesleyan.edu/libr
/wlibhome.htm

Yale University
telnet://umpg.cis.yale.edu:06520→vt100
Info: http://www.library.yale.edu

Appendix

INDEX

J

K

L

U

V

XYZ

WOLFF NEW MEDIA

Wolff New Media is one of the leading providers of information about the Net and the emerging Net culture. The company's NetBooks series includes titles such as *NetGuide, NetGames, NetChat, NetTrek, NetSports, NetTech, NetMusic, Fodor's NetTravel, NetTaxes, NetJobs, NetVote, NetMarketing, NetDoctor, NetStudy, NetCollege, NetSpy, NetSci-Fi, NetShopping, NetKids, NetLove,* and *NetMoney.* The entire NetBooks Series is available on the companion Web site YPN—Your Personal Net (**http://www.ypn.com**). And *Net Guide*—"the *TV Guide®* to Cyberspace," according to *Wired* magazine editor Louis Rossetto—is now a monthly magazine published by CMP Publications.

The company was founded in 1988 by journalist Michael Wolff to bring together writers, editors, and graphic designers to create editorially and visually compelling information products in books, magazines, and new media. Today, the staff consists of some of the most talented and cybersavvy individuals in the industry. Among the company's other projects are *Where We Stand—Can America Make It in the Global Race for Wealth, Health, and Happiness?* (Bantam Books), one of the most graphically complex information books ever to be wholly created and produced by means of desktop-publishing technology, and *Made in America?*, a four-part PBS series on global competitiveness, hosted by Labor Secretary Robert B. Reich.

Wolff New Media frequently acts as a consultant to other information companies, including WGBH, Boston's educational television station; CMP Publications; and Time Warner, which it has advised on the development of Time's online business and the launch of its Web site, Pathfinder.